# Folktales and

# Reality

# Folklore Studies in Translation
## GENERAL EDITOR, DAN BEN-AMOS

*German* Volkskunde: *A Decade of Theoretical Confrontation, Debate, and Reorientation (1967–1977),* translated and edited by James R. Dow and Hannjost Lixfeld.

*The European Folktale: Form and Nature* by Max Lüthi, translated by John D. Niles.

*The Fairytale as Art Form and Portrait of Man* by Max Lüthi, translated by Jon Erickson.

*Nordic Folklore: Recent Studies:* edited by Reimund Kvideland and Henning K. Sehmsdorf (in collaboration with Elizabeth Simpson).

*Kalevala Mythology* by Juha Y. Pentikäinen, translated and edited by Ritva Poom.

*Some Principles for Oral Narrative Research* by Axel Olrik, translated by Kirsten Wolf and Jody Jensen.

# Folktales and

# Reality

BY

## Lutz Röhrich

TRANSLATED BY

## Peter Tokofsky

INDIANA UNIVERSITY PRESS
Bloomington and Indianapolis

Translated from *Märchen und Wirklichkeit* by Lutz Röhrich.

© 1979 of the original German edition by Franz Steiner Verlag
Wiesbaden GmbH, Sitz Stuttgart, P.O.B. 347, D-7000
Stuttgart 1, W. Germany. All rights reserved.

© 1991 Translation by Indiana University Press

The paper used in this publication meets the minimum requirements of American
National Standard for Information Sciences—Permanence of Paper for Printed
Library Materials, ANSI Z39.48-1984.

⊗ ™

Manufactured in the United States of America

**Library of Congress Cataloging-in-Publication Data**

Röhrich, Lutz.
    [Märchen und Wirklichkeit. English]
    Folktales and reality / by Lutz Röhrich ; translated by Peter
Tokofsky.
        p.    cm. — (Folklore studies in translation)
    Translation of: Märchen und Wirklichkeit.
    Includes bibliographical references (p.    ) and indexes.
    ISBN 0-253-35028-X
    1. Fairy tales—History and criticism.   I. Title.   II. Series.
GR550.R613   1992
398.21—dc20                                                    90-26381

1  2  3  4  5    95  95  94  93  92

*For*
*Ingrid Dagmar*
*Jens Lothar*
*Eva Babette*
*Lambert Tillman*

# CONTENTS

         The Significance of Time and Place                  178
         The Social Milieu                                   184

VII.  The Folktale's Inner Reality                          199
         The Narrator's Ego                                  199
         The Folktale's Themes                               207

         *Notes*                                             217
         *Selected Bibliography*                             273
         *Tale Indexes*                                      277
         *Subject Index*                                     285

# Foreword

In *Folktales and Reality* Lutz Röhrich proposes a bold universal theory of folklore genres. Not since the publication of André Jolles's *Einfache Formen* in 1929 has there been such an overarching theory of genres. The abundance of examples taken from tales from all over the world maintains the discussion at a deceptively descriptive level; the use of supportive material from previously published folktale analyses disguises the innovation in Röhrich's own theory, and the digressions into historical, ethnic, and social issues obscure the conceptual unity that underlies the theory of genres that Röhrich articulates in this book.

In *Einfache Formen* Jolles offered an idealist theory of genres. For him the genres of folklore, such as *Märchen*, legend, myth, proverb, and riddle, are primary verbal formulations of the basic mental concerns that preoccupy the human mind. These concerns exist in thought without words as mental orientations, and their primary verbal formulation is in the forms of folklore. Hence folklore genres are primitive, even primeval, as they represent the primal human verbalization of thought and emotions. Each genre is a crystallization of a distinct semantic field that occurs universally in the thought of man. With the transition from orality to literacy, written forms replace the primary forms but continue to articulate the same semantic fields.

In contrast, Röhrich constructs his system of genres predicated not upon the human mind but upon human reality. Folklore genres are verbal formulations of reality that encompass social life, religious beliefs, and natural laws. They are distinct from each other in their capacity to represent this reality and in their selectivity of the specific segments that they represent. The theoretical shift from Jolles's to Röhrich's system of genres is dramatic. It is not just a switch from an idealist to a realist philosophical position but a complete change in the concept of representation that underlies theories of genres. While in Jolles's system genres represent permanent and universal orientations of the mind, and the distinctions between them are dependent upon the semantic fields that they formulate verbally, in Röhrich's theory folklore genres represent perceived, experienced, and imagined reality. The distinctions between them are predicated upon their capacity to represent particular aspects of human and natural reality, and the attitudes toward this reality that are articulated in each of them.

In Röhrich's theory, genres are contexts for symbolic representations. Each genre is a domain of specific elements of social and natural reality that acquire their symbolic significance within the frame of a particular genre. The youngest son and the stepmother in European tales, for example, are folktale symbols par excellence. They do not occur either in legend or in jest. Similarly, the stepmother figure is part of the folktale stock of characters and does not appear in either legends or jest. Röhrich analyzes in depth the folktale and the legend as a contrastive set of genres in which actions, beliefs, and figures are mutually exclusive. Those that occur in the folktale are absent from the legend and vice versa. Although on occasion, and in the folklore of particular cultures, the exclusive distribution of figures and actions between genres may not be comprehensive and it appears that there is some slippage from one genre to another, closer analysis may reveal that the symbolic figures genres share have the same role in tradition but are not the identical figures. For example, in Russian folklore witches appear both in legends and in folktales, but in fact these are two separate, differently named, traditional witch figures.

In this theory, genres constitute a universal symbolic system predicated upon representation of and an attitude toward reality. Röhrich realizes that the conception of reality has precedence over the notion of belief that has often been used in folklore as the distinctive feature that separates legend and myth from the folktale. Belief is a function of the ideas concerning the possibilities and probabilities in reality. Within a cultural system that conceives of supernatural actions and figures as part of its world, the notion of reality extends to include the same events that in another culture, which defines its range of possibilities more narrowly, will be considered part of the miraculous or the fantastic. Within a narrow rationalistic system, the acceptance of the supernatural requires an attitude of belief, whereas within a nonrationalistic system, the supernatural is an accepted part of everyday life without the formation of a special belief system. Therefore the attitudes of belief or disbelief are only functions of the concept of reality which is fundamental in the construction of any system of genres.

In Röhrich's usage the term *reality* does not refer to a single concept. Rather, it is possible to discern in it four different meanings which, for the sake of clarity, can be distinguished as *fictive reality, historical reality*, and *projected reality*, each of which obtains particular relation to the *reality of the narrators' world*. Viewed hierarchically, fictive reality is an all-inclusive concept that relates to all folk narratives, regardless of their generic distinctions. Both historical and projected realities are, by definition, fictive when they are part of stories, and nonfictive when they are part of the narrators' world.

The fictive reality is a construct of the narrative imagination and is bound by the rules that govern each genre. Folktale and legend differ from each other in their fictive reality and in the relations each genre has to the narrators' world. While the folktale employs stylistic formulas, rhetorical devices, and narrative themes to set the fictive reality *apart* from the narrators' world, the legend employs similar narrative strategies to persuade listeners or readers of the likelihood of identity between the legend and the reality of the narrators' realities.

As mentioned earlier, Röhrich considers the folktale and the legend a contrastive pair in the system of folklore genres. Their fictive realities are mutually exclusive in terms of themes, motifs, figures, and actions, drawing upon the narrators' world and selecting different elements, which are generically appropriate. They construct narratives which are distinct from each other in kind, and in the social and natural symbols they employ. Hence the fictive reality of these genres draws upon, but is not identical with, the reality in each culture, each genre representing a different domain of social and natural life. Thus Röhrich projects the concept of fictive reality into a theory of genres. The fantastic in folklore operates within generic rules that have a high degree of consistency in terms of both the selections made from the narrators' world and the construction of narratives.

However, the fictive reality is not completely a product of the imagination. In part it could be a transformed historical reality. Customs, beliefs, social organization, and material goods that were an integral part of the historical reality have been eliminated, through a process of change from the narrators' world, and transformed into the fictive reality of folk narratives, where they survived. The evolutionary concept of "survival" that has been the cornerstone of nineteenth-century anthropological theory of cultural evolution hardly explains Röhrich's notion of the transformation of historical into fictive reality. Granted, description of medieval and tribal courting behavior, belief in magic and the supernatural, funerary rites, commerce, and war have been retained in part in folk narratives, but their occurrence in the tales is not merely informative. By their retention in the tales, they have become an integral part of their fictive reality, and they are bound by the rules that govern generic distribution of motifs and themes. For the narrators they have ceased to be historical reality, let alone experienced as current social reality. They have undergone a process of transformation from history into fiction, from reality into fantasy.

Not only the past but the present as well can become part of the fictive reality. Röhrich examines aspects of culture, technology, social class, and personal psychology as they become a reality projected by narrators into the fictive realities of the different genres of folk narratives. He explains the narrative variations that occur in the same tale type told by different people, not necessarily as a consequence of faulty oral transmission, forgetfulness, and narrative improvisation that seeks to amend the story through invention or synthesis of different versions, but as a projection of the personal and cultural realities of the narrators. After all, the creative processes that are operative in narration have their roots in cultural values, religion, ethnic, historical, and social experience, as well as economic conditions. Hence it is necessary to demonstrate, as Röhrich does, that variations in narratives are in part a consequence of the reality that the narrators project into them, transforming thereby their own world to become part of the folktale world.

On the technological level, such a projected reality often may appear to an outsider incongruous, even ridiculous. The employment of planes as means of miraculous transportation instead of magic may be a rational innovation which is compatible with the narrators' world, but when it is projected into the medieval ambiance of a folktale, it verges on the comic. The projection of cultural values into tales may be more problematic. Röhrich ponders the question whether the occurrence of cruelty in German folktales is a universal trait of children's tales or a projection of German culture, and therefore can offer some explanation for how the atrocities of the Second World War were made possible. Since he finds cruelty and fright to be current in the folktales of other European peoples, he opts for the psychological-developmental explanation, considering themes of cruelty to reflect universal psychological need and to have a function in human development. Yet, in either case, these aspects of the tale reflect a reality that is projected into the folktale and becomes part of its fictive nature.

The fictive, the historical, and particularly the projected realities that occur in folktales make them a mirror of culture, class, and personality. The folk narratives of any group reflect the multiplicity of levels of meanings that is to be found in any human society. Furthermore, implicit in the application of Röhrich's theory of genres to the issue of folktales and reality is the idea that the corpus of narratives of any society offers not a single mirror but a multitude of reflections, each projecting reality from a slightly different angle, with a slightly different focus, representing each time a new image, and making reality constantly elusive.

Dan Ben-Amos

# Abbreviations

Atlantis    Atlantis. Volksmärchen und Volksdichtungen Afrikas. Veröf-
            fentlichungen des Forschunginstituts für Kulturmorphologie
            München. Leo Frobenius, gen. ed. Jena: Diederichs, 1921–28.
BP          Johannes Bolte and Georg Polivka. *Anmerkungen zu den Kinder-
            und Hausmärchen der Brüder Grimm.* 5 vols. Leipzig: Die-
            terich'sche Verlagsbuchhandlung, 1913–32.
CSL         Saints' Legends for Children (in the appendix to the Grimms'
            *Kinder- und Hausmärchen* [=KHM 200–210]).
EB          Ludwig Erk and Franz M. Böhme. *Deutsche Liederhort.* 3 vols.
            Leipzig: Breitkopf & Härtel, 1913–32.
FFC         *Folklore Fellows Communications.* (Academia Scientiarum Fen-
            nica) 1910ff.
HdA         *Handwörterbuch des deutschen Aberglaubens.* Hanns Bächtold-
            Stäubli, ed. 10 vols. Berlin and Leipzig: De Gruyter, 1927–42.
HdM         *Handwörterbuch des deutschen Märchens.* Lutz Mackensen, ed. 2
            vols. Berlin: De Gruyter, 1930–40.
KHM         *Kinder-und Hausmärchen, gesammelt durch die Brüder Grimm.* 8th
            unchanged edition. (Edited by Hermann Grimm based on the
            complete edition. Berlin, 1864.) Munich: Winkler, 1963.
MdW         Die Märchen der Weltliteratur. Friedrich von der Leyen, gen.
            ed. Jena: Diederichs, 1912ff.
RGG         *Die Religion in Geschichte und Gegenwart, Handwörterbuch für
            Theologie und Religionswissenschaft.* 3rd edition. 6 vols. + index.
            Tübingen: Mohr, 1957–64. (Original, 1927–32.)
Type        Antti Aarne and Stith Thompson. *The Types of the Folktale: A
            Classification and Bibliography.* Second revision. FFC no. 184.
            Helsinki: Suomalainen Tiedeakatemia, 1961.

# Translator's Preface

Since its publication in 1956, *Folktales and Reality* has become one of the central books in European folktale scholarship. Although Röhrich's book maintains theoretical validity (subsequent editions appeared in 1964, 1974, and 1979), *Folktales and Reality* remains relatively unknown on this side of the Atlantic. The present translation aims to correct this neglect. Perhaps the English edition of *Folktales and Reality* will exert new influences and stimulate new waves of scholarship like those spawned by the English translations of Max Lüthi's *The European Folktale* and Vladimir Propp's *Morphology of the Folktale* thirty years and more after their initial publication.[1]

This translation of *Folktales and Reality* also offers the first opportunity for English readers to become acquainted with one of the leading postwar schools of German folklore. Never before has a monographic study from the *Freiburger Schule*, founded and led by Röhrich, appeared in English. Röhrich's influence on the Freiburg approach to folklore is so great that the school's inception must be viewed in the context of his own scholarly development.

After returning from the eastern front in World War II, Röhrich began his university studies in his Swabian birthplace, Tübingen. Providing an early indication that he would not allow disciplinary bounds to constrain him, he studied German, folklore, history, music, and Latin. He completed his dissertation, "The Demonic Figures in Swabian Folklore," in 1949. Röhrich first presented *Folktales and Reality* (then bearing the subtitle "A Folkloristic Investigation") as his *Habilitationsschrift* at the University of Mainz in 1954. Its publication two years later established him as one of Europe's leading young folklorists. Röhrich remained at the University of Mainz for seventeen years before traveling to Freiburg to accept a full professorship of folklore and Germanic philology in 1967.[2]

Upon Röhrich's arrival, Freiburg had no chair of folklore. An empty former dormitory in need of renovation greeted the distinguished professor from Mainz as the designated home of the new department. Faculty, staff, students, and friends worked together gathering the essentials, building a library, and establishing a coherent curriculum. In less than twenty-five years, this building, with its protected California redwood, has become a center of folkloristic achievement.[3]

The Freiburg School characteristically approaches folklore generically. The emphasis has been on oral forms. For instance, the institute houses a legend archive, inherited from Will-Erich Peuckert, containing approximately 150,000 texts. Röhrich himself has published important articles on German legends as well as a standard reference work on the genre.[4] His achievements for the proverb are no less commendable: he co-authored the

*Sammlung Metzler* installment, and his monumental *Lexikon der sprichwörtlichen Redensarten*—for which he received the Chicago Folklore Prize in
1974—has received wide acclaim in the field of paremiology.[5] Research for
an updated, revised edition of this lexicon continues under Röhrich's su-
pervision. As director of the German Folksong Archive, Röhrich has also
established himself as an authority on this oral genre in the Germanic
languages.[6] He displays his breadth of knowledge about jokes in yet
another publication.[7] Röhrich and his emulators also apply their research to
custom and material culture. Röhrich's study of Adam and Eve considers
pictorial and three-dimensional representations of the first couple, in addition to narratives about them.[8] A branch of the Freiburg School explores
traditions of pre-Lenten celebration and costuming.[9]

The Freiburg School's approach to these materials might be labeled
*Kulturgeschichte.* This line of investigation explores the expressive forms
throughout their history, focusing on their roles in various cultures and the
transformations they undergo over time. In an exemplary two-volume
work, Röhrich explores the histories of narratives from the late Middle
Ages through the present.[10] Some of the essays collected in Röhrich's *Sage
und Märchen* provide invaluable case studies of particular narratives or
narrative cycles.[11] Although these studies may begin with an orientation
toward a particular genre, the inquiries frequently require crossing the
bounds of analytic categories. Paying little attention to the borders erected
by scholars, tradition-bearers often freely exchange *dramatis personae* and
motifs among legend, folktale, art, and belief. Thus it becomes clear that
practitioners of this method require erudite knowledge not only of folklore
but of a wide range of historical and cultural information. Röhrich's inno-
vative studies of the interrelationships among proverbial speech, folk narratives, gestures, and illustrations (including modern parodies and
reinterpretations) indicate the cross-generic demands of his approach.[12]

The present work is, in many ways, the most ambitious application of
the method. It confronts the problem of intergeneric relationships, goes
beyond Europe for its sources, oversteps the bounds of folklore to trace
recurrent motifs to some unexpected cultures and contexts, and draws
some sound conclusions about a well-studied genre. Röhrich's contributions to the study of folktales made him a logical choice for the Brothers
Grimm Prize in 1985. Thus it is quite appropriate for *Folktales and Reality* to
introduce Lutz Röhrich and the Freiburg School to the English readership.
In conjunction with works from other schools of German folklore that have
appeared in this series, a new audience now has the opportunity to examine postwar developments in German folklore studies.

I should add a few words here on the translation. In general, I have
attempted to tread the fine line between maintaining the author's style and
making the work more accessible to American scholars. German structures
occasionally required disentangling to make them more readable for their
new audience, yet, I believe, the text remains quite close to the original. In

addition to a few explanatory notes, I have "silently" aided non-Germans by including in brackets the locations of some lesser-known geographic bodies and by converting the footnotes to American style, adding some bibliographic information in the process.

Fortunately folklorists have a long tradition of international communication, which helped to solve translation problems for most technical terms, or *Fachausdrücke*, long before I could worry about them. Some, however, continue to trouble translators. The German *Märchen*, found in the title and throughout this book, is used by folklorists to refer to a specific group of narratives which, in German, falls under the larger heading *Volkserzählungen*. English-speaking folklorists refer to members of both the subgroup and the larger category as folktales. I take a flexible approach here, generally translating *Märchen* as "folktale" but bringing in additional terminology, such as "fairy tale" or simply "narrative," when needed for clarity. The same can be said for other generic labels.

I offer my own translation of several quotations which may already exist in English, such as those by Plato, by Kant, or from Germanic epics. The role of these items in Röhrich's argument did not demand the precision of specialized translators. Excerpts from the Grimms' tales are more numerous, and we are lucky enough to have Ralph Mannheim's enjoyable and accurate translation, *Grimms' Tales for Young and Old*, to follow.[13] I have adopted his translations with only an occasional change. For consistency I use his titles of the tales.

I would like to thank Joachim Roschmann, Hannjost Lixfeld, and Leonard Primiano for their help at various stages of this project. Lutz Röhrich also offered his assistance and encouragement. All these occasions proved as enjoyable as they were informative.

# *Notes*

1. Max Lüthi, *The European Folktale* (Bloomington: Indiana University Press, 1986). First published in 1947 and first translated in 1982. V[ladimir] Propp, *Morphology of the Folktale* (Austin: University of Texas Press, 1968). First published in 1928 and first translated in 1958.

2. Wolfgang Mieder, "Lutz Röhrich: Master Folklorist and Paremiologist," *Proverbium* 4(1987), 1–2.

3. Lutz Röhrich, *20 Jahre Institut für Volkskunde an der Universität Freiburg i. Br. 1967–1987* (Freiburg: Institut für Volkskunde, 1987), 1–4.

4. *Sage* (Stuttgart: Metzler, 1966).

5. (With Wolfgang Mieder) *Sprichwort* (Stuttgart: Metzler, 1977); *Lexikon der sprichwörtlichen Redensarten* (Freiburg: Herder, 1973).

6. (With Rolf Wilhelm Brednich and Wolfgang Suppan) *Handbuch des Volksliedes* (Munich: Wilhelm Fink, 1973 and 1975).

7. *Der Witz. Figuren, Formen, Funktionen* (Stuttgart: Metzler, 1977).

8. *Adam und Eva. Das erste Menschenpaar in Volkskunst und Volksdichtung* (Stuttgart: Müller & Schindler, 1968).

9. Dietz-Rüdiger Moser, *Fastnacht—Fasching—Karneval. Das Fest der "Verkehrten Welt"* (Graz: Kaleidoskop, 1986).

10. *Erzählungen des späten Mittelalters und ihr Weiterleben in Literatur und Volksdichtung bis zur Gegenwart* (Bern: Francke, 1962 and 1967).

11. *Sage und Märchen. Erzählforschung heute* (Freiburg: Herder, 1976).

12. "Sprichwörtliche Redensarten in bildlichen Zeugnissen," *Bayerisches Jahrbuch für Volkskunde* 1959, 67–79; "Gebärdensprache und Sprachgebärde," in Wayland D. Hand and Gustave Arlt, eds., *Humaniora: Essays in Literature, Folklore, Bibliography. Honoring Archer Taylor on His Seventieth Birthday* (Locust Valley, N.Y.: J. J. Augustin, 1960), 121–49; "Sprichwörtliche Redensarten aus Volkserzählungen," in Karl Bischoff and Lutz Röhrich, eds., *Volk, Sprache, Dichtung. Festgabe für Kurt Wagner* (Giessen: Wilhelm Schmitz, 1960), 247–75; and Röhrich's most recent book, *Wage es, den Frosch zu küssen: das Grimmsche Märchen Nummer eins in seinen Wandlungen* (Cologne: E. Diederichs, 1987).

13. Garden City: Doubleday, 1977.

# Preface to the Third Edition

Whoever deals with the folktale today must ask if folktales still exist. After all, didn't the brothers Grimm say that time was running out for collecting folktales from oral tradition?—and that was more than 150 years ago. Although oral and preliterate traditions are largely extinct today or have become fixed in *Buchmärchen*, folktales are enjoying new forms and functions. Folktales are a staple of every child's reading materials. The Grimm collection—although usually available only as a limited selection—is still a literary success around the globe. Comic strips have borrowed hundreds of themes and episodes from folktales and adapted them into new forms for young readers today. Folktale recordings have made hefty profits for record producers. Professional folktale tellers with repertoires of hundreds of tales travel to schools and preschools with the support of the Ministry of Education. What would the children's hour on radio or television be like without the rich materials supplied by folktales from around the world? No German theater can fail to offer Christmas tales for children if it wants to sell tickets. Families and tourist groups head for various regional folktale gardens or parks featuring familiar folktale characters, based on the model of Disneyland.

But folktales live on not only as children's folklore descended from its original adult audience. If presented properly, the folktale can also have new appeal for adults. Some tabloid magazines feature a weekly "folktale joke," which almost always entails magical folktale motifs in unexpected, thus comical, conflict with modern rational thought. Folktale cartoons and caricatures invent nonconventional folktale endings; they achieve a comic effect by failing to meet our expectations. Tales of magic shortened into joking stories use many folktale themes as they replace the older narrative form. Best-sellers consciously parody folktales, and few of their readers are children or youths. Admirers of traditional folktales justifiably criticize such violent changes. But there are also those who call for these changes in the folktale to suit an intellectual and emancipated readership.

Popular literature can also be considered a functional equivalent to the folktale. Newspapers sometimes structure coverage of royal weddings, beauty contests, and lottery wins like a folktale. Many pop songs tell of fairy-tale love and riches, frequently employing the rhyme *Märchen—Pärchen* (young couple). Finally, filmmakers are particularly interested in the folktale's sexual content as a means for filling the theaters. In this epoch of increasing consciousness, the unconscious and latent sexual symbolism in seemingly harmless children's tales such as "Little Red Riding-Hood," as well as in folktales that seem to cry out for a psychological interpretation, is made conscious for adults. We need only think of the many cinematic versions of "Bluebeard." The most recent film to use this material sets the events in our century: Bluebeard is a World War II hero, a successful fighter pilot, and later a leading Nazi. But to his, and others', misfortune, he is impotent. The war was a sort of compensation for him. Bluebeard suffers from an overly strong attachment to his mother, and he repeatedly summons her from her grave. Each time he is about to get married, Bluebeard kills his fiancée. This occurs a good half dozen times, some with horribly realistic details, others with a comic, satirical tone. An enlightened American woman is Bluebeard's last victim. Yet she escapes the fate that awaits her in Bluebeard's bloody chamber—a sort of giant refrigerator in which he preserves the bodies of the murdered women. Bluebeard is killed after our fearless American tries in vain to convince him to see a psychoanalyst and change his ways. Such adaptations allow us to see every folktale in a new light. This applies to theatrical and political manipulations of the folktale as well. We need only think of the many transformations of "The Dragon-Slayer."

The folktale has conquered all sorts of new areas. Advertising slogans and images are often structured like folktales. This is no coincidence: Ads allege that new products have magical powers like the objects in folktales. They invent supernatural beings who personify the product and suggest that it is as helpful to people as the otherworld figures in the tale of magic. The theme of wish fulfillment in the folktale is easily transferred to new contexts. The most general scheme underlying the folktale is overcoming difficulties: battle and victory, the completion of tasks, expectations and fulfillment. This scheme includes the happy ending commonly named as a characteristic of the folktale. The folktale's initial situation is characterized by a lack, a needy situation, or some other difficulty; the folktale then depicts how these problems are overcome. This schema is easily transferred to advertising. A favorite folktale and advertising figure is the king. At first glance we recognize that this figure is not designed to appeal to subliminal feelings of monarchy. On the contrary, the advertisement tries to turn buyers into consuming kings and to restore the irrational impulses which are all too uncommon in the technological world.

Although the folktale has found its way into new realms and adapted to modern means of communication, the traditional folktale has been subjected to an array of criticisms. The folktale—for centuries an undisputed, traditional means of education—is having its pedagogics, its ideological premises, and its socioeconomic background explored more consciously and critically today than ever before. Many grave objections have been raised against the folktale. For example, some accuse the folktale of being too unrealistic and anachronistic, untrue and kitschy. The folktale depicts antiquated social relations; it originated in the past, in feudal times when the king had absolute power. The good king is always right and can do as he pleases; as a father he has unlimited command over his children. The folktale also depicts a patriarchal world where men must accomplish heroic deeds. In contrast, the woman often serves others; she is degraded to a goose girl or leads the lowly life of a cinderella by the hearth. Mother Holle's maid is rewarded for diligently and devotedly shaking out the beds and sweeping the house clean; the woman keeps house while the dwarves go off to work. Of course, the folktale portrays other female types, for example, the crafty riddle princess who must be outdone in a battle of wits or a physical contest. But this can also be seen as an antiquated expectation that the man is wiser, stronger, or more intelligent than the woman.

Pedagogic reservations about the folktale are also frequently expressed: Won't folktales just arouse the child's fear? Won't children take every old woman for a witch? Shouldn't we protect our children from the folktale? The pedagogues do not limit their accusations to the "horrors of the Grimms' tales." It has been said that folktales are disciplinarian, that they express repressive, authoritarian methods of childrearing. The folktale threatens: "Don't stray from the path, don't pick any flowers in the forest, or else the evil wolf will eat you up!"—this seems to be the moral of "Little Red Riding-Hood." Similarly, the mother goat in KHM 5 expresses the idea, "Don't open the door for any strange men!" "Hansel and Gretel" teaches children "not to run away from home, no matter how badly your parents treat you; otherwise an evil witch who eats children will get you!" Don't such tales contain ideas from an antiquated culture, pedagogic relics from days long past? Don't we endanger children and make them insecure when we show them that their parents could abandon them? Or does "Hansel and Gretel" offer a lesson about the social conditions for wage-earning foresters at the start of the nineteenth century? To what extent must we retell the Grimms' tales unchanged, philologically true to their original wording? Should they be translated into modern language, as some authors have recently attempted to do? Materialistic, psychologically critical, and idealistic readings of the folktale sometimes come into conflict over this question. Franz Fühmann gave "The Wolf and the Seven Young Kids" a new function in his retelling, entitled "Praise for Disobedience":

> There were seven young kids,
> And they were allowed to poke all around,
> Except in the grandfather clock,
> That could break the clock,
> Their mother had said.
>
> There were six well-behaved young kids,
> Who wanted to poke all around,
> Only not in the grandfather clock,
> That could break the clock,
> Their mother had said.
>
> There was one disobedient young kid,
> Who wanted to poke all around,
> Even in the grandfather clock,

And he broke the clock,
As their mother had said.

Then the evil wolf came.

There were six well-behaved young kids,
Who hid when the wolf came,
Under the table, under the bed, under the chair,
And none in the grandfather clock,
The wolf ate them all.

There was one disobedient young kid,
Who jumped into the grandfather clock,
He knew that it was hollow,
The wolf didn't find him there,
And he survived.

His mother sure was happy.

Even opposing views make it clear that folktales are always models; they are didactic. The folktale offers the child models for behavior. And in this regard folktales are often not as conventional and outdated as the critics occasionally claim. On the contrary, folktales, particularly "true folktales," i.e., tales of magic and adventure, are emancipatory: The heroes find their independence; they leave their parents' home. The reasons for departure vary, but the departure, going out into the world of adventure, is always the same. The folktale depicts humans' ability to make a foreign environment their home (cf. Max Lüthi). The folktale also doesn't exactly stabilize existing social relationships; it commonly breaks structures: In the end the poor man becomes king and inherits rule over the land. The previous reign is toppled by the socially weak. The insolent princess must marry the swineherd.

The pedagogues have also recently had a few positive words to say about the effect of folktales: Frightening figures such as witches, the devil, giants, and robbers address specific problems of childhood. Many children have diffuse fears which can and must be personified in a folktale character. Thus the folktale provides a psychic means of overcoming fear. People have almost gone as far as to claim that if folktales were omitted from pedagogics, children would invent them. Regardless of one's position regarding folktales today, the folktale is a social reality that plays many roles in the lives of adults as well as children. Thus there is good cause to continue to examine folktales.

The author cannot, with a good conscience, watch the third edition of *Folktales and Reality* appear practically unchanged twenty years after it first appeared. Two decades have not failed to leave their mark on folktale scholarship or on the author himself. The emphasis of modern folktale research has changed considerably. Instead of cultural-historical, philological-literary, and comparative research, modern folklore has increasingly employed sociological, psychological, pedagogic, functional, and structural approaches. Methodological pluralism now reigns in international narrative research, and the author recently tried to demonstrate the various possibilities for folktale research in the case of a single example ("Rumpelstiltskin," in *Schweizerisches Archiv für Volkskunde*, 1973). Thus it was not easy to agree to this new edition that, because of technical limitations and costs, could only be a reprint. New literature, collections as well as monographs, could not be included. On the other hand, *Folktales and Reality* is still a book based predominantly on primary sources and one which does not need to cast the sail of its scholarship and methodology in the direction of some fashionable wind in the discipline.

# Folktales and Reality

# I.

## Introduction

Conceptually, in both objective and subjective terms, the folktale as a genre is generally defined in contradistinction to experience, reality, and religious belief. A sampling of definitions reveals this recurrent criterion: "We understand a *folktale* to be a tale created from poetic fantasy, particularly from the realm of magic; it is a wonder story not concerned with the conditions of real life." The folktale "fails to follow the laws of reality"; it presents "fantastic, miraculous events which could not realistically occur because they contradict natural laws." "The concept of folktale" denotes "a colorful story which takes place in a fantasy world void of the usual causal and natural connections." "Contradiction of reality lies at the heart of the folktale." The folktale is "fabled poetry," a product of fantasy which "does not require belief."[1] An investigation of the folktale's relationship to reality therefore drives at the genre's essence. The topic is not new; a number of studies with the same title as ours, or similar ones, already exist.[2] However, these earlier works often contribute little to our understanding of the problem. Some titles promise more than their contents offer, while other publications provide no more than risky interpretations or mere rationalism.[3] Some works identify realistic elements only in the decorative motifs added to the folktale as a part of the realistic style found in more recent collections;[4] still others consider the topic superficially.[5] Unfortunately, this critique also partially applies to a number of monographs which treat the position and function of single elements of reality in the folktale statistically. Such investigations consider, for example, the role of the king[6] and the woman in the folktale,[7] the meaning of birth and death,[8] love and marriage,[9] or rights and justice,[10] the position of plants[11] and animals,[12] or the function of the folktale forest.[13] Similarly, the articles in the *Handwörterbuch des deutschen Märchens* on specific realities such as "tree," "blood," "bread," "fountain," "money," or "staff"—some of which are quite extensive but consist mostly of examples—often do not help our discussion. We go beyond these earlier works by considering the range of issues suggested by our title as a means of gaining insight into the folktale's nature.

The topic "folktales and reality"[14] includes the question of "folktales and nonreality"; these are two sides of the same coin, and each must be considered in close connection with the other. We should ask whether folktale traits not corresponding to rational reality can be more closely defined. These traits are not completely arbitrary: Fixed norms and laws apparently govern the supernatural in the folktale. A typology of folktale wonders would consider the various origins and functions of the magical motifs. Not all of the motifs come from folk belief; some are purely fantastic and were never believed. The wonders can fantastically exaggerate real life, or they may be completely unreal. We must also consider how a given folktale uses the magical and miraculous motifs. Even within the Grimms' *Kinder- und Hausmärchen* (= KHM) we find a variety of possibilities. For example, the water of life that keeps death at bay (KHM 97), a ship that can travel on land (KHM 64 and 165), the purse that never becomes empty (KHM 101), a knapsack into which one can wish everything one wants (KHM 81), a jacket which makes its wearer invisible (KHM 92 and 93), the "table-be-set," and the "cudgel in the sack" (KHM 36) are special and extraordinary even in the folktale itself. The plot revolves mostly around the possession of these miraculous items. On the other hand, the folktale does not seem to consider many notable things as wonders at all. Organic objects made of gold, e.g., a golden bird (KHM 57 and 64), a golden fish, a golden colt (KHM 85), even a golden child (KHM 85) or the girl from whose mouth a gold piece falls with every word that she speaks (KHM 13), are seen as something special but by no means as marvels which fully contradict all biological possibilities. The folktale does not see a "wonder" when the seven young kids emerge from the wolf's stomach unharmed (KHM 5) or when Little Red Riding-Hood and her grandmother do not suffocate in the wolf's belly (KHM 26). By the same token, the wolf survives the operation in which his stomach is cut open and filled with stones (KHM 5). Other examples are even more clear: Inanimate objects that talk, e.g., bread or apples (KHM 24), a bone (KHM 28), drops of blood (KHM 56 and 89), or the talking water in "Little Brother and Little Sister" (KHM 11), are accepted as real without any rationalistic deliberation. None of these miraculous events surprise anyone. Only a certain type of wonder attracts the folktale characters' attention and produces suspense.

In contrast, "novellas" (Types 850–999) do not overstep the boundaries of reality and contain absolutely no supernatural wonders. "King Thrushbeard" (KHM 52) and various folktales about clever riddle-solvers—which often include no marvels whatsoever (e.g., KHM 94)[15]—belong to this group. We hardly notice these novellas among the other narratives in the Grimms' collection because even "wonder tales" do not emphasize the miraculous aspects of the supernatural.

The designation "unreal" does not suffice as a definition of the folktale because even supernatural and miraculous elements have their limits in tales of magic. There are things that would appear unreal even in the true tale of magic; not every conceivable wonder can occur in a folktale. By considering these aspects, we can discover the actual relationship between folktales and reality. Only these impossibilities are truly unreal to the narrator.[16] Characteristically the folktale does not wander so far from reality that it is no longer believable. If the folktale does not require *believable* miracles, then it at least demands ones that make sense and do not interfere with the order and harmony of the folktale world. As soon as a narrative overemphasizes miraculous elements, we speak of tales of lying *(Lügenmärchen)*, which usually cross the border to jest *(Schwank)*. In "true folktales"—a typical "scientific" label—the wonder does not degenerate into fantasy. Wonders are not unbounded; they develop according to a specific typology and logic. We encounter purely subjective, conscious fantasy for the first time in romantic, literary fairy tales. The folktale, on the other hand, has a bounded imagination, and fantasy does not play as freely as it occasionally does in the literary tale.

Every folktale is somehow connected to reality. Although possible and impossible occurrences recklessly mingle and the laws of causality often seem forgotten, certain causal relationships do survive. The coexistence of fantasy and reality represents an important feature of the folktale.[17] Moreover, the folktale's magical events are not isolated; the supernatural is always tied to reality. Magic always affects human heroes: kings, craftsmen, and farmers, the mother, the stepmother, and siblings—all people who exist in reality.

Folktales rarely begin as tales of magic: The narrative's initial situation is almost always possible. Only as the story develops does the narrative abandon external reality, only to recover it at the end of most tales. The folktale does not take place in a world of unbounded possibilities. It rises above reality without breaking away from it altogether. Of course, even apparently realistic opening situations go beyond reality, albeit in a different way than supernatural events. Where in "reality" do poor woodsmen abandon their children (KHM 15) or do we find a woman so evil that she allows her stepchildren to be killed (KHM 47 and 53)? The above examples, which I take only from the Grimm collection, reveal the difficulties we face studying the question of reality in the folktale. Asking about the folktale's relationship to reality drives at the crucial issue: All areas of folktale research meet at this point. Yet each discipline concerned with the folktale has its own specific questions concerning reality.

Our problem becomes considerably more complicated from a historical perspective. Investigations into the origin and age of folktales try to identify the historical epoch in which the motifs which appear unreal to us today were facts, or at least believable reality. Do these motifs still correspond to reality for other civilized or tribal cultures, or were folktales always mere entertainment? These issues begin with the simplest questions of everyday manners and customs: To what extent is the folktale a source of cultural and historical data? Yet even more exciting than such facts, the folktale seems to provide, in the midst of the modern rationalized world, a mental link between the present and an archaic, magical predecessor of our world-view that hardly any other source can match. Across political and cultural boundaries, the folktale, one of our oldest mental relics, still depicts ideas from days long past.

Differences in conceptions of reality provide a means for grouping folktales according to age. The genre is not an intellectual or historical unity but rather a complex of many sources and origins. The question of reality views the folktale in historical flux because the history of the folktale is the history of gradually changing orientations to reality corresponding to the various stages in people's sense of reality.

Although folktale motifs have remained astonishingly constant over centuries, often millennia, we nonetheless recognize considerable change in the way they are perceived. As we shall show, even where we think we see traces of belief in magic, it is often the "making unreal" of the magical (Lüthi) that is truly characteristic of the folktale. By the time our folktales attained their familiar novelistic form, much of the original belief in the reality of the magical motifs seems to have already been lost. Attempts at dating folktales must pay careful attention to this fact. Most of the printed collections, i.e., the sources we have, originate from the nineteenth and twentieth centuries and do not offer much historical perspective. However, we can construct a relative historical chronology from the concurrent folktale records.

Of course, we need ample comparison to tales current among modern tribal societies in order to trace the folktale's path from primitive belief and early prototypes to its modern European form. Yet even with comparative and historical perspectives, we cannot fix the magical world to any particular age: Archaic elements of folk tradition are not always "survivals"; these elements continue to be expressed in a variety of new ways. We cannot date folktales solely on the basis of their primitive features because each individual may treat this aspect of the folktale as a relic of prehistoric behavior or as a possible mode of thought in the present. Time has not stood still in the folktale.

The genre of "folktale" is manifold; what we summarily call a "folktale" changes from culture to culture, from place to place, and from time to time. Perhaps the folktale has persevered because of its flexibility, its lack of rigid form.

This leads us to the problem of genre classification. This too is primarily a question of perceptions of reality. A motif's function within the framework of an entire narrative, or several narratives, reveals the role it plays relative to reality. Therefore we should avoid stripping motifs from their folktale context and instead consider the problem of reality within a generic perspective.

Genres of folk narrative are conventionally differentiated on the basis of belief, but past research has, at best, drawn an unclear border between the believed legend and the folktale which is considered unreal. We need more analyses of specific examples in order to characterize how the genres depict the real world as well as unreal or miraculous occurrences. As a criterion for genre division, belief seems to be relative and subject to historical change. In any case, we do not find only fantasy in the modern folktale and pure folk belief in current legends. We repeatedly observe that folk belief constantly develops new forms rather than remaining fixed.

Our methods of classification are in danger of becoming far too abstract and schematic. A "genre" is not an end in itself; it does not exist in real life, and it is not an independent entity. A genre is a product of the human mind. We should not ask when and where the word *folktale* or some corresponding antiquated concept (e.g., "mythos" or "fabella") came about. The attitude toward the narratives and motif complexes that we call "folktales" which prevails at a given time is far more important. What do people think of the narrative? The characterization of folklore as "sympathetic magic," "fetishism," "animism," "magic," "prelogical thinking," etc., says nothing if we cannot penetrate the intellectual and psychic processes that folklore embodies. The ideal goal would be to investigate narrators' perspectives over time and space. However, in the section on narrators, we are concerned primarily with a contemporary problem: Does anyone still take the folktale seriously? To what extent has it become purely poetic fiction? To answer this we must investigate the various rationalizing influences to which the folktale has been exposed throughout its history. In particular, we consider the more recent stages of development: How is the folktale repeatedly transformed? How do new concepts replace the old? How does the folktale react to the realistic thinking of the modern technological world? How do magical and rational causality coexist? Which social classes tell folktales, and how do sociological factors affect the narratives? How does the folktale incorporate that which is beyond reality, and to what extent does it depict everyday, local realities?

Finally, we ask how realistically the folktale reflects ethnic traits. Few cultural creations are a more international property than the folktale, but it is precisely the folktale's ubiquity which enables us to investigate national differences in attitudes toward reality. In short, a folktale is not an isolated text and must be considered within the context of the ethnic group from which it originates.

The largely literary folktale research established by André Jolles and Robert Petsch and developed by Max Lüthi has, no less than other research directions, its own problem of reality. A folktale becomes "fiction" only when its magical motifs are no longer "real." This raises the literary question: What stylistic forms utilize the fictionalization of magical elements within the new, novelistic framework? Fictionalization of the folktale also leads us to consider the story's "inner reality." Even where the folktale becomes the product of pure confabulation, it still portrays general situations and conflicts which can occur and which frequently rely on the individual teller's subjective experiences. A narrator generally wants to say something meaningful and substantive. This generalization also applies to the series of tradition–bearers who have passed down the tales. The mere fact that a narrative is repeated is an indication of its inner reality. But simply documenting early texts does not tell us what actually made this item popular. It is worth pursuing the inner motivation which forms traditions and seeking psychological explanations for it: What is the basis for the general human propensity toward the folktale?

The phase of documenting worldwide distribution of folktale motifs seems to be over. We also now recognize that the other basic tool of the historic-geographic method—the typology—is an aid, not an end in itself, to folktale research. In our concern with folktale distribution, we forgot to ask why the same items appear internationally. It does not suffice merely to find new connections among international motifs; we must discover why the folktale has such appeal. Above all, we still lack an actual analysis of the folktale's nature, i.e., a systematic description of essential themes and motif groups.[18] The concept of "primary stratum" (Grundschicht)* currently at the fore of folkloristic discussion must be treated psychologically as well as sociologically.

These problems also raise the question of the narrator's inner attachment to the folktale: What makes the individual's tale "effective"? What inner mood does the individual express in a narrative? The words motif and type do not grasp the folktale's nature, since both type and motif are academic constructs.[19] Only the texts in their individual wording are realities; but these realities are individual accomplishments, not a collective possession. Modern folklore investigates how individuals uniquely mold the general property tradition passed down to them.[20] The romantic notion of Volk no longer holds sway. In this shift folktale research follows the path established by folksong research. Today we collect the materials as "true to reality" as possible, ideally with tape recorders and simultaneous filming, in order to do justice to the accomplishments of the individual teller.

We must mention one last aspect of the topic "folktales and reality" which we do not treat in more detail in this work, although it is part of the overall problem—namely, interpretation. All folktale interpretations are based on the fact that the folktale world goes well beyond experienceable reality; in other words, they too ask how folktales relate to reality. Since the folktale's manifest content does not seem to correspond to its latent content, the interpreters seek a "deeper" and "actual" meaning. The interpretation asks what the folktale "really" means. The astounding number and variety of answers this question has found raises considerable doubts about the method. Every period, even every individual, has a different relationship to "reality." Interpretations of the folktale's reality thus repeatedly change depending on when, and by whom, they are written. Even the

*The discussion of social strata refers to Richard Weiss, Volkskunde der Schweiz (Zurich: Eugen Rentsch, 1946).—Trans.

sense of a need for folktale interpretations changes over time and, in any case, is not the product of a primary reaction to the folktale. All interpretations arise from the differences between a rational reality and the folktale's "wonders." These wonders have lost their original reality, and the interpreters try to provide them with new meaning. In this sense folktale interpretation is a secondary, rationalistic approach to the folktale. Ironically, this rationalistic endeavor often shifts to an irrational belief in the reality of the interpretation.

We do not discuss individual theories of folktale interpretation here (the mythological, astralmythological, meteorological, theological, theosophical, anthroposophical, psychoanalytical, or various political or sociopolitical interpretations) since preconceived views developed outside the folktale, rather than the texts themselves, usually guide the interpreters. It is a fundamental error for an interpretation to project its outside opinions into the folktale,[21] but unfortunately the majority of interpretations do indeed bring more into the folktale than they get out of it. Such attempts at an exegesis on the folktale's connection to reality serve the goals of a specific world-view, but they go beyond the acceptable bounds of research. Interpretations must, therefore, proceed deductively from the material if they are to do the folktale justice as an item of folk poetry.

Most interpretations commit other methodological errors: Folktale interpreters rarely refer to the original form; instead they use one, more or less random text which seems to confirm their theory. In the process, not only traits which belong to the given folktale's basic form are subjected to interpretation, but also the particular version's local, individual, or incidental decorative traits, or even those penned by the publisher of a collection. The same offenders usually do not differentiate between the folktale as a whole and the individual motifs.

Of course, even a completely arbitrary interpretation can be based on subjective evidence which allows its author to experience the folktale as reality in his or her own way. Perhaps the interpreter will even be successful in leading others to the same experience. The folktale gives every person the freedom to experience the narrative individually.

The characters and objects in the folktale are, above all, simply themselves. Yet there are also images in the folktale that do not originate from some old magical belief system; rather, they are easily interpretable pictures and symbols. For example, a girl with golden hair, one who emits a gold piece from her mouth with every word she speaks, the king's daughter with a golden moon on her chest or who grows golden flowers from her hair are not intended to be taken literally; rather, they are "really" "symbols" of the girl's good characteristics. Axel Olrik observes that human characteristics are expressed as actions in the folktale, but the observation is not reversible; i.e., not every folktale action can be evaluated as a human characteristic.[22] A psychological fact can be expressed by a wide variety of plots and images; conversely, a single image provides the basis for numerous interpretations. Therefore translating the metaphoric actions back into psychic processes is always problematic. The most basic instances indicate that interpretation is possible only where the folktale has already subsumed elements of reality. As a rule, the interpreter may never forget that the folktale originates in people's minds. Thus the interpretation must begin by considering the ways of thinking which produce the folktale and with the people who mold the text. Deep, thoughtful analysis cannot proceed without a knowledge of the folktale's historical development.

We can summarily observe that the various methodologies in folktale research currently proceed without reference to each other even though they have the problem of reality in common. Folktale dating and the ethnography of storytelling, and even various methods of interpretation, literary questions of genre and style, and religious, psychological, and sociological approaches, all have an interest in "folktales and reality." This topic is of basic concern to them all and unites their divergent approaches.

# II.

# The Genres of Folk Narrative and Their Relationship to Reality

## FOLKTALE AND LEGEND

The genres of folk narrative are commonly grouped according to their various relationships to reality; the types of narrative that are believed are differentiated from those that are not. The distinctions drawn between the "folktale" and the "legend" rely most heavily on the question of reality. Therefore we must investigate these two genres together.

The Grimm brothers' definition which states that the folktale is "more poetic," the legend "more historical"[1] established a differentiation based on reality and belief that has persisted until the present. Modern theory upholds the Grimms' criteria for determining genres by arguing that both genres go beyond objective reality, but that only the legend requires subjective belief in the story's reality. In his paper delivered in Strassburg, Friedrich Ranke recently rekindled the question of the legend's and folktale's differing levels of reality and offered important new perspectives on the issue.[2] Nonetheless he basically concurs with the Grimms when he views the true legend as a believed report of experience and the folktale as a product of fantasy which is not believed.[3] Johannes Bolte also sees "the primary difference between the folktale and the legend . . . in their different relationships to the real world. While the legend claims to depict reality and requires the audience's belief, the folktale . . . cares only about entertaining, not about worldly occurrences. . . ."[4]

Folk narratives have since become more rational, but basically these differences between legend and folktale still apply. In its modern Western form, the folktale is essentially fantasy, a *fabula incredibilis*, while the legend still corresponds to people's more pretersensual side and stands closer to folk belief. Belief and knowledge can still coincide in the legend. The folk often call legends "old truths" or just "truths."[5] Confrontation with doubt actually reduces disbelief in the legend, while the folktale has, in general, long outlived such conflict. Today the folktale's emphasis on the markedly fantastic has generally led to its classification as mere entertainment. This puts the folktale in a crisis, because even rural entertainments have changed. A quick glance at recent collections reveals the extent to which the legend has superseded the folktale.[6] The legend has generally retained its vitality longer. The folk have maintained an inner relationship to the legend because it deals with knowledge: as a factual or experiential report it challenges the audience's critical intellect. The legend is also a more personal, individual narrative. Even skeptical grandchildren are interested in their grandfathers' believed experiences. Even where people have finally ceased to believe the legend, they still have opinions about its reality.

It is clear that all these questions revolve around the narrative's function for the teller and the audience. Folktale tellers and legend tellers assume different degrees of inner participation in their narratives. Because they feel compelled to tell the truth, narrators of legend reports often confess to forgetting a detail. Folktale tellers, on the other hand, use fantasy to replace what they have forgotten.[7] The folktale also often formulaically ensures its own credibility, but it uses different elements of style than the legend. The legend's subjective reality is often quite obvious; in contrast, the folktale sometimes emphasizes its fabricated reality through irony. Because the folktale is not set in the real world, it requires opening and closing formulas which move it from reality to the unreal and vice versa: "Once upon a time" and the German "If they haven't died, they're still alive today." The legend must also comes to terms with rational reality, but it uses very different techniques to settle this conflict. For example, it might explain why a numinous, miraculous apparition can no longer be seen or observed. Historical legends often offer visible proof of their accuracy (e.g., "The rock can still be seen today"). The legend needs these devices because it constantly attempts to draw nearer to reality; historical legends want to be history. Folktales, on the other hand, are stories.*

This common belief-based division between legend and folktale is, however, by no means a historical constant and therefore does not furnish an objective line for separating the genres. We may not analogically transpose the current relationship between the genres onto an earlier period. Even today not every legend is believed: The border of belief extends through the genre and is constantly in flux. Above all, the designation "believed" or "not believed" is subjective and therefore not a universally applicable generic feature. The same narrative text can be a believed "legend" for one person and a fabled folktale for another. The border between belief and fiction, i.e., acceptance or rejection of the legend's content, varies among individuals, even within a given historical period. A single person's judgment of a legend may depend on his or her situation, age, and momentary disposition toward the experience being reported. Thus the folktale-legend division appears to be purely subjective and is by no means

*A play on the German *Geschichte*, which means both history and story.—Trans.

objective. All fixed genre categorizations simplify and schematize the very complex relationships that exist among narratives.[8]

Not all legends are considered true anymore. For example, the legend that reports "It's haunted" offers a very different perspective than the one that says "It's supposed to be haunted" or "They say it used to be haunted." Despite these differing attitudes toward the reality of the content, we group all three as legends. Inner, believing involvement in the true legend is often absent today. Phrases such as "According to legend . . ." or "They say . . ." show how narrators clearly distance themselves from the peasants who actually bear the belief or tradition.[9]

The extent to which a legend is considered true depends largely on which figure from folk belief appears in the narrative. Belief in one figure may live on, while another has become material for a fabulat. Giants, for example, have long since died out from folk belief; dwarves followed. Witches have survived the longest, and belief in them lives on in many places.[10] Legends about the dead have also retained much of their credibility to the present.

Folk belief sharply limits the narrator's art when telling first-person experiential legends, but we also find more artistic forms of legend which go beyond belief without becoming folktales; dwarf and giant legends are examples of such fabulat-legends.[11] Here the generic boundary is totally unclear, and we must work with a greatly expanded concept of legend. Now that humans have emancipated themselves from the magical world, the experiential legend becomes the story-legend which is no longer believed reality, only entertainment. The experiential basis for a motif fades further and further into the background and is finally forgotten. The term *oral literature*, i.e., oral tradition already formed by literary, artistic elements, describes this sort of narrative. Of course, it is not always easy to draw the boundary between believed and invented elements because additions from the narrator's imagination often creep into the narrative unconsciously. As a result, the "belief-fabulat"[12] stands between the original report of the experience and the pure "fabulat." For example, when the "Oppele," a local headless ghost in Swabia, puts his head in the corner to free his hands so that he can clean his shoes (!), an originally numinous, experiential motif has become a humorous, burlesque narrative device.

Only the historical legend truly reveals the variety of realities to which legends correspond. While the local legend depicts extraordinary numinous events, the historical legend looks for the unusual in the purely human realm. Legends about historical figures (e.g., Karl the Great, the Great Electors, Herzog Ulrich,* and others) limit or entirely avoid wonders. The local legend, in contrast, needs wonders; without them it would be of no interest.

The legend finds a link to reality by providing a specific time and place

---

*Duke of Württemberg (1487–1550).—Trans.

and including specific people in the narrative. In contrast, the folktale does not need to specify the locale; it can take place in a "folktale land." While the historical legend takes place in the historical past, and the experiential legend in the present or the immediate past, the folktale is usually set in a fictional past, i.e., it is basically ahistorical and timeless. Time has no function in the folktale. One legend motif tells of a man who spends a hundred years among the demons beneath a mountain. His stay seems short, but when he returns to earth he finds that all his relatives have died: In the legend time continues inexorably, but in the folktale it can stand still. After Sleeping Beauty's magical sleep (KHM 50), life resumes exactly where it stopped a hundred years earlier. The heroine is as young as before; the man who returns from the demon world in the legend actually aged during the elapsed time and cannot live much longer.

Localization and dating alone by no means sufficiently differentiate the treatment of reality in the genres of folktale and legend: There are many localized folktales that are not legends (cf. pp. 181–82), and removing the locale from a legend does not make it a folktale. Obviously we need several characteristics in order to make the boundary between folktale and legend clear. A single feature does not suffice.[13]

The Grimm brothers reveal their clear-sightedness in their relative, rather than dogmatic, formulation of the difference between the genres: "the folktale is *more* poetic; the legend *more* historical."[14] Concentrating more on differences than on what the genres have in common, research during the past few decades has often failed to sufficiently heed these relationships. We must therefore demonstrate that the two genres overlap in many ways and that the division is much more complicated than generally acknowledged. The simple formulation that the folktale is considered unreal and the legend real casts the genres far too rigidly. We cannot formulaically summarize the similarities and differences between the genres so easily. Analyzing specific cases would serve us much better; in doing so we must cast our net wide and, in particular, inquire into the inner psychological structure of both genres.

To define the differences, we must proceed from the similarities. As much as has been written about folktales and legends, we still lack a comparative study of the various uses of the motifs and themes that occur in both genres. Only in this way will we get at the essential differences.

The considerable amount of material the genres have in common, due to their mutual heredity and the constant interaction in oral and written tradition, reveals their psychic proximity. Folktales and legends have many of the same otherworld figures, the same animals, and the same human protagonists. Both genres include disenchantment, battle with demonic forces, family quarrels, courtship, and other episodes.[15] Both tell of the master thief,[16] the dragon-slayer, the spirit in the bottle,[17] talking bones,[18] the dead suitor and husband,[19] and humans transformed into animals. The effects of magical instruments[20] and magic using a demon's name[21] occur in legends and folktales, as does pursuit by a demonic figure.[22] The central motif in the legend "The Wives of Weinsberg"[23] is the same as that in the tale "The Peasant's Clever Daughter" (KHM 94); likewise the motif of the ring rediscovered in the fish's stomach appears in both legend and folktale.[24] "Strong Hans" (KHM 166 as well as KHM 90) consists of the same motifs as the legend "Strong Hermel" from the lower Rhine.[25] Offerings to a demon,[26] the motif of supernatural help with spinning,[27] and "The Gifts of the Little Folk" (KHM 182) are common to legend and folktale, to name just a few examples.

The folktale usually begins with a situation of disorder, and then, after the conflicts are overcome, order is restored. The legend takes the reverse path: In many cases it ends with unresolved dissonance; i.e., it often does not end at all, instead leaving the story open for the future (the attempted release fails; the spook continues haunting, etc.). The folktale ends harmoniously. This difference is particularly conspicuous where legend and folktale utilize the same content and motifs. In a Swabian legend, for example, a man is abducted by a horde of bandits. He receives a musical instrument to play at a witch dance. Although he has never held a musical instrument before, he plays beautifully. But when he returns home he's holding a cat's tail instead of the instrument.[28]

The same story has a happy ending in the Irish tale "The Piper and the Pooka." At the start the Irish musician knows only one song, "The Black Villain." After being abducted by the Pooka and taken to the fairy house, he becomes the best bagpiper in Ireland, and he retains his skills until his death.[29]

The legendary form of this story depicts an illusion; the legend often leads to lifelong confusion. The folktale, on the other hand, leads the hero out of confusion: Portrayed as "a half-foolish man" at the beginning, "he has understanding" and can make the sweetest music after his experience with the fairies.

A narrative's opening and closing are particularly informative: Folktales almost always have a happy ending, while the legend often ends tragically. Corresponding to folk belief, legends contain human sacrifice to demonic forces. Many river demons demand a human annually, and the plague also claims a human life.[30] Human sacrifice does occur in the folktale (e.g., KHM 88), but not at the story's end. The lion which receives the girl turns out to be an enchanted prince who is later released from the spell. In other folktales the promised child is not even delivered (e.g., KHM 31) or is freed from the demon's power (KHM 60).[31] Often the hero need not sacrifice his child if he shows his readiness to do so.[32] Where the hero actually carries out the sacrifice, as in "Faithful Johannes" (KHM 6), the children are immediately brought back to life. In KHM 33 ("The Three Languages") the hero lands in an old dungeon inhabited by a pack of wild dogs to which a human must be delivered at certain hours. But his knowledge of the animals' language protects him. In the folktale, human sacrifice builds only an introductory scene or an element of tension. In the legend it forms the narrative's tragic ending. Only legends about the devil differ: For example, in exchange for building a bridge, the devil in a Swiss narrative demands "the first living thing" that crosses it. But a chamois that is "the first living thing" to cross makes a fool of the devil.[33] Here the devil *legend* transforms the old motif of sacrifice into jest.

Many legends rely on something "almost" happening for their suspenseful effects: the treasure was *almost* raised, the disenchantment came so close to working, if only . . . , etc. Conversely, in the folktale heroes *almost* meet defeat, but their failures cause only a temporary delay; tragedy persists in the legend.[34] Thus the legend has no actual "heroes" like those in the folktale.

The motifs in common show that the narratives must originally have had equal possibilities of ending positively or tragically. The generic differences between the legend's pessimism and the folktale's optimism did not exist from the start. They are, to an extent, the result of different historical developments, and partly a function of various human psychological demeanors and experiences. Generic diversity depends in part on the diversity of human attitudes and modes of experience; ways of thinking stipulate stylistic forms. It is therefore only conditionally correct to say that the legend must end tragically. More accurately, the *humans* in the legend lack the perseverance needed to raise the treasure or to free others.

The theme of enchantment and disenchantment reveals some of the most interesting aspects of how legends and folktales treat reality differently. More astounding than the differences, however, is the fact that two such different genres both contain the theme of disenchantment. On the other hand, the differences are clear: While the folktale contains no magic that cannot be undone, the legend imposes inexorable fate. Undoing spells is very difficult in the folktale, the required task seems impossible; everything seems quite simple in the legend.[35] But in contrast to the folktale, disenchantment almost always fails in the legend because fear overcomes the rescuer before the task is completed. The releaser also has no magical aid in the legend, unlike his or her folktale counterpart, who usually receives such help. Failed attempts at disenchantment in the folktale are merely intensifying or retarding devices before the actual disenchantment. The failure does not make the disenchantment impossible or defer it far into the future as it does in the legend.

Legends and folktales have predetermined disenchanters. In the folktale the hero is the chosen one. In the legend, however, the predetermined one often does not even appear in the narrative. Instead, someone who may not be born for another hundred or thousand years fills the role.

Christian blessings often disenchant otherworld figures in the legend (e.g., "God help you!"). Only in the legend do Christian cures such as saying mass, pilgrimages, pious greetings, or helpful reparations undo transformations.[36] The folktale's otherworld figures, on the other hand, are occasionally described as being unable to "smell Christian flesh." Only the legend has a need for salvation in the Christian sense; this is totally unfamiliar to the folktale. Instead we find plain, material techniques for disenchantment in the folktale.[37] Also in contrast to the legend, enchantment and release often occur unconsciously, occasionally even accidentally or playfully, in the folktale, as in the cases of unpremeditated or unintended spells (e.g., "The Seven Ravens," KHM 25; also see KHM 93). The princess disenchants the Frog King (KHM 1) without conscious intent. She never foresees the possibility that this will occur (cf. KHM 123 as well).

Yet another vital aspect merits consideration: In the folktale the rescuer, not the rescued, is usually the hero. In contrast, the legend shows much more interest in those in need of release. In the legend some misdeed causes the curse; the folktale spell affects the innocent. The legend casts a spell on or damns the offender; the folktale almost always victimizes someone deserving sympathy, not the evil mother-in-law, stepmother, or older siblings.[38] In the rare cases where the folktale punishes the antihero with a curse, there is no release: The evil king in "The Devil with the Three Golden Hairs" (KHM 29) characteristically remains unreleased from his role as ferryman at the story's end; the old witch in KHM 122 ("The Donkey Lettuce") dies from the many blows she receives as a donkey.

Folktale and legend narrators clearly have very different attitudes toward the people in their narratives and distinct views of the function of release from a spell. In the legend, release is objective, directed, and altruistic: the wanderer should find peace. In the folktale it is subjective and egotistic: heroes rescue their chosen partners and thereby attain their own happiness.

There is another basic difference: In the folktale the living are enchanted; in the legend the wandering dead are generally disenchanted. Accordingly, legends generally release people so they can die or, more accurately, die again, i.e., find their final death, their "eternal peace." The folktale transforms enchanted people back into their original human form.[39]

In the legend releasers know that the snake or other enchanted creature is a human under a spell. They are often trying to rescue their beloveds. In contrast, the princess in KHM 1 has no idea that a spell has been cast on the frog.[40] The human characters in the legend know quite well that they should expect something, good or bad, from demonic forces. Folktale heroes have no idea, at least at the outset, that help will befall them. In other words, the folktale reflects a different level of consciousness than the legend.[41]

Legend narrators also weave their egos into the narrative's *external* form. If they don't have their own experiences to report, they include their ancestors, relatives, and friends as eyewitnesses and townspeople. Somehow they bring themselves into relation with those who had the experience.[42] As a rule, the folktale avoids the first-person narrative; it is usually told in the third person. The folktale has a general antipathy toward anything individualistic. The choice of general personalities, kings, princes, princesses, etc., frees fantasy's psychological path to the ego's unconscious, to an individual as well as collective reality. Thus individual needs form the folktale as well as the legend. Psychologically speaking, the folktale is a camouflaged first-person narrative, in contrast to the experiential legend's direct and conscious first-person technique. The folktale generalizes the unconscious projections of the narrator's ego and severs them from the individual.

Folktale heroes' confidence in their instincts is related to this unconscious process. Heroes find their good fortune with the security and self-assurance of a sleepwalker, even if they follow an incorrect or dangerous path or violate an interdiction. They often do not even notice that their lives are in danger and that their fates hang by a thread. Awareness of danger constantly exists in the legend, even at the slightest challenge by a demon; humans cannot free themselves of these thoughts. The ego—the hero's as well as the narrator's—clearly has very different functions in the legend and the folktale.

For Max Lüthi, the individual's isolation is an essential feature of the folktale. The folktale repeatedly emphasizes a single, isolated figure: the only child, the youngest son, the stepdaughter or orphan, the king, the poor man, the numskull, the beautiful princess. The plot also contributes to the isolation: The hero's parents die, the hero is abandoned as a child or must wander through unfamiliar terrain, two brothers separate and go off in different directions, etc.[43] In the legend Mother Holle helps all hardworking spinners; in the folktale she helps a *single* hard-working Goldmarie. The folktale depicts the single case; the content of the legend is repeatable. The folktale's content is much more open to generalization than that of the legend: Goldmarie stands for all poor, hard-working girls. This is one of the most peculiar psychological features of the folktale. The folktale contains universals. In contrast, the legend depicts the experience of a single person.

The folktale emphasizes the hero as a single person, but the legend also "isolates"—and Lüthi missed this observation—by subjecting the person to the extraordinary, solitary experience. Moreover, the legend generally isolates the demon as well, i.e., a single supernatural figure usually appears, while in a folktale several otherworld figures can enter one after the other as the hero's helpers or adversaries. This means that the folktale teller rediscovers his or her ego in the story's hero, while in the legend the narrator's ego projection can be sought psychologically in supernatural beings as well.

Some otherworld figures appear in both genres, such as giants and dwarves, devils and witches, living dead, fairies and sorcerers, dragons, and trolls.[44] The folktale's catalog of demons has, of course, dwindled to relatively few figures. Many of the legend's supernatural figures never appear in the folktale, for example, the Kobold, vampires, grain spirits, tree spirits, Saligen,* the changeling, wild hunters, the wild horde,[45] and innumerable local and regional demons with their many unique forms and names.

Demons found in legend and folktale often have no more in common than their name. The folktale witch is a genuine demon, usually visualized as having a malformed human body. In comparison, the witch of legendry is only a magical human, but she does have a markedly demonic appearance when she rides her broom or takes the form of a cat or hare. In the folktale the witch is still cannibalistic (KHM 15, "Hansel and Gretel").[46] The folktale witch's magic is much stronger than that employed by the legendary witch; the former can change the hero to stone (KHM 60 and 85) or into a tree (KHM 123); the poison she mixes causes the hero's horse to die instantly (KHM 22). Since the folktale witch is a genuine demon, she is bullet-proof (KHM 60). The more savage folktale witch probably indicates that this genre has preserved older conceptions than corresponding legends.[47] The split between the folktale and legend witch apparently occurred quite early: We can document punishment of humans—applied or threatened—for witchcraft as early as the start of the Middle Ages. Karl the Great's ban on believing "that a man or a woman is a striga and eats humans" (*Capitulare de partibus Saxoniae*) and the Lex Salica's mention of the possibility that a striá (striga) can consume a person show that the witch's cannibalistic traits must still have been a reality in folk belief at that time. Today this conception is limited to the folktale. In the folktale we still find some warlocks as well; in the legend women have dominated the art of witchcraft ever since the *Malleus Maleficarum*** appeared.

The folktale does not account for the witch's miraculous powers; they are taken for granted. The legend explains that she inherited or learned her powers from the devil. Finally, the witch appears alone in the folktale, but according to legend and folk belief, a single village often hosts several witches, and many witches travel to Block Mountain or Brocken*** together.

Folk narratives in other countries sometimes even differentiate the folktale witch from the legend witch by name. For example, in Russia the folktale witch is the Baba-Yaga; the witch of folk belief is called ved'ma or Koldun'ia.[48] Only children still believe in the folktale witch, but in villages in many areas of Germany, women are still accused of witchcraft. Yet the alternatives "belief" and "disbelief" do not sufficiently describe the phenomenon. The level of belief in witches varies even within folk belief and legend. Wind and weather witches who cause tornadoes and thunderstorms were often witnessed in the nineteenth century, but they have,

---

*Female spirits, found in the Tirolian Alps, known for their erotic advances toward farmers.—Trans.
**Inquisitor's handbook for witch trials, first published in Strassburg, 1487.—Trans.
***Block Mountain: A fictional peak. Brocken: Highest peak in the Harz Mountains; appears in Goethe's *Faust*.—Trans.

along with the journey to Brocken, all but disappeared from modern folk belief. Heresy and pacts or affairs with the devil, a common component of the concept of witches during the late Middle Ages, play no role in today's folk belief. But lack of belief in these functions of the legend witch does not make her a folktale character because the motif groups featuring the folktale witch are completely different. There are few motifs describing the folktale witch's evil and cunning; the legend witch practices a far greater and more developed array of black magic. The folktale lacks affairs with the devil, the witches' gathering, the witches' ride, milk and butter witches, the witch who performs black magic on livestock, as well as wind and weather witches and the witch in the form of an Alp demon. These motifs are the product of a distinct course of development.

We observe similar differences for other demonic figures. The "three supernatural women" (Frauen-Dreiheiten) appear in legends as well as folktales:[49] In the latter they are constantly tied to the swan-maiden motif, but they fill various roles in the legend (water nymphs, wood maidens, sunken women or women changed into stone, castle and mountain maidens, etc.). The legend's depiction of Mother Holle is also more multifaceted than the folktale's. The motifs compiled by Lincke in the Handwörterbuch des deutschen Märchens[50] clearly indicate that hardly any motif from underworld mythology has not been attached to Mother Holle. This figure ranges from the nymph whose song enslaves the listener, to the Aufhocker,* to giantesses and witches. Mother Holle even merges with the Virgin Mary and becomes the queen of heaven. The image of Mother Holle changes radically in legend and folk belief, while it remains constant and has relatively few variants in the folktale. There is only one tale "Mother Holle"; i.e., some versions of a single international tale type have picked up a regional figure from the mythology of the underworld. In the legend this single demonic figure has attracted numerous narrative motifs and united them. Therefore Mother Holle of legendry has little in common with the Mother Holle in the folktale. The only connection lies in Mother Holle of folk belief's inspection of the maids' distaffs during the twelve nights of Christmas.[51] Mother Holle of legendry also rewards the hard-working spinners and punishes the lazy ones, but rationality has already imposed itself on the wonder in the legend: The heroine's golden hair or the disfigurement of the unkind girl would be unthinkable here. In the legend the hard-working spinners receive small gifts that they discover the next morning (the wonder itself occurs under the cover of darkness), or they receive help with their spinning or other work.

We also encounter other motifs of service to supernatural figures[52] in the folktale (e.g., KHM 13, 100, 136, 179, and 196). Roughly corresponding motifs in the legend include helping deliver a child in the underworld or playing music at the wild horde's banquet. In the folktale the hero appears

---

*A spirit which jumps on people's backs late at night.—Trans.

to be exiled into such service at first, but in the end it turns out to be for his or her own good. The legend follows the reverse course: The human hopes to gain good fortune in the underworld, but receives nothing in return for his or her services.

Similar differences exist for human marriage to a demon. Each of the two genres treats this motif in its own way. In both, certain conditions govern the marriage; e.g., the wife may not utter her supernatural husband's name, or an indication of the otherworld partner's former existence as a demon (e.g., an animal skin) must be hidden or destroyed. In both genres the taboo is usually violated. But in the folktale everything turns out well; the reunification of the couple disenchants the supernatural spouse. The legend ends with the separation of the couple or even with disease and death overcoming the human as the result of an unsuccessful attempt at disenchanting the demonic partner.

Dwarves also display very different traits in folktales than they do in folk legend and folk belief. As in the legend, dwarves volunteer their help in the folktale (e.g., the three little men in the woods in KHM 13 or the little men in KHM 91 and 113). But folktale dwarves don't wear tarn-caps or practice smithery, they do not bake for humans or borrow anything from them, and the folktale also does not tell us anything about the dwarves' departure at the end.[53] The helpful dwarves in the folktale are not insulted by offers of reward; on the contrary, they expect humans to serve them first (KHM 13 and 53). In the legend the supernatural golden reward changes, in whole or in part, into leaves, dust, or coal because the human recipient does not adhere to the accompanying conditions. In the folktale (e.g., KHM 100) just the reverse occurs: The sweepings paid to the human for seven years of service in the underworld change into gold and are still gold when he opens his satchel at home.

Folktale and legend giants have more in common because both legends and folktales about giants have become farcical, and we often cannot distinguish one genre from another. The humorous motif of the dumb giant appears in both genres (cf. KHM 183), e.g., the motif of the uneven contest in which the giant must press water from a stone while his little human rival squeezes a cheese. This motif appears in many legends as well as in "The Brave Little Tailor" (KHM 20).[54]

However, differences do exist between folktale and legend giants. Only the folktale portrays the giant as a cannibal; the legend (as with its depiction of the witch) paints a more human picture. The giant also performs many more deeds in the legend than in the folktale. For example, the folktale lacks the many aetiological motifs found in legends about giants (e.g., the giant as an architect).

Similar observations hold true for the Scandinavian troll. Undoubtedly the trolls in legends and folktales have a few features in common other than their name, but in general they are quite distinct. Trolls of legendry are demons from actual experience; the purely fictional folktale trolls, in contrast, seem to have been created solely to play the role of the hero's supernatural adversary or helper.[55]

The devil folktale, closely related to narratives about giants and trolls, has some parallels to devil legends with the same motifs. The narrative about the man who promises his soul to the devil under the condition that the devil grant him one more harvest, and who then sows acorns, is encountered as a historical legend, as a devil's legend, and as a folktale.[56] There are few differences between the "cheated devil" in legend and folktale (KHM 189 and 195). We should note here that folktales recorded true to their sources preserve much more living folk belief than literary versions. For example, "a poor servant from Lorraine meets the devil at the crossroads at midnight"[57] reads like the opening of a legend, an item of folk belief; the folktale normally requires neither the haunting hour nor the crossroads in order to include the devil. This image contrasts sharply with the conception of the devil found in the experiential legend. The devil in the folktale is a fellow with whom one can speak; for people who believe in legends, the devil is so real and demonic that anyone who dares utter his name at all, does so euphemistically. The devil himself rarely appears in the experiential legend; instead he is usually used to explain a witch's or freemason's magic powers. In the legend the devil actually comes and takes away the souls bound to him when their time is up; in the folktale the pact with the devil leads to the hero's success in the end (as in KHM 92). Associations with evil forces do not make the folktale hero an "antihero" like his counterpart in the legend who sells his soul to the devil. For example, every version of Type 812, in which the hero promises himself to the devil if he cannot solve the devil's riddles within a certain amount of time, has a happy ending: The hero outwits the devil before the period agreed upon expires.

The folktale devil often does not even have his sights set on the hero's soul, and by no means is he always the hero's adversary. More commonly he gladly rewards loyal service without any ulterior motives ("from now on you are free again"). In "The Devil's Grimy Brother" (KHM 100) the hero serves in hell for seven years before moving on with a rich payment. This completely undogmatic text replaces the devil's demonic reality with a human figure. This human devil has found his way into other narratives as well, for example, the "Magic Flight" tale type, where he takes over the role of the sorcerer: The hero marries the devil's daughter, and at the tale's end, the devil dies chasing the hero.[58] Occasionally even the devil's own grandmother helps the hero outwit the devil (e.g., KHM 29 and 125): The grandmother, sitting in a large armchair, protects the lucky hero and helps him fulfill his tasks. This markedly positive, good-natured image typifies the folktale's depiction of the devil. This grandmother is like any other and is in no way a demonic-monstrous figure.[59] The folktale sometimes takes legendary belief in the devil so lightly that it even allows Satan certain *succès d'estime:* In "Bearskin" (KHM 101) the devil gets the evil sisters' souls at the end, and he is happy to receive two souls instead of Bearskin's one. (KHM 120 is similar.)

Occasionally the devil even appears as an impartial judge who corrects social and moral abuses on earth. For example, he hires three upstanding laborers to help him prove a criminal's guilt and win over the convicted soul for himself. The devil does not abandon his workers when they get into hot water; instead he even frees them from the executioner's hand (KHM 120). The devil richly rewards the poor, hard-working butcher who naively offers him bratwurst, but he eats the rich, miserly brother.[60] We find the most positive picture of the devil in folktales where he takes the hero's evil adversaries to hell. Hell is not necessarily always a terrible place; on the contrary, it often offers a rather pleasant stopover with fresh wurst and ham.[61] KHM 100 portrays a jestfully distorted view of hell: The damned sit in large cauldrons under which the devil's grimy brother must neatly tend the fires. He performs this duty particularly well at those cauldrons in which he spots his former military superiors. In contrast to the legend, these tales no longer take Christian ideas seriously, showing that folktale tellers molded the figure of the devil independently, even in opposition to the church's version.[62]

The folktale also contains motifs obviously borrowed from other demonic figures and applied secondarily to the devil. For example, the devil appears as a man-eating monster in KHM 29 (otherwise only giants appear as such) and replaces other demonic figures such as the dragon.[63] The devil fills more than just two roles in the totality of folk tradition, i.e., in folktales, legends, and farcical tales.

The returning dead appear in both legends and folktales. In the legend these figures produce a highly numinous effect. In contrast, the dead do not return as spooks in the folktale: In the Nordic folktale, Cinderella's mother appears without sending the chill down our spine aroused by the returning dead in the legend.[64] "The Singing Bone" (KHM 28) is not a numinous object but rather "an amazing little horn that sings by itself." In the folktale it is considered the highest form of faith and devotion when a murdered mother returns to her child (KHM 11 and 13) or a dead child returns to his mother (KHM 109). In legend and folk belief the appearance of a dead person is interpreted as an unlucky omen. Only the folktale contains the dead as grateful helpers (KHM 217).*

In the legend people usually fear a man who returns from the dead, even if he is a beloved relative. In the folktale people can even happily marry the dead: Among the gypsy Taikon's narratives we find a folktale about a man who steals a woman who lives only by night; during the day

---

*Numbering follows Bolte and Polivka's *Anmerkungen zu den kinder-und Hausmärchen der Brüder Grimm.*—Trans.

she is dead. From the narrative's style we can determine that it is not a legend, and it also has a happy ending: The couple lived long and happily without ever fighting.[65]

When Death himself appears in the legend, he evokes a highly numinous feeling (e.g., Death as the leader of the wild horde; the Lenore motif). In the folktale, on the other hand, there is nothing shocking about Death personified. On the contrary, he is praised as the most just power, he can be outsmarted, and he becomes godfather to human children, bringing them fame with his gifts that make them miracle-working doctors (e.g., KHM 44). Death also occasionally functions as a grateful helper: In a Greek folktale the hero encounters Death sleeping on a precipice. Like the thankful animals before him, Death asks the hero, who threatens to shoot him (!), to spare his life. Death offers a bone as a pledge of his readiness to help the hero. When the king refuses to give up his daughter, the hero twists the bone; Death appears and takes the king away.[66]

Now we can consider the otherworld elements in legends and folktales in regard to their relationship to reality. Despite having the same names, supernatural figures in the folktale, seen as a whole, have a different foundation than those in the legend. The legend generally depicts "cursed" otherworld figures, the folktale "enchanted" ones. Even the external appearance of these figures differs greatly between the two genres. The folktale's otherworld figures almost always appear in human form; at worst they have unusual (giant, dwarf) or distorted (a hunchback in old age) proportions. The supernatural animal in the folktale is frequently a person under a spell. In the legend, demonic forces appear in animals' bodies. The animal-demon in the legend is something quite different from the transformed human-animal in the folktale. Snow White and Rose Red (KHM 161) have great fear of the black bear at first, but when he begins to speak, they immediately trust him. In the legend, talking animals are considered ghosts. This means that the folktale's miraculous world is "real" in the sense that it is normal, while the "real world" can appear very strange and induce fear.[67]

The folktale's demonic figures are visible and recognizable as a matter of course; they exist in a different reality than the same figures in legend and folk belief. Unlike the folktale, the legend contains amorphous ghosts that are not visible at all; humans can only hear or sense them. The vocabulary which describes the entrance of supernatural figures also reflects generic differences: In the legend ghosts "appear," "hover," or "suddenly turn up"; in the folktale Rumpelstiltskin "enters" (KHM 55). In the legend the devil is "conjured"; in the folktale he "knocks on the door" (KHM 101).

In the legend demonic forces dominate; in the folktale humans prevail over demons. Compared to the legend, the folktale has experienced a complete emancipation. Legendary figures belong to a real otherworld; folktale figures have become part of a fantasy world and are no longer truly "demonic,"[68] and therefore not truly "otherworldly" in the same sense as in the legend. The folktale does not know the meaning of the word *ghost*.

The legend lives in two worlds; the tension between them becomes life-threatening for humans. Mental illness and physical invalidism often result from interaction with the supernatural world in the legend. The legend consciously pits reality against the next realm. The folktale lives in only one world, where the real and transcendental coexist. This world and the next have equal rights, and therefore humans display no numinous shyness in the face of the otherworld in the folktale.[69] Of course, the folktale does contain the concept of fear (e.g., in KHM 121 and 220), but the best-known example, "The Boy Who Left Home to Find Out about the Shivers" (KHM 4), in which the encounter with the ghosts has none of the legend's horror, shows exactly how lightheartedly the folktale takes the numinous realm. The hero wants to learn about the shivers because he has heard they exist. But the beings that appear demonic to others seem quite normal to him and thus lose all their horror. Fantasy enhances fear in the legend; in the folktale it provides the vent for fear and opens the door leading away from numinous feelings.

Legends and folktales have different views of the supernatural world as well as of the real one. In the folktale, wonders do not function as such; instead they serve as repeatable truisms that shock no one and need no explanation. The talking wolf does not shock Little Red Riding-Hood, nor is the goose girl taken aback by Fallada, the talking horse, even when the dead horse's head continues to speak (KHM 89).

The folktale leads away from the mundane, but instead of returning to the routine, "the miraculous has become the routine" in the folktale.[70] In contrast, the legend's view of the world emphasizes the supernatural as something remarkable and overwhelming which happens once in a lifetime and always remains a mystery.

If the folktale, unlike the more critical legend, does not receive its impetus from impossible and fantastic events, we must consider the other forms and emphases of the folktale marvel. In the folktale, the functions fulfilled by people and objects, not their external form, are miraculous. Although we find horses that fly or speak in the folktale, there are neither horses with wings nor ones with many heads.[71] Because folktale marvels are not conspicuous, the narrative has no need for wonders as striking as those that occur in the legend. Nothing as extraordinary as the events in the legend ever happens in the folktale. The folktale employs only things necessary for the plot. In contrast, the legend contains elements intended to astonish the audience.

Characters in the legend often intentionally seek numinous experiences. They consciously try to encounter demons, and they risk their own safety while raising a treasure or disenchanting someone. Characters in the folktale, on the other hand, accidentally encounter marvels; this frees them from danger and gives them security. Folktale characters do not perform magic with their own powers, using an array of tricks and incantations like the typical characters who banish witches in the legend. Instead they effortlessly receive help from otherworld figures and their magical gifts. The folktale contains magical motifs but no magic like that in the legend. The folktale changes magic into play. In folk belief and legend, a witch's invocation of part-for-whole magic causes her victim great pain. In the folktale the hero uses a scale, hair, or feather to effortlessly invoke the helpful fish, horse, or bird.[72] Often enough the wonder is produced unintentionally (e.g., "The Spirit in the Bottle," KHM 99, or "Aladdin and the Magic Lamp"), without being sought or demanded by the character, as in the legend. In the legend a person actively, often driven by greed or curiosity, confronts demonic otherworld figures with a request (e.g., for reward, release, treasure, the dwarves' help). In contrast, folktale heroes generally do not encounter otherworld figures of their own volition; they are much less active in such interactions than their counterparts in the legend. In the folktale heroes are *tested*; in the legend people put themselves to the test.

The folktale has been called "wishful fiction" (Wunschdichtung), but the folktale teller's own wishes are often expressed unconsciously, and the desired happy ending occurs only after great effort and danger. Perhaps the label "wishful" better suits the legend, which openly expresses wishes, e.g., for the elusive treasure, for help from household ghosts, or for the maiden whom no one has been able to free.

In addition to these contrasts in demonic and otherworld reality, the two genres also depict humans quite differently: At the center of the numinous experiential legend stands the demon; the folktale focuses on humans. The folktale assigns the hero tasks which seem impossible, but in the end he or she overcomes them.[73] In the legend the offender must return from the dead to accomplish some unending Sisyphean task in order to gain release.[74] More precisely, the experiential legend has no hero.[75] The folktale describes a series of adventures with the hero at the center: This hero endures the various experiences. In the legend various people can encounter one otherworld figure. The narrative's title, if it has one, emphasizes this point. Even if the editor, not the narrator, usually provides the title, the psychological findings still hold true. The legend's title names the demonic figure: We speak of legends about the devil, giants, jack-o-lanterns, witches, etc. The folktale's title names the human hero: Hansel and Gretel, Snow White, Cinderella, Sleeping Beauty, Bearskin, Little Red Riding-Hood.[76] This is not an unimportant difference in emphasis.

In the legend the witch harms some farmer; it does not matter which, because it can happen to anyone, and she affects everyone equally. In the folktale the witch confronts only the hero (perhaps also the antihero); for others she does not seem to exist at all. In the legend the demon is timeless and permanent; it existed before humans and will outlast them. At the legend's end the demon can remain a threat to the future. In the folktale the *human* survives; his or her death always lies in the future.

The human characters' strengths peak at the end of the folktale, but in the numinous experiential legend they are often powerless. At the folktale's end the human around whom the story revolves is usually the victor; in the legend he or she is frequently defeated. In the folktale the young hero wins out, even with his lack of experience; the legend punishes the brash human, sometimes with death. Youthful spirit is dangerous in the legend; only the foresight, experience, and restraint of age can help.

In the legend, otherworld figures, not humans, conform to types. The people are portrayed individually; they have good and bad qualities and never exceed the bounds of normal human attributes. An individual may be unusually strong, but not stronger than is humanly possible. In the folktale, however, the hero is a special figure, either an ideal type who has only good qualities or a good-for-nothing, but never an average Joe. We do not need much of a description of a folktale king; we can imagine what he is like because this character hardly varies.

The folktale handles questions of ethics more subjectively than the legend, which judges objectively. The literal fulfillment of an oath clearly demonstrates the difference: The legend punishes the swindler who swears "to his creator above him" that he is standing "on his own land and soil" while hiding a ladle under his hat* and dirt from his property in his shoes. The Goose Girl in KHM 89, who swore not to tell anyone that she is really a princess, finally tells her woes to the cast-iron stove, i.e., an inanimate object, at the king's insistence. The king listens through the stovepipe and hears everything, but she still has kept her promise not to tell anyone.[77]

The legend emphasizes ethics much more than the folktale. Guilt and sin are important motifs in the legend's strict ethic. In the folktale, deceit can lead to happiness and success. The folktale does not apply ethical standards to magic, while the legend applies Christian standards and therefore condemns all magic as evil and devilish. The motif of the magic gun that always hits its target appears in both genres. In the legend the use of such hunting magic is an unpardonable sin; someone becomes a marksman only by devoting his or her soul to the devil. In the folktale (e.g., KHM 111) the hero receives the magic gun as a reward for loyal service to an apparently demonic hunter, and with this rifle makes a fortune as a sharpshooter. The folktale does not see Christian guilt in interaction with a demonic figure. The extraordinarily strict moral judgment in "Mary's Child" (KHM 3) does not contradict the thesis that folktales and legends have different ethics because this tone was added by the brothers Grimm.

The different relationships between internal and external reality in the

---

*A play on the German words *Schöpfer* (creator) and *Schöpflöffel* (ladle).—Trans.

two genres apparently account for their depicting different spheres of experience. The folktale generally excludes most external reality in favor of an inner psychic reality. The experiential legend depicts numinous astonishment at the apparent suspension of the natural laws of causality in external reality.

The events in both genres draw on a deep psychic level, but the real, external world triggers the legend, while the folktale's decisive factor lies in the internal world. The nature of the inner psychic need for communication determines where on the scale from folktale to legend the narrative will lie. The narrator's conscious choices as well as his or her inner psychic need for expression form the narrative. The formal components of the various genres of folk narrative depend on diverse basic psychic attitudes. Thus the legend and folktale reveal very different emotions. The legend is filled with astonishment, fear, shock, and agitation; belief and reason, experience, and feelings all play a large role in this genre. The internal world and the external environment, the body and soul, have close relationships here. In contrast, the folktale does not seem to know what pain is; it has little concern for emotion and feelings. It does not seem that folktales are played out in the interstice between internal and external worlds, but rather purely in the external. The folktale projects the psyche onto a material, external entity; almost everything internal is translated into external plot.[78] Max Lüthi correctly speaks of the folktale's "one-dimensionality" in contrast to the legend's "two-dimensionality." It almost sounds like an accusation when the same author says folktale characters have no inner world; folktale figures can be described as having no inner world because they *are* the inner world.

Consider the well-known ending of the Grimm tale "The Frog-Prince" (KHM 1). The loyal servant Heinrich had three iron bands around his heart to keep it from bursting with sorrow over the transformation of his master into a frog. After his master is disenchanted, the bands make a loud noise popping open, one after the other: "No, master, it is not the coach, it is a band from my heart." This transfer of the psychic into the material and external world makes the psychic itself visible. The inner world that Lüthi would like to deny the folktale lies in this external world. This concretization of psychic processes also leads us to reject Karl Spiess's characterization of people in the folktale as materialistic.[79]

Everything external in the folktale is only the visible expression of psychic processes. The shoe that fits and the matching half of a ring that identifies the correct bride seem to be completely external features of recognition, but the external constantly suggests something internal. The legend looks outward; the folktale listens inward. The folktale's language allows the psychic to become directly visible; the legend is more closely connected to the external world. Speaking metaphorically, the folktale is a dream without waking, i.e., without relation to reality; the legend is like waking up after a dream and recognizing reality's existence. The legend, which places such great value on the visual and sensual, often results from delusion, illusion, or even hallucination. The legend only seems more realistic because it always tries to maintain reason. The folktale confronts reason with its internal truth. Even as a purely fantastic narrative, the folktale maintains a certain reality of experience. The legend openly discloses experiences; the folktale conceals them behind the narrative's external development. The legend draws experiences from without, while the genuine folktale episode addresses an inner concern.

## THE AETIOLOGICAL NARRATIVE

The aetiological narrative is the only genre of oral folklore that always clearly establishes its content's relationship to external reality. The mode of thinking in this genre is the same over the entire globe: The narrative explains a lasting natural phenomenon as the result of a single past event. We must pay particular attention to the aetiological folktale's[1] relationship to reality here: Even if pure fantasy produces these narratives, they always provide concrete explanations for some phenomenon.

Aetiological narratives chart a broad mental link between European and tribal traditions. We find aetiological narratives in collections from almost all peoples, and they often outweigh all other genres. Oskar Dähnhardt and his colleagues have diligently compiled "nature legends" in their four-volume standard reference work,[2] but even this immense collection represents only a small fraction of the materials that have been collected. Antti Aarne's studies of Finnish animal stories in volumes 8 and 9 of the *Folklore Fellows Communications* also furnish rich material. A large number of aetiological narratives can also be found in the *Revue des traditions populaires*[3] under the heading "Les pourquois." Works by Adolf Ellegard Jensen[4] and Hermann Baumann[5] supply important non-European material. The volumes in the Atlantis series edited by Leo Frobenius are full of explanatory myths and folktales; and Robert Lehmann-Nitsche collected about eleven hundred aetiological narratives from South America alone.[6]

Narrators everywhere entertain an interest in the origin of things. In Europe and elsewhere, no phenomenon of note does not have a narrative to explain its current form. We find this need for causality in even the most basic realms of human life.[7] An older, purely historical-mythical question may have concerned humanity before this rational question of "rerum cognoscere causas": Was it always so? What was it like before? The question of cause develops only out of this interest in origins: Why did it change?[8] We are not constructing a psychological theory of the possible historical development of human thought. On the contrary, materials from tribal societies fully justify such statements about the historical evolution of these questions. Although both types of questions appear side by side in historical sources, it is certain that the aetiological question developed from a mythical awareness of reality. A look at the traditions of tribal cultures or at humanity's oldest religious documents reveals this course of development. The Old Testament's aetiological account of creation is still entirely within the mythical-religious realm. Among other things, the Old Testament explains why only the snake crawls on its stomach and "eats earth." The first section of Genesis concludes with an aetiology of the Sabbath. Aetiological narratives explaining sin, death, speech, the female gender, marriage, the supposed difference in the number of ribs between men and women, the sexual awakening, shame, clothing, labor pains, oppression of women, agricultural plagues, and human intelligence follow.[9] But once-believed aetiologies had already become mere fiction in Greek and Roman antiquity, e.g., in Callimachus's aetiologies or in Ovid's artistic metamorphoses, even if this material may have originated in folkloric thought.

It is difficult to pin down the conception of reality in modern aetiological narratives because they range from folk belief and legend to jest. Many of our legends are explanatory in character: They might explain why a church was not completed or why we can see the devil's footprint at a certain spot. A witch takes the blame for damage incurred by a house, stall, or field. We also identify aetiological thought in the belief that not everyone can see certain demonic figures, perhaps only children born on a Sunday or people who really want to see them. By seeking reasons for a figure's invisibility, the legend's inquiry into causality grapples with rational reality in its own way. Well-known motifs such as the death of the giant Pan, the departure of the dwarves, rewarding the spirits, the murder of the nymph, and all Christian motifs of exorcizing demons explain the cessation of a demon's appearances. The large number of motifs about disenchantment, with its innumerable possibilities and variations, also belong in this category. All of these legend-closing motifs are only variations on a theme, and all have the same aetiological purpose of showing, through the demon's demise, that people no longer believe in it.

Historical legends also contain aetiological explanations. For example, a story may explain a place name (e.g., the story of the women from Weinsberg).[10] Folktale collections also do not lack aetiological narratives of various ages and origins. Among the Grimms' tales, numbers 18 ("The Straw, the Coal, and the Bean"), 148 ("The Lord's Animals and the Devil's"), 172 ("The Flounder"), 173 ("The Bittern and the Hoopeo"), 175 ("The Moon"), 180 ("Eve's Unequal Children"), 194 ("The Ear of Wheat"), 222 ("Why Dogs Are the Enemies of Cats, and Cats of Mice"), and 223 ("Why Dogs Sniff Each Other") fit in this category.[11]

Most humorous explanations of place names are aetiological because they derive the nickname from a historical or fictitious occurrence. The saint's legend explains how and why a certain saint performed a miracle. In any case, there are so many aetiological narratives that we do not need to go out of our way to find them. In fact, attempts at tracing explanatory modes of thinking have gone too far, for example, Walter Berendsohn's attempt to show that the Grimm tale "Mother Holle" (KHM 24) is an explanatory children's story because it explains one girl's golden beauty and the other's ugly misfortune.[12] This interpretation is too far-fetched: The true aetiological folktale explains the general case, not the specific, and addresses very different subjects than KHM 24.

The grandest aetiological narratives explain the creation of the world and the human race (cosmo- and anthropogenesis), e.g., stories about ancestral parents or narratives about the origin of mortality and reproduction. The origin of sex receives particular attention; many such tales appear among the African materials in the Atlantis series.

Among most tribal cultures, legends about creation and the flood are still believed mythical reports.[13] Western Christians also tell aetiological narratives about the creation of the world. Some European legends supplement and expand the Biblical report of creation; others consciously contradict it in an undogmatic, often humorous manner. It is unlikely that we can determine the extent to which these European narratives originate from some lost, ancient mythical belief.

Antti Aarne recorded the following aetiological narratives in Finland: God created the world from mud the devil fetched from the sea's floor.[14] The earth became elongated because the Lord leans on one side of the planet, His Son on the other. Rocks used to be soft and even grew, but God commanded them to be hard. Mountains were created when the bottom of God's sieve for filtering rocks broke. Women were made from a dog's tail. The devil made gypsies as a counterpart and in opposition to God's creation of people. There are similar, sometimes obscene, stories about the origin of marriage, menstruation, genitals, baldness, red beards, the Adam's apple, the septum, etc.[15]

In a narrative from Lorraine the good-natured smith Mathis lets the devil walk away three times after duping and capturing him. The story ends by stating that "if Mathis were not so dumb the devil would still be sitting in a sack and there would be no more evil in the world."[16]

The Dutch origin legends collected by J. R. W. Sinninghe establish the origin of women, marriage, and smoking (the devil invented it). The narratives explain why the sea is salty, why dogs sniff each other, why February has twenty-eight days (it lost one day to January and one to March playing cards), etc. In addition to these humorous explanations, European tradition includes many Christian aetiologies. For example, lightning cannot strike the beech tree because Jesus' cross was made from beechwood.[17] KHM 194 uses a Christian aetiology to explain why wheat grows only at the top of the stalk. In the Danube region Christian legends explain why trees have branches[18] and why milk boils over.[19]

In many parts of Europe the biological folktale seems still to have a connection to the believed saint's legend. In Rumania the snail emerges from Christ's saliva; in Macedonia Mary's saliva produces the silkworm; in Iceland the devil's saliva transforms into the useless jellyfish.[20] But such believed explanatory legends have become rare in more recent European collections as the folk become increasingly cognizant of the fictional character of these explanations.[21]

Where these narratives address humans, they generally deal with questions about the origin and function of bodily parts, differences in skin color and body size, the causes of diseases, differences between poor and rich, etc. The stories commonly express ideas about the inheritance of acquired traits: One-time injuries result in lasting changes. For example, the female genitals resulted from a sparrow pecking at a wooden statue of a woman.[22] A Bulgarian narrative explains the arch of the foot in a story about a hero who supposedly cut meat from his own foot to feed the bird that carried him into the upper world.[23] We also find explanations for the plant world, e.g., why leaves turn red in autumn, which plants are edible and which are not and why, or how plants and their fruits attained their present form. Finally, a primitive geology explains the form of the earth's crust, the forms, types, and characteristics of rocks, and the size and course of rivers.

However, the vast majority of narratives which explain nature, in our own and in tribal cultures, focus on the animal world. Some explain why people eat certain animals; others explain why some animals molt. The aetiological narratives address the external appearance of certain animals, e.g., the color of their fur, or the origin of the fish's fins. Other stories explain an animal's form of nourishment (carnivore or not), the origin of hostile relations between particular animals, the various animal voices and what they mean,[24] the origin of animal names, the difference in appearance between the male and female, etc.[25] The explanation is not always obvious and often reveals the narrator's charming power of deduction and originality: When the devil created the mouse, God made the cat to attack it. Stories explain why there are traces of eyes on the horse's feet, why the pig has a short snout, why the hare's mouth is cleft, where the wolf got its long tail, why the spider has threads in its abdomen, and why the ant is "broken" in the middle.

These last illustrations are European examples from Finland,[26] but the narratives have almost exact parallels among distant peoples. For example, we have some expressive and inventive narratives from China: Mosquitos rise from the ashes of a monster. The dragon cheated the rooster out of his horns; now the rooster always calls for them. The crab gossiped about the cow, so the cow stepped on him, making him flat.[27] Japanese animal tales are no less fantastic than the Chinese: The pheasant is red because he is ashamed that the owl gave the best advice on how to free the king of the birds. As a consolation (!) the pheasant's meat was made tasty.[28]

We could compile a comprehensive folktale zoology from these narratives about peculiarities of the animals, but it would certainly not provide a uniform picture. In North America alone we find a dozen variants of how the raven became black.[29] One commonly finds an entire series of aetiological motifs strung together to explain several unrelated biological features at once. Animal legends and cosmogony can also combine to form peculiar narrative complexes. A Pawnee legend reports that one day mole dug a hole through the earth's crust; the light streamed through and drove him back in fright. Since then he has no eyes; the light put them out. Humans, who were still living under the ground then, went up through his hole, but the mole didn't want to come along.[30]

Even explanatory tales that are not believed reveal astute observations of nature. Those that contain no facts hold "kernels of truth" and disclose wise knowledge about life. Among these are some stories about the causes of death,[31] the origin of the white man,[32] or how intelligence was divided among the people.[33] Culture folktales (*Kulturmärchen*), which explain the origin of certain elements of civilization, are also neither completely arbitrary nor totally unrealistic. The tales are not necessarily historically accurate, but they are also not random inventions or fantasy intended solely to give some explanation. On the contrary, these stories often reflect important details about life in the given culture. Tribal narratives of this sort are based on actual observations of nature more than our own, but even aetiological fabulats often incorporate important aspects of real life. Only very specific elements of the past are important enough to be reported; therefore, these narratives about the history of civilization and the origins of human culture constantly repeat certain themes, e.g., how humans obtained the gourd,[34] the origin of hunting, of fire, and of laws and practices such as circumcision.[35] A Yoruba folktale that reports how a child was killed by his attendant closes with these words: "Since then it is Yoruba law that a woman shall not leave home before the seventh day after birth. Only after the seventh day shall she go into the bush."[36]

Highly graphic tales also trace the origins of items used in ritual. The culture hero usually plays the central role in these narratives. He brings fire, teaches the people how to make tools and weapons and how to hunt; he instructs them about rituals and ceremonies, and he even acts as a demiurge who performs cosmogonic deeds and gives the stars their regular paths.[37] Occasionally women discover and found such institutions.

We also find aetiological culture legends in Europe. For example, other narratives from Finland explain the origin of weaving textiles, distilling brandy, graves, ironworks, the organ, money, etc. But these narratives have long since left the realm of mythical belief in Europe. The same narrators explain why the priest wears a funny collar, why bald people can't enter heaven, etc.,[38] making it clear that they are telling farcical, or often obscene, stories even if they still use the old aetiological narrative devices.

Will-Erich Peuckert distinguishes two types of nature legend: an older one in which magic still plays no role, and a more recent stage in which divine or demonic forces can call forth magical transformations. Peuckert cites the tales which attribute the coloring of animals to a paint job:

> Two animals paint each other in Pomerania, among the Flemish, the Annamese, the Eskimos, the Ainu, Indians in North and South America, and Black Africans, in short, among all the peoples of earth. Only in

Germany, Holland, Rumania, and Malta—if Dähnhardt's collections are reliable—does the creator paint the animals. These clearly stand out as the products of high culture in a sea of primitive legends.[39]

Peuckert attributes all transformations without magic to a premagical time.

In addition to dividing the narratives historically, we also consider it important to ask how the tradition-bearers perceive the reality and credibility of their tales. According to these criteria, we can distinguish three types of aetiological narratives which exist in tribal societies and may still be recordable today: The first group consists of believed origin legends. Certain nature and culture aetiologies lie entirely within the religious, mythical world-view. They do not merely playfully establish causality; rather, they presuppose true belief. Occasionally we find such items even in European tradition. For example, a Finnish narrative describes the origin of the swallow: A witch kills her stepson; his sister puts his bones in a box made of bark and throws it into the sea. The swallow emerges from the remains.[40] Here we see the episodes of "The Juniper Tree" (KHM 47) in legendary, aetiological form which reflects the living folk belief that a person's vital energy lives on as a bird after death.

Of course, we encounter this sort of serious, believed text more frequently among tribal peoples. In a tale from the Moluccan island of Ceram we find an animal marriage folktale combined with an aetiological, historical legend:

> In the village Povallut on Hoamoal there once lived a young girl named Poisina. She fell in love with a crocodile who had taken human form. But she did not know he was a crocodile. One day she gave her beloved Sirih and Pinang, but the crocodile-man could not handle them and he got drunk. He foamed at the mouth and then water began to spew out. The girl Poisina fetched a clay bowl and held it in front of her beloved's mouth. The bowl filled up and she got another. This one also filled up with water, she fetched more and more empty bowls, and the water continued to stream out of her beloved's mouth. The village Povallut was flooded and sank. Now a lake of the same name lies where the village Povallut once stood.[41]

This is certainly a believed story. The story about the monkey's origin in Minahasa tradition (Celebes) bears further witness to the belief in aetiological narratives: Monkeys are considered primitive people or a special race of people; therefore monkey meat is rarely consumed.[42]

We can often still detect traces of older legendary or even mythical traditions hidden in fictional tribal folktales. Peeling back the folktale layer reveals the older elements. We repeatedly encounter aetiological folktales which seem to derive from an older myth that has been rationalized. Only at a rationalistic stage (or at least one that confronted rationalism) did the aetiological closing formula become necessary as an explanation. Often enough a discrepancy exists between the narrative and the explanation, clearly showing that the aetiological principle was added to an originally mythical narrative.

Myths are of obvious credibility and need no explanation. For example, Robert Lehmann-Nitsche asserts that the South American Indian animal tales "often do *not* explicitly emphasize the explanatory element as European narratives do with beloved additions, such as 'since then . . . ,' or 'therefore the robin has a large red spot on her breast. . . .'" He goes on to say that he has "the impression that this somewhat schoolmasterly finale does not belong to the original and was more likely added or adapted for the story's foreign listeners. The native who is quite familiar with the finest details of the local nature knows for himself, without further ado, . . . what the story alludes to." "The Indian's interpretations of the environment's peculiarities usually appear within myth and are usually of secondary importance there. They often weave the explanation into presentations of world-view, of the earth's origin, etc. Fables which directly explain a special feature are scarce; we can view these as products of fantasy developed later and which suggest the beginnings of artistic literature."[43]

The second group consists of aetiologies intended exclusively for entertainment, i.e., the explanatory folktale, a tale commonly imbued with a humorous tone and which has no religious content. Such tales were never believed, even among tribal peoples. They have no inner necessity and contain neither a mythical truth nor a deeper ethical reference. The explanatory folktale is simply a tale for a tale's sake.[44] This genre is an art form. In order to assign a tale to this group of narratives, we must consider the object of the explanation: Does it deal with some arbitrary unusual occurrence or with basic questions of human existence? The stories which belong to this group of artificial aetiological myths are usually quite rationalistic, differentiating them from true mythical reports of primeval times. The narratives in this group "have no basis in reality"; rather, they "strive to account for natural phenomena with graphic comparisons or rational attempts at explanation."[45] The method of universally supplying aetiological explanations has become a rational principle.

The aetiology as a mere play form constitutes the third group. In contrast to the other two groups, the aetiology does not construct the narrative here; rather, the explanatory element is reduced to a decorative motif: Unlike believed myths in which the explanation, if included, is believed reality, these narratives contain false, degenerated explanations. The aetiological closing "that is why . . ." is usually attached superficially, without any inner necessity, to extensive narratives without any apparent relationship to the narrative's primary content. For example, a dragon-slayer tale in central Sudan closes with this sentence which does not belong to the tale: "Ever since . . . the Hausa build Birnis (walls) around their cities."[46] At the end of an African version of "Cinderella" we learn the fate of the evil stepsister: She threw the eggs she received from Abaga the panther on the ground, and out came the lion, boa, and jackal. The tale closes: "The people would not admit the girl with her animals, so she had to return to the bush. That is why the lion, boa, and jackal still live in the bush today."[47] We find the following ending in a version of "The Wolf and the Young Kids" from Auvergne: "The wolf ate both of the big kids, but the smallest hid in his mother's shoe, and the wolf bit off the end of his tail. Since then goats have a very small, stubby tail."[48]

Almost all folktales which end with the questions "To whom does it belong?" "Who is right?" or "To whom do we owe it?" contain decorative aetiological motifs.[49] These questions have been added to the original tale. Even the lengthiest tribal folktales often have unnecessary aetiological endings. The tale certainly did not develop around the aetiology. It is therefore easy to judge these narratives. Presumably the narrative and the aetiological closing often did not originally belong together. Instead a later narrator combined them, and we can therefore assume that the tale is older than the amended explanation.

Narratives with this type of aetiological embellishment may once have been believed myths, or they may be narratives always intended merely for entertainment. One thing is certain, today they are no longer believed reality. Instead, these tales use a believed mythical form for entertainment. The explanatory element has become a closing formula. The aetiological folktale thus derives its fictional relationship to reality from the true myth's believed reality.[50] Yet it is interesting that the desire for a relationship to reality survives even in the fantastic realm of the folktale. The tale fulfills this need by formulaically borrowing from the once-believed aetiological legend.

## SAINT'S LEGEND AND FOLKSONG

The Christian saint's legend requires belief in the reality of its content, yet, as with other legends, we cannot always clearly separate it from the folktale because the saint's legend's[1] perception of reality has also changed throughout its historical development. Neither the extent and type of the holy miracle nor belief in it has remained constant. Originally, as with Gregor of Tours, Gregor the Great, and others, the saint's legend maintained a historical basis. Only since the Merovingian period, particularly because of influences from Oriental saints' legends, have reports of miracles by Christian saints become more and more fantastic, leading to the Council of Trent's (1545–63) declaration that worship of saints is useful and salutary but not necessary for salvation. The decree ruled that "all superstition about the invocation of the saints, worship of the reliquaries, and the use of icons shall be abolished."[2] This curtailment of overly fantastic outgrowths also meant that the folklore genre of the saint's legend would remain within the realm of religious reality. Humanism, the Reformation, Enlightenment, and rationalism all leveled criticisms at the saint's legend, resulting in the genre's constantly changing picture of reality. The saint's legend of the late Middle Ages is different from the modern saint's legend which occasionally appears in folktale collections (e.g., those by Angelika Merkelbach-Pinck, Gottfried Henssen, Matthias Zender, Father Pramberger, and others).

Historical and individual differences in the saint's legend's conception of reality aside, i.e., regardless whether the legend is believed religious reality or is told only for its poetic truth, strong emphasis on miracles is an essential feature of the genre. This represents the main difference between the saint's legend and the folktale: In the folktale miraculous events usually occur with a degree of matter-of-factness; in the saint's legend they are astonishing divine acts which command reverence. The saint's legend wonder is an extraordinary reality. If God himself or a saint does not perform the miracle, then angels carry it out (e.g., children's saints' legends [CSL] 1, 2, and 6 included in the appendix to the Grimms' tales). The miracles in the saint's legend themselves also differ considerably from the folktale's supernatural occurrences. For example, the miracle of the new sprouts from dry wood (CSL 6) and the motif of grave flowers (CSL 4) are typical saint's legend miracles which do not appear in the folktale (if they do, we can trace them to a saint's legend).[3] "The Heavenly Wedding" (CSL 9) contains a miracle specific to the saint's legend: A poor peasant boy shares his food with a "wood statue of the Madonna and the Christ child." The statue "began to fill out, and the people didn't know what to make of it." The story ends when the boy falls dead at his turn to take communion and goes to the "eternal wedding."

In this we can observe a basic difference between the folktale and the saint's legend. The folktale hero attains a worldly happiness; the saint's legend extends into holy eternity. The majority of the children's saints' legends in the appendix of the Grimms' tales (CSL 3, 4, 5, 6, 8, and 9) end with the death of the main character.

Yet at the same time the saint's legend claims to report true events. Like other legends, this genre bolsters its credibility by stating the time and/or place it occurred. "This was in Christ's time, when the Lord wandered the earth with his apostles preaching all over. In doing so he occasionally came to Wustweiler-Roth-Hambach on his way from Metz-Forbach-Hundlingen to Silzheim. . . ."[4] "The king of Bohemia wanted to know what his wife, the queen, had confessed to St. Johannes of Nepomuk. . . ."[5] "My mother was not yet born. I don't know what year it was, but I can figure it out. It was sometime between 1813 and 1825. In July there was a procession for Donatus. When the statue of Donatus was carried through the village. . . ."[6]

In contrast to the folktale hero, the figure depicted in the saint's legend is usually a historical personality. Of course, we also find saints with no historical precedent, for example, "the maiden with the beard" who appears in a saint's legend in the 1815 edition of the Grimms' tales.[7] She is the result of a misunderstanding: People mistook old Romanesque images of Christ wearing a skirt and crown for a woman. But the saint's legend historicizes even ahistorical saints. Thus the maiden with the beard was supposedly the daughter of a pagan king of Portugal; according to other versions she is the daughter of some other historical or pseudohistorical ruler.

Although it provides particular dates, the saint's legend still openly plays with time. For example, the Grimms' CSL 2 begins with an exact specification of time: "Three hundred years before the birth of Our Lord Christ." The twelve apostles are brothers born three hundred years before Christ, but their guardian angels rock them into a three-hundred-year sleep until the "night the Savior was born. Then they awoke and were with Him on earth." CSL 8, in which the little old mother sees her children in church as they would have been had they not suffered early deaths, also marvelously mixes real and unreal time: "The one was hanging on the gallows, the other tied to the wheel. 'You see,' said the aunt, 'that's what would have happened to them if they had lived and if God hadn't called them to Him while they were innocent children.'" Such a strange split between possibility and reality does not occur in the folktale. If the folktale depicts a vision or a dream (e.g., KHM 181), it becomes reality.

Despite all their differences, the folktale and the saint's legend constantly interact. Facilitated by a once more similar conception of reality, the genres have exchanged numerous motifs during many centuries of adjacent development within oral tradition. Motifs that appear purely fantastic to us today and seem more part of the folktale's unreal world once dominated the saint's legend. For example, we find the motif of the hero's unusual or supernatural procreation and birth in the saint's legend as well as in the folktale: St. Olcanus's mother lay in her grave seven years before her brother Patrick woke her to bear her child.[8] Even dressed as a folktale, this saint's legend lays claim to belief. Saints' legends contain other folktale motifs: talking and helpful animals,[9] tests of intelligence, riddle and other contests.[10] Some of the children's saints' legends in the appendix of the Grimms' tales also correspond to well-known tale types and often contain motifs otherwise foreign to Christian saints' legends. "St. Joseph in the Forest" (CSL 1) basically consists of the folktale scheme of the kind and unkind girls who each serve an underworld figure and receive reward or punishment according to their good or evil behavior.[11] St. Joseph replaces Mother Holle or the three little men (KHM 24 and 13). Some saint's legend heroes, such as the king's son (CSL 4), the mistreated youngest child (CSL 1), etc., are typical folktale figures. The aetiological principle which occurs in these saints' legends (e.g., "The Hazel Branch," CSL 10; CSL 7, which explains why the cornbind is called "Mary's glass"; and "Eve's Unequal Children," KHM 180, which explains the origin of occupations) is also not an original element of the Christian legend.[12]

We can identify folktale–saints' legends, i.e., saints' legends which have borrowed from the folktale, as well as hagiographic folktales which resemble saints' legends. For our topic the second group is of more interest. In particular we must ask how, and to what extent, the saint's legend's perception of reality and miracles penetrates the folktale. The Grimm collection alone offers rich material for examining this question. For example, "The Griffin" (KHM 165) contains the St. Christopher motif about the tall man who doesn't know why he has to carry all the people across the river. In KHM 76 ("The Carnation") the queen has "no children because the Lord had shut her womb." God then answers her prayers for a child: An angel comes down from heaven and promises her a son. "Two angels from heaven in the form of white doves" bring the queen her daily food when the king immures her in a tower. At the end of the tale she dies: "When she was buried, the two white doves . . . which were really angels from heaven, perched on her grave." In contrast, her son follows the career of a true folktale hero, and his part of the story contains no Christian motifs.

We find another example of saint's legend motifs penetrating the folktale in KHM 33, at the end of which the cardinals in Rome elect the hero to be pope. Other versions of this tale have true folktale endings without the pope motif. It seems the tale about understanding animal languages was applied secondarily to a pope.[13] Despite the election of the Swiss count's son to the papacy, the Grimm tale remains a true folktale about a hero who understands animal languages.

Other folktales have also taken on Christian motifs without losing their folktale character in the process. Guardian angels appear in "Snow White and Rose Red" (KHM 161); parents "baptize" the son they desired even though he is born as an animal (KHM 108); the brothers fail to fetch "baptismal water" (KHM 25); and a mother gives her youngest son the Biblical name Benjamin (KHM 9). Even the water nixie in KHM 79 attends a Christian church. The fisherman's wife's greatest desire in KHM 19 is to become pope, but for model folktale heroes, eternal salvation is most important (KHM 87).

One of the two traveling companions in KHM 107 justifies his carefree attitude with moving trust in God: "I trust in God and don't worry about a thing." "God must be glad that I'm so merry." But this is only an isolated Christian motif, and we cannot speak of Christian miracles for this folktale because the traveler, like a true folktale hero, finds his good fortune by chance. Christian elements such as praying in the face of danger, thanking God when it is endured, and the parents' blessing are merely decorative motifs in the true tale of magic.[14] A folktale does not become a saint's legend just because the parents' prayer for a child is answered, even if "God fulfills their wish" (e.g., KHM 144). Likewise, the heroine's prayer that she and her brother be rescued in some versions of "Hansel and Gretel" (KHM 15) does not make the tale a saint's legend. The tale remains a true folktale despite this Christian feature.

Of course, in some cases the generic borders are still in flux. "The Star

Talers" (KHM 153), for example, appears legendary: The poor girl acts out of Christian charity, religious compassion, and trust in God, and she is richly rewarded for her kindness. This seems like a saint's legend even if the figures who test the girl's compassion are not saints and the tale does not emphasize that the rain of stars is a miracle from God.

A series of tales in the KHM are neither true folktales nor true saints' legends, but rather "religious stories" (Types 750–849) in which the characteristics of both genres merge. These tales differ from the saint's legend because an anonymous pious person, rather than a particular saint, is the central figure. For example, an unnamed miller's daughter is the heroine in the strongly religious tale "The Girl without Hands" (KHM 31). In the actual saint's legend, a Christian saint must overcome the temptations of the evil world; in these saint's legend–folktales a person must prove his or her piety (or fail to do so) in an encounter with an unrecognized saint or holy person. Such is the case in KHM 3, where a Christian figure (the Virgin Mary) tests the child (in a Sicilian version St. Franz of Paula plays the girl's godfather).[15] In contrast to most of the Grimms' children's saints' legends, "Mary's Child" has a true folktale happy ending even though the protagonist (we can't really call her a heroine) did not prove herself. To be sure, folktale luck or chance does not trigger the heroine's change of heart, but rather a clearly Christian miracle. The miracle occurs when the queen, sentenced to burn at the stake for cannibalism, repents: "Immediately the heavens sent rain that put out the flames, and above her a light flared, and the Virgin Mary descended with the two little sons at her sides and the newborn daughter in her arms. She spoke kindly to her, 'All those who repent their sins and confess will be forgiven,' and she handed her the three children and loosed her tongue, and bestowed happiness upon her for the rest of her life." These are absolutely the powers of the saint's legend.

"The Girl without Hands" (KHM 31) also resembles the saint's legend. The motif of an angel closing a sluice in response to the girl's prayer, so the moat dries out and she can cross, does not appear in other folktales; it is clearly a saint's legend miracle.[16] And when the outcast queen prays in the forest, the "angel of the lord" appears again and leads her to a hospitable little house. There a "snow-white maiden" greets her and explains: "I am an angel sent by God to care for you and your child." God also sustains the royal husband while he searches for his outcast wife, although he does not drink or eat the entire time. And finally, God also allows the heroine's hands to regrow. Nevertheless "The Girl without Hands" follows the folktale scheme of the innocent persecuted woman. Folk belief in magical causality and Christian miracles coexist in this tale: The girl's immunity from the devil is based partly on magical warding-off practices (such as drawing a circle with chalk and washing herself) and partly on the Christian image of the tears which, as a sign of contrition, disempower the devil.[17]

The effective powers in other folktales also oscillate between those typical of the saint's legend and those ordinarily associated with the folktale. "Mary's Child" (KHM 3) is the best-known instance in the Grimm collection. A comparison of the versions suggests that saint's legend figures have replaced the folktale's older demonic otherworld figures. For example, a little black man appears instead of the Virgin Mary in a Swabian version of this tale type.[18] In other versions we find other demonic figures such as a fairy, a mysterious black woman, a sorceress, in Sweden the "Grey-Coat," and in Algeria the demonic ghoul.[19]

Other tale types also interchange the folktale's marvel and the saint's legend's divine miracle. In the Grimm tale "The Juniper Tree" (KHM 47) the murdered boy's bones magically transform themselves into a beautiful bird, and through the guilty stepmother's death the bird magically becomes a living boy again. But a Palestinian version attributes the same events to a miracle of God: Here the sister lays the bones under the chicken trough after the father eats the boy. When the father asks his wife about the boy, a cock appears: "God created it from the boy's remains."[20] The Palestinian version seems more rational than the Grimm version's purely magical events: The former *explains* the occurrence as a miracle, but this does not make the tale unreal; it remains believable. This is a common development in narrative reality: When belief in magical causality falters, a saint's legend miracle can save it. In other words, folktales occasionally become saints' legends in order to preserve their credibility. In a modern Greek version of KHM 36, for example, Christ himself gives a poor man a "table-be-set."[21] In Russian folktales St. Nicholas often plays the role of supernatural donor.

Similarly, the mother of God, the apostles, and the Lord himself perform the deeds originally attributed to fairies, sorcerers, and enchanted animals. In some French tales "the folktale hero crosses himself and puts himself at God's mercy before he begins his adventure." He receives his magical items from God or St. Peter. "The folktale princess's disease is caused by carelessly throwing away the host."[22] In a Spanish folktale the grateful dead man is not a debtor for whose burial the hero pays, but rather a soul in torment whom the hero helps free from purgatory.[23]

We also find similar items in German folktales. Christian saints appear instead of the three little men (KHM 13), elves, fairies, and water nixies.[24] Mother Holle becomes a heavenly woman, St. Sunday, an angel, or the Virgin Mary.[25] And the German folktale has an affinity for religious closings: The poor goatherd receives compensation for his suffering in heaven;[26] the hero leads the rest of his life in solitude; the princess enters a nunnery to learn nursing.[27] Some narratives conclude with religious maxims;[28] upon his death the devout hero returns "his soul to God."[29] Under the influence of Christianity, prayer replaces magic and folktale fate is no longer undeserved. The hero no longer succeeds because he is the chosen one naturally helped by all the supernatural powers; instead he also needs to demonstrate human thoughtfulness, take precautions, and above all remain very pious.

In a Carinthian folktale a prayer book causes the robber to mend his ways.[30] The worried heroine of another Austrian folktale kneels in prayer for a while and then says an extra Lord's Prayer for the poor souls who need protection. Her little sister promises the Lord she will make a pilgrimage to Einsiedeln if he leads her out of the wild forest.

The princess in a Pomeranian folktale cowers before the horrifying fight between her rescuer and the dragon and asks God to assist the stranger.[31] A folktale from the Harz Mountains tells of the king's troubled child: "Her only consolation was her good conscience, her only support was prayer; this kept her from abandoning all hope and gave her courage."[32] The hen girl in a Tirolian folktale wants nothing to do with marriage to a snake. Only after an image of Mary tells her exactly how to disenchant the snake does she declare herself ready to marry the animal.[33] Similarly, in a Styrian folktale the minister is consulted, and only after his reassuring recommendation of nine candles and nine garlands of roses is the disenchantment successfully carried out.[34]

The folktale's inclination toward the saint's legend only partly changes its picture of reality. Deeds no longer believably attributable to demonic figures are ascribed to supernatural powers referred to by dogmatized high Christianity. In other words, the folktale's supernatural occurrences no longer appear believable unless they are transplanted into a current religion and changed into Christian miracles.

But the incorporation of Christian miracles does not always fundamentally change the basic ideas behind the folktale. Praying the rosary while trying to break a spell *magically* increases one's power. Consistent with the Catholic belief that priests possess magical skills, folktale characters use sacred objects and religious customs to strengthen or oppose magical powers.[35] Here the folktale's and Christian folk religion's world-views meet within the same reality.

Numerous miracles have also streamed from saints' legends to folksongs. For example, the motif of flowers on the grave appears in German folksongs such as "Graf Friedrich" and "Die entführte Graserin."[36] The miracle of the branch also passed from the saint's legend to the ballad "Der Tannhäuser."[37] The miraculous sprouts from the dry branch indicate that Tannhäuser's sins are forgiven. We also find legendary features in the ballads "Wegwarte" and "Das Versteinerte Brot."[38] Saints often intervene in folk ballads, preventing a tragic ending: St. Thomas returns the royal Moringer[39] to his home in time for him to prevent his wife's second marriage. St. Julie brings another well-known ballad figure, the Margrave of Bakenweil,[40] home to defend his rights as a husband. Heavenly powers intervene and save other innocent ballad heroes from execution (e.g., "Der Spielmannssohn")[41] or keep them young and healthy during many years of imprisonment (e.g., "Edelmann und Schäfer").[42] A sign from heaven predicted by the dying ballad hero proves his innocence (e.g., "Raumensattel," "Scloß in Österreich," "Alter Mann und Schüler").[43] In all of these cases we can clearly recognize that the narrative saint's legend donated the motifs to the songs. Moreover, we have no reason to suspect that people consider miracles in the folk ballad any less real than those in the saint's legend itself. Pursuing the relationship between these two genres of folk poetry further would be a profitable endeavor, but we must now turn to the largely neglected area of the many interrelationships between folktale and folksong.

Folktale collections occasionally include tales that seem to be folksongs in prose. The tale "The Soldier" from Lorraine[44] provides an example of a song that lives on in narrative form. In the ballad a greedy mother unknowingly kills her own son. The recorded tale is clearly an early, transitory form: The narrative includes entire stanzas from the song, and the narrator herself still remembered the bear trainers who brought the song to the village. The ballad and the narrative passed off as a "folktale" contain the same level of realism in their report of a gruesome news item.

We also commonly find the opposite relationship between the genres; i.e., folksongs pick up elements from folktales. For example, a number of children's songs are based directly on folktales. Children's games involving the princess who is walled in and then released[45] seem to be based on "Maid Maleen" (KHM 198). Likewise, the song "Briar Rose Was a Beautiful Child"[46] developed from KHM 50. Using historical literary sources (e.g., works by Johann Fischart and Andreas Gryphius), Johannes Bolte compiled numerous folktale fragments in children's songs.[47] Children's songs and games imbue folktales which have lost their element of reality with new dramatic reality.

Yet more interesting for our questions about reality are folktale motifs in adult folksongs. The extent to which folksongs include folktale motifs varies from country to country. Folk narrative has a particular tendency to take the form of a ballad in England[48] and in the Scandinavian countries, where the troll ballad derives its materials from the folktale.[49] The folktale motif of the snake kiss appears in Scandinavian and English folk ballads; "The Singing Bone" (KHM 28) also supplies material for a ballad distributed throughout Scandinavia and Great Britain.[50] The Danish folk ballad "Algrev and the Queen" tells of bringing a dismembered and cooked person back to life.[51]

In Scandinavian ballads, as in folktales, the dead mother returns to her children to take care of them.[52] The ballad "The Waterman" describes marriage to a supernatural figure. The Danish ballad "The Maiden and the Wolf"[53] depicts transformations caused by the evil stepmother. Maximilian Lambertz reports that a good deal of folktale material lives on in Albanian folksongs, particularly ballads.[54] Cinderella (KHM 21) is also found in a Greek ballad.[55]

The relationships between ballad and folktale merit a more exhaustive treatment. We can choose only one example here: The magic flight and the contest of transformations[56] are found in numerous folksongs throughout Europe. In a French ballad a maiden refuses a young man's visit, and in order to escape from him, she changes into a rose; he changes himself into a bee so he can kiss her. She then becomes a fish, he a fisherman. In turn, she becomes a hare and he a hunting dog, etc. A Scottish ballad depicts a similar contest of transformations which concludes as follows:

> Then she became a silken plaid
> And stretched upon a bed,
> And he became a green covering,
> And gaind her maidenhead.[57]

These folksongs are derived from the tale type "The Magic Flight," yet their perspectives on the reality of magic are much more modern than the folktale's. In song, transformations are only poetic fiction, images of two lovers coming together. Transformations into a dead man and the earth which "swallows" him, into a nun and a priest, into a star and a cloud which "engulfs" it, into a silk blanket and the accompanying green covering, no longer have a magical reality; they are images which do not conceal their eroticism very modestly.

The German songs corresponding to these French and English-Scottish ballads are similar. For example, Erk-Böhme (III, 1083) include a song about a contest between a maiden and a young boy:

> "If I were a little mouse,
> I'd crawl into the little house."
> "If I were a cat,
> I would want to catch you like that." (3rd stanza)

Here, too, reality plays a completely different role than it does in the tale of the magic flight. The song no longer contains real transformations, only "crazy wishes"—as the heading in Erk-Böhme indicates. The wishful folktale situation remains unrealized as it does in numerous songs,[58] many of which begin with: "If I had the tolls on the Rhine and Venice were mine . . ." (EB 1088). "I wish to God I were a beautiful little bird in the forest . . ." (EB 1082). "If I had three wishes . . ." (EB 1081). "If I had the power to make seven wishes . . ." (EB 1081). These are sentimental songs about wishes unlikely to be fulfilled.

Other wishful songs depict unreal situations: For example, the extraordinary tasks the suitors in Erk-Böhme 1090ff. must complete are impossible and therefore do not lead to marriage. Other songs turn folktale motifs into deliberate lies (EB 1095ff): e.g., "Schnudelputzen's Hausstand" (EB 1097f.), which describes a crazy household, or the parody about absurd folk remedies (EB 1099). Songs about the world upside down (EB 1104) and about Cockaigne (EB 1095f.) include the same unreal, exaggerated motifs of the ship that sails on land, the blind man who sees a rabbit, and the roasted doves that fly away with their stomachs turned toward the sky that appear in "The Ditmarsh Tale of Lies" (KHM 159; cf. KHM 138) and "A Tale of Cock-a-doodle" (KHM 158).

## FOLKTALES WITHOUT THE HAPPY ENDING

The happy ending is one of the folktale's most important defining features. It belongs to the very essence of the tales we call, following Antti Aarne's designation, "true folktales" or "tales of magic" (*Zaubermärchen*). But novellas (*novellenartige Märchen*) also have happy endings, thus linking them to the other main group within the genre of folktale. The more difficult and thorny the hero's path and the more serious the conflicts he faces, the greater his happiness will be.[1] After all the difficulties and despite all the magical barriers, ultimate success is always certain in the folktale's fantastic world. The hero fulfills the tasks, solves the riddles, and wins the princess's hand despite all the opposition he faces. People under spells and curses are freed, the animal-bridegroom regains his human form, and Sleeping Beauty awakes from her magical sleep. Lovers are reunited and live happily ever after. The slandered and outcast wife is rehabilitated, and the couple's marriage continues in happiness; the abandoned children return to their parents' house. The water of life revives the dead. The princess is not really dead and is brought back to life (Snow White). In the end the hero defeats his demonic adversaries and surmounts all danger; freedom from giants, sorcerers, witches, and dragons is gained. The hero wins the contest with the demonic monster; a last-minute ruse saves the soul promised to the devil.

In the social realm as well, everything turns out fine in the end: the poor become rich, the poor farmer and his one ox becomes the richest farmer in the land, and the apprentice becomes king and lives a magnificent, happy life. Many closing formulas express this stereotypical happy ending: The folktale would not be the same without it. Hundreds and thousands of folktales contain the happy ending, which is part of the narrative's standard form.

We can easily check this assertion: Folktales without the happy ending are often fragmentary or mutilated. Comparison with other versions indicates that the tale type does indeed follow the rule of happy endings. Let us look at two examples from the Grimms' collection. The Oelenberg manuscript* of the Grimms' tales includes the tale about the two young chimney sweeps who eat the magic bird's heart and liver. According to prophecy, anyone who does so will become rich and be emperor. The tale ends when

---

*Forty-nine tales collected by the Brothers Grimm and sent to Clemens Brentano in 1810. Never published by Brentano, they were discovered in the Oelenberg monastery in Alsace in 1920. These early transcripts reveal the changes made by the brothers before publishing the tales.—Trans.

the goldsmith, who wants to marry their sister, chases them out of the house.[2] Thus the Oelenberg manuscript text is a folktale with an unhappy ending, but this variant is clearly an anomaly. The folktale's epic laws require fulfillment of the rhymed prophecy at the heart of the tale:

> Wer ißt mein Herzelein,
> der wird bald Kaiser seyn,
> wer ißt mein Leberlein,
> findet alle Morgen unterm Kissen ein Geldbeutelein
>
> (whoever eats my little heart
> will soon become emperor,
> whoever eats my little liver
> will find a little moneybag under his pillow every morning)

The verse makes sense only if the rest of the tale refers to it, but this does not happen in the manuscript version. We can accurately describe the variant with the abrupt ending as corrupted. The Oelenberg manuscript version of "Little Brother and Little Sister" (KHM 11) also lacks the happy ending.[3] In such cases the brothers Grimm tended to use other versions to help produce a composite printed text which corresponds to the tale type, including the happy ending.

In any case, the happy ending is so basic to the true folktale that we must question the mere concept "tragic folktale." Isn't a "folktale with an unhappy ending" an oxymoron? Let us examine some narratives with unhappy endings and ask whether we can refer to them as "folktales."

We begin with "antifolktales" in which the protagonist is a negative hero. A number of courtship tales direct our sympathies overwhelmingly toward the man by juxtaposing him with an unworthy woman (occasionally the roles are reversed). The person is sometimes portrayed so negatively that the tale cannot end happily, even though the other spouse's behavior is irreproachable. In the following examples, the female antihero prevents a happy closure to narratives that seem like folktales. "The Three Snake Leaves" (KHM 16) has a tragic ending because the princess, whose hand the hero wins only with great effort and sacrifice, turns out to be unfaithful and must be condemned to death. In other words, the tale portrays the wife so negatively that it cannot possibly have a happy ending. In "The Fisherman and His Wife" (KHM 19), the wife's insatiable greed leads to catastrophe; the typical folktale good fortune is wasted, and the fishing couple end up where they started, poverty-stricken. This tale contains an odd mixture of elements from the tale of magic (i.e., grateful animals) and the Christian world-view. The religious hubris motif accounts for the negative ending: The fisherman's wife is punished for her sinful desire to be pope, or even God. In both KHM 16 and 19 the unhappy ending belongs to the normal tale type.

Certain tale types about suitors normally end with the wedding, but individual variants end negatively. Narrators seem to consider the proud princesses who pose impossible tasks unworthy of marriage. In an Albanian variant of Type 329 ("Hiding from the Devil"), the hero successfully hides from the princess, but the defeated princess "burst with rage," thus preventing the usual folktale wedding.[4] The wedding is normally an essential part of this tale of magic: Why else would the hero put himself through her tasks? We can explain the fact that the hero does not marry in this variant only by assuming that the narrator did not want to allow the proud, conceited princess to have a happy folktale wedding. A Swiss folktale also tells of an insolent young woman who loves a young man but won't show him any affection. She rejects his advances while accepting his many gifts. This folktale also ends tragically: The suitor renounces his sweetheart, and she then waits for him in vain.[5]

Excessive moralistic considerations diminish the true folktale's lightness. Only the farcical tale (*Schwankmärchen*) can depict these antiheroes without moral reflection. To maintain their effectiveness, a number of folktales depict the hero in a series of failures, rather than in his usual progression. Type 1450 features a peculiar antifolktale hero. "Hans in Luck" (KHM 83) may not be an antihero in the moralistic sense, but he is an antihero to the happy folktale (*Glücksmärchen*). Through a series of bad trades, Hans forfeits his happiness himself. But he doesn't notice that he has lost everything he owns, and he does achieve true folktale happiness in his own subjective imagination. Objective reality judges Hans negatively, and the tale's effect relies on this difference. Folktales often utilize such contrasts to achieve an effective surprise ending. At the end of a Portuguese folktale, a monkey falls into a well while listing his good fortune.[6] We find some very creative narratives that imitate the happy folktale to achieve the surprise negative ending. An Armenian folktale offers an example: A poor man goes out to find God. He wants to ask why he is poor even though he works arduously. On the way he meets three animals. Each requests that the man ask God a question. The man finds God, receives the answers, and delivers them to the animals on his way back. He declines the rewards for his efforts, trusting in God's promise to help him. As a result of his stupidity the wolf-man, who wanted to know why he had been sick and leprous for seven years, eats him. The man had delivered the answer: Eating a dumb human will cure the wolf-man.[7] Such is the tragic close of this tale, which maintains the fiction of a happy folktale until the very end so that the audience actually expects a happy ending. "Godfather Death" (Type 332, KHM 44) also ends with the hero's death, despite all of his fantastic successes and miraculous healings, because in the long run Death can't be outsmarted.

If the folktale includes a moralistic lesson, it may not mix well with a happy ending. Moralistic tales provide frightening warnings as well as shining examples. A number of "religious stories" (Types 750–849) close with a cautionary exemplum. "God rewards and punishes" is the central theme of these moralistic tales, which usually end with a negative example. The true folktale reverses the sequence, and the hero's success follows others' failures. In KHM 87 ("The Poor Man and the Rich Man"), the negative example follows and contrasts with the happy one. A medieval literary version of this tale (Type 750) in Stricker's *Mären* already shows this purely didactic trend: Egotistical wishes bring harm to the rich man.[8] Punishment of the rich and greedy is a well-loved theme: In Type 751 Christ and St. Peter punish the greedy peasant woman by changing her into a woodpecker or making her take two snakes as foster children. We can also add a number of "binary" tales to this category: In "Mother Holle" (KHM 24, Type 480) the unkind girl's horrible fate is made more effective by the contrast to the kind, helpful girl's preceding adventures.[9] "Simeli Mountain" (KHM 142, Type 676) and "The Fires of Youth" (KHM 147, Types 752 and 753) also follow this pattern. In the former a greedy attempt to repeat a lucky adventure ends in death; in the latter a blacksmith burns his mother-in-law trying to repeat God's miracle.

Types 780ff., which depict how a crime is discovered and the perpetrator punished, also have unhappy endings. KHM 115, "The Bright Sun Will Bring It to Light" (Type 960), and "The Singing Bone" (KHM 28) are prime examples. Sin and reprisal, not true folktale elements, dominate these moralistic tales so much that they don't even mention bringing the innocent victim back to life. These tales focus on the antihero's crime, how it is miraculously discovered, and the identification and punishment of the criminal, not the hero's deeds. The "beautiful grave" and "proper burial" are the victim's only consolation. Some versions do have a conciliatory ending in which the murdered man is restored to life in typical folktale manner, and sometimes the murderer even receives a pardon. This strange combination of features makes Type 780 ("The Singing Bones") a cross between a tale of magic and a moralistic, didactic legend.

Other religious folktales, such as those grouped under Types 750ff. and 780ff., also belong to this group of moralizing folktales with unhappy endings. In "The Dog and the Sparrow" (KHM 58) the sparrow avenges his friend the dog, whom a farmer maliciously runs over. In the end the farmer's own wife kills him. The Aarne-Thompson index classifies this tale as an animal tale in the subgroup "Birds" (Type 248), but it is actually a moralistic tale which reminds us that recklessly killing an animal will be strictly and severely punished.

Moralistic considerations even alter the character of a series of "true folktales" by eliminating the usual happy ending. Punishment of disobedience is a common closing motif; since the hero must be penalized, a carefree, happy ending is out of the question. If the farcical tale "The Master Thief" (Type 1525) fails to charm the narrator with its characteristic playfulness, he or she may find it necessary to impose moralistic considerations and punish the thief.

Many versions of "The Singing Bone" (KHM 28) resemble legends because they fail to bring the dead man back to life. Some versions of "The Juniper Tree" (KHM 47) include the typical folktale happy ending, while other, more legendary versions lack the bird and the reincarnation of the boy from his bones.[10] Are these legendary variants of the well-known folktale (Type 720) fragments or relics of an archaic form? The verse about collecting the bones which appears in most versions ("my sister Marleenken gathered up all my bones . . .") allows us to conclude that the archetypal form included the reincarnation from the bones. The legendary variants without the happy ending show just how similar folktales can be to the believed legend.

Not coincidentally, we find two variants of "The Juniper Tree" with the unsettling ending in Hertha Grudde's east Prussian collection alone.[11] Narratives in this collection often lack happy endings; few of the texts correspond to international tale types 300–749.[12] For example, in tale number 38 ("The Seven Brothers," pp. 71ff.) a king drowns his seven sons. Although this narrative follows the structure of a folktale, it does not have a positive outcome: The king loses his throne, but no one brings the seven brothers back to life: "And they chased the king into the woods, where he died!" Characteristic of the texts in Grudde's collection, reincarnation does not accompany the punishment.

The people turned to stone in a few variants of "Faithful John" (Type 516), like the boy in "The Juniper Tree," are not brought back to life. Nor does the faithful servant always succeed in averting the prophesied fate.[13] Tales such as these (cf. KHM 28 and 47) are clearly related to archaic folk belief and often approximate the legend.

The general focus of a number of narratives in the Grimms' collection clearly makes them legends without happy endings.[14] The inclusion of these items in the KHM does not represent a methodological error by the brothers Grimm; rather, it reveals their artistic aim of making the collection more diverse. But even in the Aarne-Thompson tale type index, many of the entries under "Tales of Magic" (Types 300–749) are clearly legends. For example, "Lenore" (Type 365) is actually a legend: The abduction of the bride by the dead bridegroom is a frightening numinous event—as only legends depict—often linked to a moral about not conjuring the dead by crying too much. "The Vampire" (Type 363; not in the Grimm collection) also ends negatively. In an Estonian version of Type 363, a girl marries a man who enters a church during their honeymoon and devours the corpses while the pastor is consecrating them. When the wife finally tells her husband that she saw him do this, he bursts into rage (he had told her not to watch him) and strangles her while letting out a bloodcurdling roar.[15] This is clearly a legendary unhappy ending. Type 366 ("The Man from the Gallows") and other narratives about the hanged man who comes back from the dead to demand the return of his liver (heart, clothing, etc.) from the poor man who took it from the corpse are equally legendary (e.g., KHM 211, according to Bolte-Polivka's enumeration). The tale about the witch's house (related to Type 333) often ends tragically. KHM 42 ("The Godfather") is a legendary narrative, particularly in the second half: The hero unknowingly finds the devil's house full of strange things and flees in fright. We find most texts of this tale in legend collections.[16] In the Grimm version (KHM 42) the hero successfully flees—as we would expect in a folktale—but in other, more legendary versions, the person does not escape from the devil's or witch's house alive.[17] The related tale "Frau Trude" (KHM 43) is definitely a warning tale. It shows what can happen to a little girl who goes to the witch's house against her parents' will.

Warning or scare tales compose a special group of folktales without happy endings. The best-known case is "Little Red Riding-Hood" (Type 333). Research by Paul Delarue and Marianne Rumpf[18] confirms what Robert Petsch, among others, had originally conjectured,[19] namely, the *Urform* of this tale must have had a tragic ending, and the positive close was amended later. Little Red Riding-Hood and her grandmother were first rescued from the wolf's belly—like the kids in KHM 5—in the Grimm version (KHM 26). This positive ending makes the tale more like the typical tale of magic. Other warning tales have also shifted to the positive ending by allowing the villain to be outwitted. But this is not an original feature of "Little Red Riding-Hood"; most versions have a tragic ending. This means that such tales were told primarily as a warning and had to include the frightening tragic ending to achieve the desired pedagogic effect. Only the Grimms' artistic workover, including the addition of a happy ending, made this tale conform to the typical folktale style. Other warning tales, including the Scandinavian tales about man-eating monsters,[20] the Italian Caterinella tale,[21] and the scare tales (*Schreckmärchen*) documented in various oicotypes and regional forms throughout Europe by Gottfried Henssen, follow the same development.[22] The warning tale with an unhappy ending was certainly not randomly composed just so adults would have some story that would keep the children away from the dangerous forest. A closer look reveals traces of belief in these tales: The wolf in "Little Red Riding-Hood" probably originated as a werewolf or some other people-eating demonic figure which developed into an ordinary animal over time. In France, where "Little Red Riding-Hood" originated, belief in the werewolf was still very much alive around 1700, when Perrault replaced it with an ordinary wolf for the first time.[23] In other words, warning tales, like other folktales, do not simply contain entertaining fictions designed to arouse fear in children. On the contrary, their original unhappy endings and demonic figures link them to the legend.

A few short comments suffice for other types of folktales without the happy ending. Foremost among these is the cumulative tale: A pig finally eats the "thick, fat pancake" after its long travels and numerous encounters.[24] Hen's funeral procession (KHM 80), made increasingly large by the cumulative technique, finally becomes too heavy, and the coach falls into the brook, drowning everyone. In "The Louse and the Flea" (KHM 30) everything and everybody mourns the louse's misfortune until the spring begins to gush so furiously that they all drown. This is the only effective way to end these unending tales. The number of participants keeps growing until a sudden collapse which, as a rule, results in a negative ending for all.

Different laws require an unhappy ending for many aetiological tales. These tales presuppose the former existence of an ideal, delightful state of nature, a paradise. The tales explain how some event altered paradise, and ever since the world has been as we know it today. In other words, the tale attributes a permanent feature of today's environment to an earlier, one-time occurrence. It is striking how often the tales describe the decisive event negatively. The flounder's crooked mouth (received as a punishment in KHM 172) and the rabbit's cleft lip, the "broken" ant, and the crab which walks backward are all negative deviations from a more perfect world.[25] The only tale of this sort in the tale type index is Type 565, "The Magic Mill": "A ship-captain steals the saltmill and takes it aboard ship, where he commands it to grind salt. He cannot stop it and it sinks the ship and keeps grinding. This is why the sea is salty." Again a negative event leads to a lasting state of nature.

We find the most folktales without happy endings in collections of narratives from tribal societies. In these tales good by no means always overcomes evil. This clearly shows us that the designation of the happy ending as a generic feature is based specifically on the European tradition of folk narrative. We find particularly striking contrary examples among the Indian folktales from the Cordilleras[26] and the Siberian folktales in the *Märchen der Weltliteratur* series.[27] Even if the tale itself has a happy ending, the closing often gives the plot a tragicomic accent. For example, a Siberian folktale concludes by noting that "they were so happy they died." With that the story ends.[28] The young hero of an Eskimo folktale smashes everything in a fit of rage. In his grief he changes into a wolf and trots out into the world; no transformation back to human form occurs to give the tale a happy ending.[29]

African tales also frequently lack the happy ending: An east African Chagga folktale ends when the earth swallows up the hero, who unwittingly breaks a vow.[30] African folktales often close with a tragic, lasting separation rather than reunion.[31] A folktale from the Sudan ends when "the young woman left and went back to her family. The young man [who had mistreated her] didn't find another wife. From then on he always had to cook for himself."[32] The Fijian folktale about the sun's child who disobediently chooses the wrong gift from the moon, thus assuring his own death, also ends tragically.[33] We could provide many more examples, but it should already be clear that tribal narratives do not conform to genres to the extent that our European folktales do: Tragic endings often follow a "typical" folktale plot. The farther away from Europe we go geographically, the less we can assume that folktales will have a happy ending. Wolfram

Eberhard offers a graphic example from the Near East: During an evening of folktale telling, a member of the audience threatened to shoot the narrator if he let the hero die. Since then this story has had a happy ending.[34]

In conclusion we can say that the tale of magic is a narrative about the fulfillment of happiness. In this genre the hero endures negative "motifs of minimal harm," but they detract little from his lasting, overall happiness. The happy ending is part of the wonder tale's characteristic lightness; it is an essential defining feature of this genre. Narratives which regularly end unhappily form certain groupings and subtypes within the genre of folktale, suggesting a revision of the Aarne-Thompson tale type index: A series of numbers must be separated from the "true folktales." Moreover, this reiterates the need for the long-overdue catalog of legend types.

The appeal of the happy folktale has encroached on other genres of narrative (e.g., legend, exemplum, warning tale, etc.). The addition of happy endings has reduced the distinction between these narratives and folktales. There are many possible explanations for the development of the happy folktale—i.e., of an entire genre whose chief characteristic is the happy ending within our intellectual history—all of which require further investigation. The tale of magic's happy ending is the product of a cultural, historical development. This development probably occurred quite early in Indo-Germanic tradition: Even our oldest written folktales tend to have a happy ending, e.g., Homer's Cyclops, Rhampsinitus's treasure chamber (in Herodotus), and "Amor and Psyche" in Apuleius's *Metamorphoses*. But we can discover even earlier tendencies in folktale collections that have not been poetically worked over. Narratives from tribal societies reveal that folktales did not always have happy endings. This feature results as "genre" develops into a sort of constraint on the narrator. The motifs still shared by folktale and legend in modern European tradition substantiate this observation. We need not repeat the list of these here;[35] we only remind the reader of disenchantment, supernatural and magical figures, human sacrifice, service to spirits, death personified, people returning from the dead, women prophesying a child's fate, etc. Those tales which have the typical folktale happy endings in some versions and unhappy endings in others are particularly interesting. The "happy ending" as a basic component of an entire subgenre of folk narratives becomes possible only once the folktale has lost its believable and realistic character, i.e., when it is made unreal. This has, as a rule, already occurred for the European tale of magic. Even novellas *(novellenartigen Märchen)* are much more realistic than the European tale of magic.

The generic concept of the happy folktale is therefore historically relative. We have identified (a) narratives which end unhappily and have *not yet* been stylized as typical folktales, and (b) narratives *no longer* stylized as folktales, which tend to be more realistic than typical folktales. Rationalistic trends require that even the tale of magic reconcile itself with reality in the end. Whenever reflections of real life enter the tale of magic, they reduce its traditional optimism. For example, a Swabian folktale explains why the couple is not happily reconciled at the end: "Because the hunter was so gullible and believed his wife was a witch, her brothers wouldn't let him keep her. They took her away and cared for her until her death and never forgot what their faithful sister had done and endured for them."[36] Elisabeth Koechlin correctly points out that the French folktale often lacks the conciliatory ending because the audience has realistic expectations. Thus the French animal marriage tale sometimes ends tragically.[37] One may view this as a disharmonious breach of the "true" folktale's character, but what do we really mean by "true folktale"? Narrative genres are not a priori entities; traditional folklore texts, even entire genres of folk narrative, undergo gradual historical change.

## JEST*

"Maybe it's not true," apologized the Hessian peasant girl for believing in her rendering of "Hans the Gambler" (Type 330; cf. KHM 82)[1] even though she herself considered the story about the liar sneaking into heaven "jest." The characteristics and wording of this narrative collected by Kurt Wagner indeed warrant the conclusion that the narrator believes it. Wagner rightly concludes that "the jestfulness does not hamper belief in the content's reality. If we compare this 'believed' jest with 'The Three Lazy Sons' (KHM 151) or 'The Ditmarsh Tale of Lies' (KHM 159), we see that 'jest,' as a narrative form, does not have a homogeneous relationship to reality. The generalization with which L. F. Weber[2] groups jest as a homogeneous form contradicts the facts."[3] The Hessian peasant's comment is not an isolated case. Matthias Zender notes a similar remark by an informant about jest: It "could be true, but it doesn't have to be." Zender also provides evidence that narrators sometimes believe "The Master Thief."[4]

Jestful tales about tricking the devil sometimes still resemble devil legends. Gottfried Henssen assures us that "some narrators consider the events in these tales as real as those in legends about the devil."[5] Henssen groups a version of the farcical tale *(Schwankmärchen)* about the devil who must catch a man's (broken) wind (Type 1176) with legends "because the narrator told it in all seriousness, as if the events were real."[6]

There are even real parallels to Trina in "Wise Folk" (KHM 104): Trina asks a con man how her husband (who died thirty years earlier) is doing. Since the con man says he knows her husband, she gives him a care package to take up to heaven. As if following this example, an Upper Bavarian family sent their dead daughter "letters to heaven" containing thousands of marks via a crafty con man in 1897.[7] Incidents of this sort,

---

*The German term *Schwank* covers an array of jestful narratives, e.g., jokes, anecdotes, tales of lying, farcical tales, and parodies of other narrative genres.—Trans.

which we still read about in the newspaper, are farcical tales come true. Thus it is no coincidence that narrators often localize farcical tales: "In Jevenstedt there was a good-natured smith . . .";[8] "In Mülldorf a man and his wife had a loud argument . . .";[9] "Up on that mountain a farmer was raking . . ."[10]; etc. In printed texts it is not always clear whether such localizations are merely fictitious or if actual events inspired the tale. But this in itself demonstrates that the boundary of reality runs through the middle of the genre "jest." Regional and individual differences, as well as the genre's range from humorous anecdotes about actual events to freely invented fantasies, reinforce the notion that we cannot generalize about jest's relationship to reality. A difference obviously exists between a story about Eulenspiegel and one about Friedrich the Great, between one that tells about a particular farmer, tailor, smith, or pastor and one that portrays *the* typical representative of the given occupation, between the tale set in a particular place and the one that takes place in Schilda,* in hell, or at heaven's gate. The sexual jest has a different significance than the tale of lying, the saint's legend–jest differs from the *Schwankmärchen;* and all this doesn't even consider the genre's historical development from humanistic facetiae up to its present form.

The farcical tales in the Grimm collection are no longer believed or taken as true. The freedom from magical thought exercised by such texts has allowed jest to become, along with jokes and anecdotes, the most common form of folk narrative today. Even in the most remote alpine valleys, jest has superseded all other genres of folk narrative.[11] When the magical world loses its hold, jest flourishes and mixes with almost every other genre to form new genres, each with a different relationship to reality: the *Schwankmärchen,* the jest-legend, and the jest–saint's legend. Jest can appear in every form of folk narrative; the comic can take hold of any narrative genre. The hero in certain tales of magic in the Grimms' collection finds himself in comic, laughable situations. For example, in "The Two Brothers" (KHM 60) the lion puts his master's head on backward in his haste to resuscitate him. The hero, lost in his sad thoughts, first notices his new anatomy when he tries to eat lunch. "Bearskin" (KHM 101) and "Hans My Hedgehog" (KHM 108), both with the animal bridegroom motif, contain strong jestful features. But all of these tales remain true tales of magic despite the incursion of isolated comic, jestful features. In general we can clearly distinguish hybrid *Schwankmärchen* from the true jests in the KHM. The genuine folktale giant, for example, distinguishes "The Brave Little Tailor" (KHM 20) from purely farcical tales, e.g., "Farmer Little" (KHM 61), "Clever Hans" (KHM 32), and "Frederick and Liza-Kate" (KHM 59).

Even such extreme tales of lying as "The Ditmarsh Tale of Lies" (KHM 159) have some of the material, if not rational, connection to reality that

*The residents of the fictional city Schilda are known for their stupidity.—Trans.

finds its way into modern jest and farcical tales. This Grimm tale does not involve miraculous magic but rather the conscious reversal of natural laws, e.g., an anvil and a millstone swim, roasted chickens fly, and a blind man sees. This tale is unbelievable because it perverts everyday items and events. In other words, the more unbelievable a tale, the more closely it must openly border on reality.

Jest and farcical tales seem to operate on a supernatural plane only if we approach them from a rationalistic point of view: The Grimms' "Hans the Gambler" (KHM 82) beats all takers, dead or alive, in the tavern, hell, or heaven, at cards. But in both worlds the atmosphere of a real inn prevails and the same laws apply. Jest distorts natural expectations, but it does so within an earthly realm without magic. When the supernatural appears in jest, it is usually unreal rather than miraculous; jest often has a clearly disbelieving, rationalistic attitude toward magic. "The Tale of the Snow-child" used the folktale motif of magical procreation ironically as early as the tenth century.[12] Jest freely distorts numinous, supernatural events through joking and irony; it perverts the numinous into the comic. Thus there are even jests about blessings.[13] The devil's grandmother (KHM 29 and 125) is also a jestful, comic addition to an otherwise serious matter. "The Boy Who Left Home to Find Out About the Shivers" (KHM 4) also contains elements of jest: The hero, using his healthy, rational human intellect, laughs off an arsenal of fabricated and real legendary ghosts. He unmasks the numinous, leaving it laughable and powerless. The hero finally learns about the shivers through a completely "real" event: His wife throws "a pail full of minnows" into his bed while he is asleep "so that the little fish wriggled around all over him." Here jest takes the demon out of the shivers and evokes fear through "disgust" instead.

"Hans in Luck" (KHM 83) jestfully parodies a tale of wishes (*Wunschmärchen*): All of Hans's wishes come true, but they lead to the loss of everything he owns. Parody also alters the folktale's ethics: Only the farcical tale unquestioningly approves of laziness. In true numskull tales the dumb hero changes or proves that, contrary to what others think, he is actually not dumb at all. In the farcical tale he *remains* dumb even if he is as successful as the true numskull.

In jest the hero's supernatural abilities have become a mere boast, as in "The Brave Little Tailor" (KHM 20). Although it seems miracles have occurred, only coincidence and trickery underlie the events. The "seven in one blow" are flies, the stone thrown so high that it never comes down is, in reality, a bird, and the stone from which the hero squeezes water is cheese. "A Good Stroke of Business" (KHM 7) ridicules the ability to understand animals. In jest and farcical tales (e.g., KHM 104), the belief in miracles benefits only the trickster who uses it to exploit and con backward people. Jest often exaggerates supernatural motifs to the point of laughability. For example, a jest from the Lower Sieg River tells of "a man in

Vinxel who had a pig. Each morning he went into the stall and cut off a piece of the pig, as much as he needed. By the next morning it had grown back. It was a magical pig that ate cocoa and pudding."[14]

When jest mixes with the saint's legend, miracles also receive an ironic tone. Miraculous deeds are made into quackery: "I know a little something about doctoring," St. Peter jokingly tells Brother Scamp (KHM 81), and they wander off together. Sometimes only a small step separates the miraculous from the bizarre: The hero's attempt to imitate the miraculous rejuvenation or reincarnation misfires (KHM 81). The farcical saint's legend also suspends our sense of justice: The Lord and St. Peter are almost powerless against Hans the Gambler (KHM 82), even though they gave him the cards that always win. Hans uses the gift to hold Death at bay, to beat the devil in hell at cards, and finally to force his way into heaven.

The farcical saint's legend freely plays with the tradition of the saints, sometimes disrespectfully. Saints even appear as cattle dealers or beggars if necessary.[15] This is particularly clear in gypsy folktales. In one tale God marries a man (his godchild) to his own daughter (!).[16] In another story God and St. Peter call on a woman giving birth; because they do not know about such things and, besides, it is not a man's business, they must expend considerable effort finding a midwife. Then they must listen to what three women (Schicksalsfrauen) foretell about the child's fate and cannot undo the prophecy.[17] In a tale recorded by Johann Reinhard Bünker, a gypsy even beats up the Savior; he is pardoned because, other than this, he has a very kind heart.[18] This lack of respect can go so far that the Lord God himself becomes a sort of Master Thief.[19] In the Latvian folktale "The Surreptitious Lord," the Lord finds nothing to eat on earth, so he has no other choice than to beg for food from the devil's sister.[20]

A widely distributed farcical tale (Type 791, "The Savior and Peter in Night-Lodgings"; also see Type 752A, "Christ and Peter in the Barn") depicts Jesus and St. Peter traveling. They sleep overnight on a farm, and in the morning the farmer wakes them to help with the threshing. Weary from their travels, they don't get up, and their host beats St. Peter. The two trade places to prevent this from happening again. When the farmer comes back, he hits the lodger in the other bed; i.e., poor St. Peter again receives the blows! The Silesian farmer says to them both: "I won't put you up here, you lazy dogs; if they're supposed to help a little with the morning's threshing, they stay in bed."[21]

Of course, Christ generally remains sacrosanct in the farcical saint's legend; the tales mock only St. Peter. Even when he shares sleeping quarters with Jesus, St. Peter receives a double dose of beating rather than each getting an equal share. Farcical saints' legends depict St. Peter in the widest variety of fantastic situations. Some tell how his mother (KHM 221)[22] or his wife and daughters used to be pigs and geese, among other things.[23]

St. Peter has become the favorite figure for mixing holy and jestful, even bluntly profane, elements. For example, St. Peter throws dice for the souls of the damned.[24] More commonly he is beaten and duped, particularly in the many tales about the human hero who outwits heaven's gatekeeper. The dishonest tailor convinces St. Peter to let him into heaven (KHM 35). St. Peter gives Brother Scamp (KHM 81) a magical knapsack into which he can wish anything he pleases. At the end of the tale Brother Scamp uses the knapsack to dupe St. Peter at heaven's gate by returning the gift and then wishing himself into the bag, thus gaining admittance to heaven. In some versions of KHM 81 and 82 the hero of the jest is a smith from Jüterbog, Bielefeld, Apolda, Mitterbach, etc. (localization!). He throws his leather apron through an opening in heaven's gate and then asks permission to retrieve it, thus finagling his way into heaven.[25]

St. Peter seems to have grown more popular as a figure in the farcical saint's legend over time.[26] In any case, he was added secondarily to many items: For example, in some versions of KHM 189 he replaces the sly farmer,[27] and he appears with Christ in versions of "The Buffalo-hide Boots" (KHM 199).[28] The same is true for versions of "Brother Scamp" (KHM 81): A tale in Martin Montanus's *Wegkürzer* (1557) still depicts God and a Swabian traveling together and mocks the Swabian, the most popular jest character at the time, who won't admit he ate the lamb's liver. Later St. Peter replaces God (as in KHM 81) and is cheated out of the lamb's liver (in Grimm it is the heart). In some versions Jesus and St. Peter travel together, and St. Peter himself won't admit he consumed the liver.[29]

Even the wildest jests about St. Peter have some basis in reality. The Malchus scene in the New Testament (John 18:10) establishes Peter as the rash, unthinking character who wants to play the role of God himself. His three denials of having been with the Lord (Matthew 26:69–75) provide a real model for the St. Peter who disobeys the Lord in the versions of KHM 81 mentioned above and in KHM 35, and for the St. Peter who is frequently deceived and duped. Incidentally, St. Peter frequently plays the comic figure among the apostles in religious drama: The folk are still punishing him for betraying the Lord.

This alone shows that St. Peter jests have a serious relation to reality. Notably these tales are not found in Protestant regions and therefore should not be understood as "anti–saints' legends." The most animated St. Peter jests come from predominantly Catholic regions, particularly the Rhineland. Even the most risqué farcical saints' legends do not actually violate Christian belief, and even St. Peter's most suggestive acts depicted therein do not denigrate the respect for him in Rome.

In summary, we can say that every type of folk narrative fluctuates between the poles of reality and nonreality, making generic classification according to differences in realism very problematic.[30] If a genre's relationship to reality determines its content and form, then clearly a genre is not a rigid, timeless, universally valid entity. The numerous motifs common to legend and folktale allow us to assume that the genres were originally closely related despite the differences in the way these motifs are used. The reality in the saint's legend also once resembled the folktale more closely. The autonomy that the genres have formed over time should not obscure the fact that many hybrid genres break the rules, thus disappointing those who find pleasure in constructing an abstract system of classification.[31] With folktales, legends, jest, and saints' legends, we have shown that the dichotomy "believed/not believed" collapses under scrutiny, even within each of the genres. We cannot press the effort to differentiate the genres according to this dichotomy too far. Even the concept itself is not constant. The border between real and unreal is relative and shifts over time and space: The status of reality in folk narrative today is different than in the days of the brothers Grimm; it is different in the Balkans than in Germany or France. The concepts of genre obtained from one folk often break down completely when applied to the oral traditions of other folk groups, and every historical period produces its own peculiar art forms.

The experience of reality from narratives we call "folktales" seems to differ from time to time. The plot construction is generally more stable than generic classifications and characterizations: While genres change, motifs remain. Various versions and variants of a particular folktale can belong to very different genres according to the truth and reality of their content, which, in turn, depends on whether God or a saint, the devil, or a demonic figure performs the miraculous deed—to name one possible variation. Thus the same motif complexes occur in very different realms of belief and are told with very different attitudes toward their reality. Does the genre "folktale" have any validity if we also find "folktale motifs" in the Old Testament,[32] in classical[33] and Germanic legends about gods,[34] in heroic legends,[35] in tribal mythology,[36] and in literature from every century?[37] Many "truthful" genres, e.g., myth, saint's legend, and legend, have flowed into the folktale, losing their basis in reality in the process. Thus we cannot consider generic questions without simultaneously inquiring into the narrative's historical formation. We may not, as Max Lüthi does in his essays, which otherwise have taught us so much about folk narrative, work from a fixed European model of the folktale, i.e., from an a priori, completely poetic form which has attained a finalized style. These tales include anything that corresponds to this "folktale style" and make anything else conform to it. This completely ignores the countless transitional forms between folktale and legend, as well as the folktale's earlier forms and the transition from believed non-European tales. In any case, it does not suffice to limit ourselves to a "genre" in which supernatural, miraculous events have already lost their reality and become the genre's essential feature. Therefore, in the following chapters we must explore the folktale where it is still reality.

# III.

## The Folktale and the Reality of the Magical World-View

### MAGIC

Few of the miraculous elements in folktales seem to have a link to living folk belief. Some of these ideas have already died off and disappeared from modern folk belief. When the archaic world-view is no longer understood, new, more believable ideas replace older elements. But some folktales have become so fantastic that it seems they never had a real relationship to folk belief. The folktale probably had a fantastic, fabulizing tendency from the start. The "table-be-set," the "cudgel in the sack," the knapsack from which entire regiments march forth, the bird that lays golden eggs and makes anyone who eats it ruler, and rubbing the magic lamp to make a genie appear are all purely fictional wishes that certainly never had anything to do with folk belief.

But where miraculous motifs are still tied to the magical world-view, they are not the product of a completely unbounded imagination. When we peel back the layer of fantastic exaggeration, we frequently uncover the underlying elements of belief on which the folktale is based. Of course, only some of this corresponds to modern folk belief because, even among "primitive" peoples, belief is always changing; its substance is in constant flux. Ideas from various ages may merge in a single folktale. In this section we use a few examples to elucidate the degree to which "survivals," i.e., rigidified elements of belief and custom which have lost their original meaning, exist in the folktale and to what extent the folktale is based on conceptions of reality from an archaic world-view.

The folktale contains the globally distributed concept of magic based on the principle of like produces like (similia similibus).[1] A well-known example of this sort of magic is the tribal practice of producing or imitating rain in order to stimulate natural rain. We find a clear example of this magical method in one of the oldest known folktales, "The Magic Flight" (Types 313, 314): In KHM 79 two children, a brother and sister, flee from the water nixie. "The little girl threw a brush behind her which grew into a mountain with thousands and thousands of bristles and the nixie had a hard time climbing over it. When she finally succeeded and the children saw her coming, the little boy threw a comb behind him and it grew into a mountain with thousands and thousands of teeth, but the nixie managed to keep her footing and finally got across. Then the little girl threw back a looking glass, which turned into a glass mountain, so slippery, so very slippery, that the nixie couldn't possibly get across it." By the time she returned with an axe to break the glass, the children were far away.

The sequence of motifs in "The Magic Flight" described here is distributed over the entire globe.[2] The fleers usually escape by throwing back some objects which magically transform and become insurmountable obstacles for the pursuer. Considered superficially, these events seem to fantastically exaggerate, as folktales do, the otherwise natural act of throwing back something which hinders one's flight and may even delay a pursuer. This seems obvious and natural enough: Even some versions of "The Magic Flight" depict such simple, "realistic" flight. In a Serbian version, for example, the objects thrown back do not change; instead the pursuer stops to pick them up. In an Indian folktale the hero throws three cakes to the three dogs chasing him. We find similar realistic depictions in African narratives as well.[3] We can also trace the purely rational depiction of the flight historically: Hippomenes, Atalanta's suitor, wins a race by dropping golden apples from the Hesperidian tree which Atalanta, trailing him, picks up.[4] In the legend of the Argonauts, Medusa kills and dismembers little Absyrtos while fleeing from Kolchis and throws the pieces in the sea to impede Aëtes (the boy's father), who is pursuing her.[5] In both of these classical examples the tricks work without any magical transformation of the objects thrown back. The ancient Egyptian "Tale of the Two Brothers" also contains the flight motif without magical transformation of the obstacles: A god casts a stream full of crocodiles between the two brothers pursuing each other. Similarly, in ancient Germanic texts Rolf Kraki does without magic by throwing money back to his pursuers, who then fight over it.[6]

However, most folktales do depict a magical transformation of the thrown objects. But even this is not merely a fantastic exaggeration of reality; rather, it too has a close relationship to folk practices and belief. More specifically, this folktale motif is based on very serious impediment magic: Throwing back magical objects is part of ancient magical practice. Ethnographic research indicates that similar folk beliefs still exist in many places. For example, modern inhabitants of the upper Gangetic forests believe that a person who crosses a pass or ridge should throw back a pebble or piece of wood so that evil spirits are not carried into the next valley.[7] According to Vladimir Bogoraz, similar practices exist in the Chukchee cult of death in Siberia: When returning from a funeral, the Chukchee throw objects back in order to prevent the dead from following.[8]

In folktales the fleer's blood, spit, clothes, and tools often magically obstruct the pursuer. The folk belief that a part can represent, and even magically assume the functions of, the whole (pars pro toto) is part of the larger conceptual complex of contagious magic. More precisely, the law of sympathy states that all things that have been in contact once continue to suffer the same fate. In folk belief the law of sympathy means that things and people that belong together have a lasting connection even after their separation. In a folktale a horse's or bear's hair, a fish's scale, or an eagle's feather can summon the animals themselves when the hero needs their help. This folktale motif's basis in the belief in pars pro toto is quite clear: The person who has a part can also influence or have power over the whole. For this reason folk belief warns against throwing away nail clippings or cut hair. Also related is the part-for-whole role hair plays in love magic and in beliefs about the dead:[9] People must be careful with their hair not because it contains their "soul" but because they otherwise expose themselves to harmful magic propagated by someone else. According to folk belief, if the new owners of a dog put some of the animal's hair in their boots, the pet will grow accustomed to them more quickly.[10]

Even if it seems like jest, it is no coincidence that the hero in KHM 29 ("The Devil with Three Golden Hairs") must pull out the devil's hairs. The original text recorded by the brothers Grimm makes it clear that this motif is based on part-for-whole magic, which was the most important element of the tale. The text concludes with this sentence: "Therefore whoever does not fear the devil can rip out his hair and have the whole world."[11] These are ancient ideas for which early evidence exists. A story in Saxo Grammaticus's history of the Danes[12] parallels the Grimms' "The Devil with Three Golden Hairs": Thorkill arrives in Utgard, which is described as a living hell, and pulls a hair from Utgardloki's long beard, creating an awful stench. In Greek mythology one of Poseidon's grandchildren, Pterelasos, has a golden hair that guarantees him victory and immortality. He dies when his daughter pulls out this hair.[13] The Biblical story of Samson, whose hair provides him strength, is even better known.[14]

The idea that strength resides in the hair, as found in these ancient Jewish, classical, and Germanic sources, seems to be a secondary development from the idea of contagious magic. The central idea here is that the hair represents the hero, not simply that he loses his hair and thus his strength: Whatever happens to a man's hair will happen to him. Thus when an otherworld figure gives the folktale hero three hairs with which he can summon the donor, it seems the folktale has preserved an ancient belief in contagious magic.

Other well-known folktale motifs reflect this archaic magical conception of reality as well. For example, the saliva of the fleeing heroes or some other object associated with them answers for them as they escape. Talking saliva appears in versions of KHM 15 ("Hansel and Gretel"): Gretel's saliva answers the witch for the children, who have flown, until it dries up.[15] In

KHM 89 an amulet with three drops of the mother's blood assures motherly protection for the king's daughter on her journey. The blood clearly represents the mother's power. We discover the magical importance of these three drops of blood only when the girl loses them and the evil waiting maid "gloated, for now she had power over the bride who, without the drops of blood, became weak and helpless." The drops of blood speak for the mother: "If your mother knew of this!" In "Darling Roland" (KHM 56) the drops of blood answer for the murdered sister. In truly folkloric French versions of "Little Red Riding-Hood," the dead grandmother's blood is set before the girl to drink. When the child puts the cup to her lips, a voice laments: "You are drinking my blood!"[16] The trail of blood which shows the way to an otherworld or enchanted figure in some folktales (e.g., KHM 88) is a rudimentary, rationalized form of the ancient sympathetic conception of blood added to the folktale after the magical connection between the blood and its donor was no longer believed.[17]

We can trace to a distant past the idea that blood can speak for that person from whom it came. For example, blood has an independent function in the "ordeal of the bier"; Christian belief in judgment by the Lord became metaphorical only relatively recently:[18] God's statement to Cain's murderer in Genesis 4:10, "The voice of your brother's blood cries to me from the earth," was certainly not originally a metaphor. Modern idioms such as "spilled blood cries out to heaven" (vergossenes Blut schreit zum Himmel) and "the voice of blood" (Stimme des Blutes) still reflect the original belief. Our folklore does not contain literalized metaphors; rather, it depicts part of an archaic magical conception of reality which has a latent existence in the modern mind. Pacts with the devil must be signed in blood because the blood itself represents the person, not because people believe blood houses life or the soul,[19] and not because blood merely "symbolizes" the soul or life. Like hair, blood is a part representing the whole, according to a general sympathetic, contagious connection.

Such instances of contagious magic which still occur in our Western folktales are only remnants, but we find these ideas far more frequently in the tales of tribal peoples, where they are sometimes still magical reality today. Human excrement, as well as secretions,[20] can represent its creator: Clearly it is absurd to speak of "agents of the soul." In a Wongaibon (New South Wales) folktale, excrement answers for the fleeing hero.[21] In a Chukchee tale the evil spirit captures a boy, empties his bowels in his chamber pot, and orders the excrement to guard the boy.[22] In Northwest American Indian folktales, culture heroes such as raven and coyote can magically bring their excrement to life: The great raven transforms his own excrement into a beautiful woman and immediately falls in love with her.[23]

It is also notable that sympathetic relationships work even after death. For example, the blood in KHM 56 answers for the dead daughter.[24] The best-known example is KHM 28: Here the dead man's bone is made into a musical instrument which reveals the murder in a song. Once again the part gives information about the whole.[25]

In the Grimm version (KHM 28) the singing bone betrays the murderer, thus leading to the punishment he deserves, but no magical resuscitation of the dead man occurs. However, other versions of this tale (Type 780) do include bringing the dead man back to life.[26] The motif complex of bringing people back to life from their bones appears in all sorts of narratives. For example, in "The Juniper Tree" (KHM 47) the sister collects the boy's remains, which then transform into a bird, and the bird back into the boy. The heroine in KHM 46 ("Fowler's Fowl") finds both of her sisters, murdered and chopped up by the wizard, lying in a basin in the forbidden chamber: "But she got to work and gathered the pieces and put them in their right place, head and body and arms and legs. When nothing was missing, the pieces began to move and knit together, and the two girls opened their eyes and came alive again." This motif of dismemberment and resuscitation has also become one of the many methods of disenchantment. For example, in an Austrian folktale the enchanted princess must be cut in half, right through her heart, with a sword, then cut into pieces and cooked in a kettle for an hour.[27]

Even the farcical saint's legend "Brother Scamp" (KHM 81) doesn't hesitate to employ this motif. Here St. Peter brings the dead princess back to life:

> "Bring me a cauldron of water." When the water was brought, he told everyone to leave the room and only Brother Scamp was allowed to stay. St. Peter cut the dead girl's limbs off, threw them in the water, made a fire under the cauldron and boiled them. When all the flesh had fallen off, he took the smooth white bones out of the water, put them on a table, and arranged them in their natural order. When they were ready, he stepped up to the table and said three times: "In the name of the most Holy Trinity, rise from the dead." The third time the king's daughter stood up alive, healthy, and beautiful.

Brother Scamp later attempts to repeat this feat but fails, not because he lacks the apostle's holy powers but because he does not know how to arrange the bones "and got them all mixed up." From the point of view of the psychology of religion, this failure is completely pre-Christian.

A Russian version of KHM 100 ("The Devil's Grimy Brother") depicts the motif complex "death and resurrection from the bones" in a different context. Before the hero can marry the czar's daughter, he must refrain from cutting or combing his hair, blowing his nose, cutting his nails, or changing his clothes for fifteen years. When the fifteen years are up and preparations for the wedding are underway, the devil cuts the hero into little pieces, throws him in a cauldron, and cooks him. He then takes the hero out and puts the pieces back together, bone to bone, joint to joint, sinew to sinew. He then sprinkles water of death and of life on the hero: The unwashed soldier stands up as a spruce lad. He then happily marries the czar's youngest daughter.[28]

The same motif complex also occurs in our folk legends, for example, in the story of the drowned child whose mother collects his bones in a kerchief and carries them into the church. There the child comes back to life, starts to cry, and frees himself from the cloth.[29] Folk ballads such as the ancient Danish "Mariboes Spring" also contain this motif. It also appears in the Finnish epic *Kalevala* when Lemminkäinen's mother collects her son's remains from the water.[30]

This widely distributed motif, which figures differently in a variety of genres of folk narrative, might strike us as unbelievable fantasy if we did not also find the collection and revival of bones in myth, such as the classical story of Pelops, who is resuscitated when his pieces are cooked in a cauldron.[31] Germanic mythology also contains the motif: In the Eddic story Thor's bucks are slaughtered, cooked, and eaten. A god revives the bones, which land on Thor's hide.[32]

What is the basis for this rebirth from bones within the history of religion? It is clear that the human or animal usually magically comes to life from his or her bones. Bones apparently function as the most important part of the body. Moreover, bones remain after an animal is eaten and take the longest of all body parts to decay. Thus even after death they could well appear to be the seat of the creature's lasting and renewable power of life. The skeleton was indeed a symbol of life before it came to represent death.[33]

We find this concept among hunting societies the world over; in some cases the motif still functions in their folk belief. Certain rules relate to this belief: Many hunting societies forbid breaking, burning, or throwing away the hunted animal's bones. Instead they preserve the bones in a particular place without losing a single one.[34] Adolf Friedrich has provided voluminous north Asian material about the idea that bones possess the power of life. Karl Meuli, proceeding from the strange division of the sacrificial animal in Olympic ritual, draws our attention to the ancient hunting ritual of setting aside specific parts of the animal, particularly the bones, from which new game is created.[35]

The north Asian data collected and investigated by Friedrich do not include tales only about bringing animals back to life from their bones; the concept applies to humans as well. People sometimes trace their lineage to the bones of an animal.[36] For example, we clearly see this concept in a Yukaghir tale from Siberia: The vicious raven kills his two brothers-in-law one at a time, pushes them into a heated bathhouse, and eats the roasted bodies. He then tells his wife to clean the bones, gather them in a bag, and hang them high in a tree. The wife cries bitterly, collects all the bones, even the smallest ones, puts them in a bag, and hangs it up as instructed. Later her third and youngest brother kills the raven and then asks his sister where she put their brothers' bones. She climbs up the tree and brings them down. He takes the oldest brother's bones, arranges them, and sprinkles them with the water of life and of youth. The first time he does this, flesh covers the bones; the second time, skin covers the flesh; the third time, the young man stands up and speaks: "Oh, oh, I have slept too long; but I feel quite refreshed anyway." The same occurs with the second brother.[37]

Gathering the bones in a cloth and preserving them in a particular place (a tree) calls to mind the verse in "The Juniper Tree" (KHM 47): ". . . gathered up my bones, / Tied them in a silken kerchief, / And put them under the juniper tree. . . ." Likewise, the motif about cooking the bones in "Brother Scamp" (KHM 81), in the Russian version of KHM 100 mentioned above, and in the legend of Pelops is not a random invention; it too has parallels in real north Asian concepts and customs. The Siberian tale summarized above is not a "folktale" in our sense of the word because it corresponds to real concepts of belief and custom. Vladimir Bogoraz, who recorded the tale, notes that "the ancient Yukaghir preserved the bones of their dead by gathering them in bags or hiding them in secret places."[38]

Similarly, according to belief among these people, initiation to shamanism includes being killed and eaten by the spirits. The bones are then scattered, gathered up again, thrown in a kettle, and cooked until the shaman awakens with magical power. The initiate must die and rise from the dead before being transformed into his new spiritual existence as a shaman.[39]

This phenomenon is not limited to north Asian hunters. Mexican Indians in Guazacualco and Yluta also place the bones of the dead in baskets and hang them in trees so that their spirits will not have to burrow through the earth when they return to life. According to the ancient Egyptian Book of the Dead (ch. 25), all bones must be kept together for the resurrection.[40] Bringing people back to life from their bones apparently was also current in the world of the Old Testament: In Ezekiel 37:1–14 this image appears as a visionary parable for the resurrection and reunification of Israel. Pelops is slaughtered and brought back to life, but he lacks his shoulder blade because Demeter ate it. Thor's buck is lame because one of his bones was damaged. This motif of the missing or artificially replaced bone causing slight harm is also widely distributed in folktales.

A Scottish tale tells of the resuscitation of a sheep from its skin and bones, but the animal turns out lame because its hooves were eaten.[41] In an African Kabyle folktale the hero must bring back an eagle's nest from atop an unclimbable cliff. He succeeds with help from his beloved, the daughter of a Wuarssen (the cannibalistic giants in Kabyle lore). The girl tells the hero: "Take this knife and this perfume. Cut me up with the knife. The pieces will stick to the cliff so you can use me as steps and easily climb up and bring down the eagle's nest containing seven eaglets. As you climb back down, bring my pieces with you. At the bottom put all the pieces back together, and when everything is in order, blow the perfume into my nose. I will be alive just as before." He does as told, but after coming to life the girl tells him, "You did everything right, but you left my little toes stuck to the cliff and forgot to bring them down. Now I'm missing them."[42]

Almost the exact same narrative occurs in an Irish folktale: The hero is able to fulfill the task of climbing a 900-foot glass mountain only by killing his helper, taking the bones from her body, and using them as steps. On the way down he must gather them up, but he forgets one. When he reaches the ground he puts the bones back together, covers them with flesh, and sprinkles them with water from the spring of life at the foot of the tree. His helper comes back to life, but she is missing a toe.[43]

We find the same motifs in German-language legends, only in a different context. The "hazel-witch" lives in Seis (southern Tirol): A farmhand says he saw her at a witches' feast. The other witches cook and eat the hazel-witch, except for a rib which one threw at the boy when they noticed him. Instead of eating the rib, the boy pocketed it. The witches replace the missing rib with a piece of hazelwood in order to successfully resurrect their meal. Later the boy tells the farmer that there is a hazel-witch in the house: She was sitting among them and fell dead from her stool.[44] In the legend about a child resurrected from his bones in church,[45] "the little finger on his right hand is missing a knuckle."

Even this motif of the missing bone (rib, toe, shoulder blade), which seems purely fabular, has parallels among north Asian hunters. Commonly the shaman is missing a bone after his resurrection. But then one of his relatives must die.[46] In a Siberian tale the great raven's daughter has her missing leg replaced with the leg of a wild goose.[47] A Yakut tale describes how a man, insulted by a shaman, kills the offender twice and scatters his bones. But the shaman's spirits gather the bones, and he miraculously comes back to life. The man kills the shaman a third time and cuts him into little pieces; he burns the shaman's jawbone at the stake. The shaman rises from the dead for a third time, but he no longer has a jaw. His relatives replace it with a calf's jaw.[48] Thus the motif about missing bones also leads us back to peoples who, as we saw above, have a traditional belief in resurrection from bones. The folktale motif derives from this belief but seems to have taken the first step toward becoming a part of more aestheticized narratives: This new tale complex adds a vital element of suspense to the pure report of folk belief, gradually reducing the reality of the older form.

Whenever folktales mention sympathetic animals, plants, or objects, we are dealing with an archaic belief in contagious magic. The objects the hero leaves at home before departing on a journey, so that his relatives will know how he is doing, work through sympathetic magic. The knife stuck in the tree in KHM 60 ("The Two Brothers") reveals whether the brother out in the strange world is still alive. The golden lilies which blossom from pieces of a magical fish and the golden twins produced by other pieces turn out to have a sympathetic relationship: When a witch turns one brother to stone, one of the golden lilies falls over at home (KHM 85, "The Golden Children").The sympathetic flower is the hero's "alter ego," which dies when he does. This motif also appears in the ancient Egyptian folktale: One brother places his heart in an acacia flower; as long as the tree is standing, no one can defeat the hero. He dies only when the tree is felled. Here we have the same connection between a plant and human life (the heart may be a later aetiological addition to explain why the hero's life is connected to the tree).

This conceptual complex may seem like pure fantasy at first, but actually it still has parallels to living folk belief. In many places people used to, or still, plant a tree when a child is born: Since they have a common fate, the tree may not be cut down during the child's lifetime. The tree may even hinder the development of an entire farm. Following a basic concept about the contagious relationship between a human and a plant, the child grows and weakens parallel to nature; he is "like a flower of the field."* Trees are a favorite choice for a sympathetic relationship because trees have a strong vital energy and longer life span than humans. The opening of "Snow White and Rose Red" (KHM 161) also contains a clear reference to reciprocal existence between humans and nature: "A poor widow" had "a garden with two rosebushes growing in it, one of them bearing white roses and the other red roses. She had two children who resembled the two rosebushes, and one was called Snow White, the other Rose Red" (cf. the end of the tale as well). The twelve lilies in the twelve brothers' garden (KHM 9) have a magical, sympathetic connection to the brothers' lives: When their sister picks the flowers, the twelve brothers change into ravens. This magical parallel between the flowers and the brothers' fate is neither merely "symbolic" nor simply based on the notion of a "soul"; rather, it suggests an actual parallel identity. The old woman, who happens to be standing there when the sister in KHM 9 picks the flowers, confirms this interpretation: "They [the lilies] were your brothers, and now they've been turned into ravens forever."

The tale about the grass snake (KHM 105) depicts a sympathetic relationship to an animal. A girl has a symbiotic relationship to a snake: "When she began to eat, a grass snake slithered out of a crack in the wall, dipped its little head in the milk, and ate with the girl. The child was delighted." The child's friendly relationship to a snake is definitely not mere fairy-tale fantasy. The German Michael Heverer reported on his 1592 journey southward from Nyköping, Sweden, that while changing horses he thought he would stop for a meal, but in every house he saw children sitting on the floor sharing their porridge with tame snakes; he lost his appetite.[49] In the Grimm tale the child's relationship to the snake ends tragically: The girl's mother kills the "good little animal," and—as told in KHM 105—after the snake is slain, "a change came over the child . . . and soon the child lay in her coffin."

The idea of a sympathetic snake in this tale is ancient; Friederich von der Leyen correctly places this text near the start of his attempted chronological arrangement of the KHM. To be sure, this distinctive Grimm text does not belong among the very oldest folktales, because here the belief

*Psalms 103:15.—Trans.

that the snake guarantees life, or at least brings good luck, is no longer an obvious reality. But in many places people clearly recognized this function of the snake until very recently: According to Adolf Wuttke, for example, Bohemian folk belief includes the idea that a family of snakes lives in some houses, and each member of the snake family "represents a member of the human family, [and] everything which befalls the snake also happens to the respective family member."[50] In the village of Magden in Frickthal [Switzerland], Ernst Ludwig Rochholz reports, domesticated house snakes "watch over the rearing of children, protect the milk animals in the stall, guard the adolescent daughters, and find them a man according to their merit. Sometimes a house has two [snakes] that live and die with the mother and father of the house."[51]

A folktale from Lorraine treats the motif of the snake as the spirit of a house somewhat more thoroughly than KHM 105, in a sense completing the Grimms' fragment while also displaying more typical folktale characteristics. Here the snake and the rich, hardhearted farmer's cows have a sympathetic relationship. The cows thrive as long as the maid feeds the snake milk. When the farmer chases the maid away for wasting milk, the snake abandons the stall, and misfortune befalls the farm and household. The snake gives his little crown to the maid, bringing her happiness and success. In the end the snake lives with the maid, "and the house prospered; God clearly blessed their household."[52]

A gypsy version of "Bluebeard" contains a sympathetic toad: The fiend dies when he eats his life-toad served up roasted by his third wife, who was supposed to feed the animal.[53] Sympathetic folk remedies rely on the same human-animal connection when they transfer a human disease to the animal. Thus the animal saves the human rather than causing his or her death.[54]

The folktale depicts other items outside the body which magically sustain life. For example, in the widely distributed tale type "The Ogre's Heart in the Egg" (Type 302), the hero must destroy the monster's heart hidden in an egg in order to free the maiden from the ogre's power.[55] For added security this egg lies inside an animal living in some secret place. The heart is often protected by multiple encasements; the heart's locale varies but is usually an egg inside a bird.[56] The grateful animals help the hero destroy the ogre's heart, and the ogre dies.

This motif seems so fantastic that it appears to have no relationship to even the most archaic reality; modern readers must find it hardly conceivable that any belief underlies this motif. Nonetheless we can establish such belief: The basic idea is that people can place their souls in material objects, thus providing themselves with a sort of life insurance. In the folktale only demonic monsters can still protect themselves in this manner, but originally humans themselves employed this practice as a general defense against black magic of all sorts. In the ancient Egyptian "Tale of the Two Brothers," the hero himself (Batu) deposits his heart in an acacia flower for security. When the flower with the heart is cut, Batu falls down dead.

Even today tribal peoples do not find this conception odd. We find the motif of placing a heart at the top of a tree to protect human life in a Cherokee Indian tale.[57] We also have evidence of this practice in black West Africa, where, for example, a medicine man puts the natives' hearts in a jar until some perceived danger has passed. Someone may also "entrust his heart" to an animal: Only the medicine man and the heart's owner, who guards the animal and hence himself from harm, know which animal has the heart. Accordingly, this particular motif about life being connected to a plant or an animal also plays a large role in tribal narratives. Rather than being limited to one tale type, the motif is a common narrative element among tribal societies, indicating its significant relationship to reality. For example, the Wuarssen, a man-eating demon in Kabyle folktales, says: "My soul is in safekeeping. . . . My soul is a hair resting in an egg inside a partridge. The partridge lives in a camel's stomach, and the camel lies under a boulder in the sea."[58]

A Koryak story from Siberia tells the motif as follows: In the Triton-man's tent stands a box containing his heart. When Ememqut abducts the Triton-man's wife, the Triton-man, who is out grazing his reindeer far away, says: "My heart is really pounding. Something must have happened back home." Ememqut finds the box and throws it, heart and all, into the fire. When the heart begins to burn, the Triton-man becomes very ill; when it burns completely, he dies.[59]

These tales in which humans, not demons, hide their hearts reveal the older belief. In a Siberian folktale, seven Samoy hang their hearts on the tent poles when they come home and then sleep without their hearts.[60] In an ancient Asian folktale, the brothers hang their hearts in a tree before going to sleep.[61]

Here we must briefly address the places the ogre hides his encapsulated heart: In Nordic versions[62] the princess tries to get the ogre to tell her where he hid his heart. He tells her it's under the threshold, but he tricks her and it's not there. The maiden decorates the threshold in his honor. The second time the giant alleges that the egg containing his heart is in the hearth. Since he mistrusts the princess, she gets him to reveal the secret only through trickery.

But perhaps the heart was originally hidden where the giant first claimed; the threshold and hearth were, after all, the most important places in the old peasant home. Long ago, when funerals were held at home, people were buried at these spots. Perhaps later narrators, searching for a more artistic and developed composition, considered these places too simple. Perhaps the Celtic versions prove that the heart was indeed originally stored in these locations: Here the giant's heart actually lies under the threshold or under a tree in his garden.[63] This evidence carries considerable weight because Celtic folktales are among Europe's oldest.

The seemingly fantastic folktale motif of the glass mountain was also once part of belief; it belonged to the concept of the realm of the dead. Jacob Grimm refers to the Lithuanian custom of burying lynx or bear claws with the dead so they could climb the steep mountain and reach the throne of the holy judge.[64] In her investigations, Inger Boberg correctly draws parallels to the Celtic "Glastonbury" and the ancient Nordic "Glaesirvellir."[65] Jan de Vries points out,

> it must be noted that this is a motif about the otherworld. In the most varied parts of the world great dangers and monstrous difficulties threaten the dead on their journey to the next world. . . . The ride up the glass mountain is as much a part of the journey to the beyond as, for example, the ancient Persian belief in crossing the Zinvat bridge. Thus we doubtless find mythic elements in this folktale.[66]

Numerous folktales depict the mysterious power of *magic formulas*: "Open sesame!" opens the secret treasure chamber in the mountain (Type 676; cf. KHM 142). In KHM 19 the fisherman repeatedly conjures the magic fish with the incantation "Little man, whoever you be, Flounder, flounder in the sea. . . ." The magic table (KHM 36) serves up the finest delicacies, but only when it hears the magic formula "Table, set yourself!" Similarly, the formula "Little goat, bleat, bring me a table with good things to eat" in KHM 130 magically produces a freshly set table. In the same tale the heroine puts her sister to sleep with a magic spell. Upon hearing the words "Shake your branches, little tree, Throw gold and silver down on me," Cinderella's tree supplies the most beautiful dresses ever seen (KHM 21). Cinderella repeats this magic formula three times in the course of the story. The queen's magic mirror in "Snow White" (KHM 53) answers the formula: "Mirror, mirror, on the wall, who is the fairest of all?" Cinderella (in the Cap o' Rushes tale type) escapes the prince by saying: "Behind me dark, before me clear, So no one sees which way I steer."[67]

Gretel implores the white duck to take her and Hansel across the large body of water in the witch's forest: "Duckling, duckling, here is Gretel, Duckling, duckling, here is Hansel. No bridge or ferry far and wide— Duckling come and give us a ride" (KHM 15). The Goose Girl (KHM 89) uses the incantation "Blow, wind, blow" to magically produce a strong wind. The discharged soldier in KHM 199 paralyzes the robbers with a formula for thieves.[68] A magic formula frees Joringel from the witch's spell: "Greetings, Zachiel! When the moon shines on the cage, let him go" (KHM 69). We could easily provide many more examples of magical speech.

The magic formulas work only if the wording is exactly right. If not repeated perfectly, the magic produces disastrous consequences: In "The Sweet Porridge" (KHM 103)[69] the heroine's mother cannot stop the magic pot because she forgets the formula "Cease, little pot!" The flood of porridge is finally dammed when the daughter comes home.

We can easily trace the use of such formulas in the folktale to living folk belief, but their formulation is certainly not recent, and therefore we cannot draw any conclusions about a particular archaic conception of reality. However, it is striking that written magic (using numbers and/or letters) plays absolutely no role in the folktale even though it has an important place in belief. Surely this implies a criterion for dating the tales: If folktale magic uses no writing, it must originate from a time before writing existed.[70] The folktale depicts a stage of development in which even a mere word still had direct power, i.e., an almost material effectiveness. As soon as anyone expresses or even thinks an effective thought, particularly wishes and curses, the deed is done, the thought becomes a real material fact. "I wish you'd turn into a raven and fly away, then I'd have some peace and quiet," the queen tells her little daughter, and "the words were hardly out of her mouth when the child turned into a raven" (KHM 93; cf. KHM 25).[71] Again folktales from tribal societies offer particularly telling examples, because they do not limit this process to a few exceptional transformations and instead depict the word's powerful effectiveness in everyday life as well. In an Eskimo folktale, for example, a blind man's speech has the power to call other people's eyes into service.[72]

Naming a person or a supernatural being also clearly has magical potential. For example, ancient Egyptian sorcerers gain power over the gods by ascertaining their true names.[73] An Old High German house blessing aims to ward off all demons by reciting their names: "Well, Vicht, you should know that your name is Vicht." This suggests that people's names are linked to their existence, they are part of their essence. Thus the king's son merely calls helpful "Iron Hans" three times, and he immediately appears (KHM 136).

Tribal peoples avoid revealing their names to strangers because they could be used in black magic. Tribal peoples can even mortgage their names, and according to this *habeas nomen* concept, whoever has the name has the man. In our own folk belief, a dying man can "give away" his name; and we can still occasionally observe an aversion to state one's name.[74] Our culture contains yet other remnants of these ancient concepts about names. For example, when parents name their child after a dead person, they do so—at least unconsciously—believing and hoping that the child will have many of the namesake's characteristics, if not that person's "soul." Likewise, the poor occasionally name their children after rich persons. People avoid giving their child the name of someone who recently died in the fear that the child might suffer the same fate, perhaps even die of the same cause. Some tribal peoples view giving a child a dead person's name as a type of rebirth. We also find this idea in the oldest folktales: In the ancient Egyptian "Tale of the Two Brothers," the hero, Batu, is turned into a tree. A splinter from the tree produces a baby boy whose name is also Batu, and he *is* the same hero Batu.

"Rumpelstiltskin" (KHM 55; Type 500), generally cited as the model example of the power of name magic, actually seems to have nothing to do with this: A girl promises her first-born (in other versions her hand in marriage) to the dwarf who helps her spin. The demonic helper comes to collect and will allow the girl to renege only if she can guess his name within three days. Most analyses cite the power of the name to explain how the demon loses the bet: The demon apparently loses his power because the girl says his name. But the demon's downfall actually results when Rumpelstiltskin bursts into excessive rage because she guessed his name and he loses the reward. This is a type of riddle-bet, not name magic. The girl could be required to guess something other than the name: In some versions she must not *forget* the demon's name,[75] and in others she is supposed to guess his age.[76] Neither task is easy: The demon's age is incalculable, and he doesn't have a human name. An archaic feature of "Rumpelstiltskin" and other riddling contests is that the prize is existential: Life itself is at stake. One either guesses or perishes. When the riddle is solved, the Sphinx plunges into the abyss; the Eddic dwarf Alwis turns to stone when struck by sunlight.[77] But the wager itself, not name magic, determines the contestant's fate.

Numerous other agents of magic play a role in the folktale. Music, for example, often has a persuasive magical power. Particular music compels those who hear it to dance: When "Darling Roland" (KHM 56) plays the violin, the witch must dance whether she wants to or not. The hero in KHM 110 ("The Jew in the Brambles") also wishes for a fiddle which makes everyone who hears it dance. In a Kabyle folktale people cannot continue working when they hear the magic flute; the birds become silent, and even the walls of the houses bend down to listen.[78] Music also breaks spells: In a gypsy folktale a girl born as a rose regains human form when a musician plays the violin.[79] Magical sounds also empower the horn with which the hero can call for help (cf. *Song of Roland*). In KHM 54 the walls and fortifications fall like those in Jericho when the magic horn sounds. Other magical music in the folktale puts everyone to sleep. The folktale also depicts other ways of putting people into a magical sleep: A prick from the enchanted spindle sinks Sleeping Beauty into magical sleep (KHM 50); a poisoned comb puts Snow White into her deathly sleep (KHM 53). Folktales from tribal societies contain forms and practices of sleep magic that our living folk belief lost long ago. For example, a Siberian tale plainly explains how a woman throws her thimble on her husband when she wakes up in the morning, making his sleep so deep and sound it seems as if he is dead.[80]

Even folk beliefs about the evil eye occasionally find their way into folktales. In an Eskimo tale the hero kills people and animals by looking at them.[81] The sorcerer Balor, who has a single eye in the middle of his forehead and another in the middle of the back of his head, appears in Irish folktales. The eye on the back of his head would kill everyone, like a basilisk, with its evil squinting glare and its poisonous shining colors if

Balor did not keep it closed. He opens it only when he wants to turn his enemies to stone.[82] Here fantasy builds on folk ideas about the evil eye.

In contrast, the Irish folktale hero Fionn, who can recognize anything simply by biting himself on the thumb, sounds like the product of pure fantasy.[83] But we find similar motifs in other Irish tales: The thumb possesses curative power; the hero draws wisdom from his or her burned thumb; biting the thumb can help one see into the future.[84] Surprisingly, similar narrative elements appear in African folktales: When the clever heroine of a Kabyle tale asks the fingernail on her little finger for advice, it provides information and help.[85] Again the folktale depicts an ancient practice for increasing magical power that living folk belief has lost: According to Plutarch,[86] Isis nourished Malcander's child by sticking her finger in his mouth. According to Jewish legend, the angel Gabriel fed Abraham with his finger. Nursing a child with a finger also played a role in the Virgin miracle in the Middle Ages.[87] Today this notion survives only in some idiomatic phrases. The German saying "sich etwas aus dem Finger zu saugen"* was not originally a metaphor but rather magical reality during the stage in human evolution preserved for us in the folktale.

Our narratives also contain remnants of hunting magic: After slaying the seven-headed dragon, the hunter in KHM 60 ("The Two Brothers") cuts out its seven tongues, wraps them in a cloth, and guards them closely (cf. KHM 111). In folktales and medieval heroic epics, this motif usually serves as the hero's proof that he really killed the dragon. But this hunting trophy originally had a different purpose. The hunter prevents the animal or beast from getting revenge by cutting off an essential part of its body (other trophies include horns, ears, tail, and teeth). Before skinning a bear, Siberian hunters cut off its paws, poke out its eyes, and sever the tendons in its feet. If through their carelessness the bear should suddenly free itself, it would no longer pose any danger. The hunters consider the bear truly dead only after they break out its teeth and remove its claws.[88] The folktale has lost the original meaning of this ancient hunters' custom.

In numerous versions of "The Blind King" (Type 551), a wise man tells the king that he can regain his sight only with the blood from a dragon's heart. In an Italian version of "Little Brother and Little Sister" (KHM 11), the blind king must smear his eyes with his own daughter's blood.[89] In a Greek version of "The King's Children," the Egyptian king wants to cure his leprosy by bathing in a royal child's blood.[90] Again, all this sounds like pure fantasy designed merely for the sake of storytelling: The blood from a dragon's heart is particularly difficult to obtain and thus provides a basis for the folktale hero's adventure. Requiring human blood also sets up conflict or tension which the narrative then disengages in the typical folktale manner. But again the reality of belief conflicts with this "purely fictional"

---

*Literally, "to suck something out of your finger"; meaning, roughly, "to pull something out of thin air."—Trans.

interpretation. Belief often ascribes magical power to blood, and many past and present remedies prescribe blood as a curative agent. Before a division between folk and scientific medicine existed, Hartmann von Aue's "Poor Heinrich" suggested using the blood of a virgin to cure lepers.

Folk medicine may not go so far as to claim that dew from the gallows can restore a blind man's sight (as happens in KHM 107, "The Two Traveling Companions"), but we do find a basis for this idea in folk belief: Everything associated with the gallows and people hanged there somehow has magical power.[91]

In KHM 16 the hero observes how a snake brings its friend back to life with three special green leaves. According to folk belief, a snake in distress signals all the other snakes in the area to come and help.[92] Likewise, a folk belief collected in the upper Palatinate which says that at a certain time of year toads sit in fountains and draw in all the poison that falls from the sky, corresponds to the fountain-toad motif in KHM 29.[93] In KHM 165 a king's daughter wastes away because a toad took some of her hair to build a nest; she will recover only if she gets her hair back. We find a similar view in folk belief: In Bohemia it is said that if a toad builds its nest with someone's hair, that person will waste away and cannot be saved by anyone.[94]

We can mention only briefly other magical practices which appear in individual folktales. Folktales frequently contain all sorts of fertility magic. Women become pregnant after eating fish (KHM 85).[95] A gypsy folktale describes at great length the detailed recipe for fertility obtained by the barren queen.[96] A salesman in a Palestinian tale shouts: "Magic eggs for sale! Eat one and you don't need a man to become pregnant!" A woman feeds her stepdaughter pancakes made from the eggs, and she really becomes pregnant.[97] An Italian folktale prescribes a concoction made from three hairs from the devil's beard for the childless queen.[98]

Fertility magic in folktales among tribal peoples seems still to have a closer relationship to living folk belief. A girl in a Kordofan folktale eats the bone meal from a crushed skull to become pregnant.[99] In an Oceanian tale, blood from a man's finger produces a daughter.[100] The European folktale naively mixes pre-Christian and Christian motifs: Parents respond to successful fertility practices by saying, "God has answered our prayers."[101] Even Jesus and St. Peter impregnate a woman with an apple "full of hope."[102] Individual motifs about magical procreation may be fantastic, sometimes even absurd, but in principle they correspond to the folk belief in a magical world.

All of these motifs about magical practices are older than the word magic mentioned above. But in both cases the folktale depicts a real picture of belief in magic. We have cited only a few examples of this archaic reality in the folktale, but we already see that even modern "tales of magic" are not mere fantasy. These tales were living "reality" in an archaic world where magic was real and completely natural and did not yet have a numinous effect. In the folktale this archaic world meets the enlightened world-view which no longer recognizes magical forces. This later view of reality freely employs these magical motifs and mixes them with pure fantasy to achieve a poetic effect. We must ask how the folktale, a product of fantasy, preserved archaic elements. How can we explain the folktale's unique mixture of primitive and artistic components?

The question itself contains the answer. The modern European folktale's status as conscious fiction enables it to maintain and preserve themes, traits, and motifs that have ceased to be part of belief. The folktale, unlike the legend, no longer has any reason to pay attention to belief. Even the oldest recorded Mediterranean folktales had already begun to outlive the belief they depict. However, because the content was no longer believed, the tales retain elements of the old magical world-view.[103] For the same reason, Christianity has had little significant influence on the European folktale.

We cannot, however, fail to recognize an entirely different factor in the folktale's development. Because primitive magic, the law of sympathy, contagious and homeopathic magic are not bound to a particular religious world-view, they have been able to survive up until the present by continually renewing themselves in folk tradition. The enlightened artistic world-view and belief in magic exist side by side in the folktale. For very different reasons, both of these elements of the folktale have helped preserve the magical world-view. The artistic guise preserves magical thinking as a product of fantasy; the magical world-view maintains it as reality.

## MAN AND ANIMAL—TRANSFORMATION AND DISENCHANTMENT

We have already pointed out the symbiotic relationship between man and animal in terms of their sympathetic connection in certain folktales. An investigation into grateful and helpful animals in the folktale also seems to take us back to an archaic world. These animals behave independently in the folktale and often fulfill an important function in the plot by determining what will happen to the hero. For example, three animals repay the kind-hearted hero's favors by helping him complete three tasks (e.g., KHM 17, "The White Snake"; 62, "The Queen Bee"; 191, "The Mongoose"; and 126, "Faithful Ferdinand and Faithless Ferdinand"). Occasionally the grateful animals help the hero find and destroy the monster's hidden soul and thus obtain the king's daughter. In "The Faithful Animals" (KHM 104a) a man pities some animals and frees them. They return the favor by later freeing him from prison.[1] There are a number of reasons the animals may be grateful to the hero: The hero either rescues individual animals from some danger (e.g., KHM 17 and 62; Type 554), or he lets an animal he could have killed get away unharmed (e.g., as a hunter in KHM 57 or as a fisherman in KHM 19, Type 555). The tale type "The Girl Who Married Animals" (Type 552) also portrays helpful animals: A bankrupt man marries his three daughters to three animals, usually an eagle, a bear, and a whale. The girls' brother visits them and discovers that his brothers-in-law periodically take on human form. With the animals' help, the hero survives further adventures and finally gains the hand of a princess.

Horses frequently provides humans with advice (according to folk belief, horses can see spirits), as is the case in the Irish folktale about the king's son and the bird with the beautiful song.[2] The horse also plays this role in the Grimms' "The Goose Girl" (KHM 89). The fox is also commonly a helpful animal (e.g., in KHM 57).

The animals usually intervene to show their gratefulness, but this must be partly a result of later psychological developments in the folktale: For compositional reasons, an aetiology is added to demonstrate the hero's readiness to help and explain how it pays off. But there are numerous folktales that offer no specific cause for the animals' helpfulness. For example, doves help Cinderella (KHM 21), and the goat helps Two-eyes (KHM 130) for no particular reason.

The particular tasks with which the animals help are certainly often the product of pure fantasy. Nonetheless, the facts that they help at all and that they are the most common folktale helpers (outnumbering supernatural and human helpers) offer some basic insights into the nature of the folktale world. Despite all of the epic and fabular stylizing the folktale undergoes, the animals still usually use their natural, real abilities to help: Fish retrieve things that fall into the water (KHM 17 and 126); ants crawl through the keyhole or help the hero pick up millet seeds (KHM 17); birds help separate the bad lentils from the good (KHM 21). Moreover, since the helpful animals are as a rule wild, not domesticated, these motifs appear to be derived from hunting societies. The folktale treats exceptions, e.g., the donkey which emits gold (KHM 36), as objects, not subjects of the plot. Helpful animals appear as independent characters; they are the hero's partners.

Only tales introduced after farming displaced hunting incorporate domestic animals as well. The donkey commonly appears in these folktales (e.g., KHM 5, 36, 130). KHM 169 ("The House in the Forest") emphasizes the farming ethic of giving top priority to the livestock (and not because they are people under a spell). In the course of the folktale's evolution, wild animals become less dangerous. For example, the bear eventually becomes the shaggy, good-natured Meister Petz, a teddy-bear character who appears in farcical tales. Intelligent domesticated animals begin to prove themselves superior to the wild animals: The dog, cat, and rooster collectively overcome the wolf, fox, and bear;[3] the goat (KHM 5) and even the birthing sow[4] outwit the wolf. But our folk narratives which still contain ideas from hunting societies portray animals very differently: Here hunters often obtain magic from its original possessor, the animal. Both European and non-European folktales have preserved this ancient concept.[5] Helpful animals in the folktale know where to get the water of life, the water of beauty, or the root of life which cures the decapitated hero (e.g., KHM 60). In another folktale the swans know that moistening the heroine's eye sockets with morning dew will restore her sight.[6]

Sigmund Freud goes too far when he calls the motif of the helpful animals primeval man's "family story,"[7] but the motif does lead us back to an archaic level of reality. To interpret this reality, we must again turn to tribal tales. Recent ethnological research, e.g., by Hermann Baumann, brings the folktale about helpful animals into connection with totemic origin myths, i.e., aetiological tales which establish a close relationship between an individual or a clan and a type of animal: Helpful animals become the totemic animals of the tribes they rescue. For example, the Ibibio tell of a battle between cities on opposite sides of a river. One side successfully crosses during an ebb, but high water keeps them from returning. A large python answers their distress by bridging the river; they walk to safety on its back. When the enemy tries to cross the bridge, the snake dives under and they all drown (in another version a crocodile bridges the river). As an expression of their gratitude, the victors no longer kill or eat the python (or crocodile). In other tales an animal saves people or brings them good fortune after making them promise never to kill or eat the helper's species.[8]

In these examples the seemingly fantastic motif of the helpful animals is still part of a believed clan tradition or tribal legend. African, particularly Sudanese, tales about acquiring magic also present this motif as believed reality: A hunter trails a wild animal, but the animal asks him to spare its life. To show its thanks, the animal gives the hunter knowledge of all magic, particularly hunting magic.[9] This motif of the animal who repays the hero for letting it live also appears in European folktales, but in Africa it is completely embedded in believed "legends" about all sorts of hunting magic.

It is always an individual who procures the hunting skills in this way. The relationship of the individual to an individual animal is perhaps even older than social organization into totemic groups. The motif complex of the helpful animal seems quite similar to the idea of a personal guardian animal that we find in the most basic tribal narratives. A protective animal spirit gives an imperfect human the animal's superior skills. An Eskimo tale, for example, tells of a young woman who cares for a young, two- or three-day-old polar bear. Because she has no children of her own, she feeds and treats the bear like her own child. When the bear grows up, it goes hunting and provides her with plenty of food. Other members of her tribe grow envious and want to kill the bear. The woman discusses the situation with the bear, and they must part in tears. But the woman frequently goes to meet him, and he continues to provide her with food.[10]

These tales depict a very ancient relationship to animals: The animal is not a second-class creature but rather the human's equal or even superior. Animals are seen and treated as humans. The bond to the animal kingdom can put humans and animals on the same level or even lead to the experience of an animalistic alter ego.

The folktale "The Bear's Son" probably belongs among the European folktales which depict this archaic relationship to the animal world. The tales of this type[11] usually begin with the abduction of a woman by a bear. The bear holds her captive in his cave, and she bears him a son. Tales in which an animal (bear, mare, she-wolf, or dog) suckles the hero also contain remnants of this world-view.[12] At first glance, descent from an animal seems to be only an aetiological fabulat invented solely to explain the hero's superhuman powers, but it is entirely conceivable that this too was originally a believed line of descent. The tale probably first began to focus on the bear's son after sensitivity to the story's perversity pushed human-animal marriage into the background.[13]

An Irish folktale also seems quite archaic: A hunter spots a rabbit, but he spares the animal's life. In gratitude the rabbit promises him a child. Nine months later the hunter's wife does indeed bear a child, even though she is over fifty years old and hasn't delivered a child in their twenty years of marriage. When the father dies, the rabbit's family adopts the child.[14]

Of course, these motifs are rare relics in Europe. In contrast, tribal tales describe human descent from animals far more frequently, sometimes in mythic reports of cosmogenesis and anthropogenesis. According to an Australian tale, "in the beginning" the earth opened up, and the totemic animals came out one by one: raven, parrot, ostrich, etc. Since they were not yet complete beings, lacking limbs and sensory organs, they lay down on the dunes. As they lay in the sun, their power and strength increased; they finally attained human form, and they got up and went off in all directions.[15]

According to a North American Indian tale, the ancestor of all forms of life was a swan. A magpie, a wolf, and a coot emerged from the swan. One day the magpie suggested to the wolf that he get some earth so that the coot could have solid ground under its feet. The wolf found the earth and then sang and played a rattle while the magpie dumped the earth over the water. This is how the land and sea attained their present state. The magpie, the smartest of all animals, changed into an Indian, establishing the human race.[16]

It remains a mystery how humans descended from the totemic animal, but we should point out the interesting observation that African, Native American, and Australian folk narratives apparently developed the idea that humans and animals originally belonged to the same family independently. Even in Europe we still occasionally encounter this sort of anthropogenesis: A Finnish folktale, for example, tells how bear, frog, and man descended from three brothers.[17] Today this tale is obviously only aetiological fiction, but the comparative ethnological data suggest the possibility that our culture also experienced a totemic phase.

We do not want to enter into the problem of totemism and the extensive ethnological discussion of it here.[18] We also cannot possibly discuss whether all people, including Europeans, necessarily go through a totemic stage. Here we intend only to examine folktales to see whether the relationship between humans and animals in the texts reveals some sign of an ancient reality. In doing so, we cannot ignore the materials from tribal peoples which undoubtedly contain important clues: The relationship between humans and animals is one of the tribal folktale's main themes, particularly among hunters. Animals also play a large role in the European folktale relative to their place in our civilized world, which has entirely ousted nature, or at least suppressed its natural character. In contrast, folklore describes the original humans living in immediate contact with the other creatures. Animals had not yet become subhuman; they existed within the same cosmos as man. Humans had not yet recognized the order of life as specifically human and therefore followed the natural order which put them on equal terms with animals. The simple human thinks only in human terms and assigns human characteristics to animals. Thus tribal folktales humanize an animal's adventures and transform a human's adventures into an animal's.[19] This interchangeability clearly shows the belief that humans can also tend to their affairs in the body of an animal.

Only with the progressive intellectual development of human self-consciousness did an increased awareness of the differences between humans and animals form. But some aspects of the close relationship between the two have sustained themselves for a long time and do not seem to be limited to the past culture of a single society. The medieval trial and punishment of animals, which in some cases lasted into the modern era,[20] reveals how animals were treated as human and legally responsible. Albert Wesselski has compiled extensive medieval evidence to show that we can still recognize the original totemic animal-human connection in the modern abhorrence for such perverse relationships.[21]

As late as the twentieth century, country folk reported the death of the man of the house and important dates, e.g., Candlemas (Feb. 2), to the bees, cows, and horses. Pets have their own names, animals receive special holiday meals on Christmas, and, according to folk belief in many places, animals have their own special section in heaven.[22] These customs reveal an ancient, close relationship between humans and animals. The spirit of Enlightenment killed many such ideas—Descartes equated animals with machines—but perhaps we can still detect a trace of the time when animals were humans' equals in our relationship to a few domestic animals, particularly dogs and horses.[23]

Tales in which the ability to understand animal languages plays a role give us a taste of the many different historical layers of humans' attitudes toward animals that can exist in the folktale. In some folktales this ability has not yet become a "motif"; in other words, it is accepted as obvious and needs no further explanation. In other folktales only a chosen hero has this ability, with which he or she attains folktale happiness.

We must clearly distinguish two aspects of this phenomenon: Either the hero understands animal languages, or an animal speaks a human language. The first group of folktales, in which a person learns and understands animal languages, branches out a great deal: For example, Faithful Johannes hears what three ravens say to each other while flying by "because he knew their language" (KHM 6); i.e., his individual ability to understand the animals has a decisive influence on the rest of the story. The hero of KHM 17 ("The White Snake") achieves happiness by using his ability to understand animal languages. In a well-known Russian folktale, the numskull is the only one in the family capable of understanding animal languages.[24] The tale type about the man who understands animal languages and his curious wife also belongs to this group of tales, in which the knowledge of animal languages is an exceptional gift or a peculiar acquired ability.[25]

The second group of folktales consists of those in which an animal miraculously speaks a human language. For example, the ability of the princess's horse (Falada) to speak in KHM 89 is unusual enough that Conrad, the girl's geese-tending companion, reports the girl's conversations with the dead horse's head to the king. Even in tribal folktales, an animal that speaks a human language may be seen as something unusual and miraculous. For example, the Swahili farmer in an east African folktale is surprised to find out that the gazelle he bought can talk.[26]

In addition, there are folktales in which the animal endowed with human speech, like some of the humans who understand animal languages, is taken for granted. Here humans need not magically learn the animal's language in order to converse; the two address each other in the same language and exist on the same plane. The flounder asks the fisherman to throw him back (KHM 19). The goat in "The Magic Table, the Gold Donkey, and the Cudgel in the Sack" (KHM 36), the raven, the fish, and the fox in "The Mongoose" (KHM 191), not to mention the humans who retain their language after being transformed into animals (e.g., KHM 1, 11, 106, 108), all speak without surprising anyone. None of these tales explain how humans and animals understand each other.

Here we quite clearly have a very ancient conception of reality in which it still goes without saying that humans understand animal languages. We find this view in other tales, for example, the ancient Egyptian "Tale of the Two Brothers," where a talking cow can warn the younger brother, Bitiu, about his older brother without any commentary about a special ability to understand animals being necessary. Achilles' horses warn their master about his imminent death.[27] A later rationalistic age seems to have first viewed the talking animals as somewhat unusual and therefore developed them into new motifs. But many folktales still recognize that humans and animals must once have spoken mutually intelligible tongues. Formulas such as "in the days when the animals could still speak" express this notion.[28] Tribal folktales and myths frequently emphasize this idea: A

Kabyle folktale tells us that "in the beginning all the rocks, wood, water, and earth spoke."[29] An Eskimo tale says, "There was a time when man and animal were not very different: Their languages differed only as much as dialects do, and if the animals wanted to speak with people, they changed into people."[30]

We can distinguish a variety of views of animals which seem to correspond to historical differences in conceptions of reality. First, real animals contrast with animals possessing marvelous abilities. There are animals endowed with human speech and those that humans can understand only once they have learned the animal language. There are also demonic animals that always retain their animal form, and humans magically transformed into an animal's body. This last group breaks down into humans changed into an animal by some evil adversary and those who transform themselves. Some folktales contain several of these possibilities, even if they belong to very different historical stages. Both "real," but "tame," doves which help sort the lentils and the "supernatural" white bird in the tree on the mother's grave that throws down everything the heroine wishes for appear in "Cinderella" (KHM 21). In KHM 108, real animals (pigs that are butchered), supernatural animals (a rooster that is shod like a horse), *and* humans transformed into animals (a child in the body of a hedgehog) strikingly occur alongside each other.[31]

Broadly generalizing, we find positive and negative attitudes toward animals in folktales. One view sees animals as related, equal, or even superior to humans; the other sees them leading a miserable, subhuman existence purely to serve man. In either case animals are always perceived in human terms: Humans measure animal physiognomy, anatomy, poise, and way of life by their own standards. It is only a small step from this conception to the idea that animals are transformed humans.

In our folktales, transformation into an animal is usually a tragic fate which degrades the victim into a nonhuman. The human innocently suffers this fate brought about by an evil witch or a curse, e.g., when the parents unwittingly wish for it to happen. In these cases the victim is not actually guilty, but violating a taboo produces a sort of magical guilt: For example, in "Little Brother and Little Sister" (KHM 11) the boy drinks from the bewitched spring and changes into a deer. Transformation into an animal caused by someone's wish which immediately and unexpectedly comes true (e.g., KHM 25 and 93) results from violation of the implicit taboo against cursing. This taboo exists because the effects of cursing are taken very seriously. In "King Lindworm" (Type 433B)[32] the mother disregards instructions and gives birth to a monster. Violating taboos also causes transformation into an animal in the saint's legend–folktale where transgression of Mosaic or Christian codes results in the change. In one tale, Jesus and St. Peter transform a miserly woman as a punishment (Type 751). We can construct a psychological bridge from these religious examples to the well-known motif of transformation into an animal which is the basis for the Grimms' "Hans My Hedgehog" (KHM 108, Type 441): The parents have been childless for so long that they wish for a child even if it is a hedgehog, a donkey (cf. KHM 144), a snake, or a pig. Punishment of the impatient, impetuous wish for a child and the wish that unexpectedly comes true have become traditional folktale clichés, but they also have a basis in living folk belief. In general, according to belief, an expectant mother must heed various rules if she wants to have a healthy, normal child: For example, if someone sins during delivery, it is said that the child will become a werewolf.[33] This one example embodies the folktale motif from "Hans My Hedgehog" modified into a legendary form which corresponds to Christian morals, and transferred to a figure (the werewolf) current in modern folk belief.

The person transformed into an animal is usually damned to lead an idle existence while patiently waiting to be disenchanted. But in some very different cases the animal body increases, rather than reduces, the human's abilities. This latter, far more ancient view of reality appears in tales in which transformation is not a punishment but rather an ability the hero acquires through friendly coexistence with animals. The grateful animals frequently lend the hero the ability to change into animal form, and the hero actively uses this gift to gain happiness: "I want to thank you," the grateful crow in a folktale from Holstein tells the hero. "Whenever you want to be a crow, just say 'I want to be a crow!' Just like that you'll be a crow."[34] In contrast to the legend, which no longer contains grateful or helpful animals and where transformation occurs only as a punishment, this folktale motif complex embodies the much older notion that humans can take on and cast off the appearance of an animal at will. People also change from human to animal bodies as a matter of course in tribal folktales. For example, the hero in an Alaskan folktale visits the walrus people, i.e., "walruses in human form."[35] An African Hausa tale describes the inhabitants of a certain city who regularly change into hyenas, leopards, buffalo, and lions.[36] Such narratives seem to lie at the start of a development that also eventually encompassed our European folktales.

We now see that transformation into an animal was not originally a punishment or the result of black magic. There is nothing strange or unnatural about these transformations because divisions between the animal and human worlds have not yet been drawn; humans and animals coexist on equal terms. An Alaskan Eskimo tale depicts this original state: "Animals could change into people, and people into animals. And the people walked on their hands, they crawled around on all fours."[37] A different Eskimo tale takes place "in the days when one could easily be man or animal."[38]

Societies with totemic structures have already developed a clear awareness of the difference between man and animal, but the way of thinking depicted in these tales reveals, to use the ethnographic term, a "proto-totemic mentality" which recognizes only one group of living creatures. In Africa only the apparently ancient animal mythology of the bushmen still contains a believed proto-totemic mentality, but relics of this mode of thinking abound in the many African folktales about transformation of animals. For example, a tale from the Gold Coast tells of a man who goes with his wife to her fish relatives and lives among them as a fish himself.[39] The first wife of a man who remarried changes herself into an elephant and joins her herd. She is brought back only because her child finds her and tells the father.[40]

The point is that in these narratives the humans are not transformed, but rather they *transform themselves*. Moreover, this has not yet become an act of magic; the self-transformation occurs slowly as the humans constantly associate with the animals. For example, an Indian folktale from the American Northwest coast describes how a man who visits the seals gradually becomes a seal himself: "His relatives set out in boats to look for him. There they saw him in the distance lying among the seals. The second time they found him, again with the seals, he had whiskers and hair on his back. The third time they noticed that he had a seal's markings on his stomach." They try luring him into coming back several times:

> One day the seal-man came back to the village on his own along with his seal-wife and their child. He slept in his house, but the next morning he was gone. This happened several times. His brother and others implored him to stay, but he said, "Don't worry about me; I lead a happy life among the seals under water because it is more beautiful there than up here on earth." So they let him go and no longer paid any attention when they spotted him on the rocks or in the water.[41]

European folktales contain few willful transformations like those in tribal folktales, and certainly none that are still believed. "The Magic Flight" (Type 313) is one of the few: In some versions (e.g., KHM 51 and 56) the fleeing lovers change *themselves* into a rosebush with a rose, then into a priest and a church, and finally into a duck and a lake.[42] We also still find these antique motifs of self-transformation in "The Magician and His Pupil" (Type 325): A magician's apprentice changes himself into various animals. His father sells the animals, which then run away from the buyers, who do not have the magic reins. Finally the magician buys back the boy, but the apprentice has become a master magician himself, and in a contest of transformations which usually last several rounds, he defeats his teacher. The Grimms' "The Thief and His Master" (KHM 68) includes this series of motifs.[43]

This motif complex about the ability to repeatedly transform oneself, an ability not granted in other folktales, seems to be pure fantasy which dispenses with all reality. But like the self-transformation motif in "The Magic Flight," we can trace the motifs in this tale to older motifs not otherwise found in tales of magic with their limitation of transformations to the result of black magic.[44] In Greek and Germanic mythology, only gods and demons possess the ability to transform themselves. When self-transformation still occurs in our European tales, only witches and wizards have this ability (e.g., KHM 69), or the rational explanation has already set in that the hero was apprentice to a magician (KHM 68) or that his lover is a witch's stepdaughter and uses her magic wand (KHM 56). In contrast, tribal folktales do not require supernatural forces for transformation. In these tales no gap exists between experience and belief; nothing is more natural than transformation. Karl von den Steinen reports an incident he experienced: The Bacairi were pursuing a fugitive black slave. They couldn't catch him, but they noticed a tortoise in the bushes nearby and were appeased because they were absolutely convinced that the boy had turned himself into the tortoise.[45]

This incident describes a self-transformation which occurs without any magic, as is still frequently the case in tribal folktales. The ability to transform oneself is accepted as an obvious reality. A Sudanese tale simply states that "one day Gulu [the vulture] changed himself into a man. Ewoako [the boa] changed himself into a man. . . ."[46] Leo Frobenius attests that Ethiopian folktales contain no motifs of magical transformation, only factual reports of plain, natural transformations.[47]

The concept that humans have a single identity which could manifest itself in two or more forms may have existed before the notion of transformation. This world-view is not "premagical"; on the contrary, it teems with magical practices, but something as commonplace as transformation requires no magic. Transformation without magic is much older than that which requires magic: Magical transformations first appear at a stage in the folktale's development where supernatural occurrences require an explanation. The voluntary ability to change one's external form predates magic spells. Perhaps even the Frog King could originally change his form at will: The *Panchatantra* contains a frog who is grateful for being saved from a snake. He retrieves the king's ring from the fountain and then changes himself into a human and marries the king's daughter.[48]

We can schematize the various levels of the idea of transformation into groups characterized by these statements:

1. "So and so *is* an animal," or can be an animal as well;
2. "He *transformed himself* into an animal";
3. "*Someone changed* him into an animal."

These groupings simply describe the types of transformation and are not intended to suggest a sequence of rationalistic development. Rather than separating into historical phases, all three types coexist in modern folk narrative; they build a magical-mythical whole dominated by different members at different times.

One aspect of transformation makes the difference between the tribal folktale and the European folktale particularly evident. Transformations that occur in tribal folktales need not be undone at the story's end. The

European folktale experienced a decisive change in its perception of reality: The tale of magic developed from the proto-totemic story and no longer contains the premagical ability to switch from human to animal form; a magical act must trigger the transformation into an animal. Moreover, not everyone has the magical power to change her- or himself into an animal; only certain notable people can perform this magic.[49] In a final stage, the Christian world-view attributes demonic evil characteristics to this magical person (e.g., the witch), and transformation into an animal becomes the prime example of these characters' ability to perform harmful magic. The legend even goes a step further than the folktale: The legend doesn't seem to trust the witch with such far-reaching magical abilities anymore; thus only God transforms people as a punishment. The legend also eliminates the concept of "bewitchment." As the folktale finally becomes a "genre" formed according to artistic rules, it loses its original realistic character and becomes a mere play form. Transformation into an animal becomes a humiliating dehumanization, but it has no lasting effect on the victim; it only helps increase the story's tension. The folktale has become "happy fiction" (*Glücksdichtung*), which by artistic necessity requires that the concluding motif be the main task in the hero's series of adventures; namely, return to human form. To summarize: Transformation was originally a reality in the folktale, but later it became a mere "motif"; i.e., it sets up the disenchantment and the happy ending.

The folktale about marriage to an animal offers an abundance of important enchantment and disenchantment motifs. Although the motif complexes are distributed among various tale types (Types 400–459), the scheme itself ("Transformation into an Animal and Disenchantment through Marriage") is quite general, and more versions of this tale have been recorded around the world than any other.[50] The animal in this tale can be a dragon, a lion, a wolf, a raven, a hedgehog, or even a glowworm. In the Danish, Swedish, Icelandic, and Finnish versions, a white dog, a bear, a horse, a deer, a rat, or a snake plays the role of animal bridegroom.[51]

It is no coincidence that in the very first tale in the Grimms' collection, the frog transforms into a king's son once he gets into the princess's bed. In KHM 108 the hedgehog-child Hans weds the king's daughter, and a king's son born as a donkey in KHM 144 finds a princess's love and thus finally regains his human form. In exchange for the "lilting, leaping lark"[52] the father must marry his youngest, most beloved daughter to a wild lion (KHM 88). Snow White marries the king's son who had been changed into a bear (KHM 161).

Even with all these cases of marriage to a human transformed into an animal in the Grimms' folktales, the tales never depict sodomy; no marriages between a human and an animal are consummated. It always turns out "really" to be a marriage between a man and a woman, and transformation back into human form occurs *before* they actually consummate the marriage. The lion in "The Lilting, Leaping Lark" is a lion only during the day; at night, when he is with his wife, he has a human body (KHM 88). The king's daughter in KHM 1 does promise to let the frog sleep in her bed, but the Grimm tale mentions marriage only after he changes back into human form. In "Snow White and Rose Red" (KHM 161) Snow White marries the bear only after the dwarf has been killed and the bear's skin falls off, exposing a handsome prince. "Hans My Hedgehog" (KHM 108) takes off his hedgehog skin before getting into bed with his chosen princess. The princess in KHM 144 is only "engaged" to the donkey; the marriage is between two humans.

Because of the influence of the Grimm collection and its limitation on human-animal interaction, German scholars speak of the "animal bridegroom" (Tierbräutigam) in contrast to the English term "beast marriage." Indeed, the "animal bridegroom" seems to have replaced the older "animal husband"; numerous folkloric texts still openly use the later term to describe the relationship. But regardless whether it is an animal bridegroom or an animal husband, can we say that these tales have any relationship to reality? They cannot, of course, reflect actual sexual relationships, because marriage to an animal has never been a reality. Despite the abundant materials, we cannot adequately answer this question on the basis of European tale types, and we must once again turn to tribal folktales. We find the same development in the attitude toward the reality of marriage to animals in these tales that we did for transformation. In tribal folktales, marriage to an animal does not yet have negative connotations of perversity and does not yet require special magic to transform or disenchant the animal. The tales often depict marriage to an animal as something quite natural: Humans who live close to nature consider the animal their most important partner for survival; human and animal worlds merge. For example, in Siberian folktales marriage to an animal is quite ordinary: One day two very pretty polar bear–women came onto the river bank. A man sitting on the beach saw them, married one of them, took her home, anointed her, as is customary at weddings, and together they had children.[53] Primitive hunters in Greenland also still believe in marriage to foxes.[54]

In African folktales, humans often marry animals without thinking twice. For example, rooster and elephant may contend for a woman.[55] A Yoruba tale begins: "A woman had a daughter. Ikoko [hyena] came and said: 'I want your daughter to be my wife.' The woman said: 'You shall have her!' "[56] In West African folktales, tortoise quite naturally woos a human girl.[57]

The frequent connection between these tales and cosmological myths shows just how seriously the tales treat the motif of marriage to an animal. For example, Akun, the tortoise in Yoruba folktales, appears as both an animal bridegroom and the figure who unites the sexes and introduces intercourse to the world. In another Yoruba tale, a girl who declines all other suitors marries Alamu, the lizard, but then runs away from him:

"Ever since, the lizard always raises its head when sitting on walls and trees. Alamu is on the lookout for his wife, but he doesn't find her."[58] A western Sudanese tale explains the origin of a common matrimonial custom with a story about an animal husband.[59] A believed Malay clan legend that explains the central Javanese Lalang people's special status tells of a princess impregnated by a dog; the son thus produced becomes the father of the clan.[60]

Among primitive hunters, the animal marriage occasionally has a close connection to hunting magic. In a Pawnee Indian tale from North America, a boy brings the buffalo under the control of humans by marrying one: He becomes a buffalo himself and lives among the animals for a while. He then returns to his human tribe and teaches them how to find and kill buffalo. Even this tale itself has a practical function as part of hunting magic, because the Pawnee believe that telling the story lures the buffalo.[61]

In the European folktale, human company, love, and marriage restore the animal to its human form. In tribal folktales, on the other hand, animals often transform themselves into humans, marry, and then change back into animals later. European and tribal folktales treat this theme in fundamentally different ways: In the European folktale, talking animals who play a role in the story are not really animals but rather humans under a spell. The hero marries an exceptional animal, i.e., a transformed person. In tribal folktales, real animals often marry humans; of course, they can often freely choose between their animal and human forms. Only by understanding this important aspect of the animal-marriage narratives can we possibly comprehend the fact that characters in tribal narratives sometimes express their desire to marry an animal: For example, a Yoruba girl rejects all suitors until Akuko, the rooster, comes around. She says: "I want Akuko to be my husband!" The rooster hears her, says he'd like to marry her as well, and they become a couple.[62] The girl in a Moluccan tale wants to marry a fish-man at all costs; her father opposes the idea and kills the fish-man. The daughter commits suicide. The father then revives them both with some medicine and allows them to marry.[63]

Tribal tales about marriage to animals do not yet have a need for disenchantment because the type of transformation they depict is completely different from that in European tales. Tribal tales also completely lack humiliation of the person transformed into an animal and of the person who marries one. Even the very concept "disenchantment" is not present in these simple folktales because this concept is linked to enchantment and curses, to powerful black magic, punishment, and guilt. Transformation into animals as a curse or a punishment first appears in later cultural stages when humans have emancipated themselves from the animal world. In the European folktale, what starts out as marriage to an animal results in disenchantment as soon as the human says "yes" or at the moment they are married.

Most of our folktales have a happy ending. In contrast, animal marriage tales among tribal societies often end tragically; after temporarily taking on human form, the animal spouse again becomes an animal. An animal marriage tale from Ceram, which otherwise has much in common with the European form, clearly shows this difference: Some siblings lay their hands on a tree that belongs to a snake. The snake demands the sister become his wife as a penalty and in exchange for releasing the brothers. During the day the snake takes human form; at night it becomes a snake again. The brothers trick the snake-man and kill him. The dead man changes back into a snake, but the brothers throw it into the river.[64] In this case the girl marries an animal in human form, not a man transformed into an animal, and the tale ends with the snake-man's death.

There is clearly a connection between animal bridegroom motifs in tribal and European folktales. Some sporadic relics reveal that disgust over marriage to an animal is not universal, even in the European tales. For example, the king's daughter in a modern Greek folktale expresses her desire to marry an animal. She tells her father that she will marry only a man who can become a wild animal.[65] A girl in a Norwegian folktale who has no husband would even settle for an animal, and she finally marries a fox.[66] We occasionally find the transformation of animals into humans in Russian folktales. For example, a fish transforms itself into a beautiful maiden who marries the numskull.[67] The marriage is not judged negatively; on the contrary, God tells them to marry.

There are also short legendary tales in German that describe bonds between hunters and animals without mentioning disenchantment. A Silesian tale briefly reports the events as facts without any narrative adornment: "A man and a girl were picking blueberries. Suddenly the girl was gone. The man poked a stick under a rock he saw moving. And when he stuck the stick in the hole, a mole came out and sang:

> This home is very fine,
> here I keep my beautiful love.[68]

As a last example, consider the image of the werewolf, still alive in folk belief in Germany during the nineteenth century. This image preserved until very recently the idea that the beast switches from animal to human form.[69]

These European exceptions only confirm the rule. In general, a strong ethical stance against sodomy superimposes itself on the European animal marriage tale, while tribal versions still depict the older view of such relationships. In European tales, associating with animals is below human dignity. It is certainly not coincidental that at the start of many of these tales, the animal tricks or extorts the father into giving up his daughter. These tales can accept marriage to an animal only by making the father decide between giving up his own life or marrying his daughter to the animal. The motif of the girl's devotion and love to the animal, which disenchants him, can develop only from this initial situation. But above all, these tales depict the daughter's love for her father, which leads her to go to the animal, not her love for the animal itself.

Picturing the animal as a temporarily transformed human tones down the feeling that the marriage is perverse: "Once there was a king's son who was a bear for six days, and on the seventh day a man."[70] These periods during which the enchanted person is free from the animal's body are not merely fantastic inventions designed to give the animal marriage tales some variation, nor are they rationalistic devices added to make the biological possibilities of the marriage more believable; these narratives correspond to certain beliefs in tribal societies. The Eskimo, for example, believe the seal is a transformed man who takes off his fish skin every nine days and regains his human form.[71] A North American Indian folktale describes an entire village of eagle-people with eagle skins hanging all over the place. The young people have young eagle skins, the elders, skins of older eagles. At home the "animals" go about in the form of humans.[72] In a tale from Oceania, when the chief's daughter turns fifteen she falls in love with a frog who can remove his skin, and who sleeps with her and marries her in human form.[73]

This common motif about the ability to remove temporarily the animal "skin" seems to be a survival from the ability to freely switch between human and animal form. We also find a few Grimms' tales in which the animal-person throws off his animal pelt rather than actually being disenchanted (e.g., KHM 144, 161, 108). The prince in KHM 144 remains human only after the king burns the donkey skin. Notably, the word *disenchantment* does not appear in this tale. Moreover, the princess does not protest her marriage to the animal.

The ability to remove the animal "skin" is not a rationalized form of transformation into an animal; i.e., the transformation is not explained away merely by describing the animal as a person masquerading with an animal pelt draped over his or her body. On the contrary, this motif reflects an ancient concept which maintains that animals literally have a human core, and when they take off their animal skin they *are* human.

Accordingly, we do not find transformation back into human form by taking off the animal pelt only in folktales. This process occasionally plays a role in believed magical practices in some cultures. An Eskimo woman, it is reported, let an old woman come into her hut even though her husband had told her not to. On her way out, the old woman turned into a fox. During the night the young woman woke up with a terrible headache. She felt her head and noticed that antlers had sprouted. By the time she left the hut, she already had the head of a reindeer. Her husband followed her, found her in a herd, and freed her by pulling off the pelt as he was told to do. He had to throw her on her back and be careful not to kill her while removing the pelt.[74]

From here we easily take the next step to a number of methods of releasing people from animal bodies. These practices are not, as Hans Naumann and Friedrich Ranke assert, derived from a primitive view of death;[75] rather, they are quite ordinary reality from a time when humans believed in the ability to remove the animal skin to reveal the human within. This purely material method of disenchantment seems surprising only when viewed from the perspective of later developments in the folktale which stipulate disenchantment through human company, love, and bodily and spiritual interaction. The folktale hero himself is often afraid to perform this process; he cannot bring himself to chop off his beloved animal's head when she asks him to. "Shoot me dead and chop off my head and paws!" says the helpful fox in "The Golden Bird" (KHM 57). The hero is afraid to do it (because he no longer understands the original nature of transformation) and says: "Fine gratitude that would be! I couldn't possibly do that." The formula "disenchantment through death" is completely out of place in this tale. It belongs to nothing other than the belief reflected as reality in the Eskimo tale mentioned above, i.e., the ability to return to human form by removing the animal body.

Like the Eskimo tale, European folktales often depict disenchantment through a concrete, bodily, often even violent process; in short, the disenchantment is material rather than spiritual. In the folktale, disenchantment affects only the body. Originally disenchantment merely consisted of changing back, taking off the animal shell, and hiding or burning it (e.g., KHM 108 and 144).[76] Disenchantment through decapitation, stabbing, or other methods of killing, such as the more recent adaptation of shooting, work only because the transformation is conceived as an external phenomenon. Disenchantment through these methods is the most violent way of doing magic. The king in KHM 135 decapitates his true bride, who had been turned into a duck, at the very moment she swims through the gutter into the kitchen. In some versions of "Little Brother and Little Sister" (KHM 11), the queen who turns into an animal (usually a duck) each night is also changed back into human form in this manner. Decapitation also occasionally removes the spell from the animal bridegroom. The lion who plays this role in a Hungarian-German folktale is decapitated and disenchanted with three swings of a sword.[77] According to the animal's request, the hero cuts off the head or paws of the enchanted person, stabs him, or beats him to a pulp with a switch.[78] These are not different types of death but rather a variety of ways of removing the animal "covering." More recent motifs of killing someone, such as the living dead in the legend, so that person will be free to rest in peace have nothing to do with the destruction of the enchanted animal in the folktale.

The worldwide tale "The Swan Maiden" also still reflects the old belief in the ability to voluntarily remove the animal garb; i.e., it does not yet contain the later folktale development of an actual transformation. In this tale the hero steals the swan skin from a bathing swan-maiden. She must then retain her human form, and she marries the hero.[79] Interestingly,

"The Swan Maiden" is also one of the few tale types that appear over the entire globe, in European, Asian, and primitive traditions, without any apparent connections. Tribal peoples often tell this tale as a believed cult legend as well as a folktale. For example, a story in volume 12 of the Atlantis series tells of a hunter who secretly watches the buffalo take off their hides and bathe as humans. The hunter damages one of the hides, and when the buffalo put their hides back on, one of them falls off a buffalo-man, who flees with the others in his "naked" human form. The smith repairs the hide and makes it into the mask of the buffalo cult.[80]

We also find the swan-maiden motif in reverse: Stealing human clothing means the victim remains an animal. For example, "The Dove Woman" from western Sudan "changes herself into a pretty woman, moves to the city, and sets up house. A man sees her and marries her. She lives very well with the man, but every morning she changes back into a dove." When the man takes her clothes, she remains in the form of a dove.[81]

The Grimms' "The Six Swans" also clearly retains something of the original concept of transformation: The witch-queen throws shirts over her stepchildren, and they fly away as swans. The children can take off their swan skins and have human form only for a quarter of an hour each evening. The spell is broken by (human) shirts that their sister throws over the transformed swan-brothers (KHM 49). This tale clearly shows the old conception of transformation as a covering. The change back in this case exactly reverses the original transformation.

Transformations other than into or from an animal follow the same rules in the folktale. "The Cast-iron Stove" only covers the transformed prince; the prince himself is not changed. In order to release him, the princess must "scrape" a hole in the oven until the enchanted prince can squeeze out (KHM 127).

Folktales in which love and marriage bring about disenchantment belong to a different developmental stage of reality.[82] The Grimms' tales make it seem as though disenchanted people always marry their rescuers. Tales such as "The Six Swans" (KHM 49), "The Seven Ravens" (KHM 25), or "The Twelve Brothers" (KHM 9), where sibling love, not love between a man and a woman, breaks the spell, are exceptions.

Folktales contain disenchantment *leading* to marriage and disenchantment *through* marriage. Individual cases do not always rigorously differentiate between disenchantment dependent on, i.e., preceded by, marriage, and disenchantment as the precondition for tying the knot. In any case, disenchantment and the disenchantment-marriage belong together and presuppose each other. In the folktale, anyone ready for disenchantment has, by definition, reached a marriageable age.

In a Silesian folktale, for example, the princess with a horse's head who must eat a man in the church every eight days says to her disenchanter: "You have freed me, now I will marry you."[83] A disenchanted princess from Pomerania makes herself equally clear when she tells her hero: "You are my savior, you kissed me, now you also have to marry me."[84] It would be completely contrary to folktale style if the princess did not want to marry her savior and if he had set out only to free the princess and not to find a wife (but see pp. 192 and 196).

Heroes and heroines disenchant their beloved, but males and females go about the task differently. Women disenchant with pity and service, men by freeing captives. Males often effect disenchantment with markedly erotic motifs, most commonly a kiss and the consummation of marriage.[85] Of course, our trusty Grimms' "tales for children" avoid all erotic motifs. For example in the original text of "The Frog King" (KHM 1) the nasty frog unambiguously tells the king's daughter: "Bring me into your bed, I want to sleep with you!" And when she throws him against the wall, "he fell down into the bed and lay there as a handsome young prince; then the king's daughter lay down with him."[86] Other versions of "The Frog King" are even clearer: The frog is allowed to sleep in the princess's bed for three weeks. When he joins her in bed, she places a sheet, a diaper, or a skirt between herself and the frog; or the foreman lies between the two, but the frog jumps over him and finally gets the princess to kiss him.[87] "Wilhelminke, I want to jump on your lap," sings the toad in an east Prussian version.[88]

Recent collections which record folktales in their adult form are particularly unabashed: In "The Venus-Bird" from Holstein, the numskull awakens the princess from her magical hundred-year sleep by sleeping with her.[89] The soldier who disenchants the queen from a spell gets into bed and sleeps with her for three nights.[90] Other folktales are more subtle but are nonetheless unmistakably erotic. The motif of the three tormenting nights seems to have sexual connotations (cf. KHM 92). Similarly, a kiss disenchants spooky legend figures in the form of a snake or toad. The disenchanter must let the snake-girl crawl on him or wind herself around him; he must embrace her, hold her tight, wrestle with her, stay with her for a night, etc.[91]

The fact that this disenchantment motif also appears in legend (although it lacks the happy marriage afterward) indicates that it developed more recently, when transformation was believed to be the result of black magic, and the generic expectation of a happy folktale ending, i.e., marriage, already existed. The idea of disenchanting love has indeed become a favorite motif fairly recently, and the erotic disenchantment motif has spread only as a result of the folktale's development into an artistic love story. Disenchantment at the moment the lovers' lips touch or as soon as they embrace increases the dramatic effect of this method of breaking the spell. Transformed people regain their human form as quickly as they magically lost it. This aspect of the European folktale contrasts with the earlier conception of transformation as we occasionally find it in tribal narratives. In particular, the idea that human company in general, not only through marriage, can return someone to human form seems very ancient.

Not a single act but rather gradual assimilation to the surrounding human society restores the human form. Disenchantment through love is simply the novelistic stylization of this believed notion of disenchantment through human company. The Pygmalion story also corresponds to this notion: Daily human contact humanizes the subject. Like Pygmalion in the Greek legend, a wooden statue of a girl comes to life in a Turkish folktale.[92]

The recent expansion of the idea of disenchantment has proliferated motivations for undertaking the task, particularly in ethical and psychological respects. Pity, love, the willingness to help, the desire to undertake an adventure, or even the selfish pursuit of profit may inspire disenchantment.[93] In addition to deliberate efforts at disenchantment, we also find unintended disenchantment (e.g., KHM 1).

The more the folktale distances itself from magical reality, the more formulaic disenchantment becomes, until it finally becomes a merely stylistic element used to construct a model folktale. In other words, disenchantment provides the necessary stereotypical release from the spell and leads to the expected happy ending. A few folktales include "disenchantment" even though no spell or transformation occurred in the first place. "Disenchantment" finally comes to mean any sort of release, and it is now only a happy "resolution" without its former connection to magical reality.

Similarly, the European folktale completely subordinates to stylistic considerations the connection between enchantment and guilt. The modern artistic folktale often does retain magical guilt—little brother in KHM 11 is transformed because he drinks from the enchanted fountain—but we nonetheless almost always have the impression that spells affect the innocent. The happy folktale completely abandons reality in order to free the hero and his or her partner of burdens. In contrast, the legend continues to take guilt very seriously: It has brought the old conception of magical guilt into close connection with the Christian idea of sin and punishes both violations equally severely because it sees both concepts as completely real. Because transformation and disenchantment are so closely bound to the concept of guilt, the folktale takes great pains to protect its hero from accusation: The hero almost always disenchants and is never disenchanted. As a rule, it is the folktale hero's partner, rather than the hero, who is transformed.

The legend's disenchantment, which usually fails,[94] has a completely different relationship to reality. The folktale did not follow the legend's rationalizing direction because its disenchantments had already distanced themselves from reality. In the legend, disenchantment is a serious matter which has also found a close connection to Christian notions of salvation. Only the legend depicts disenchantment through Christian remedies such as saying mass, pilgrimages, piously giving thanks, and religious greetings. Even though the legend's motifs of reparation as a precondition for disenchantment reflect a primitive ethic of retribution, we cannot imagine them without the influence of Christianity.[95] Christian influences also introduce the idea of release to eternal peace into the legend. In contrast, the folktale conceives of disenchantment in earthly terms. Folktale disenchantment does not transcend time in a Christian sense; rather, it frees characters so they can enjoy their worldly existence.

The differences between folktale and legend disenchantments correspond to the different historical stages of reality they embody. The original belief in transformation does not recognize the concept of disenchantment. Magic gradually replaces the universal ability to voluntarily change back into human form, and finally only disenchantment can undo transformations. The last stage coincides with the historical development of religious belief in salvation. Only the established high religions speak of "salvation"; early religion did not yet express this need.[96] Belief in disenchantment has developed through a series of stages: from breaking the spell by taking off the "covering," to killing and decapitation, and finally to a purely spiritual disenchantment through Christian remedies and acts of love.

Primitive elements in our European folk narratives are not always the oldest. The folktale can reproduce any of the historical stages of transformation and disenchantment, producing a different accent in each case. A given narrative, however, emphasizes one aspect over the others.

## MANNERS AND CUSTOMS

Magic is only part of an entire world that once existed. We have inquired into the magical realm of this world, now we must also investigate other human activities that appear in the folktale and ask what they tell us about a past world-view and its conception of reality. Folk belief is not the only aspect of an archaic, once-believed reality that we recognize in the folktale. The folktale also provides historical information about actual ways of life. Of course, a narrative's cultural shading does not always indicate the actual age of the story: Cannons and cars can replace older requisitions in folk narrative. The magic rifle and bullet that never miss their target developed from the magic sword. Any clues that we do uncover apply only for the given text, not for the entire tale type, particularly when decorative motifs not essential to the plot contain this information.

Exemplifying this fallacy, Josef Prestel dates "Rumpelstiltskin" (KHM 55) to the baroque period, when (and because) spinning gold was in its heyday in order to supply the lace industry.[1] But clearly this is a false conclusion because it fails to recognize the folktale's central motif. It is also a mistake to ascribe "Rumpelstiltskin" to the sixteenth century and the discovery of the spinning wheel, because the spinning wheel is also not a vital element in this folktale's reality and therefore does not provide a criterion for dating, particularly because older versions of the tale about help with spinning mention the spindle.[2]

Humans and domestic animals live in small quarters in the folktale

(KHM 169). Hans Naumann draws conclusions about archaic ways of living on the basis of the giant who comes home and says, "I smell, smell human flesh" (cf. the devil in KHM 29). He sees this formula as proof that primeval man lived in homes or caves without windows or lighting. Only in such a house could the inhabitant smell if someone he could not see had crept into the dwelling while he was away.[3] Naumann's interpretation is not very convincing. The hero hides in the monster's house and therefore would not be visible even if it were well lit. Folktale demons obviously have an instinctual ability to detect the presence of a human in their home.

We cannot determine the age of KHM 87 on the basis of the potatoes that the poor man's wife puts on the fire even if we know that potatoes have been cultivated in Germany only since the middle of the eighteenth century. This tale type (Type 750) appears in Stricker's *Mären* from around 1250. Millet, which has tenaciously held its ground in the folktale (e.g., KHM 103), would provide a better historical index of folktale civilization: Its shallow roots make it workable with a hoe, and thus millet has long been one of the primary cultivated grains. Millet was the main source of nourishment among the lower classes from Germanic antiquity until the Middle Ages, by which time the upper classes had already switched to bread.[4]

The lace that the German Snow White (KHM 53) buys from her evil stepmother has been dated to the rococo period, but lace adornments date to at least the thirteenth century.[5] Besides, Icelandic versions of this tale contain rings, shoes, and belts, all of which are much older, instead of lace.[6] In short, we cannot date the tale type on the basis of the lace in the German text.

The folktale's depiction of occupations is also so varied that it does not allow us to draw a precise picture of some historical or social reality. Ancient Germanic wild men appear alongside medieval knights; discharged soldiers who apparently fought as mercenaries in the Thirty Years War meet craftsmen who could have lived in the late Middle Ages as well as the nineteenth century. All of these figures are largely interchangeable.

In this chapter we ask: To what extent does the folktale depict real manners and customs? In doing so we encounter familiar methodological problems. In a well-known effort, P. Saintyves attempts to trace Perrault's tales to ancient seasonal celebrations and initiation rituals. Sleeping Beauty is nature waking to the new year, Cinderella the bride oracle on Valentine's Day, Cap o' Rushes a Fasnacht costume, Little Red Riding-Hood the May Queen, Thumbling the consecration of youth, Bluebeard the ritual testing of a wife, Puss in Boots the indoctrination of the newly chosen king.[7]

False interpretations often take up customs that appear only in the folktale's decorative elements. For example, we can find evidence that the practice depicted in "The Three Feathers" (KHM 63) of blowing a feather into the air in order to decide which direction to follow has a basis in reality.[8] But even though the Grimm tale takes its title from this custom, its appearance in the Grimm version is an exception and merely ornamental; it tells us nothing about the tale type. Other versions of this narrative (Type 402, "The Mouse, Cat, Frog, etc. as Bride") do not depict this custom.

Occasionally folktales pass something off as an "old practice" just so the hero follows the correct path. A modern Greek folktale, for example, describes a city where "according to an old practice, the first person to appear at the gate of the city after it was opened in the morning would replace the king who had died."[9] In this case the custom is invented for the sake of the story. Similarly, we cannot simply label cannibalism motifs in the folktale remnants of prehistoric times when cannibalism may have existed, especially since we can document criminal commissions of cannibalism as late as the nineteenth century. The folktale no longer depicts cannibalism in its original, magical form; instead it condemns it as a crime.[10] The emotional appeal of gruesome subjects seems to be a more important motive for including cannibalism in the folktale. In particular, the eating of children, like the common folktale motif of abandoning children, clearly first appeared as a motif designed specifically for the "warning tale," which was devised to frighten children. Thus we cannot conclude that abandoning children was once an actual practice. Jacob Grimm's documentation of the historical roots of abandoning children because of poverty and need (and then only immediately after birth) in his study of ancient law and the depiction of this practice as "an old custom" in certain folk narratives[11] do little for our understanding of "Hansel and Gretel," for example, where this cruel motif seems to have been invented only for the construction of the plot. The motif is absent in a large number of the versions.[12] We have no proof that the tale has a relationship to historical reality.

Since we cannot discuss every manner and custom here, we have chosen a single area to cover, namely, engagement and marriage in the folktale.[13] August von Löwis of Menar calculated that a hero's seeking a bride is the focal point in 72 percent of all tales of magic.[14] The folktale climaxes and ends when it reaches its goal of marriage. Of course, the wedding is occasionally simply a convenient formula for the happy ending. The folktale does not always logically require a wedding. A Russian folktale affixes this sentence at the end: "The daughter married a good man and lived happily and satisfied."[15] Despite the folktale's tendency to include a happy marriage, it is not a love story. The story is not about two people who belong together. The *obstacles* to marriage are often more important than the actual love and marriage.

We cannot expect the folktale to provide detailed descriptions of wedding customs because weddings occur so frequently at the story's end. We generally find such details only in recently recorded, often somewhat verbose narratives that describe a village wedding (cf. pp. 197–98, for example). But we have better sources than the folktale for details about modern country weddings. When the folktale does directly describe engagement and marriage customs, reality is often quite clearly abandoned. For example, the man's method of deciding whether to remarry in KHM 13 has nothing to do with real marriage oracles. He tells his daughter: "Take this boot with a hole in the sole up to the attic, hang it on the big nail, and pour water into it. If the water stays, I'll remarry; if it runs through, I won't." This motif appears only in the Grimm version. Even another version collected by the brothers themselves lacks this opening.[16]

In other folktales, details about engagement and wedding customs are relatively recent decorative additions that reveal nothing about the tale type's age. "Darling Roland" (KHM 56) reports that "in that country it was the custom that a proclamation be made for all the girls for miles around to attend the wedding and sing in honor of the bridal couple." But this tells us very little. Wilhelm Grimm adopted this custom from Hessian folklife. Other narrators of this tale use different motifs in order to bring the true bride and Roland together once again.

We are more interested in asking whether the folktale can tell us anything about ancient wedding practices that no longer exist but that were once a real part of folklife. Even if the folktale seldom depicts the wedding itself, the conditions the tales require for marriage are a rich enough topic for the study of manners and customs. We are not trying to simply analyze the wedding's place in the folktale's structure and form; rather, we must attempt to place the folktale in the real historical, psychological, and sociological context in which its style corresponds with the way of thinking it depicts.

Some analyses date the folktale's strong emphasis on courtship to the Middle Ages, when love supposedly first became a poetic motif. But in the majority of folktales about courtship, love, oddly enough, plays almost no role. Those tales that do depict love, e.g., KHM 6 ("Faithful Johannes"), in which the young king becomes enamored of the portrait of the Princess of the Golden Roof, seem to have acquired this feature more recently. Falling in love with a picture surely does not belong to this folktale's original form, because in the majority of versions the hero becomes acquainted with the princess in some other way. The same applies for "The Black and the White Bride" (Type 403), where the Grimm version (KHM 135) again contains this motif.[17] In general, the folktale portrays love and marriage much less romantically: Notably, the folktale doesn't mention love when the hero's adventure is primary and the ruler's daughter is merely his reward. Similarly, there is no mention of love when a father promises his daughter in exchange for his freedom, without the engaged couple even knowing each other. In any case, the folktale does not depict marriage for love. As was often the case among peasants, people in the folktale often marry for practical reasons: The king wants to marry the girl who supposedly can spin straw into gold (KHM 55), or, more realistically, the queen chooses a girl who can spin three rooms full of flax to be her daughter-in-law (KHM 14). The silver tree with golden fruit is also a welcome dowry (KHM 130). A knight wants to marry a "dragon" that has already killed two husbands simply to get its farm.[18] A peasant must take economic factors into account when choosing a wife who will provide important help with the work. The seven brothers decide to marry so they won't have to keep house themselves.[19] In one folktale, the king's son even marries a poor orphan because she is so industrious and skillful (KHM 188). In other tales a clever woman seems particularly desirable (KHM 94).

Not only stylistic demands prevent the folktale from requiring an extended period of engagement before the couple actually marries. In the folktale, engagement and marriage coincide; marriage immediately follows successful disenchantment. Although the folktale frequently speaks of true and false brides, it never mentions engagement and seldom a church wedding.[20] But folktales certainly contain the old practice of promising to give one's child in marriage, and the promise has greater validity than the marriage itself. According to the folk, "the Lord considers an engaged couple to be married." Thus in the folktale a marriage is easily absolved, even during the wedding celebration itself, if the former bride who can prove the groom promised to marry her reappears. This frequently occurs with the motif of the old and new keys (H1292.6), which perhaps derives from a legal formula.[21]

In "Cinderella" (KHM 21) the prince cunningly manages to attain one of the fleeing heroine's slippers and declares, "No girl shall be my wife but the one this golden shoe fits." Jacob Grimm traced the motif of using a shoe to discern the correct bride to a Germanic engagement custom.[22] We also find parallels in modern customs: Primarily among Romance peoples, the groom sometimes removes the bride's old shoes before the wedding. In Lorraine, for example, everyone at the wedding tries to remove the bride's shoes, but only the groom succeeds.[23]

But the folktale also seems to echo far more ancient wedding customs. The folktale's use of marriage to reward great deeds or accomplishment of difficult tests corresponds to the trials required to attain manhood in tribal societies. Before a young man may marry in these societies, he must prove himself at hunting or at war; he must bag a certain animal or kill a certain number of enemies. These tasks the suitor must undergo embody a basic folk idea: A woman can, and must, set conditions before she gives herself away; a man must prove his masculinity to the woman, he must be capable of bringing offerings even if he risks losing his life. Of course, the folktale fantastically exaggerates this reality. For example, before marrying the king's daughter in KHM 29, the suitor must bring the king three golden hairs from the devil's head back from hell; others must fetch the water of life. In other folktales the hero must wash black yarn until it turns white, sort rye and wheat (in some versions of KHM 113), or empty a pond with a thimble (KHM 193). In "The Griffin" (KHM 165) the suitor must build a ship that travels in water and on land, then he must take a hundred rabbits out to pasture and tend to them all day, and finally he must bring a feather from the griffin's tail. As we said, the folktale consciously fabulates these tasks, freely inventing details. However, in other cases we discover real manners and customs when we peel back the folktale's exaggeration.

For example, the suitor's tasks of cutting down an entire forest (KHM 193), planting a vineyard, and building a house or castle (in some versions of KHM 113) closely resemble tribal requirements for marriage.[24] The requirements usually have something to do with farming, such as cultivating, digging, sowing, harvesting, draining ponds, cutting wood, building shelter, and protecting and caring for animals (since farmers also have livestock). Each of these tasks tests the suitor's ability to provide for the family. Of course, in tribal narratives the suitor's tasks correspond much more closely to real customs: For example, in West African Kpelle narratives the suitor must bring fruit, a chicken, or rice from the other side of a river; he must build a house on the cliffs, cut down a tree, or play a board game with the princess's father. Occasionally he must guess what is inside an amulet.[25] In South American Indian tales, the suitor must be able to build a house and a plantation for his father-in-law.[26] These tasks still correspond exactly to real customs.

The way in which the European folktale places these demands on the hero reflects ancient methods of contracting a marriage: The bride's father sets conditions that benefit him alone for his approval of the marriage. Tale 81 in Bünker's collection even depicts negotiation of the price for the bride. Such tales, like tribal narratives, seem to reflect the practice of buying a marriage.[27] Other tales—as well as numerous medieval ballads—indicate the possibility that brides were once stolen. This also applies to tales in which a king's daughter is abducted, even if the addition of a merchant gives the abduction a bourgeois guise (KHM 6).[28]

Many of the folktale suitor-hero's extraordinary feats have clear parallels among tribal initiation customs. This is no coincidence because in tribal societies, demonstrating the attainment of maturity through initiation originally meant that the initiate was ready to marry as well. The wedding immediately followed initiation. The initiate and the folktale hero who wants the princess must prove their strength, endurance, and wisdom. Many folktale tasks are designed to kill the hero. Those tales in which he does die and is then revived with the water of life (e.g., KHM 92) remind us of the initiation process that often imitates death and rebirth. The initiate experiences death before attaining maturity. Conversely, many tribal peoples think of death in terms of initiation.[29]

The solitary indoctrination which the tribal medicine man undergoes preceding the test of worth also reminds us of familiar folktale situations. Many versions of "Iron Hans" (KHM 136) depict one such situation: The wild man takes the young king's son into the forest and assigns him a task. Similarly, in "The Thief and His Master" (KHM 68) a magician raises a child away from the parents' home. In both cases a supernatural figure or a sorcerer rears the boy away from his normal environment. This indoctrination prepares him to pass the difficult tests he faces later.[30] A magical adviser in the form of a wise old man appears in innumerable folktales. There are many possible interpretations of this figure,[31] but the parallels to real initiatory leaders are striking: Like an initiator during ceremonies of maturation, the old figure in the folktale tests the hero's character and gives him the advice needed to accomplish the tasks. Likewise, the twelve brothers who live in a lonely house in the forest (KHM 9) and their declaration, "Whenever we meet a girl, her red blood will flow," remind us of the isolation of young men before their initiation and their strict seclusion from girls of the same age. The fact that the folktale hero who must leave home has hardly outgrown childhood and usually has not yet married also speaks to the parallels between initiation rites and the folktale: The boy in the folktale is exactly the same age as the initiates.

In tribal societies young girls are also strictly isolated and must live in solitude before they mature. As soon as a girl menstruates for the first time she is put in a puberty hut, where she must stay for a certain period. This female isolation also seems to have found expression in many folktales. Many scholars have shown the connection between "The Maiden in the Tower" (Type 310) and the girl's puberty hut. This provides an interpretation for Rapunzel (KHM 12, also see KHM 198), whom a witch locks in a tower at the age of twelve and who is then set free by a prince.[32] The fourteen-year-old Sleeping Beauty (KHM 50) also magically sleeps in a tower apart from the court society; when the prince awakens her, she is ready to marry. The folktale often exaggerates the duration (e.g., "Sleeping Beauty") and severity (e.g., the three stolen princesses, Type 301, who may not walk under the open sky before they turn fifteen) of the confinement,[33] but even these fantastic tales seem to rely on actual practices. Some tribal societies even use a tower as the girl's puberty hut, so that dangerous menstrual blood does not come into contact with the ground and destroy its fertility.

Before initiation, girls are also taught what they will need to know in their new social position. An old woman from the tribe usually provides the instruction. The folktale reflects this reality: Only the witch herself may visit Rapunzel in the tower, and she closely guards against anyone else gaining entrance. The development of the folktale described above makes it understandable that a witch has replaced the earlier magical attendant figure.[34]

Russian scholars have recently pursued the similarities between folktale motifs and actual social practices in much greater detail. They see the folktale's oldest and sole basis in initiation rites. Vladimir Y. Propp and Dmitrii Zelenin consider folktale motifs of sex change, abandoning children, abduction by a forest spirit, cutting off a finger, cutting the hero into pieces, and, in general, all motifs about the wandering hero who must bring something from a faraway land, survivals of puberty trials. For females, the motif of beauty in a chest (Cap o' Rushes), the forbidden chamber, abduction of a girl by a dragon, and all motifs about magical birth have the same origins.[35] It is difficult to say just how far such explanations may go and whether one can infer a historical evolution on the basis of approximate parallels between tribal customs and folktale motifs. Viewing these customs as the folktale's actual basis says little about the folktale's modern form and, in any case, leaves questions unanswered about how the folktale evolved from a simple factual account to the fixed-form product of fantasy that we call a "folktale" today. We simply lack the basic evidence required to construct such a bridge. In any case, parallels among our own customs have more to do with the European folktale than the often constructed similarities to tribal customs. We now turn our attention to European tradition.

Riddling commonly provides amusement at peasant weddings.[36] Guests pose riddles for the couple and among themselves. The practice of solving riddles at weddings seems to be very old; perhaps an actual test of the suitor provides the basis for this playful fun. We do find parallels to a serious test in tribal maturation rites: The suitor must prove his knowledge as well as his endurance and strength. In the Eddic story, Thor riddles the dwarf Alwis, who wants to marry his daughter, all night. Obtaining a bride by solving riddles also appears as early as the Latin story of Apollonius of Tyrus.[37] Samson's wedding depicted in Judges 14 certainly belongs to the same group of motifs. Here the groom himself riddles the guests:

> Out of the eater came something to eat
> out of the strong came something sweet. (14:14)

The guests arrange for the bride to trick Samson into revealing the solution. The riddle refers to one of Samson's adventures: A bee swarm had nested in the stomach of a lion that he killed.

A well-known folktale (KHM 22) contains exactly the same type of riddling, and here too solving the riddle is the precondition for marriage. A princess "let it be known that she would marry the man who posed a riddle she couldn't solve, but that if she did solve the riddle his head would be cut off." The hero turns his experience of killing twelve robber-murderers with a soup containing poisoned raven meat into a riddle: "Here is my riddle: One killed none, yet killed twelve." The princess can't solve the riddle, and in the end she must marry the hero.[38]

Of course, riddles also appear in very different contexts in the folktale, for example, in "The Shepherd Boy" (KHM 152) and "The Peasant's Clever Daughter" (KHM 94). The devil also asks riddles, and the person who has sold his soul to the devil can annul the pact by solving them (e.g., KHM 125). But it is striking how often the folktale requires solving one or more riddles as the precondition for marriage.[39] In other tales the hero must guess what kind of birthmarks a girl has (KHM 114 is similar): Only the suitor who guesses that the rich gypsy's daughter has a star on one breast and a moon on the other is allowed to buy (!) her as his wife.[40] In KHM 212 the hero must guess what material was used to make the king's daughter's dress. Through trickery he learns that it was sewn from the leather of a louse.[41] In some versions of "The Cast-iron Stove" (KHM 127) the false bride cannot solve the riddles, but the king's daughter knows the correct answers.[42] All of these examples suggest an ancient connection between solving riddles and actual wedding customs.

In the Grimm tale "The Mongoose" (KHM 191), the king's daughter will marry only the man who can hide himself so well that she cannot find him by looking through her twelve magic windows. A raven, a fish, and a fox help the hero to fulfill the task: The raven hides him in an egg, puts it in his nest, and sits on it; the fish swallows the hero and dives to the bottom of the lake. After the king's daughter finds him in both hiding places, the fox transforms the hero into a mongoose.[43] The mongoose-hero hides under the princess's braids, and she cannot spot him by looking through her magic windows. The princess gives up and the hero marries her. In other versions a horse hides the hero in its tooth.[44] Sometimes the hero must find the princess; in other words, a test of his ability to search replaces the hiding contest.[45] Occasionally both the hero and the princess hide from each other.[46]

Of course, these hiding places are typical folktale fantasies, but the hiding game itself is the well-known and common wedding custom of the bride and groom hiding from each other on the morning of the wedding or when returning from the ceremony. First the groom must find the bride. Then the groom suddenly disappears, perhaps during the wedding dance, and the bride must search for him. This custom was not always a game; it has roots in folk belief, where we can find its serious meaning. Paul Sartori calls this custom a "ritual refusal": The bride and groom are not allowed to change their marital status too quickly because evil powers enviously have their eyes on all transitions. Thus each new stage in life should be made to look as if it is forced upon the participants, who cannot be held responsible for the change.[47]

Another motif complex appears to be closely related to guessing and hiding: In numerous versions of Type 313 the hero must pick out the correct bride from among many women wearing similar veils. A helpful animal (a fly or a bird) lands on the correct girl (cf. KHM 62), thus allowing the hero to identify her. In other cases he recognizes his bride by some particular feature; e.g., she is missing her little toe or part of a finger.[48] The Snorra Edda contains the reverse form—i.e., the bride must pick the groom out of a group—in its description of how the giantess Skadi became the god Njord's wife: Skadi demanded compensation from the Aesir for killing her father; namely, she wanted to marry one of the gods. But when choosing, she was allowed to look only at their feet. She chose the one who had the smallest feet, convinced that it was Baldr, but it was Njord. Thus he became her husband.[49] This humorous tale has already modified the original meaning, but the practice itself still corresponds to actual customs. Various peoples require the groom to identify his bride from among a number of women solely by looking at their feet. This is a particularly common wedding custom in France, Italy, and Serbia. Moreover, we can still recognize ancient ideas in this game. The idea is to deceive the demonic and evil powers so they cannot identify the actual couple getting married, i.e., the people in danger because of their transitional status. Perhaps bridesmaids, still common today, are a last remnant of this idea.[50]

According to Sartori, other wedding customs have the same meaning: For example, a small girl or an ugly old woman sometimes accompanies the groom when he goes to get the bride. The correct bride joins him only after this switch, which may be repeated several times.[51] In Egerland [a German-speaking area around the city of Eger in northwestern Sudetenland, now part of Czechoslovakia] a maid or day laborer in disguise, i.e., someone less desirable to the groom, greets him in place of the bride. People call this disguised substitute the "old bride," and she produces wedding presents the groom supposedly gave her. Finally the groom induces her to remove the costume by offering a monetary gift; only then does the real bride show herself. According to popular belief, the "old bride" takes the bad luck out of the house. This too is an apotropaic artificial premarriage. The harm threatening the true bride falls upon the false bride.[52] This substitution, like the folk customs mentioned above, supposedly diverts the danger away from the couple. This strongly reminds us of the folktale motif of the *substituted bride*, which also seems to have a basis in actual wedding customs. The folktale's altered, often fantastically expanded usage of this motif should not obscure the narrative's relationships to actual customs. On the way to the wedding, the stepsister, who is "as black as coal" and "ugly as the night," disposes of the white bride and takes her place (KHM 135). "The old witch [i.e., the stepmother] so beguiled the king and so deceived his eyes with her arts, that he let her and her daughter stay. In the end he decided that the daughter wasn't half bad and actually married her." In "The Cast-iron Stove" (KHM 127) the king's son is already planning to marry a different girl when, at the last moment, the correct bride appears; "The Lilting, Leaping Lark" (KHM 88) is quite similar. Maid Maleen (KHM 198) must stand in for the prince's unworthy bride during the wedding, but then she reveals herself as the proper bride who was once engaged to the groom.[53] In some folktales the substitution occurs at the young wife's childbed: In KHM 11 the evil stepmother replaces her stepdaughter, who had married the king, with her real daughter, "who was as ugly as the night and only had one eye," after the birth of the queen's first child. Some folktales include the motif of the substitute bride in completely different contexts: In KHM 127 the king and his daughter send the miller's and the swineherd's daughters to the unwanted suitor so the princess won't have to marry him. These efforts are usually in vain, as in many versions of the animal bridegroom tale.[54]

The false or substitute bride is not always a rival; the true bride's friend can also take her place. The latter case approximates the actual custom to a greater degree. A few folktales depict this proper substitution on the wedding night: In a few Danish and Icelandic versions of Type 401, the princess is changed into a sparrow or a deer on her wedding night. A friend or servant takes her place until the husband burns the animal skin at the right moment or breaks the spell with a blow from his sword.[55] These tales depict old protective customs used during weddings against magic of all sorts, as well as the actual dangers that can threaten the couple. A few narratives, such as "Faithful Johannes" (KHM 6), actually portray these dangers. Faithful Johannes sacrifices his own life to protect his master and his bride from the three magical, demonic events that threaten to keep the couple apart. Versions of "The Grateful Dead" in which the otherworld helper fights a demon or a dragon that tries to kill the groom on the wedding night show the extent of the dangers threatening the couple.[56] Again folk belief provides a background and starting point for these fantastic motifs.

Real wedding customs in all societies are full of taboos: Marriages may not take place during particular months and on particular days; the bride may not help bake the cake or work on the wedding dress; the bride should not be happy to move out of her parents' house and should not say "I do" in a happy tone. The wedding procession must follow a particular path and remain tightly knit; certain foods should not appear on the wedding table, and so on. Violating these proscriptions results in all sorts of bad luck.[57]

Obstacles to the folktale wedding are the same as those that folk belief says may interfere with real weddings. Carelessly breaking taboos, no matter how trivial they may seem, has dire consequences for the bride and groom: In numerous animal bridegroom tales the young wife is not allowed to see her husband; if she does, intentionally or not, the man must leave her. In "The Lilting, Leaping Lark" (KHM 88) the animal bridegroom cannot come into contact with "a ray of candlelight." The hero often forgets about his bride because he kisses or simply speaks to someone else against the wife's prohibition (e.g., KHM 127; cf. KHM 113, 186, and 193).[58] These taboos often refer to the couple's relationship to their parents (KHM 127 and 193). In KHM 186 the king's son forgets his true bride when he goes home one more time to obtain his father's approval of the marriage. We find the same motif in "The Drummer" (KHM 193): "Oh," the king's daughter tells her fiancé, "I implore you. When you get home, be careful not to kiss your parents on their right cheeks, because if you do you'll forget everything, and I'll be left here alone and forsaken." The king's son in "The Prince and the Princess" (KHM 113; also see KHM 56) also falls into a magical state of forgetfulness when his mother kisses him. According to folk belief, a kiss can magically cause forgetfulness as well as remembrance. In particular, someone can steal the bride by kissing the husband, thus making him forget her. But a kiss also brings back the memory, as "Sleeping Beauty" (KHM 50) clearly demonstrates.[59]

Folk belief prescribes "Tobias nights" (cf. Tobit 6:8) for the same reason it suggests delivering a false bride to the groom. In many places the couple must (or used to) practice abstinence during the first days and nights of marriage in order to protect themselves from various sorts of harm.[60] We find similar practices in the folktale: In some versions of KHM 93 ("The Raven"), the hero sleeps next to the princess for three nights without touching her.[61] We can also assume that a wedding without sexual intercourse takes place in the tale about the eighteen soldiers who sleep with eighteen princesses in order to disenchant them: "The oldest said: 'Tonight you must complete the disenchantment; each of us will sleep with his fiancée, but everyone must lie there calm and quiet next to the princess without talking or moving until they play reveille.' And that's what they did. All thirty-six slept together and bravely endured the night. Only the drummer almost ruined the whole thing."[62] The three nights with her husband that the true bride buys (KHM 88, 113, 127, 193) also probably relate to this custom.[63] The sword placed between the man and woman is also a clear indication of a taboo that requires maintenance of chastity. The tale "The Two Brothers" (KHM 60) uses the sword motif in this way when one of the brothers sleeps with the other's wife. But the young queen no longer understands the custom's original meaning: "She didn't know what to make of it, but didn't dare to ask." This motif also appears in the *Nibelungenlied* and in the heroic legends of other cultures. But this practice was not always a motif designed to serve the epic purpose of proving the brother didn't touch the other's wife. Placing the sword between the couple was an actual legal custom that we can trace quite far back in history. For example, at both of Maximilian I's weddings, to Maria of Burgundy and to Maria of Brittany, someone stood in for the emperor. The substitute, fully clothed, lay beside the bride in the presence of the empire's dignitaries, and an exposed sword was placed between them.[64]

The need for customs designed to magically protect participants in a peasant wedding extends to the bride's bed.[65] People try to cleanse the place where the marriage will be consummated of all demonic influences. Any ritual or cultic purifications of the people themselves found in German wedding traditions, however, are only remnants. Sprinkling the bride with water can be included here. In Uckermarck [on the Oder River in eastern Pomerania], washing the bride's laundry provides an occasion for a small prewedding festival. In ancient India, Greece, and Rome, the bridal bath (λουτρὸν νυμφιχόν) was among the most important wedding preparations. This custom has lived on in eastern Europe, where the bride bathes and is whipped with birch switches. According to Olaus Magnus, wedding baths took place in Sweden as often as weddings.[66] Such rites are supposed to purify the bride of all harmful influences.

We find somewhat similar elements in "The Monster's Bride" (Type 507A), a widely distributed folktale particularly well known from Andersen's "Traveling Companion."[67] A princess's lover is a sorcerer. Every night she goes to him to request help against her suitors. She then asks her suitors to guess her thoughts or to find a hidden object. The hero succeeds with the help of a grateful dead man. But before the princess can marry the hero, she must be purified of her contact with the sorcerer. In Bünker's, Ey's, Andersen's, and Asbjörnsen's versions, only a bath on the wedding night works.[68] In a Norwegian version[69] the hero must whip the princess with nine green birch switches and then bathe her in milk products; first he washes her in a vat of whey, then he rubs her down with sour milk, and finally he rinses her with sweet milk.

The groom must also undergo similar purification ceremonies before the folktale wedding if he has had contact with demonic powers. In "King Lindworm," one of the most beloved Danish folktales (Type 433B), the heroine must whip her husband in the bridal chamber with switches soaked in lye. Then she washes him off in sweet milk. The men from the king's court laugh at the bride and tell her such cleansing "works only in the peasant's imagination." But she turns out to be right: The process finally removes the spell from her lover, and "they congratulated the couple more than ever before."[70]

Some versions of "Faithful Ferdinand and Faithless Ferdinand" (KHM 126) also depict the groom bathing in hot milk. The ritual bath has become a test of courage in this tale. A king orders the hero to win him a princess; he does so. The girl places demand after demand on the king that the hero must fulfill for him before the marriage. In the end she declares that she will marry only the one who dares to bathe in hot milk. Again the king sends the hero in his place; but the hero's helpful magical horse blows the bath of boiled mare's milk cool for him, or the hero protects himself by covering his body with the horse's froth. Rejuvenated and beautified, he climbs out of the bath. The king tries to do the same but burns himself and dies. The princess marries the hero.[71] Treating the groom with water or milk and hitting him with birch switches is not "fertility magic," it magically purifies him of demonic influences before the marriage. The contexts of the folktale motifs reveal this more clearly than the actual customs, which have outlived their original meaning. Some customs practiced today are often not understood and no longer believed reality. On the other hand, the folktale, which on the surface seems to have been invented merely for entertainment, often describes living reality from the past.

The same observation applies to the motif complex to which we now turn as we move from engagement and wedding customs to the birth of the folktale hero. In particular we want to look at the special case in which the hero is promised to a demonic figure at birth—that is a motif complex which seems to lack any reference to reality.

It is striking how commonly and in what a variety of tales in the Grimm collection this or a closely related motif plays a role: The witch in "Rapunzel" (KHM 12) tells the man who has intruded into her garden, " 'You may take as much rapunzel [a type of lettuce] as you like, but on one condition: you must give me the child that your wife will bear.' In his fright," the Grimm text continues, "the man agreed to everything, and the moment his wife was delivered the witch appeared, gave the child the name of Rapunzel, and took her away." The miller in KHM 181 promises the nixie of the pond that which "was just born in his house." " 'What could that be but a puppy or a little kitten?' thought the miller," but when he got home his wife had just given birth to a little boy. He doesn't fulfill his promise until the nixie herself finally comes and takes the boy to the pond. Rumpelstiltskin (KHM 55) "shouts" the well-known verse: "Brew today, tomorrow bake, / After that the child I'll take," because the girl who must spin straw into gold promised him her first-born in exchange for his help. She had already given him her necklace and ring.[72]

In other Grimm tales the child is promised sometime after birth, but the basic motif of giving a young person to an otherworld figure remains the same. The lion in KHM 88 ("The Lilting, Leaping Lark") tells the frightened man: "Nothing can save you unless you promise to give me the first creature you meet when you get home." The man finally gives in, and "when he reached home, the first creature he met was none other than his youngest, most beloved daughter." "An old man whom he had never seen before came up to" the poor miller in KHM 31 ("The Girl without Hands") "and said: 'Why wear yourself out chopping wood? I will make you rich if you promise to give me whatever is standing behind your mill.' " Without knowing what he is doing, the miller promises his daughter to the devil.[73] Similarly, the merchant in KHM 92 ("The King of the Golden Mountain") turns over his little boy to the black dwarf.

In "Mary's Child" (KHM 3) the poor woodsman who can no longer feed his family gives his only child to the Virgin Mary, who takes the girl to heaven. The Grimms' tale and other versions which approximate the saint's legend should not obscure the fact that this is simply a more recent branch of the tradition under discussion. In other versions of this tale (Type 710) the father gives the child to a demonic figure rather than a Christian figure.[74]

Bolte and Polivka's *Anmerkungen* document the distribution of this motif in tale types that do not contain it in the Grimm collection. In particular we should mention the numerous versions of "Iron Hans" (KHM 136): The wild man helps a childless couple get a son, but they must give him the child after a certain period.[75] In some versions of KHM 113 ("The Prince and the Princess") the father rashly promises the prince to a sorcerer or a witch,[76] and a few versions of KHM 206 ("The Three Green Branches") include the motif of freeing a boy given to the devil by his father.[77]

The reasons for giving the young person to an otherworld creature are quite diverse in these tales. Some offer a very explicit reason, such as the momentary desires of a pregnant woman (KHM 12) or a poor man's greed (KHM 31, 92, 181); in others the parent unknowingly gives the child away because the demand for the child is not direct (e.g., KHM 31, 92, 181). In another group of tales the parent knowingly (albeit out of need) promises the child to the otherworld figure (KHM 3, 12, 55). Folktales often depict this motif as a sort of substitute sacrifice: Someone who falls into the power of an otherworld figure is freed after promising to sacrifice his or her child instead (KHM 12, 88). But in every case the basic motif of transferring a child to an otherworld figure remains the same. The folktale portrays a variety of otherworld figures on the receiving end: males and females, local demons of all sorts, the devil, the Virgin Mary, and various Christian saints. Various beliefs and aspects of reality appear to mingle in these tales, but above all they depict belief in the child-stealing demon. We also find this notion in the form of the changeling in folk belief. This belief is manifest in "Rumpelstiltskin" (KHM 55): When the queen offers him "all the riches in the kingdom," he makes it clear that "something living is worth more to me than all of the treasure in the world." The basic idea behind belief in the changeling is that dwarves want to get their hands on human children.[78] Pacts with the devil as we know them from legends about witches and freemasons also provide a basis for the child-stealing figure. Interestingly, the folktale usually speaks of "promising," not "signing over": Dr. Faustus and every folk legend character from the Middle Ages to the present who sells his soul to the devil signs himself over. Apparently the folktale reflects an older cultural practice than the legend, as it often does. The only devotion of one's soul to a demon that still appears in the legend is a pact with the devil empowered by signing oneself over in blood. In contrast, the folktale seems to have secondarily replaced some otherworld figures with the devil, and only these few cases (KHM 31 and 92) mention "signing and sealing" the agreement. All other transfers appear to belong to preliterate cultures.

The consequences of belonging to a demon in the folktale also occasionally differ considerably from the fate of the person who sells his soul to the devil. The witch in "Rapunzel" promises that the child "will have a good life and I shall care for it like a mother" (KHM 12). "Mary's Child" also has a good life, even in the versions in which she is given to a demon. In the versions of "Iron Hans" mentioned above, the golden boy does not suffer. The demon even tells him he "must" go out into the world; he "can't stay here [with the demon] any longer" (KHM 136). The boy's sojourn with the demon does not appear to be coerced upon him; we cannot compare this to a medieval pact with the devil and its notion of an apprenticeship to demons or the devil himself. Bonds to demons in the folktale seem to draw on an older stage of culture.

Otto Höfler has recently compiled the many instances of this motif in Germanic antiquity, where it is related to belief in Odin.[79] The Nordic tradition of King Víkar, which encompasses several ancient Scandinavian texts, is one example. The Hálf saga describes Víkar's birth and youth; the Gautrek saga and Saxo Grammaticus portray his death. Taking these texts together, we see the close connection between the king's death and his birth: As determined before his birth, because his own mother "gave" her unborn child to Odin, Víkar's life ends on the gallows as a sacrifice to Odin. The Hálf saga depicts the mother's promise of the unborn child: Alrek, the king of Hordaland, was married to the princess Signy. A servant extolled the beauty of another woman, Geirhild, to Alrek. Höttr then approached Geirhild. The saga makes it clear that Höttr was none other than Odin, and Höfler correctly assumes that this was not a merely personal whim on the part of some scribe but rather the narrative's original meaning. Höttr then promised Geirhild that she would marry the king if she promised always to turn to him (Höttr) when she needed something. And so Víkar took Geirhild as his wife. But of course the king could not keep both wives. He promised to choose the one who brewed the best beer. Signy turned to Freyjo for help, Geirhild to Höttr. Höttr put his spear in the brew and, in exchange, demanded whatever was standing between Geirhild and the vat. The beer turned out well, and King Alrek said, "Geirhild take care! The beer is good—if nothing bad follows; I see your son hanging high on the gallows, woman, sacrificed to Odin." (This speech forms a stanza.) The same year Víkar was born, the son of Alrek and Geirhild.[80] Although this story already contains the folktale formula of unknowingly promising a child, the human sacrifice to Odin indicates that it also still embodies mythic belief in gods.[81]

The "Great Saga of Olaf" about Eyvind Kinnrifa renders a particularly striking account of this custom. This powerful north Norwegian chieftain, a pagan opponent of the converted Norwegian king Olaf Tryggvason, was devoted to Odin and therefore could not be baptized. The saga believingly reports the reality of the events. The story begins when the obstinate Eyvind is cunningly captured and brought before King Olaf:

> The king commanded him to take the baptism along with the others. Eyvind declined. The king kindly asked him to accept the correct belief and told him about Almighty God's many works and glory; the bishop did the same. But this did not move Eyvind. The king then offered him glorious gifts and large tracts of land and promised him his full friendship if he would reject paganism and take the baptism. But Eyvind brusquely rejected it all. Then the king threatened to torture or kill him, Eyvind would not be moved. The king had a basin of embers brought in and placed on Eyvind. And his body burst open. Then Eyvind spoke: "Take the basin off of me. I want to say a few words before I die." It was done. The king said: "Will you now believe in Christ?" "No," he said, "I couldn't be baptized even if I wanted to, because my parents' children always died, and they went to some Finns versed in magic and paid them a lot of money to magically help produce a child. They said that they couldn't do it. But the Finns said that my parents could possibly have a child that would live if

they took an oath that this child, if it lived, would serve Thor and Odin all
his days. Then I was born and they gave me to Odin. I grew up and as
soon as I was independent, I fulfilled their oath. I have served Odin with
love ever since and have become a powerful chieftain. I have served Odin
and been devoted to him more than once so I could not possibly break the
oath, nor do I want to." At that Eyvind died. He was a man well versed in
magic.[82]

The increasingly demonic and diabolical depiction of the pagan world
finally brings our motif of dedicating a child into the numinous world of the
legend and the folk ballad. For example, the Danish song of Germand
Gladensvend, for which we have six sixteenth-century texts, tells of a
young childless queen who—in distress at sea, but also out of a desire to
bear a child—pledges the fruit of her body to a demon who appears in the
form of a bird. The demon, who appears as an eagle, a raven, an invisible
sea-troll, and finally a vulture, wants "his" boy. The sobbing mother con-
fides the boy's secret background to her son. When he is fifteen years old,
he wants to visit his bride in England and asks his mother to lend him her
"feather shirt" so he can fly to his beloved. Before he flies off, his mother
warns him that if he encounters the raven, he is lost. Despite her warning
the youth flies away. He meets the raven:

> "Welcome, Germand Gladensvend,
> Where have you been all this time?
> Before you were born of this world,
> You were to be mine."

The youth asks permission to visit his bride before turning himself over on
the way back. The demon concedes but wants to "mark" the boy first: He
cuts out his right eye and drinks half of his blood.

Germand Gladensvend reaches his bride pale and bloody. She combs
his bloody hair and curses his mother. He defends his mother and tries to
console the girl. She puts on a feather shirt herself and slaughters all the
birds in flight, but she can't catch the evil raven. In the carnage she finds
only the boy's right hand.[83]

The best-known example of this motif's diabolical form is the legend
"Robert the Devil." The duke and duchess of Normandy long in vain for
an heir. In her despair the duchess promises that any child the devil
grants her will belong to him. The marriage immediately becomes fruitful
and the boy, born at great pain to the duchess, grows strong and handsome, although he does have a devilish evil streak. His bad deeds are
depicted with disgust: Finally he becomes a thief and murderer.[84] The
second part of the story depicts typical legend penance. The various local
features of this "legend," which are depicted as actual events, prove that
our motif appears here, for the last time, as believed historical reality.[85]

In addition to these demonic and diabolical forms, Höfler also traces the folktale's subdued versions back to the mythical motif of human sacrifice in ancient Germanic ritual. He sees a clear survival of Germanic devotion to Odin in the promise of a child to a demon.[86] Despite the many examples from Germanic antiquity Höfler provides, we should mention a few alternative ideas. Even if the folktale's fantasy-shaded motif of promising a child to a demon reflects an ancient believed reality, an ancient ritual, and actual family actions, we still do not know when this motif lost the element of reality in the folktale. Demonic and diabolical forms of the motif have appeared at least since the sixteenth century. The folktale's formulaic use of this motif to create tension from the start for the hero seems quite a bit more removed from the original belief than the Danish ballad and the Robert legend. How can we explain the motif's relatively late distribution in folktales around the world? The folktale motif's international distribution, which extends well beyond the Germanic area, makes it far more probable that the motif's early history does not belong only to Germanic antiquity. In this regard Höfler was too biased.

The motif's similar manifestations in ancient Jewish thought pose a particularly difficult stumbling block for Höfler's theses.[87] For example, Hanna, the mother of Samuel, was "greatly distressed, prayed to the Lord, and wept bitterly" because she had no children. "She made a vow and said, 'O lord of hosts, if Thou wilt indeed look on the affliction of Thy maidservant and remember me, and not forget Thy maidservant, but wilt give Thy maidservant a son, then I will give him to the Lord all the days of his life, and a razor shall never come on his head." Samuel—his name means "granted from God"—was dedicated to the Lord: "For this boy I prayed, and the Lord has given me my petition which I asked of Him. So I have also dedicated him to the Lord; as long as he lives he is dedicated to the Lord." (1 Sam. 1:10ff. and 27ff.).

The Old Testament calls a person dedicated to God a "Nazirite" (Hebrew Nazir). Numbers 6 devotes almost an entire chapter to extensively setting forth how one must fulfill this vow, and in Exodus 22:28, Mosaic law demands that "the first-born of your sons you shall give to Me."[88] Samson also is a Nazirite dedicated to the Lord, as described in Judges 13:

> And there was a certain man of Zorah, of the tribe of the Danites, whose name was Manoah; and his wife was barren and had borne no children. Then the angel of the Lord appeared to the woman, and said to her, 'Behold now, you are barren and have borne no children, but you shall conceive and give birth to a son. Now therefore, be careful not to drink wine or strong drink, nor eat any unclean thing. For behold, you shall conceive and give birth to a son, and no razor shall come upon his head, for the boy shall be a Nazirite to God from the womb; and he shall begin to deliver Israel from the hands of the Philistines. . . .' Then the woman gave birth to a son and named him Samson; and the child grew up and the Lord blessed him. (Cf. ch. 16:17)

Finally, John the Baptist is also described as a Nazirite devoted to God like Samuel and Samson: His mother, Elisabeth, was barren and on in years, but the son promised her by an angel of the Lord was also supposed to be dedicated to God (Luke 1).

This ancient Jewish idea, which contains no demonic elements, could have gradually developed into the folktale version. With the advent of Christianity, religious interest in Nazirite tradition ceased because according to the new religion, all people are the children of God. Accordingly, a new form of discipleship replaced the Naziritic form.[89] In any case, Höfler ignores Nazirite tradition. But we cannot leave this realm aside when considering this motif. The question of the origin of this folktale motif must, of course, be the subject of a separate monographic investigation. The Old Testament's conception was clearly not limited to Judaism but rather is a general Oriental belief. It is plausible that the folktale derives from the eastern Mediterranean region. Gunkel, Peuckert, von Sydow, and Baumgartner have already conjectured this path of diffusion for other folktales.[90] Most important, the international distribution of this folktale motif suggests that we should not trace it only to a Germanic origin.

A number of this folktale complex's details are indeed more similar to the Nazirite narrative than to sacrifices to Odin found in the sagas. In contrast to the ancient Germanic conception in which Odin first receives the child when it dies or the child must actually be sacrificed, the folktale figure, like the Hebrew god, obtains the child during its lifetime. Life, not death, is dedicated to the supernatural figure. Folktales and Hebraic thought also both pose obligations for the child. The Old Testament's frequent demand that "no razor shall come upon [the Nazirite's] head" reminds us of the obligations set upon the folktale hero during his service to some otherworld figure: The devil's grimy brother (KHM 100) may not wash or comb his hair, trim his beard, or cut his nails for seven years. Rapunzel's hair finally grows to a length of twenty ells (yards), and when she violates her isolation, the witch cuts it off (KHM 12; cf. KHM 3). Perhaps an element from "Iron Hans" (KHM 136) also belongs here: The prince does not cut off the golden hair he acquires while serving Iron Hans; instead he hides it under his cap, which he never takes off so people won't see the hair.

While Germanic antiquity depicts dedicating only sons to a god, the vow of a Nazirite (Numbers 6) also explicitly includes dedication of women. In "Mary's Child," "Rapunzel," and "The Girl without Hands" (KHM 3, 12, 31), the parent gives a daughter to a supernatural being.

In Germanic tradition the child becomes Odin's warrior and spends his life killing Odin's enemies. The Old Testament requires strict separation of the Nazirite from death: If a Nazirite comes into contact with a dead person, his vow is contaminated, and he must precisely follow certain purification rites. A Nazirite shouldn't even contaminate himself with the death of a close family member (father, mother, brother, sister—Numbers

5:6ff.). In other words, the child is isolated from his family. The parallel Germanic figures do not face this restraint. But *all* of our folktale heroes do: They abandon their mother and father and live in complete isolation while serving the otherworld being to whom they were given.

The vow of the Nazirite lays down other taboos: Above all, the devoted souls must not contaminate themselves. This is also a well-known feature of the folktale. The golden boy has to protect Iron Hans's spring from contamination (KHM 136—"I want you to sit beside it and make sure that nothing falls in, for then the spring would be defiled"). After the boy violates this interdiction, he no longer has a close connection to Iron Hans. Other folktale heroes must also keep something clean while serving an otherworld figure, for example, in "Mother Holle" (KHM 24). The devil's grimy brother (KHM 100) must "clean house, carry the sweepings out the back door, and in general keep order" in hell. Only from the perspective of our modern concept of hygiene do these duties seem to contradict the promise not to cut one's hair and not to wash oneself. These conditions no longer have a meaningful function in our folktales; they even have a humorous tone. But as the vow of the Nazirite clearly shows, the prohibition against washing was originally an indication that no one should touch the child and thus violate his cultic purity.

## CRUELTY IN THE FOLKTALE

Sharp criticism of the cruelty sometimes depicted in the folktale is not new. Plato's critique expressed by Socrates in *Politeia* is itself older than the oldest recorded European folktale: "Shall we simply allow children to listen to folktales, randomly invented by some unknown person, so that they take views into their soul that often contradict those that they should, in our opinion, have in later years . . . ? We must dismiss most current folktales."[1] Kant is as avid an opponent of the folktale as Plato: "The child's imagination is strong enough without them and need not be stretched even more by those stories."[2] A more recent pedagogue believes that telling folktales "rouses a need for magical drinks and opiates: Imbibing in folktales is followed by gaining pleasure from novels, which leads to the delights of the demi-mondaine. Folktales lead youthful intellect down the false path. And no wonder that after consuming stories about magic and spooks the intellect can no longer defend itself from the sick monstrosities of misguided novelesque writing."[3]

Even the Grimm brothers' *Tales for Young and Old*, which Wilhelm Grimm extensively reworked to make the stories more appropriate for children, have been harshly criticized for the cruelties they depict. Achim von Arnim objected to the brutality of some Grimm tales from the start, particularly to number 22 in the first edition ("How Some Children Played Slaughter Together") and "The Juniper Tree" (KHM 47). But the brothers defended themselves, positing the need to accurately record tradition, and they correctly argued that the cruel elements are an important aspect of folklore.[4] This defense raises an important issue for our investigation: Despite the many external refinements imposed on the tales, numerous aspects of their cruelty remain because they are among the tale type's basic components.

Nonetheless, compiling the cruelties that still appear in the oft-revised Grimms' tales makes for a startling list: Nasty foster parents torture (KHM 21, 24, 130, 185, 186), abandon, cast out of their home (KHM 15, 201), or even kill (KHM 13, 53) children, particularly orphans. A loyal friend can be brought back to life only with the blood of two innocent children killed for this purpose (KHM 6). A father threatens to kill his twelve sons if his wife gives birth to a girl (KHM 9). Witches capture and fatten children to prepare a good meal for themselves (KHM 15). A mother bestially slaughters her son and serves him to his father as a meal (KHM 47). Another father mercilessly cuts of his daughter's hands for disobeying him (KHM 31). A town supplies hundreds of young girls to feed an evil dragon (KHM 60). We find motifs of horrible cannibalism (KHM 15, 47) and human sacrifice (KHM 6, 60). Fratricide occurs (KHM 28, 60), and even the killing of spouses (KHM 16, 126). A mother still lying in childbed is locked in the bathroom to suffocate (KHM 11). People are blinded (KHM 107, 121), atrociously chopped into pieces (KHM 47), and buried alive (KHM 16). A princess mercilessly has rejected suitors executed and puts their heads on the palace wall (KHM 191). A sex murderer brutally kills a large number of girls he has locked in his house by chopping up their bodies and throwing the bloody pieces into a basin in the forbidden chamber (KHM 46). All this occurs in the Grimm brothers' tales for "children" and the "household" alone! Thus Wilhelm Grimm's comment in the introduction to the second edition doesn't seem to be completely correct: "The same purity which makes children seem so wonderful and blessed runs through these tales; both have the same blue-white, unblemished, sparkling eyes."

After the Second World War a tidal wave of press against the "horrors of the Grimm tales appeared."[5] A German press agency reported on August 7, 1948, that a British military memorandum had considered the use of folktales in German schoolbooks and concluded that folktales, saints' legends, and legends should not be completely removed from the books but should be reduced to a minimum so that pagan ideas would not veil Christian teachings.[6] The Anglo-Saxon occupational powers temporarily forbade the printing of any new folktale collections because folktales made the German people cruel; folktales, they claimed, had played a major role in the development of the methods used in the concentration camps.[7] There was also no lack of German authors of the same opinion. For example, Günther Birkenfeld commented that in light of the Grimm tales, it no longer seemed inconceivable that the German people could commit the cruelties of Belsen and Auschwitz.[8]

Neither the attacks nor the defenses offered by folktale lovers have gone much beyond the surface. Defenses include justifying the Grimms' tales by pointing out that tales from other nations also portray cruel behavior. People have also argued that children do not consciously recognize folktale episodes. However, parallels in the folktales of other peoples neither explain nor excuse the cruelties that actually occur in the folktale. Moreover, now that depth psychology has taught us the importance of the unconscious and how it can influence real, conscious situations, we should not take the child's unconscious reception of these elements too lightly. Couldn't the child's fear of the stepmother and the witch affect him or her as an adult? In short, we should not discount this question with an apologetic "It's not so bad." The phenomenon has not yet been discussed seriously and thoroughly enough: The *Handwörterbuch des deutschen Märchens*, for example, contains only a very short article, "Grausamkeit" by Groth,[9] and the index of the *Handwörterbuch des deutschen Aberglaubens* refers us to the article "Animal Torture," which is completely irrelevant to our quesiton.[10] Folklorists have generally allowed child psychologists and pedagogues to enthusiastically, or rather, overenthusiastically, discuss this question and bring about direct, practical changes in children's literature. But the paradigmatic interest in a few spectacular folktales, citing the cruelties they contain *without* mentioning the entire narrative context, and judging the tale exclusively from modern perspectives, does not suffice. Mostly we need a complete compilation and exhaustive review of the folktale materials which fit this characterization. Then we must place them in cultural and historical context and question their psychological penetration; in short, we must ask: What relationship to reality do folktale cruelties have? In this chapter we will show, with a few primary motifs, the extraordinary diversity of cruelty both cultural-historically and psychologically. We will show that we cannot universally reproach or approve of these motifs, that we cannot claim they reveal national character or modern political references before we examine the origin, distribution, and function in folk tradition of the specific motifs.

1. *Little Red Riding-Hood and Her Grandmother's Blood.* In KHM 26 the evil wolf devours Little Red Riding-Hood and her grandmother, but then a hunter comes along, cuts open the sleeping wolf's stomach, and frees them. French versions from the nineteenth and twentieth centuries deviate from the Grimm text significantly: Here too the wolf eats the grandmother, but apparently not all at once (thus leaving her intact). Instead "he put the leftovers in the cupboard and put her blood in a bowl on the table." When Little Red Riding-Hood gets to her grandmother's house, the wolf offers her the flesh and blood of her own grandmother. She eats and drinks until the wolf eats her. Since a slaughtered grandmother whose flesh and blood the child has eaten cannot be retrieved alive from the wolf's stomach, the tale ends tragically with the death of both.[11]

Other versions adorn this aspect with even more horrible details: Little Red Riding-Hood must first stew the grandmother's thickened blood in butter; the girl eats the grandmother's teeth like beans or rice; the bones lie under the bed like firewood; the intestines are mounted to the door like a lock. Ernst Tegethoff, editor of the French folktales in the *Märchen der Weltliteratur* series, believed these cannibalistic traits suggest that cruelty characterizes the French folktale, but Marianne Rumpf has shown that these details appear in Italian and Tirolian versions as well as in three-fourths of the French versions; indeed they belong to the normal form of the "Little Red Riding-Hood" tale.[12]

Presumably Perrault did not take up folk tradition's cannibalistic tendency because he felt it was cruel and tasteless. Throughout his tales we can see how Perrault softened and changed his sources where good taste, the sense of moderation, and the views of morality during his time could have been offended. Perrault even voices this practice in the introduction to the fourth edition of his "Griseldis" (1695): "The desire to entertain never infringed on my guiding principle, namely, never to write something which could offend decency and decorum."[13]

Perrault's version was possibly a model for the Grimms' informants. The Grimms explicitly mention in the notes to the respective tales that the same informants from whom they recorded "Little Red Riding-Hood," the Hasenpflug family, provided other stories of French origin, even some from Perrault. We can assume that the characteristic German folktale happy ending was later added to the original tale with its tragic ending, perhaps even by someone who sent the tale to the Grimms. The motif of putting stones in the wolf's stomach occurs only in the Grimms' version and was presumably analogically borrowed from "The Wolf and the Seven Young Kids" (KHM 5)[14] We can see that in folktales told and recorded in writing by bourgeois preservationists, cruelties have been expurgated. On the other hand, folkloric texts do not provide a basis for generalizations about national attitudes toward cruelty. It is therefore not possible to draw conclusions about a people's psychology on the basis of this aspect of the tales. We must also ask, to what extent are these folktale episodes real? Marianne Rumpf has shown that "Little Red Riding-Hood" originally belonged to the genre of "warning tales"; i.e., it is actually a story told to children in order to warn them about the dangers of the forest, of the wild animals and sinister people who live there and wait to prey on children.[15] Whether this is pedagogically appropriate surely remains to be seen,[16] but "Little Red Riding-Hood" does presumably have a certain relation to reality. Namely, it is entirely possible that Little Red Riding-Hood's devourer was originally a *werewolf* which Perrault first replaced with an ordinary wolf. In no fewer than seven modern French versions the culprit is still a werewolf. Moreover, the records we have from the many werewolf trials during the sixteenth and seventeenth centuries show that the accused were frequently charged with having killed and eaten children. Perhaps parents warned their children about these events back then; folk belief and legends also describe werewolves who store the leftover meat from their victims.[17]

2. *Bluebeard and His Forbidden Chamber.* Hardly any element of a folktale has had a greater impact or found as much popularity as the theme of the wife-murderer who has already killed a number of girls and who is finally outwitted by a brave young maiden. Ever since Charles Perrault made this folk narrative about the murderer appropriate for literary treatment, numerous plays and operas have employed the story: from Gréty, Ludwig Tieck, Taubert, and Jacques Offenbach, to Béla Bartók's opera *Duke Bluebeard's Castle*, to name a few. The combination of sexuality and crime makes Bluebeard, like the Don Juan motif, a popular subject for frequent treatment. A modern French author, one of the most recent adapters of Bluebeard, seems to describe Bluebeard's appeal the best when a figure in his play observes: "Everywhere they speak of Bluebeard's bloody chambers. And yet the fair sex deifies him. Madam, you don't suspect what these fools are capable of. Some run after him with golden scissors and try to get a small piece of the feather in his hat. Others constantly carry one of his beard hairs in a precious locket. And all this only to end up in the horrible Ehebett!"[18]

All of these literary treatments distance themselves quite far from the folk narratives, in which we find no trace of the titillating appeal of sexual crimes. While dramas, operas, and films cast the sex murderer as the story's hero or antihero, the folktale is far more interested in the fate of the heorine who outwits the fiend. To be sure, the folktale depicts enough cruel scenes: A large, bloody basin stands in the middle of the forbidden chamber; "in it lay dead, mutilated people; next to it stood a wooden block, with a sparkling hatchet on top." And the fate that threatens the heroine is exemplarily demonstrated by an unlucky predecessor: "He threw her down, dragged her in by her hair, cut off her head on the block, and chopped her up so her blood flowed onto the floor. Then he threw her into the basin with the others" (KHM 46). The folktale does not depict the heroine's sister's heinous fate just to include a bloodcurdling scene; rather, these episodes appear to suggest a possible danger to the heroine herself, and the details are intended only to provoke tension. The heroine in KHM 40 ("The Robber Bridegroom") also watches another girl suffer the fate she faces: The cannibalistic robbers "came home, dragging another young girl. They were drunk and paid no attention to her screams and moans. They gave her wine to drink, three glasses full, one white, one red, and one yellow, and her heart burst apart. Then they tore off her fine clothes, put her on a table, chopped her beautiful body into pieces, and sprinkled them with salt." In other versions the robbers hang the girls on the wall: Nineteen women's corpses are hanging on hooks; a twentieth hook is conveniently unoccupied when the heroine arrives at Bluebeard's house. The "Halewijn-Ulinger" ballads employ a similar situation to produce dramatic tension: Seven girls whom the murderer has already killed hang from a tree. All this is certainly atrocious enough, yet the audience maintains a certain detachment because the heroine herself does not suffer this fate;

Bluebeard's murder is not sensed as real, it is only a possible fate confronting the heroine. These images provide an epic formula for creating tension; when the tension peaks, the story takes a good turn, the heroine outwits the evil creature, he is punished, and the story avoids a tragic ending.

We must add another important consideration: The sadistic sex crime does not belong to the original folktale tradition. Bluebeard is not by nature a profane sex murderer, but rather a sorcerer or even a demon. Jacob Grimm conjectured that Bluebeard symbolizes leprosy; the murderer, like "Poor Heinrich," wanted to cure himself by bathing in the blood of virgins. But murdering one girl would suffice, and moreover in the folktale Bluebeard does not use the blood from the murdered girls. Hanging the girls, as the murderer does so often in the "Halewijn-Ulinger" ballads, also doesn't help the murderer get the girls' blood.[19] Hans Naumann's claim that Bluebeard derives from belief in vampires[20] and Ernst Tegethoff's thesis that attributes Bluebeard's origin to the Germanic image of dwarves also lack sound evidence.[21] Nevertheless, it is indeed correct that Bluebeard, as well as his counterpart in the folk ballad of Halewijn-Ulinger, was originally a demonic nonhuman figure who abducted and killed young girls for some unknown reason. More recent tradition has developed a completely human murderer who sadistically kills girls. The Grimm version (KHM 46), where the murderer is a wizard who uses his powers of transformation and magic to prey on the girls, testifies to the originally magical motifs which we, of course, can no longer recover. He can sing in two voices, the decapitated heads talk and can possibly heal, and the murderer's magical horn summons his friends.[22] If we wish to explain the popular reception of Bluebeard in the nineteenth and twentieth centuries by asserting that his crimes still seem real today, i.e., they actually happen, we must not forget that Bluebeard's original deeds took place on a magical, not a real, plane.

3. *Human Sacrifice.* It is not uncommon that a human must be sacrificed in the folktale, that the princess must be delivered as a tribute to a dragon or some other monster. KHM 60, for example, depicts a seven-headed dragon who lives on a high mountain outside the city and demands a pure maiden every year on the threat of ravaging the entire country. In the folktale, human sacrifice has already become a "motif" and usually functions only as an epic formula to produce tension: A princess must be sacrificed so the hero can later free her (KHM 60), or perhaps the monster to whom the heroine is sacrificed will turn out really to be a prince under a spell and the sacrifice disenchants him (KHM 88). Since the folktale sacrifices the hero or his partner, the horrible situation more easily turns out for the best. In other words, the folktale needs the hero or heroine for epic reasons, and thus it cannot allow them to perish; conversely, the hero needs the sacrifice motif because facing death makes his victory over evil all the more flashy. The folktale sees human sacrifice from a purely narratological perspective; sacrifice is never a lasting tragic reality, it always remains a frightening possibility. The folktale never includes drastic depic-

tions of the dragon devouring the sacrifice or of the cruel procedure of delivering someone, because the heroine is never actually sacrificed. It suffices to mention her predecessors' fate without elaborating the details.

Nevertheless, folktales about human sacrifice recall real sacrifices from the past.[23] Epic laws do not affect the more realistic legend as much; thus these narratives have preserved these memories more accurately and provide a last remnant of actual sacrificial customs. The legend contains human sacrifice at regular intervals (like those to the folktale dragon) to river demons who threaten to cause floods.[24] Humans are also sacrificed to prevent disease and hunger. Legends sometimes describe human sacrifice in excruciating detail. A report from Carinthia depicts events in 1715: The plague demanded a human sacrifice. It was secretly arranged that the first person to exit the church after the next service would be chosen. A young girl was selected and mercilessly thrown into a pit and buried alive.[25] This sacrifice strikes us as unusually cruel, but it is not cruelty for its own sake. This serious effort to magically cure and end the plague has its roots in folk belief: In this particular form of human sacrifice, namely, burying someone alive, the victim's vital energy directly provides magical protection.[26]

In the legend's report a young girl is coincidentally chosen as a sacrifice to the plague. The real reason for this selection, here and in other cases, lies in the belief that the death of an "innocent child" or a young girl who has not spent her vital energy has particularly strong magical powers. Folktale dragons certainly do not demand a "pure maiden" exclusively for "epic reasons." Moreover, the heroine's unlucky predecessors have in fact saved the folktale city from devastation, thus fulfilling the purpose of actual human sacrifices (KHM 60).

A gypsy tale that tells of an unusually cold-hearted and cruel king who is finally, like the bishop in the legend of the mouse tower, devoured by mice also relates to this theme.[27] The tale's closing, which reports that the summer after the ruler's death was fruitful and the harvest a hundred times greater than ever before, brings to mind the sacrifice of Germanic kings which took place during famines in exchange for regaining the fields' fertility. The famous reference in the eighteenth chapter of the Inglinga saga provides a parallel: In the first year of famine an ox was sacrificed, in the second a human, and when that did not help the king himself was sacrificed to Odin in the third year.[28] Of course, ancient Nordic examples have entered the realm of the "legend" and no longer reveal historical reality.[29] In summary, we can reiterate that both folktales and legends maintain human sacrifice as a survival, but the folktale has taken the reality out of this cruel practice and turned it into a formulaic device that increases the tension in the hero's adventures.

4. *Cannibalism.* Modern ethnology has taught us not to judge tribal anthropophagy and cannibalism by our own standards of cruelty. All of the cases in which human flesh is eaten in order to acquire some power or ability the sacrificed person had, in which the human flesh serves as

medication or as nourishment for a shaman, or in which human genitalia are consumed to increase potency are not cruel, profane atrocities but rather part of "magical cannibalism."[30] The enemy's head magically increases the head-hunter's strength. Even consuming live bodies, as some tribal peoples do, is not designed to cruelly torment the victim; rather, it stems from the need to ingest the victim's vital energies as directly as possible.[31] For our purposes, however, we must ask whether we can classify cannibalism in the folktale according to its cultural history.

We have evidence of "profane cannibalism"[32] in a Russian folktale in which hungry parents who have nothing left to eat slaughter their own son and store his flesh in the storeroom.[33] The ending of a folktale from Lorraine contains a trace of fictional cannibalism associated with an execution; after the guilty are punished, the narrator comments: "They were burned in oil, they must have tasted good."[34] Both tales are, however, exceptions among European folktales and of little interest for social history. Instead we should ask which characters consume human flesh in the folktale and how they are morally judged.

Our folk narratives certainly do not apply some archaic standard when judging the ethics of cannibalism. These tales mention the deed only with abhorrence, and only demonic figures are believed capable of such a crime. Thus it is almost always a giant, a sorcerer, or even the devil who expresses his cannibalistic desires with the stereotypical words: "I smell, smell, human flesh." More than anyone else, witches seek to consume children (e.g., KHM 15, 51, among others). Not infrequently someone accuses the heroine who has just become a mother of having eaten her child after giving birth, and being accused of cannibalism is the worst thing that can happen to the folktale heroine because without further investigation, the accusation almost always leads to her being labeled a witch (e.g., KHM 3 and 49).

Naturally the folktale also contains cannibalism motifs that provide the story's typical tension: The witch's cannibalistic intentions bring the mortal danger facing Hansel and Gretal (KHM 15) to a dramatic climax. Mute heroes and heroines bound to silence also never fail to be accused of cannibalism (KHM 3 and 49). In the Grimms' "Foundling" (KHM 51), preparing to kill and eat the hero brings the actual story of "The Magic Flight" into play.

But why does the folktale mention cannibalism so frequently? The need to create tension alone cannot explain the abundance of instances, since depicting other dangers achieves the same end. The fact that the folktale always portrays cannibalism as a criminal evil does not rule out possible parallels to tribal societies which do not condemn consumption of human flesh. Documentation of folk belief in the nineteenth century shows that people still ascribed anthropophagy and cannibalism to certain demonic figures at that time. For example, a Swabian legend tells of a farmer who lends his dog to a hunter in exchange for part of the catch. An hour later a human foot is thrown through his window, and he realizes that he helped the wild hunter kill a human.[35] Man-eating witches no longer appear in folk belief and legend,[36] but on this topic the folktale has undoubtedly preserved older forms of belief. We already mentioned that Karl the Great made it punishable "to believe that a man or a woman is a striga and eats humans" (*Capitulare de partibus Saxoniae*). Folk belief must still have attributed cannibalism to witches at that time.

It is more difficult to explain *why* witches eat human flesh. The few folktales that still provide insights on this matter clearly contain remnants of "magical cannibalism." The case of "Snow White," where the evil step-mother wants to eat Snow White's lungs and liver, is not completely clear. In KHM 53 it appears that the queen attempts to become more beautiful by consuming beautiful Snow White's organs. We could label this "magical cannibalism" without further deliberation if both of the Grimms' earlier texts did not completely lack cannibalism.[37] We can also find other equiv-ocal cases; for example, an Albanian folktale discusses whether the witch wants human flesh only to cruelly torture people and concludes that a witch is, by nature, a cannibal, even when this causes her to act against her impulses.[38] A Swedish folktale explicitly explains that an old witch steals and eats children "to increase her magical powers."[39]

While the folktale usually restricts actual cannibalism to witches, we do find many cases in which someone kills a human to obtain the blood needed to magically cure a disease. For example, a prince's blood can cure the king in a modern Greek tale, and before the prince is killed he must be fattened up for forty days.[40] In an Italian version of KHM 11, the blind king must smear his eyes with his own daughter's blood.[41] "Faithful Johannes" (KHM 6) provides the most impressive example of this deed: The king can bring his faithful servant back to life only with the blood of his own children.

All this corresponds to folk belief in the magical power of blood, which we can trace into the modern era. In Hartmann von Aue's *Poor Heinrich*, the blood of a virgin is supposed to cure leprosy, i.e., folk and scientific medicine had not yet diverged. Folk medicine employed, and still employs, blood in a variety of cures. After the execution of a robber-murderer in Hanau in 1861, people stormed the scaffold and drank from the steaming blood. In 1864 in Berlin, the executioners dipped lots of white hand-kerchiefs in the blood from two murderers and sold them for two talers apiece.[42] We can see that the folktale's anthropophagy and cannibalism does not necessarily have to be traced to prehistoric times. We have used court records as one means for tracing belief in magical cannibalism up until the nineteenth and twentieth centuries. Here we mention one of several other cases, namely, a murder trial in Oldenburg in 1888. Two testimonies confirm that the accused believed that whoever consumed the flesh of a young innocent girl could do anything in the world without having to be held responsible. Thus he killed two girls, ages six and seven, slit their throats, and cut off and ate a large piece of flesh from their buttocks.[43]

5. *The Juniper Tree and the Motif of Cutting the Victim into Pieces*. In KHM 47 a young boy's stepmother decapitates him by slamming the top of an apple chest on him. Later she chops the corpse into pieces, cooks them in vinegar, and serves the boy's remains as a stew to the father when he gets home. We can divide these gruesome events into three motifs: (1) the stepmother's malicious murder of the boy, (2) the Atreus meal, and (3) cutting the corpse into pieces.

The trick of getting someone to look for something in a chest and then suddenly slamming the lid occurs in a Hessian version collected by the brothers Grimm themselves, as well as in the Low German text collected by Philipp Otto Rung that appears in the Grimms' *Tales for Young and Old*.[44] It apparently belongs among this tale's fixed motifs. Early uses of this cruel method of murder appear in Gregor of Tours's *Historia Francorum*[45] and the Eddic "Song of Wieland,"[46] in which the smith gets the two princes to look into his supply chest. But it is unlikely that these items have a connection to the folktale. Similarly, the Atreus meal motif in the folktale clearly has no direct relationship to the more ancient "Way of Atlit"[47] or to the Greek legend,[48] which contain the same motif. Numerous items of folk and high literature include the extreme crimes of inhumanely murdering someone with the lid of a chest and unknowingly consuming one's own child[49]— possibly, but not necessarily, in connection to real crimes—without the need for any traceable interdependence. These cruel actions are no longer historical or mythical reality in the folktale; they have become fixed "motifs." They are, from the perspective of narrative technique, the peak, or better yet the low point, of the hero's adversary's horrendous behavior, i.e., extreme cases used again and again because of their epic effectiveness. Even Goethe quite consciously acknowledges the motif's effectiveness when he has Gretchen sing the victim's song from "The Juniper Tree" while in prison (*Faust* I, ch. 18).

Similarly, the motif of cutting up and cooking the corpse in the folktale has lost all reality. This motif, which strikes us as dreadful in "The Juniper Tree," tends toward jest in other tales. In KHM 81 St. Peter cuts off a dead princess's limbs, cooks them, puts them back in place, and brings the princess back to life. Although this, one of our oldest folktale motifs, is still a bloody crime in "The Juniper Tree," it has become part of merry, yet successful, quackery in "Brother Scamp."

Cutting up the corpse before bringing it back to life by collecting and properly organizing the bones, forms an important motif.[50] Besides parallels in the classical legend of Pelops[51] and the ancient Nordic legend about reviving Thor's bucks,[52] we can clearly trace this motif's origins back to ancient hunters, and we still find it among north Asian peoples today. These tribal hunters forbid breaking, burning, or throwing away the bones of the animals they catch. Instead they preserve the bones in a special place, and none of them may be missing.[53] Even cooking the bones in "Brother Scamp" (KHM 81) and in the legend of Pelops, and collecting the bones in a handkerchief and storing them in a special place (under a tree), are not randomly invented ideas; they correspond to real north Asian beliefs and customs.[54] The Siberian hunters see a reincarnated animal, whose meat he ate and whose bones he carefully collected and deposited according to custom, in the animal he encounters while hunting. Moreover, these practices are not limited to animals; they also govern the hunters' ideas about human death and rebirth. For example, these peoples identify their clan by saying "from the bones of so and so." Vladimir Bogoraz shows that the ancient Yukaghir gathered the bones of their dead in bags and cared for them in a secret location. Most important, according to the beliefs of these peoples, shamans are killed, cut up, and cooked, and then brought back to life from their bones.[55] Thus the folktale motif reflects a worldwide belief complex, but it clearly lost its mythic-religious reality long ago as it became a fixed narrative "motif." In the process the motif underwent a complete transformation. In fact, ethnological data suggest that the folktale motif as it appears in "The Juniper Tree" has made a complete reversal: Cutting up was originally designed to preserve life, not cruelly murder someone. Reincarnation from the bones, not the horrible process of mutilating someone, was the goal.

The folktale depicts other occasions for cutting people into pieces, and not only after their death. This deed is also not always an abominable crime perpetrated by the hero's adversaries; on the contrary, even the hero performs it: The tales in which the hero accomplishes his tasks with help from a sorcerer's daughter commonly include a related motif. The hero can complete one of the tasks only by cutting up his helpful lover and using her bones as a ladder to climb a tree, cliff or tower, where he finds the necessary object, or by throwing the pieces of the girl's body into the water containing the object he must retrieve. We find this motif complex (slaughtering, sticking the pieces on the cliff, and then bringing her back to life) as an episode in "The Magic Flight" in all of western Europe, Ireland, Scotland, France, Spain, and north Africa.[56]

Clearly the motif has acquired a completely different meaning in this context. Here base motives do not drive the hero to murder and secretly destroy the body. Apparently no blood flows when the hero cuts up the body; he accomplishes the entire deed without the cruel tone that "The Juniper Tree" gives the motif. The conditions under which the mutilation occurs are completely different here. The deed is not ethically judged: Possession of the life-giving substance guarantees from the start that the hero will bring his lover back to life. The victim herself agrees to being cut apart; indeed, she suggests the plan, which seems justified because it will help the hero accomplish the task and thus make it possible for the lovers to live happily every after. In other words, this deed pertains to a different level of consciousness than the stepmother's consciously evil crime in KHM

47. The helpful mutilation is not cruel, it is an element of epic retardation and tension confronting the suitor-hero during his last and most difficult task. Moreover, this deed usually leads to the motif of slight harm.

In addition to epic functions, this motif has a deep psychological meaning, but clearly we will not find it using Freudian psychoanalysis. For the psychoanalyst, the dismemberment motif is as a rule a symbol for castration or castration anxiety[57]—a thesis I cannot accept. Instead we must always derive a folktale's psychological meaning from the plot itself. In this case that seems quite straightforward. Cutting up the lover and using her body parts as a ladder or bridge is only the realization of this folktale's psychological process. As we know, the folktale concretizes everything by converting inner processes into material episodes. In order to reach the "ultimate" goal, the characters must "sacrifice" something. The hero's lover shows her willingness to help even if she must sacrifice herself; she is capable of "bridging" his difficulties. Thus she—completely concretely—becomes the "ladder" to his success. For his part, the hero sees that he can attain their common goal only with her help, and that reaching this goal requires a joint effort as well as temporary separation. As in the masonic test of worth in Mozart's *Magic Flute*, they must work together to achieve the last and decisive sacrifice. That is not cruelty but rather the symbol of a general human psychological situation.

6. *Disenchantment through Repeated Death*. In contrast to the legend, the folktale contains a number of truly unique means of disenchantment that appear quite cruel at first, particularly in cases where someone close to the hero (a helpful animal, a grateful dead man, or his transformed wife or lover), rather than his adversary, is subjected to harsh torture. The hero often disenchants these figures with decapitation, stabbing, or killing, or, in newer adaptations, shooting. Thus the king in KHM 135 cuts the head off of his bride who was transformed into a duck, at the very moment she swims up the gutter into the kitchen. The queen who returns nightly in the form of an animal (usually a duck) in many versions of "Little Brother and Little Sister" is changed back into human form in the same way.[58] In a Hessian version of "The Three Feathers" (KHM 63) the toad asks the numskull to put him on a bed and to cut him "straight through the heart" with a sharp knife; the numskull abides. There is a loud noise, but then a beautiful maiden is lying there instead of the toad. Similarly, the hero in a Tirolian folktale smashes an enchanted cat against the hearth "until there was nothing left of her." Instead of the cat's hind legs he now has the hem of the disenchanted princess's robe in his hand.[59] As a rule, all this occurs without fuss; the disenchanter only occasionally raises slight moral scruples about doing it, e.g., the soldier returning home in an east Prussian folktale: "An old woman asks him to cut off her head, and he says to himself: You had to do it often enough during the war. One more soul can't make much difference."[60]

This odd manner of disenchantment is much older than the use of

Christian formulas in the legend. It relies on one of the oldest forms of belief in transformation,[61] the idea common in tribal societies that the transformed figure can temporarily be removed.[62] Only more recent folktale heroes, in the nineteenth and twentieth centuries, have guilt complexes about doing it. The original method of disenchantment involves nothing cruel because it originally entailed simply removing the animal covering and hiding or burning it. That completed the entire transformation (e.g., KHM 108 and 144). The more recent method of killing people in order to release them into eternal peace, such as the legend requires for the living dead, has nothing to do with the destruction of the animal covering in the folktale. Disenchantment through decapitation does not annihilate the victim, it undoes the spell. Thus the misnomer "disenchantment through repeated death" was not originally cruel; people began to perceive the process as cruel only after they no longer understood its original meaning.

7. *The Twelve Brothers and Their Fate.* One of the least intelligible examples of cruelty occurs at the beginning of the Grimms' "The Twelve Brothers" (KHM 9): A king and a queen live in peace and harmony with their twelve sons until one day the king says to his wife: "If the thirteenth child you bear is a girl, the twelve boys must die so that her wealth will be great and that she alone inherits the kingdom." As a precaution the king has twelve coffins prepared, and the dreaded event does indeed occur.[63] However, the cruel threat of death does not come true: The boys save themselves by fleeing. After these opening events the real story begins. It almost seems like the king threatened the sons merely to provide the epic conditions for separating the brothers from their sister and to set the adventure in motion. After the cruel threat fulfills its epic purpose, it is quickly forgotten and never mentioned again. Nor do we hear anything more about the parents, even at the end of the story, and no one holds the old king responsible for their fate.

Although this motif is clearly designed only to provide the tension which sets the story in motion as well as to establish the necessarily tense dynamic between the heroine and her twelve brothers, the father's cruel demeanor toward his twelve sons to benefit his unborn daughter nonetheless poses a strange riddle. The motif is one which we apparently cannot classify historically. Although it has been attempted, we cannot simply identify the introduction to KHM 9 as a survival from matrilineal societies where people prefer a daughter to a son. The support for this matriarch thesis does not hold up under scrutiny because Wilhelm Grimm added the king's explanation for his cruel command "so that her wealth will be great and she alone inherits the kingdom." In the original text the king does not explain his cruel statement: "I would rather cut their heads off myself than allow a girl to be in their midst."[64] It is certainly not surprising that the parents of twelve sons might like a girl for a change, but that is no reason to kill the sons.

I would gladly agree with the psychologists who see this as the classic example of the Oedipus complex if other folktales did not depict just the opposite scenario. A Greek folktale king, for example, definitely wants to have a boy and threatens to have his wife beheaded if she bears him a girl. When, in the king's absence, the queen bears a girl, she quickly exchanges her for a neighbor's boy.[65] In Norwegian and Irish versions the mother is willing to give away all her sons in exchange for one daughter.[66]

Opening situations of this sort commonly appear in the folktale. They are "typical" and therefore resist psychological interpretation; i.e., they do not necessarily characterize the particular narrator who selects this introduction from fixed tradition. Nevertheless, common narrative components such as this one do have psychological significance: If they become "common property," they must also somehow correspond to general human psychological situations. But how can we grant the king's cruel and deviant behavior toward his sons in KHM 9 general psychological validity?

Perhaps Josephine Bilz's work with the dreams of (healthy) women during and immediately following pregnancy provides the clues we need if we are to understand the psychology of this cruel behavior at all. In particular, these women commonly dreamed about the loss, death, or murder of their earlier children, even if they were in perfect health. Bilz reports a number of dreams that generally correspond to the situation in KHM 9: The older siblings must die so that the unborn child will receive everything. Bilz correctly interprets these typical pregnancy dreams: "The mother herself unconsciously senses that the new child will, so to speak, harm the previous child by making him or her do without exclusive love. The only child no longer has sole claim to the mother's loving care when a younger sibling shares the household."[67] There is no actual murder, only a symbolic death. Like a magnifying glass, these dreams translate psychic processes into a graphic story. The direct parallels between a typical folktale motif and a typical dream during pregnancy perhaps make some sense of the king's otherwise inconceivable cruelty in KHM 9. This helps us understand why this "unmotivated motif"—i.e., apart from its epic utility, which some other introduction could just as easily accomplish—has become part of tradition. Moreover, this example indicates the intricacy of the complex elements we have labeled "cruelty in the folktale." We always need to combine several possible interpretations in order to penetrate this world of ideas.

8. *One-Ox and "Killing the Elderly."* In the search for the rudiments of early history and clues about the social life of "primeval society," certain scholars have recently tried to discover remnants of the practice of "killing the elderly" in the tale "Farmer One-Ox."[68] Of course, we also have historical and legendary reports of such customs in Europe. Jacob Grimm[69] was the first to outline the details, and Paul Sartori later compiled the evidence.[70] The Wends supposedly killed their old up until the sixteenth century, albeit as part of certain ceremonies.[71] It is doubtful that we can

draw general conclusions about the custom of killing the elderly from such isolated evidence. The cases preserved in historical documents and in legends have been handed down precisely because of their exceptional singularity as particularly cruel events. The evidence has thus long been in need of a new, exhaustive interpretation. Above all, we can largely rule out rationalistic explanations like those that provide almost the entire basis of Sartori's conjectures. The interpreters have surely oversimplified the matter with their egotistical, material explanations which argue that in cases of need, older people must be abandoned as useless consumers and eventually eliminated in cold blood if younger, stronger people sense an impingement on their *Lebensraum*. As an alternative we must, if possible, consider the belief that the sick are possessed by demons. This could cause the old and sick to appear taboo. Tribal conceptions of reincarnation, such as the religious-psychological view of the "head-hunt," which require removing or killing the old before new life can be created may also provide insight into this practice.

From this point of view, it also seems absurd to draw a connection between the tale of One-Ox and real instances of killing the old. In the oldest text of this story that we have, the Latin Unibos poem from the tenth or eleventh century, Farmer One-Ox smears his wife with blood and has her play dead. He then claims he has a way to bring her back to life and blows into a reed flute; his wife arises more beautiful than before. His enemies buy the flute and kill their own wives, who don't come back to life.[72] Clearly One-Ox was a farcical tale from the start. The hero's successful con and lies are the crucial elements. We were never supposed to take the murder of the antagonists' aging wives and the failed effort at bringing them back to life with the allegedly magic flute as a bloody reality. This is merely one of many stories illustrating the blindness of the cunning farmer's foolish opponents. It is also a humorous perversion of the folktale motif of rejuvenation.

More recent versions of this widely distributed farcical tale also have no connection to the actual practice of killing the elderly. In addition to the ancient Unibos motif about the allegedly magic flute that seems to wake the dead woman, we commonly find another variation on the theme of killing the elderly. Here someone "kills" the hero's mother (or grandmother), who is already dead, and must compensate the hero for his loss. The best-known instance of this motif sequence is Andersen's "Big Klaus and Little Klaus," which draws exclusively on folk tradition.[73] Humor reigns over this tale, in which Little Klaus makes a deceitful but profitable deal using his dead grandmother while Big Klaus tries in vain to sell his own dead grandmother. The murder is no longer taken seriously, and is certainly not seen as cruel. The murder humorously contrasts with the respect given elders in the folktale, and even the hero's adversary is not punished for murder—he can atone with money, thus making the sly hero even richer. In other words, this tale is not necessarily about "killing the elderly," and therefore this motif does not have to appear in the One-Ox tale type. In the Grimms' version of "Farmer One-Ox," Farmer Little (KHM 61) does not kill his wife, mother, or grandmother. From here all the way to the Far East, versions in which the cunning farmer succeeds using some other con preponderate over those with the murder.[74] The farcical tale never imagines that it might depict a cruel "practice" of killing the elderly; for the success of its "hero," every con and means of trickery is acceptable.

9. *The Cruel Princess and Her Suitors.* We find a particularly impressive account of the proud princess who unscrupulously has countless suitors beheaded, because they cannot successfully hide from her or solve her riddle, in the Grimms' "The Mongoose" (KHM 191). Anyone who fails to win the princess's hand has "his head cut off and mounted on a pole." The heads of ninety-seven suitors are already impaled on stakes in front of the palace when the hero and his two brothers subject themselves to the test.[75] The unlucky riddle-solvers wooing the princess are decapitated in most versions,[76] but this doesn't make the punishment any less peculiar. One version even provides the probable historical basis for this method of execution by suggesting that losing one's life to a sword is a privilege granted only to aristocracy; defeated suitors of lower lineage get the rope.[77] We have plenty of historical evidence for the difference between hanging as a specifically disgraceful criminal punishment and beheading as a capital punishment for royalty and aristocracy. Likewise, in the Middle Ages and the modern era, beheading someone who deserved the rope was like a pardon.[78] The princess's suitors are not disgracefully hanged but rather executed honorably.

But there is more to this story than execution. The dreadful manner of decorating the palisade with the impaled heads of the unlucky suitors to scare off others is truly characteristic of KHM 191 and almost all other versions. This motif's frequent appearance in northern and southern Slavic epics, as well as the milieu in which it appears, clearly suggests that it originated in the Orient. August Löwis of Menar has already pointed this out.[79] Ingrid Hartmann teaches us a great deal about the motif's basis in reality and its use in literature: This was clearly an actual Oriental war custom. For example, the Saracen put the heads of fallen enemies on the castle's battlements.[80] Adolf F. von Schack adds that Al Motadid Billah, an Abbasid despot in eleventh-century Spain, "had the garden next to his palace decorated with the heads of his enemies that he had killed, and he enjoyed the view that filled others with horror." The same ruler, a patron and admirer of literature, was a poet who exalted his own glorious deeds:

> . . . Many an army I have put down in disgrace!
> One after the other I lay them to rest
> And then I decorate my castle gate
> With the heads of soldiers who have met their fate. . . .[81]

We also have evidence that the Scyths hung the skulls of defeated opponents in a circle on their temple.[82] Apollonius of Tyrus (sixth century) tells of a local king in Asia Minor who had the heads of his daughter's suitors who lost a riddling contest hung on his palace.[83] These references clearly suggest that the custom of putting the heads of defeated opponents on stakes had its origin and currency in the Orient. Characteristically, the custom, using the crusades as a vehicle, found its way into minstrelsy, where it became a poetic motif used primarily to describe pagan potentates: The Middle High German Ortnit epic depicts the pagan king Machorel's castle:

> If you come to Muntabure look at the castle's embattlements.
> Seventy-two heads are on them
> Which he cut off for his wife.
> Whenever I think of it, I complain to God.[84]

Similarly, Wolfdietrich D depicts the palace of King Belian:

> One tower was higher than all the others:
> And it had the heads of the evil pagans on it.
> And the entire battlements were covered with heads.
> He believed it must have been a thousand, as he remembered it![85]

This in no way proves that the cruel motif of the ninety-nine decapitated heads on the city wall first entered the folktale by way of the medieval epic. Rather these references indicate that the tale type (Type 329) is limited to southwest and eastern Europe, as Hartmann has shown. Notably the only two German texts of this tale type come from former language islands in the east and southeast. The brothers Grimm took tale number 191 ("The Mongoose") from Haltrich's collection. Elements of Oriental folktales have had a significant influence on precisely the area this collection covers, namely, the southeast portion of Europe. Thus this motif, like the Persian princess Turandot herself, originates under immediate influence from Oriental folktale traditions on southeastern Europe, and there it became a fixed element of the "Mongoose" tale type.

Therefore the motif's basis in reality should not be sought in Germany or anywhere in the Occident. Nonetheless, European tradition zealously picked up this motif and shaped it into a fixed element of folk and literary works. This cruel motif "made an impression," it became the topos for cruel treatment and undeserved punishment. By leaving its cultural and historical milieu and entering areas where similar events never really existed, this motif subjected itself to epic law. It is quite clear that narrators use this motif to achieve a frightening effect on the audience as well as within the tale. The hero's accomplishment seems all the more phenomenal if the narrative depicts a greater danger for him: The heads of the hero's ninety-nine predecessors decorate the wall, an explicitly epic number that cries out for rounding off. No risk is too great, no punishment in the case of failure too horrifying for this narrative technique.

A Transylvanian gypsy version of "The Mongoose" deserves separate mention because of its particularly repulsive cruelty. The princess has all of her suitors who fail to hide from her castrated. After the hero twice fails to successfully hide from her, she tells him: "If I find you a third time I will grant you your life, but I will have you castrated because I want to completely adorn that tower with male members before I die." And she shows him the tower in the middle of the court, which is almost completely covered with male genitals.[86]

We can indeed find some evidence for the practice of castrating defeated opponents. Historically it was an actual punishment, for example, against Jews who had violated a Christian woman, and earlier, peasants were sometimes castrated during war.[87] As we know, this still occurred during World War II on the southeastern and eastern fronts. This atrocity cannot be explained simply as perverse torture of prisoners of war or necrophilism, but rather must also be seen in relation to folk belief. But this does not sufficiently explain the occurrence of castration in the gypsy version of the "Mongoose" tale type. Perhaps we require a more psychological interpretation: This tale is about taming the obstinate young woman who does not want to get married. The gypsy version makes her abnormal psychological complex obvious; castrating the suitors merely concretizes this folktale's psychological function. Only the man who can solve the woman's riddle can marry her. We can also suggest another psychological possibility: Perhaps the princess hopes to magically increase her own strength by acquiring her opponents' genitals. This virago collects the male attributes needed to become a man herself. We can find ethnological and psychopathological parallels for this as well.[88] It is not possible to determine which interpretation hits the mark here, and caution is always advised with sweeping interpretations. This particular case could be clarified only by a psychological analysis of the tale's narrator, which is not possible because the text was recorded in the middle of the last century. But it is apparent that historical, epic, and deep psychological elements constantly intermingle, and we cannot always clearly distinguish among them.

10. *Cruel Punishments*. The list of the various forms of execution that occur in the folktale is almost longer than a list of the offenses themselves. In addition to the death penalty, the folktale contains horrible mutilations, sometimes only as a torturous prelude to actual execution. In a folktale from Lower Saxony, for example, the executioner cuts off the robbers' fingers before throwing the delinquents into a cauldron of oil and frying them.[89] In other tales evil fiends are blinded,[90] broken on the wheel,[91] or torn apart by wild animals (KHM 11). In KHM 76 ("The Carnation") the king has the evil cook torn into four pieces (the same occurs in KHM 111). Other tales depict more severe punishment in greater detail. "He deserves

to have his hands and feet tied to four old horses that move nice and slowly as they rip him into four pieces."[92] Another punishment, which entails tying the culprit to a horse's tail and having him dragged through the city, seems to be related.[93] In an equally common punishment, the convicted offender is drowned in a bag or in a barrel with holes in it: For example, the man who murders his brother in KHM 28 is "sewn up in a sack and drowned." In KHM 9 the evil stepmother is put in a barrel filled with boiling oil and, in a paradoxical case of excess, poisonous snakes. Tricky Farmer Little is also unanimously condemned to death and is supposed to be rolled into the water in a barrel with holes in it (KHM 61). As a drastic intensification of the punishment, this barrel is often lined with nails: In KHM 13 ("The Three Little Men in the Woods"), the evil stepmother and her daughter are rolled from the mountain into the river inside such a nail-lined barrel. The false bride in KHM 89 ("The Goose Girl") is also "stripped naked and put in a barrel studded with sharp nails on the inside; and two white horses should be harnessed to it and made to drag her up and down the streets until she dies."[94] This punishment actually outdoes all other folktale atrocities.

Setting unfaithful wives out to sea in a rudderless or leaky ship does not directly result in death, leaving the final judgment to the Lord. In KHM 16 ("The Three Snake Leaves") the unfaithful wife and her accomplice are put on a ship with holes in it and sent out to sea, where they soon drown in the waves.[95]

Most of these cruel forms of execution correspond to actual punishments in history. We can document mutilations of all sorts, such as hacking off hands and feet,[96] blinding,[97] quartering,[98] and dragging to death,[99] as well as drowning in a barrel or sack with all the possible additions,[100] in legal history. These folktale punishments are reminders of past judicial systems. The punishments occasionally reflect reality (i.e., historical law) far more accurately than the fantastic folktales which house them.

We shall pick out a few examples to show how closely folktales correspond to actual legal history. Only women are buried alive or immured in the folktale. In an east Prussian tale the witch is thrown in a well, which is then filled.[101] In KHM 76 ("The Carnation") the king has his wife, who is accused of cannibalism, immured in a tower. The king in a version of "The Golden Children" has his wife buried alive when he is told that she gave birth to a dog and a cat. When he discovers that she was innocent, he has her dug up and revives her with the water of life.[102] These examples accurately reflect cultural history because living burial was *the* death penalty for female criminals until the late Middle Ages; men were hanged or broken on the wheel.[103] Women are also drowned in a barrel or sack and burned to death in both folktale and historical justice.[104]

We can clearly divide burning, the folktale's most common punishment, into two groups: (1) The burning of witches and evil women. The witch or evil stepmother is burned at the stake in numerous Grimm tales (KHM 11,

49, 60, 96, 193). (2) The heroine is accused of witchcraft or cannibalism and sentenced to be burned at the stake (e.g., KHM 3 and 9), but at the last second the execution is prevented. In both groups the sentence applies to accused witches. Clearly historical witch trials have affected both groups. The fact that the folktale applies this punishment exclusively to women corresponds to the facts of legal history: Women were never hanged or broken on the wheel, only burned or drowned.[105] Occasionally neither royal nor judicial decree condemns the woman to be burned: Like the "Brenna" in the ancient Nordic saga, some folktales depict a vendetta.[106] A revengeful girl's blood relatives "locked all the doors so no one could get out and set fire to the house, and the wizard and all his crew were burned alive" (KHM 46).

Karl von Amira saw a sacred act in all of these punishments: Burning at the stake is a sacrifice to the god of fire, hanging a sacrifice to the god of storms, putting someone on the wheel a sacrifice to the sun god, decapitation a sacrifice to the god of lightning, and live burial an offering to the genius loci or other "special gods," etc.[107] We can generally consider reading of the cruel punishments in folktales and reality as "cultic punishments," and sacral acts ("sacral theory") as outdated today, especially because we also find these cruel punishments in the tales of peoples without any contact with Germanic tradition. Moreover, deriving evidence about pre-Christian justice with the relatively late sources (mostly thirteenth and fourteenth centuries) that Amira uses is certainly problematic. However, there is no doubt that these punishments had some relationship to folk belief. These punishments are cruel, but not cruel in our modern sense. Torture is not an end in itself here; it is not devised to bestially torment the victims. People believed they had to purify themselves of the sinister harm brought upon them by criminals: Fire and water are simply the most purifying elements. Therefore, not only ancient Germans burned or drowned witches and sorcerers. Moreover, nothing eradicates the harmful figure and prevents it from returning more effectively than fire.[108] Some executions resemble an act of reparative magic. The folktale still offers a clear picture of this conception which Christian teachings about the devil and demons largely displaced from historical records. Punishing the witch undoes her black magic. For example, when the witch in "The Two Brothers" (KHM 60) burns, the enchanted forest opens itself up and becomes bright and shining. In "Little Brother and Little Sister" (KHM 11) the brother changes from a fawn back into human form the moment the witch is burned to ashes (KHM 47 contains a similar event). Clearly witches were burned primarily to undo their evil deeds, not out of cruelty. The punishments for witches aim at the total destruction of their bodies: burning, scattering the ashes in the wind, ripping apart, and drowning. These are not just random forms of punishment; according to folk belief, only total destruction guarantees reversal of the witch's magic.

Even punishing people by having horses rip them apart—which seems like pure folktale material today—has a long history stretching from antiquity into modern times. The Romans used this procedure, and from there it passed into the Merovingian-Carolinian judicial system.[109] In his Franconian history, Gregor of Tours describes the execution of Queen Brunechild: She was tied to a horse's tail and ripped into pieces. In A.D. 515 over two-hundred captured Franconian girls were supposedly ripped apart by wild horses. The *Song of Roland* also includes this punishment:

> Genelune was bound
> Hand and foot
> And tied to the tails of wild horses:
> Through thorns and hedges,
> On her stomach and back
> She broke into pieces.[110]

This horrible punishment remained in practice throughout the Middle Ages. It was last used on the notorious French king killer Robert Damien in 1757.[111]

The earliest record of the atrocious nail-studded barrel is the Carthaginian death penalty.[112] They supposedly cut off the Roman Regulus's eyelids, put him in an open *Nageltonne*, and left him to the mercy of the sunshine. Amira tried to separate the historical elements from the folktale elements of this punishment. The historical evidence he provides indicates that the folktale punishment is not merely a variant of the classical Regulus legend.[113] The "iron maiden," a chest in the shape of a woman lined with spikes which pressed against the person inside, was similar to the *Nageltonne*. However, in this case we can see the folktale's limits as a source of legal history. This is particularly important for our discussion of cruelty in the folktale. Despite the fact that many of these cruel methods of execution did take place historically, the folktale sometimes plays fast and loose with historical precedent. Notably, the death penalty is practically the exclusive punishment in the folktale, and the crime committed often has no bearing on the severity of the sentence. The folktale also cruelly punishes minor offenses such as mere curiosity (KHM 46), envy (KHM 21, 101, 142), arrogance (KHM 24), impatience, indifference or mere laziness, greed, mercilessness, and other asocial behavior, i.e., offenses that are not crimes according to the law. The various degrees of guilt often do not correspond to gradations in the sentence. Thus the false bride who is only a passive tool in her mother's evil scheme to marry into the royal family always suffers the same fate as the instigator herself.[114] Finally, the folktale also includes cruel punishments which have no historical precedent, such as ripping the witch into pieces with twenty-four horses so that "no sign of her remained,"[115] or, at the end of a Sicilian version of "Little Brother and

Little Sister," cutting up and salting the false bride and sending her as tuna fish to her mother, who enjoys the meal.[116] Here the folktale clearly uses the historical punishment of quartering as the basis for fantasy; we can trace many of the folktale's gruesome excesses to a receding historical kernel. Other tales have even devised unique legal procedures to meet their particular narrative needs; i.e., they fashion a form of punishment that creates as much suspense as possible. For example, in "Snow White" (KHM 53) the evil stepmother must step into red-hot iron slippers and dance in them until she drops dead.

Of course, all punishments that employ supernatural methods are also products of the folktale's fantastic exaggerations. This includes all cases of cruel transformation as a punishment; for example, the prince whose wishes come true pronounces an inhumane sentence on the deceitful cook: "You shall turn into a black poodle with a golden chain around your neck, and eat glowing coals and belch fire" (KHM 76).

We must ask why the extremely cruel methods of execution found in history did not suffice for the folktale. Clearly not only history accounts for the cruelty in the folktale. A number of cruel folktale punishments correspond only in part to actual laws; epic laws also clearly have a formative role. Archaic justice is largely based on the maxim "I do unto you as you do unto me": The punishment must have a logical connection to the crime.[117] The criminal receives the same treatment as his victim: A murderer pays with his life. Specific parts of the body involved in the crime are punished: The perjurer loses the hand used in taking an oath, the slanderer has his tongue cut out, and even today, as we often hear, thieves in Saudi Arabia lose the hands with which they stole. Folktale punishments also apply this principle; cruel punishments often correspond to the cruel offense. The Grimms' "The Two Traveling Companions" (KHM 107) takes "an eye for an eye" quite literally: The shoemaker who cuts out his traveling partner's eyes in exchange for some bread is blinded himself at the end of the story. The witch who intends to bake and eat Hansel is put into her own oven and burned (KHM 15). The heroine's brothers cut up Bluebeard and "put him in the blood chamber with his female victims" (KHM—1812 ed., no. 62). The evil stepmother and her daughter who drown the queen by taking her from her bed and throwing her in the river that flows beneath the window are themselves put in a *Nageltonne* and rolled into the water (KHM 13; KHM 16 is similar). The untrue friend who libels the queen in a tale in Zaunart's collection receives the same sentence that her betrayal led to for the queen, namely, live burial. This tale clearly illustrates that the punishment must correspond to the offense because other attempts at putting the friend to death fail: The ropes breaks when she is hanged, the river throws her back out, only the earth accepts her in the end.[118]

Correspondence between punishment and crime is indeed, as we said, a common means for choosing a sentence, but the demands of narrative technique also influence the choice of sentences in the folktale. Axel Olrik's law of polarity applies: An artistic metaphor balances the scales of justice. Allowing folktale criminals to pronounce their own sentences in the folktale achieves this effect: The accused hear their own crimes and are asked, "What does someone who did this deserve?" The criminals then pass their own judgment without knowing it.[119] Historically the condemned did sometimes have the right to choose their own form of death. Perhaps the game of forfeits is a last remnant of this legal custom. But clearly the folk have preserved this practice for its narrative effects, not because of its historical precedents. The most essential aspect of this method in the folktale is that the criminals have no idea whom they are sentencing. The folktale repeatedly employs this scheme to surprise its audience. Epic purposes alone led to the inclusion and wide distribution of this scheme in the folktale. Now the folktale can mention the cruel punishment twice, once when the criminal declares it and once when it is actually imposed. This increases the tension and impact produced by the punishment. In addition to this epic law of repetition, the narrator's desire to clear the hero of responsibility for the punishment's severity may also motivate this device: it is the adversary, not the hero, who devises the severe punishment. We commonly find this scenario when the punishment is particularly cruel. This and similar motifs often emphasize that the hero himself would not stoop to such practices. Sometimes animals must enact the punishment so that the hero doesn't have to. Thus the doves poke out Cinderella's jealous sisters' eyes (KHM 21), and in KHM 107 two crows swoop off the gallows and hack out the evil shoemaker's eyes.

Epic necessity also often demands that sentences be passed and the cruel punishment imposed in the folktale without any investigation into the crime. For example, a women is sentenced to death or rejected by her husband merely on the basis of unsubstantiated or slanderous accusations. This is not a remnant of historical justice but rather a clear case of injustice. But epic laws are also at play here: The heroine must be temporarily humbled and her opponents laden with guilt so that later, after general reconciliation and rectification of the injustice, the heroine looks even better.

Epic laws, more than legal history, also guide punishments imposed on the heroes themselves or other sympathetic characters. Most important, these punishments cannot go beyond reversibility. For example, in KHM 135 ("The White Bride and the Black Bride") the king has the heroine's brother thrown into a pit "full of adders and snakes." He barely hangs onto his life until he is freed from the snake pit at the end of the story. The necessity to rescue the heroine, not legal precedent, causes a delay in her death in "Bluebeard." In some tales the heroine is rescued from the stake in the nick of time, e.g., KHM 9 ("The Twelve Brothers"): "She was already tied to the stake and the fire was licking her clothes with red tongues when the last moment of the seven years passed" and she was freed (almost exactly the same occurs in KHM 3, 49, and 116). We clearly recognize artistic devices for creating suspense here—an epic law of "almost"—not remnants of historical law.

The folktale loves extreme cases: The cruelest and most unusual punishment always has the greatest effect. Only this explains the preference for punishments such as the *Nageltonne*, which appears far more commonly in the folktale than in history. The nail-lined barrel is beloved because it is an extreme. The desire for extremes causes the folktale to exaggerate cruel medieval punishments into *even more* horrible practices; likewise, the "standard" death penalty, hanging on the gallows, is relatively uncommon in the folktale.

The folktale shows good and bad in extremes. Thus the villain receives no pity, only radical annihilation. The hero ignores the dragon's pleas for mercy after it has lost six heads and proceeds to cut off the seventh as well.[120] The folktale depicts cruel details only at the story's end; Olrik calls this "the weight of the stern." After the witch is burned in the final episode, the narrator of an Albanian tale yells out, "There was nothing left of the old witch! It's over! She's done for!"[121]

Cruel punishments characterize folktales as much as wishes come true. The folktale's epic structure requires outright destruction of the adversary at the story's end: This chastisement effectively contrasts with the hero's rise. Epic laws also necessitate cruelty at the start of the narrative to create a conflict situation. This sets the story in motion: The parents' abandonment of or cruel threat to kill the hero provides the story's starting point and the beginning of the hero's successful climb. Such treatment earns the hero the narrator's and audience's pity and "sympathy,"[122] increasing the effect of his success story. If the mistreatment the hero endured during his childhood is not essential to the story and it successfully fulfills its epic purpose of pushing the hero out of the restricting environment of his youth into a world full of experiences, he often forgets the past and has no need for revenge.[123] We can also detect the epic law of the weight of the stern motivating the proud princess's cruel punishment of her defeated suitors: Ninety-nine suitors have failed to solve the riddle; their heads or even their castrated genitals are impaled on stakes surrounding the palace. But the hundredth suitor, our hero, solves the riddle. The tests given the hero must appear impossible; they must pose an overwhelming deterrent in order to sufficiently demonstrate the hero's courage and the significance of his victory. Gerhard Gesemann's observations on the depiction of battles in simple Montenegrin reports are interesting for our topic: The defeated enemy *must* have his head cut off. The story cannot be told without this element.[124]

Clearly epic laws determine folktale cruelty to a greater extent than ethical laws. Epic laws override even historical precedent: These punishments live on in the modern folktale because the narrative's psychological needs, not the desire to accurately depict history, or even coincidence, favor them. The need for epic effects and suspense, the desire to depict exaggerated extreme cases, reduces the realism of historical practices. Extremely exaggerated cruelty lacks the reality of its historical precedent; it "does a flip" before entering the folktale's unreal world.

11. *The Immoral Hero.* So far we have examined cruelties perpetrated by the adversary or imposed on him or her as a severe retribution. We have seen that the folktale constantly tries to purify its heroes from even the mere thought of an evil act, and that it often inserts special motifs for this purpose (such as allowing villains to sentence themselves and having animals perform the execution). But there are also numerous cases in which the main character clearly acts immorally and yet still succeeds. In fact, such behavior seems perfectly acceptable if it helps the hero attain a desired goal.[125] Despite violating interdictions and revealing secrets, the hero finally has his way. For example, he settles a quarrel over inheritance by taking everything and using it for himself; he lets the arguing parties kill each other or even disposes of them himself. In other words, he behaves egotistically and immorally, yet he still succeeds and is not held responsible for his actions. In KHM 110 an "honest" fellow makes a Jew,[126] who has done him no harm dance around in some thorny bramble-bushes and shamelessly coerces him purely out of malice. In a tale from Lower Saxony a soldier (we can't really call him a "hero") hits an old woman, who unselfishly helped him become rich, for no reason at all.[127] In a Latvian folktale the hero wins a beautiful princess for his king, but she finds the king too old and has him beheaded. The hero becomes king and marries the princess, without a single ethical objection being raised.[128] Of course, the hero's lover, not the hero himself, has the king executed, but the hero is a knowing accessory to the murder. This is also the case in numerous versions of "The Magic Flight": Even if it is a sorcerer or a witch that the hero and his lover kill, it is, after all, the hero's father- or mother-in-law. In a gypsy tale the daughter of an evil underworld fairy helps the hero kill her own mother.[129]

The most flagrant example I know of an unpunished immoral hero occurs in a Kabyle tale: A young man kills his seven adopted sisters so he will be the exclusive heir. He pushes them, one at a time, off a mountain so they break their necks. After a number of other bloody deeds (the last one with the help of his wife), this mass murderer and his wife "returned to their village and lived happily ever after."[130] The tale doesn't mention anything about discovery of the crimes, a bad conscience, punishment of the "hero," or atonement! On the contrary, the folktale even grants this "hero" a happy ending. This is an extreme case most likely unequaled in European folktales. But this narrative is characteristic of the cruel, immoral stories that also appear in European tradition. No one questions how the hero reaches his goal; his success vouches for his personal qualities.

Moral judgment in the folktale is not "objective," it is always applied from the hero's point of view. Accordingly, cruelty is cruel only if the hero suffers, not when he treats others this way. To understand why the folktale never treats the hero's immoral deeds as immoral, we must realize that the narrator and the audience sympathize with the hero; i.e., the narrator's ego has a psychological relationship and tacit analogy to the folktale hero. The folktale's unique egocentric perspective, which judges everything in the hero's favor, results from this relationship. In one case the hero even kills his own children without a moral shadow falling on him (KHM 6, "Faithful Johannes"). Likewise, only the adversary's magic is evil; the magic the witch's daughter learns from her mother and uses to save herself and her lover is completely acceptable (e.g., KHM 56, "Darling Roland"). The bride's stepmother's or stepsisters' death at the hand of cruel torture doesn't dampen the joy at the concurrent wedding feast. The folktale often forgets minor characters after their initial appearance; the injustices they suffer remain unretributed. All this shows how much the folktale focuses on the hero. The narrative's happy ending makes even the most traumatic stories turn out fine for him. The folktale can disregard morals and ethics because the naive narrator and audience are not actually aware of this egocentric orientation.

The cruel crimes committed and suffered in the folktale are not actually portrayed as concrete current events. The folktale knows no pity; torture is not painful. In other words, the folktale removes the reality from crime as well. Punished adversaries do not complain about the cruelty they suffer; they say nothing about their pain. The folktale does not reflect on the wolf's chances of surviving the cruel operation which puts stones in his stomach while he is sleeping (KHM 5 and 26). Self-mutilation is also apparently painless. It is quite a while before the hero of a South American Indian tale notices that both his feet were completely charred by fire and the flesh is completely burnt off of his shin. Without hesitating, he scrapes the rest of the flesh off and sharpens his shin bone with a knife.[131] Fingers (KHM 25) and heels (KHM 97) can apparently be cut off without spilling any blood and without actual pain. "The Girl without Hands" (KHM 31) describes only the girl's helplessness against mutilation, not her pain. The folktale doesn't mention pain when the poor tailor pokes out one eye and then the other, only that he can no longer see (KHM 107). The French version also suggests that the folktale does not intend for poking out two eyes and then putting them back in their sockets to be taken as a bodily reality.[132]

People in the folktale have no "feelings." We can see this in folktale situations other than those which lack pain, e.g., courtship and marriage. Will-Erich Peuckert has shown with the examples of KHM 111 and 133 that the folktale does not contain real love, that it is not an "erotic narrative," as Walter Arthur Berendsohn claimed. Hate, like love, is also fundamentally absent.[133] Only a rationalist can call the folktale harmful because the folktale itself does not treat cruelty rationally; it neither contemplates nor notices anything alarming about these occurrences.[134] Thus the child also does not consider the folktale cruel. Children are not yet sensitive to cruelty, they still do not pity, they do not yet know what they are doing when, for example, they torture animals and cut up earthworms. We must recognize this to understand the "brutal offences of childhood."[135] This is why the child does not consider cruelty in the folktale out of the ordinary. We can speak of actual cruelty only when there definitely is conscious intent. Children can imagine the *Nageltonne* and death, but they do not think about the details. Interestingly, folktale cruelty first began to disturb pedagogues when people no longer naively read folktales and instead consciously deliberated over them. Unconscious cruelty is simply not cruelty.

The brothers Grimm themselves provide an impressive example of this phenomenon, "How Some Children Played Slaughter Together" (1812 ed., no. 22). In this game the children actually slaughter a boy—as the butcher does a pig. The tale then asks: Is this conscious, cruel murder, or do the children not consciously recognize the horror of their actions? A wise old man suggests that "the chief justice take a beautiful red apple in one hand and a Rhenish guilder in the other, and then call the boy and stretch out his hands to him. If he takes the apple he should be set free, but if he takes the guilder he should be put to death. The judge follows the old man's advice, the child grabs the apple with a laugh, and he is set free without any punishment." This is, of course, a balladeer's chiller, not a folktale; the choice between an apple and a gold piece as a wise method of reaching a judicial decision about holding a child responsible has a long literary tradition dating back to antiquity.[136] The brothers Grimm presumably dropped the piece from the next edition of the KHM for pedagogic reasons. To reiterate, this is not a folktale, but nothing provides better evidence that children do not consciously recognize cruelty than the "game of slaughter." Real cruelty does not originate from memories of folktale episodes encountered during childhood. Neither pedagogues nor criminologists can cite a single case in which folktales have exercised a harmful influence on the child's psyche, yet investigations into many crimes committed by youths have found proof that reading cheap novels and viewing films about gangsters and criminals stimulate certain crimes. Reality itself, not folktales, provides a model for the children to imitate in their "game of slaughter."

Nonetheless, the brothers Grimm chose to exclude the piece from later editions. Their editorial policy contrasts with the attitude of later folktale collectors. Since the Grimms' day, folktale audiences have become increasingly conscious of narrative content, and most recently cruel elements have increased along with the intrusion of sentimentality into the folktale. Parallel developments change the folk ballad into the broadside which supports the conscious desire for sentimentality with illustrations. Popular literature has not been investigated enough for us to determine what sort of developmental paths and tendencies it follows, but the effects of our realistic epoch on folk narrative are unmistakable. Not only modern techniques for recording folk narrative which present the original text more accurately—often resulting in a very different tone from the one we find in the Grimms' tales—account for the more realistic style of modern folktales. The more realistic, and thus more consciously cruel, style is a sign of the times.

While epic necessity accounts for numerous cruel episodes in the Grimm tales (e.g., KHM 40 and 46), some more recent collections take a certain delight in gruesome details. We can detect this shift as early as Ulrich Jahn's collection, which started the modern era of folktale collecting at the end of the ninteeenth century. For example, the water of life is used to revive the old witch eight times just so she can be tortured to death again. Finally they let her die.[137] Another narrative in Jahn's collection depicts ripping out eyes and tongue in excruciating detail.[138] The narrator of a tale in Elli Zenker's collection seems to get a certain pleasure out of the details of the cruel execution of the evil stepmother in a nail-lined barrel: "And they put the countess in a nail-lined barrel and brought it up a glass mountain and let it go from the top. It didn't just roll down but went faster and faster down the hill, and some holes in the barrel left a trail of blood. The guests had come along, and the crowd yelled, 'She deserves it, she deserves it. She's a murderer.' "[139]

The tales in Hertha Grudde's east Prussian collection return the reality to typical folktale punishments. The evil stepmother is led before a court in the city and beheaded,[140] as was actually done before the abolition of the death penalty. But it is precisely this realism that makes the crimes and punishment shocking: A cruel count immures a girl he was unable to rape;[141] a rich farmer kills his wife on slight provocation and hangs her in the smokehouse;[142] a king drowns his seven sons and bites himself in the arm to keep from breaking out in laughter over his wife's sorrow and lamentation;[143] a jealous count has his wife ripped apart by dogs and then returns to his guests "and ate and got drunk with them."[144] The absence of typical folktale elements and their epic laws make the cruel episodes in Grudde's collection so gruesome. When these drastic narratives about clever malice and heinous deeds are told merely to excite horrified reactions, gruesome acts and cruelty are no longer fictional. We cannot fail to recognize the pleasure these narrators gain from describing hideous scenes of mistreatment,[145] partiuclarly because most of the texts in Grudde's collection lack a conciliatory ending. For example, in both versions of "The Juniper Tree" in this collection,[146] the murdered boy is not changed back into living human form, and the tale ends tragically.

We find a similar tone in collections from other areas in Germany. A collector of unpublished folktales from the southern Black Forest learned from one informant that "children [!] mostly want to hear the horrible, sinister, gruesome parts usually played down or simply omitted from books of tales for children. Grandfather Schwarz has to describe these elements in particular detail without leaving anything out if he wants the little ones to go home afterward. He also remembers these 'cruel little stories' the best."[147] I have recorded tales that half resemble folktales but are based on crime novels or stories from tabloids.

When folktales are no longer naively apperceived, cruelty becomes conscious and thus disgusting and horrible. This makes folktales more dangerous pedagogically, and we cannot defend tales of this sort. Even if the moralistic opposition to these narratives is an arrogant bourgeois "Thank God I'm not like that!", we cannot deny that interest in sensationalism and cruelty has increased in modern society. Today cruelty receives special publicity.

It makes no difference if this general tendency toward increased cruelty is designed to "actually" say something else by depicting cruel realities, to "merely" reflect unconscious acts, as in some of Kafka's works[148] and in surreal poetry,[149] or if it is a completely unmasked neo-veristic use of the bare cruelty in advertising. The publishing industry extols a novel by a modern Nobel Prize winner with the following: "F's most gruesome and most famous novel. The insipid illusion of virgin civilization is mercilessly torn apart. . . . A chain reaction of human cruelty, the brutal destruction of human futility. . . ." We hardly need mention actual "folk literature" in the twentieth century, the dime novels, crime novels, and other stories "in which the people make very funny remarks among mutilated corpses,"[150] or the films which depict human evil and cruelty for aesthetic pleasure. In all of these examples cruelty is real, and thus it has become atrocious, even if it is unadorned or excuses itself as the "dictate of unconscious processes."

The general civilizing process of making real and conscious has also affected the folktale, causing it to undergo interesting structural changes. We see these changes most clearly in folktale illustrations and films which make the cruel episodes visible. The illustrations in folktale books reveal how visualization affects these episodes by completely changing the gruesome situation. The illustration is always more horrible than the folktale situation itself, not only because it freezes the ghastly moment, giving it permanance, but also because it moves the unconscious into the conscious by making it visible. Pictorial representation, by definition, makes the image conscious. Only Otto Ubbelohde's* illustration makes the hero's utopian wish, "All heads off except mine" (KHM 92, "The King of the Golden Mountain"), a bloodcurdling, visual, cruel reality—even though Ubbelohde probably accommodates the folktale's inner spirit more than any other illustrator. Other illustrators such as Gustave Doré and Max Slevogt, who composed masterful ink drawings of Bluebeard, intentionally make the episodes conscious in their illustrations to achieve a realistic effect. The moment the story is frozen in pictorial representation, the folktale's cruelties become real.

Extending such detailed illustrations into the dimension of time through film not only would destroy the character of the folktale, it would

---

*A well-known illustrator of the Grimm tales.—Trans.

also be unbearable for viewers. In the original folktale, suggestive language sufficed; films would have to make the atrocious bloodshed visual and screams of death audible. Interestingly, folktale films do not do this, even though there are plenty of other historical and fictional films that do not spare any neo-realistic gruesome scenes.[151] If a folktale film tries to depict the cruelties while remaining bearable for the audience and maintaining the nature of the folktale, it must inevitably deviate from the folk narrative. Insofar as film, as a realistic medium, concretizes the folktale's content, it must also do without some of the tale's reality. In Walt Disney's *Cinderella*, for example, the heroine's sisters do not chop off their heels. In the film, Bluebeard does not murder and multilate his wives; instead they live happily and pleasurably in a sort of harem. People say Bluebard is a sex murderer only because young girls disappear without a trace into his castle. This deviation from the folktale is characteristic: The film could not show the bloodbath; it is not visually conceivable, only narratable.

In summary, we can say that our interpretation of cruelty in the folktale leads us in many directions; i.e., we must consider several very different aspects of these cruel acts. First we must place the narratives in their original ethnic and cultural contexts. Doing so reveals that it would be completely wrong to judge the episodes with our current standards alone. The cannibalistic elements, for example, turn out not to be cruel; they are survivals of an ancient but integral and meaningful magical world. Boiling a dead person's bones and putting them back together (e.g., "The Juniper Tree") has its meaningful home among hunting societies, where it is an essential element of reincarnation, a sign of eternal life. The folktale also did not invent human sacrifice; instead it picked it up as a remnant of actual customs. Many of our folktale episodes became gruesome only when we no longer understood their original meaning, as with the falsely labeled "disenchantment through repeated death."

All of these motifs lead us to very ancient practices; the folktale's cruel punishments often freeze remnants of medieval justice. These punishments also make it clear how narrative laws influence the folktale. The narrative shapes history according to its needs rather than simply replicating it. Inquiring into the role of epic laws provides entirely different insights.

Thus we must always begin by examining the historical, cultural, and legal facts before we can recognize epic laws and narrative functions. Then there is a third, more psychological plane that we can mention only briefly here: To what extent do the folktale's unique forms allow these episodes to become conscious? What do they mean if they are received and told *un*consciously? The answers may vary considerably—for example, the individual psychological significance of tales told to children clearly differs from that of tales composed for adults; more recent folktale collections differ considerably from the Grimms' collection.

Much of what appears horrid to us has a completely different effect on children. A child takes it for granted that the hero slays the dragon or the fire-breathing dog. It would not occur to any child to sympathize with the poor giants. Children never accuse the old goat who cuts open the wolf's stomach and puts stones in him to replace the kids of cruelty to animals. They also are not astonished when the kids jump out of the wolf's stomach fresh and frisky. The concept of death is still foreign to the child's mind. The folktale contains no real death, only a constant transition from life to death and from death to life, from dark to light, and from evil to good. In reality, too, what we see as a child's brutality is more often simply a lack of knowledge, not actual cruelty.

The folktale uses a language of images: images of threat and rescue, of evil and good, of scarcity and abundance, of happiness and sorrow, of beauty and ugliness. The child immediately accepts the images without needing any clarification.

Anything else is not a folktale. We must carefully choose books of folktales we give to our children. It is certain that folktales themselves do not glorify atrocity. But recent and current events have naturally made us particularly attentive to these questions.

We must be especially cautious with pictorial representations of the folktale, particularly in films. On the other hand, we must not, in our overcautiousness and uprightness, stimulate the child's fantasy only with distilled water. Children want to and should take part in real life, and thus the dark and evil sides of human life also have a claim to a place in the folktale and in children's books. An anecdote seems to express this opinion best, even if it isn't true: A young American couple were afraid to let anything near their son that might arouse a complex of fear in little Johnny. Everyone who came into contact with the child was forbidden from telling him folktales, and the parents were proud that they were raising their little son free of superstition. Everything seemed to go according to their wishes until one day the boy didn't want to be left alone in the dark and began to cry bitterly. The worried parents rushed in and asked what was wrong. "There's a complex under my bed," the boy sobbed, and it was a long time before he calmed down. Poor little Johnny was hopelessly at the mercy of his fear because, in his little heart, he had no power of opposition such as that the folktale provides. He had no way to defend himself. Thus we are not necessarily doing children a favor by keeping them away from every possible danger. Most important, we should think about these problems and not buy children's books because they have a colorful cover or because the price is appealing. Above all, we should read them ourselves before we give them to children.

# IV.

## The Modern Folktale as Believed Reality

### TRIBAL NARRATIVES

Ethnographic parallels have repeatedly helped us find meaning and determine the degree of reality in our own folktales. Unfortunately, folktale research by Germanists has shyly avoided tribal tales, and a large gap still separates ethnological and folkloristic folktale research. Not coincidentally, there is, as yet, only a handbook of German folktales which contains, for example, no article on ethnological folktale research.[1]* Even Bolte and Polivka's comprehensive five-volume work largely neglects non-European folktales. The *Märchen der Weltliteratur* series, which compiles narratives from around the world in forty volumes, does not include any comparative investigations. Even attempts at describing the nature of the European folktale as a whole (e.g., by Max Lüthi) make no effort to contrast the specifically European folktale with its counterparts in the rest of the world. Nonetheless, the genre of folktale provides a unique link between high and tribal cultures that perhaps no other product of the human mind can equal. Moreover, our results so far show that we cannot explore the folktale's history on the basis of European materials alone.

Perhaps the academic environment is more favorable for new research directions now than ever before: Folklore is crossing national boundaries with increasing frequency, and ethnology has abandoned the idea that tribal peoples are fundamentally different from us. Lucien Lévy-Bruhl[2] saw a large gap between "primitive" thought and our own, but he finally recanted his theory that primitive thought is "prelogical" and called it a "hypothese mal fondée" himself.[3] Tribal peoples are not a different species

---

*In Germany, *Volkskunde* (folklore) has tended to limit itself to European materials, while *Völkerkunde* (ethnology) deals with other societies. Postwar academic revisions have begun to bridge the gap, but often students with double majors are the strongest link between the departments.—Trans.

of human than we, as Lévy-Bruhl first assumed; human thought is not "logical" in one case and "prelogical" in another. Every culture categorizes experiences differently, uniquely emphasizing different aspects. As folklore, particularly the study of folk belief, has repeatedly shown, this applies to our own culture as well: The designation "rational" describes the twentieth-century European in his totality just as little as the concept "primitive" or "prelogical thought" does the tribal citizen.

Here we are interested only in what tribal folktales can teach us about the origins of the European folktale and how its picture of reality differs from that in our own tales. We find folktales that are *still believed* in tribal societies. Tribal folktales are often simply somewhat embellished accounts of real events that serve as clan or local history or heroic legends.[4] In particular, it is striking how much stronger the non-European tale's relationship to belief is than the European tale's: Fantasy and belief do not necessarily contradict each other here. In any case, tribal societies often draw the border between "believed" and fictional narratives very differently than we do. Thus we cannot use the polarity between the European genres of legend and folktale as a gauge for other cultures and must generally guard against measuring tribal folktales with European standards. The primary critique of the "Finnish School" points out that the "original forms" of our folktales were certainly not the "most logical"; i.e., we must avoid imposing our present perspectives onto past folktales. Doing so may make the early forms of the tales seem completely illogical and absurd to us.

Numerous folktale motifs taken for pure fantasy in Europe today are considered real and true by tribal peoples. For example, the missionary Peter Banza reports that an old shaman in Christian Yucatan (Central America) confessed on his deathbed that he had often transformed himself into wild animals.[5] We should no longer marvel at such a claim after having traced the concept of transformation back to belief in self-transformation. Similarly, the helpful animal has become a merely formulaic *deux ex machina* in our European tales (and we no longer find any helpful animals in the believed legend), while tribal peoples still accept these episodes as true. They play a large role in tribal totem narratives which usually explain how an individual or an entire tribe acquired a particular animal's help.[6]

The narrative complex "The Grateful Dead" still occasionally appears in believed form: A Palestinian narrator, for example, accepted a story about the undertaker who refused to bury an indebted man as a real event that supposedly happened in Es-Salt in east Jordan,[7] and Knud Rasmussen reports a similar case from Greenland.[8] Motifs that lost their reality in Western tradition long ago still appear as motifs of believed magic elsewhere. The master thief (cf. KHM 192), for example, is a sorcerer, not simply a clever thief, in Togo: "He knew how to put people to sleep with magic. He robbed them after they had fallen asleep. . . ."[9]

The hero's acquired or magical abilities, not "epic laws" (i.e., the narrator's psychological relationship to the hero), often make him the central figure in tribal narratives. For example, it is no coincidence that twin brothers are frequently the heroes in African Kpelle tales: According to Kpelle folk belief, twins are born with a magic horn or a "little satchel" (i.e., magic) under their arm or somewhere else on their body; they are sorcerers from birth.[10] Because the narrator's needs do not always dominate the tale, the narrative may emphasize quite different aspects of the story than a European folktale with identical motifs. While magic is possible at any time or place in tribal folktales, considerations of narrative form determine how magic is used in the European folktale. The artistic construction of the European folktale disallows unmotivated magic. Tribal narratives, in contrast, paint a completely different picture. Even where the tribal world-view has clashed with our technological world-view, it still preserves some of its old belief in folktales; i.e., "cultural contact" does not necessarily lead to rationalization of the magical view of reality. Instead technology itself becomes a marvel and only reconfirms the old world-view's belief in wonders.

Stith Thompson recorded a version of "The Lazy Boy" (Type 675; one of the most widespread tale types not in the Grimm collection) from the Ojibwa Indians on Sugar Island, Michigan. In the tale the hero builds a magical wagon that moves by itself, making the princess laugh. The Indian narrator included this tale in a series of narratives about the Ojibwa culture hero, resulting in the tale "Rummy and His Little Ford." Thompson notes, "The little Ford car was Mr. Joseph's idea of the self-moving wagon."[11] The narrator does not accept the factual reality of the civilized world as such; instead he rationalizes it and incorporates it into the old world-view.

We know that many black peoples call the radio "the voice of the clouds" because of its demonic inexplicability. Tribal peoples fit inconceivable technology and the white man's superiority into their belief in magic. Among the Kai of Cape Kingwilliamsland, Nemunemu created heaven and earth, but they call Europeans by the same name. When white man came in the first steamships, they called the ships Nemunemu's boats.[12]

Andreas Lommel recently provided a vivid example of how the influences of European civilization can confirm and reinforce belief in the killing and reincarnation of a human that we traced (cf. pp. 61–64) from the European folktale back to its believed stages among tribal societies. An aborigine in northwest Australia tried to make his report about the slaying and reincarnation of a person more believable by depicting exactly the same process white doctors use. He described an operation, with witnesses, performed on a black man in a hospital. The man lay there as if dead. The white doctor had killed him, then opened up his body and took his innards out, washed them, put them back in the body, and closed the opening. After a long time the "dead man" came back to life. Like a medicine man's subject, this patient couldn't remember a thing about the operation.[13]

In contrast to the growing effort to record information about European narrators' attitudes toward their tales and to include as much accompanying commentary about the informants as possible, publications of tribal narratives seldom include similar entries, and the collectors include only very general comments about their informants' relationship to the materials. Nevertheless, numerous fieldworkers confirm that tribal societies of various sorts accept the folktale as a depiction of actual believed events. Wilhelm Wundt summarized this conclusion relatively early: "The more primitive the ideas are, the more clearly the character of direct reality clings to them." "The tale of magic actually corresponds to belief in magic;. . . magic and wonders do not separate true from false, they belong to stories passed down as true and are assimilated into general norms of belief."[14] More recent researchers and collectors confirm this opinion. A native Greenlander's comments to Danish ethnologist Knud Rasmussen typify the deep-seated belief that all oral narratives are true: "All of our legends (this includes folktales and myths) depict people's *experiences*. They are the *truth*. Our wise forefathers did not pass down thoughtless jabber or lies. If many incidents appear untrue to modern people, it is only because they are of more delicate constitution than the ancestors who gave us these stories."[15]

Commenting on African Kpelle tales in which animals interact with humans, Diedrich Westermann observes that "the totem stories are not fairy tales; rather, they report actual events."[16] Paul Hambruch assures us that for the most part the [Oceanian] native believes his stories; to him they are true and real. . . . It goes without saying that he believes the narrative's content. . . . [The aboriginals'] folktales and other narratives verbalize actual observations subjected to the native world-view; the tales contain almost no poetic fantasy."[17]

A number of formal features of the tribal folktale result from this largely believing attitude toward folktale tradition. Audiences which consider the folktale true and real will not tolerate variation; they demand that the narrator maintain the traditional text word for word. Individual contributions are immediately rebuked. Many cultures still have no artistic forms that play with the folktale. Some North American Indians and other tribal societies lack narrative forms such as the cumulative tale (cf., e.g., KHM 30 and 140) and other more playful narrative forms that never claim to depict reality.[18] The European folktale is more of a formal whole than the aboriginal tale; the latter does not always form an artistic unity because its primary concern is to report reality, not aesthetics. Of course, these tribal tales which report belief and fact are no more intended for children than the European folktale originally was, or sometimes still is today.

The narrator's performance sometimes reveals this believing attitude toward the folktale. Walter Krickeberg explains the tendency of Aztec and Inca tales preserved in numerous Spanish chronicles and reports from the discovery and colonial periods "towards repetition, symbolic expression, and ceremonial rendition "by the fact that" the narrative is often still perceived as part of cultic activity."[19]

Narration itself is frequently still a magical and dangerous affair. Hambruch reports that during his sojourn in the Caroline Islands, "the death of one of my chief informants on Ponape hindered my tale collecting a great deal because the natives immediately ascribed it to his having given me information, which I had invited by giving him gifts unauthorized by the spirits."[20] Dorsey reports that North American Indians attribute nothing short of a magical effect to the narration of stories about the transformation of animals, even though they consider these narratives fictional. This reveals just how fluid the boundaries between fact and fiction really are. Indians attribute narratives about the human conquest of the buffalo with the magical power to prevent buffalo herds from dwindling.[21] The Omaha Indians believe that telling stories during the day or in the summer will bring snakes bearing bad luck. The Sulka of New Pomerania also tell stories only in the dark or at night, otherwise—it is said—the narrator will be struck by lightning; and the Batswana of southern Africa refuse to narrate stories before sundown to prevent the clouds from falling on their heads.[22] The Kabyle allow the Timuschuha (folktales) to be told only in the evening or at night; people who tell them during the day will lose their hair.[23] Among the Alaskan Ten'a, the narrator puts out the lights before beginning; the same rule also applies among the Basutos and the Sulka in New Guinea.[24]

Paul Sartori has compiled numerous other examples of tale telling's magical function in a paper entitled "Narration as Magic": For example, some Indian tribes tell narratives with happy endings only during certain festivals. Depicting heroic deeds was originally designed to ensure the hero's renown and victory in the future as well.[25] The Kai of New Guinea believe that old stories and folkloric legends may be told only after the new crops sprout. They attempt to improve the plants' growth and development by telling stories and thus hope to obtain a rich harvest.[26] The Koryak of northeast Asia have a tale that describes how the great raven and his son must fly up to heaven to end unceasing rains. This story should be told only as a means for calming rainstorms, and never during nice weather.[27]

Sometimes it seems that the folktale itself is even considered a sort of demonic entity. For example, almost every African Kpelle tale begins with the fixed opening formula: "It once fell down on . . .," and then the tale's characters are named. The tales close by saying, "It fell down, plop, it's your [their, his, etc.] tale." Among the Ewe, folktales also usually begin, "It fell down on . . ." Or "It came rushing down on. . . ."[28] Who or what falls down remains unclear; but Westermann says that it is possible "that initially the folktale was thought of as an entity that possessed the dramatis personae and drove them to play out the events."[29]

We find it difficult to label narratives which are still very much a part of folk belief "folktales." Certainly they have not yet become fabular fantasy in the modern European sense. In tribal narratives, many marvels and much magic have not yet become objects of entertaining narratives. Tales collected from other cultures often do not appear to be "folktales" to us, and clearly much of what Europeans have labeled the fantasies of tribal peoples are mythic reports rather than folktales. Almost all nations, cultures, and times are represented in the *Märchen der Weltliteratur* series, but many volumes, for example, the one containing Aztec narratives, contain absolutely no folktales in our sense of the word.

Apparently there are still tribal societies without folktales. According to Adolf E. Jensen, for example, there are no fabular stories resembling folktales, only believed mythic narratives, on the Moluccan island of Ceram: "The world of wonders that appears in" these tales, says Jensen, "is not a folktale world, its narrative form is not a literary experience for the Ceramese; it is a reality, and not everyday reality but rather a marvelous reality. A Ceramese . . . encounters the spirits in his narratives not once but many times in his life, occasionally daily. He knows other living humans who lead secret lives as spirits."[30] Folk narratives on Ceram offer "an unusual picture of a hermetic mythical world. The folktale is as good as unknown, as is the playful animal fable. Some narratives, such as the one about the transformation of a piece of fruit into a man, may superficially resemble folktales, but these narratives differ from our European folktales. Every element which occurs in the former—such as the transformation of the fruit into a man—is still completely part of these people's reality."[31]

The volume of Siberian narratives in the *Märchen der Weltliteratur* series also shows us a preponderantly mythical world. The tales are full of magic and wonders, but they lack fantasy and optimistic endings. They report believed reality; they are "folktales" in the "legend's" garb.[32]

Even where tribal narratives have crossed the border from believed reality to the "folktale" in our sense, we can still detect an older layer of mythical reality living on in the typical folktale fantasy. We already observed this phenomenon in our consideration of anthropogenesis and cosmogenesis: While these stories are often no longer believed today, many still mirror an extinct mythology (cf. pp. 27–34). For example, in African folktales we frequently find entire mythic complexes that have been subjected to rationalizing processes. The most significant work on this shift appears in Hermann Baumann's study of African myths about creation and primeval times. A northern Hausa folktale, for example, tells how a leaf from a cotton tree falls onto a woman's body and how she puts it under a pot at home. The leaf grows into a tree from which a boy emerges. This echoes the idea that humans originated from trees found in mythic anthropogenesis throughout Africa.[33] In other African narratives, heroes are miraculously born of a woman's leg or knee. The motif of birth from the knee also appears in some examples of African anthropogenesis, for example, in a Nandi myth which describes how the original person's leg swelled until a girl emerged from the outside of the thigh and a boy from the inside; they became the ancestors of the human race.[34]

The connection between myth and folktale is more conspicuous for those cultures where the same gods and demons still appear in both categories. For example, the nine-headed bird who carries the princess away to his cave in Chinese versions of "Strong Hans" is a well-known spook who also plays a role in the Chinese belief in demons.[35] Leza is the deity of the peoples on the upper and middle Zambezi; he is the creator and a rain god who lives in the sky. But he also appears in folktales. A favorite motif depicts bluejay's marriage to the god's daughter. But Leza has a family only in folktales, never in myth.[36]

In African tradition, animals frequently appear in both mythic and folktale form. For example, chameleon plays a large role in both African mythology and folktales. In West Africa, e.g., among the Yoruba, Akun the tortoise has a central role in narratives from various realms of belief: He is the hero, i.e., cunning animal, in the animal fable. In addition, Akun appears as a god, again most often in connection with cosmogonic motifs, by bringing the sexes together. In the folktale Akun appears in a sort of "table-be-set" motif.[37] The mantis is the principal hero in the animal tales of the bushmen and also the mythical creator of the world.[38] In these cases the narrative genres have not yet become distinct; the spectrum of overlapping narratives ranges from animal fables to mythology. One figure can appear in all genres, as an otherworld god or as an everyday animal, because for these tribal societies everyday life has a much more intensive connection to belief in gods.

On the basis of these and similar examples, Jensen concluded that the folktale would be inconceivable without a mythic model.[39] Jensen believes that older concepts of deities sank from myth to folktales, as is particularly apparent in the depiction of ghosts and demons in tribal narratives. For example, spirits commonly have unusual bodily characteristics in tribal narratives: Some have only one eye,[40] others an iron tail, iron teeth,[41] or pointed legs; some consist only of a head, and the two sides of the body differ on others.[42] While folktales usually include these spirits only because of their grotesque features, Jensen conjectures that all of these spirits were once real mythic figures whose bodily features originally served some purpose.[43] Jensen considers the motif of a male spirit's excessively large genitals, which frequently appears in the corpus of tribal folktales,[44] a relic of a deity's attributes. A god, Soido, whose genitals are unusually swollen because he devoured the crops without chewing them, appears in the myths collected from the Kíwai of New Guinea by Gunnar Landtmann. The myth then depicts how the god spread his semen containing all the produce over the earth, thus creating the first plants. In other words, this fertilizing god's unusually large genitals are not merely symbolic; the myth concretely states that they contain the world's crops.[45]

Occasionally even superficial appearances reveal how closely the demonic figures in folktale cohere to mythic-religious ideas. For example,

Siberian folktales depict a completely oversized "evil spirit": "One of his lips reached up to heaven while the other touched the earth. In between was an open mouth ready to devour everything that came by."[46] Siberian folktales contain another frightful figure, the seven-headed forest devil.[47] Deep in the African jungles lives the Kpelle forest devil, an ugly monster who terrorizes all peaceful villagers. He feeds on humans (dead or alive) and animals.[48] The numinous, frightful appearance of these demonic figures in tribal narratives often makes them more similar to the experiential aspects of our legends than the otherworld figures in our folktales. The demons in tribal folktales are often the same as those in folk belief, and they have a greater connection to the believed figures than just the same name (as is the case in our folktales). These demons have a completely different religious function and a much wider range of action than the demonic figures in European folk traditions. They are spiritual figures who play roles in the culture's entire religious life. They are forest gods, animal gods, gods of the grain harvest, hunting spirits, and they encroach deep into human life as spirits of sexual union and of disease.

A connection to the reality of belief also protects these demons from overly fantastic exaggeration. For example, dragons in tribal tales resemble actual animals much more closely than they do in European tales; they are simple, not fantastically adorned like classical, European, and East Asian dragons.[49] We cannot fail to observe dual processes—one driving toward fantastic creations, the other rationalizing the content—at work in the texts collected by ethnologists: Ancient mythical folktales battle newer folktales for domination in almost every collection of tribal narratives. But the similarities often still observable between demonic figures in myth and folktale traditions provide evidence that the two realms were once more similar, that the distinctions between the genres did not always exist, and that folktales were once believed.

Before returning to European folktales, we should mention the peculiar status of reality in the Indian folktale. Here elements from myth, theology, and the folktale form odd company. Indian folktales often stray so far from our conception of reality that we have difficulty even following them. Moreover, wonder stories considered purely fantastic fiction in Europe are still believed in India. Of course, the Indian folktales available to us are mostly literary productions (*Kunstmärchen*). Our lack of resources prevents us from determining what the folkloric predecessors of the literary tales looked like and which folktales the Indian people tell today. Besides, investigating this cross-disciplinary topic requires close collaboration with Indologists, especially because numerous manuscripts are yet to be published. Therefore we can refer only to Johannes Hertel's fruitful preliminary work, which points out that the Indian folktale has a completely different conception of reality than the European folktale. Hertel writes:

> For the Hindu, history and folktale, reality and poetry are completely intertwined. They consider all narratives in their great literatures equally

true or at least equally plausible. Therefore their folktales . . . also lack the uncertainty of European tales; they do not begin with a general "Once upon a time"; instead they almost always name a city and state, king and chancellor, even if they play absolutely no role in the given narrative, and of course the hero is named. Many narrative collections and tales that we would label folktales are connected to historical figures in India (Wikramāditja, Mundscha, Bhōdscha). What we consider folktales, saints' legends and legends all have the same value for the Indian that history or a realistic novel does for us. The Indian believes in all the narrative's miraculous figures and events which, he is convinced, influence his activities and his life every hour of every day. Even if unusual episodes dominate the narrative, as they do in "Sura and the Witches" and in the folktale-novel *Mahabala and Malajasundari*, an explanation appears which the Indian sees as completely natural: At the story's end an all-knowing monk tells the heroes who they were in an earlier life and what they did; thus their marvelous experiences in the present result from past activities."[50]

## EUROPEAN NARRATIVES

In Europe we still occasionally find a "believed folktale," undisturbed by the enlightened rationalistic world-view of the nineteenth and twentieth centuries, which has not yet become a purely fictional narrative. Wherever modern civilization has not completely painted over the past, an older, believing attitude toward folktales still surfaces: We find its remnants in remote mountain areas, particularly in the Alps and Pyrenees, in the old Celtic regions of Ireland and Scotland, in Iceland, in the Baltic provinces, on the Balkan peninsula, and among gypsies. It is significant that we find belief in folktales in such ethnically diverse regions.

Beginning our tour of these relic areas in Ireland, we encounter a unique conception of reality that differs from every other European style of narration. The Irish folktale's sober certainty and realism do not result from enlightenment or decay but rather from the conscious belief that these tales depict facts. Listen to the start of an Irish folktale:

> There was once a respected, brave man from the Eoganacht clan of Ninus named Ailill Ochair. He was Maelduin's [the tale's hero] father. But his mother was a young nun, the mother superior of a cloister, and the birth occurred as follows: Once the king of the Eoganachts led a procession to a foreign land; Ailill was among them. They set up camp; at midnight, when everyone was asleep, Ailill went to the cloister nearby just as the mother superior was going to toll the night bell; Ailill grabbed her by the hand, held her firmly, and raped her. "We shouldn't have done that," she said, "I'm likely to get pregnant." She asked him his name and clan, and they parted.[1]

The style of this Irish narrative is more reminiscent of ancient Icelandic history than of a folktale. Icelandic sagas also begin by naming historical figures. Both depict the crude realities of life; the violent rape scene that leads to the birth of the hero is bare and doesn't take notice of any feelings. However, the rest of this narrative is more like a proper folktale which describes a sailor's odyssey, including many marvelous adventures.[2]

No extensive separation between legend and folktale appears to have yet entered Irish tradition.[3] Like legends, these folktales introduce characters by giving them a specific name. Fantastic wonders and reality, often from the modern environment, uniquely mingle in Irish narratives. Even the "Irish Fairy Tales" published in Germany by the brothers Grimm contain what amounts to reports of folk belief and legend told somewhat novelistically. The collection's character resembles the Grimms' *German Legends* much more than their *Kinder- und Hausmärchen*.

The Ireland volume in the *Märchen der Weltliteratur* series also captures Irish folk tradition's strange, characteristic mix of legend and folktale. For example, this style is particularly marked in "Balor the Sorcerer" (no. 4). The Irish folktale's use of a number of believed, antique motifs that often seem primitive, and that no other European folktales contain, also reveals its peculiar conception of reality. For example, the hero of an Irish folktale is left with only a wether and a sheep after the death of his grandmother, who had raised him after his parents died young. One night a wolf kills the wether. But the sheep speaks and tells the hero how he can bring it back to life with the wolf's heart. The hero says, "O you, my darling! I'll do whatever you tell me. But why did you wait so long to speak to me? I've been so forsaken ever since my grandmother died! God bless your soul!" The sheep then says,

> "Quiet! It *is* your grandmother who's talking to you! And your grandfather is lying there under the gable. You marvel at the fact that we are in the bodies of sheep. But wait until you hear the whole story: When your mother was dying, she made us promise to take care of you, whether we were dead or alive, until you were twenty-one. We promised her we would. When we came before the eternal judge, he sent us back like this so we could fulfill our promise."[4]

This odd mixture of Christian reasoning and the idea of animal ancestors, which suggests traces of totemism, the most ancient belief in folktales, is characteristic of the Irish folktale.

Elements of living folk belief which often have nothing to do with the tale type's plot frequently appear in Scandinavian folktales. For example, in a Norwegian version of "The Black and the White Bride" (Type 403; cf. KHM 135), the heroine is sent to the "Huldra" to borrow some shears. In another Norwegian folktale (Type 400), underworld figures steal the bride because she goes out alone wearing her bridal array, which is forbidden by Norwegian folk belief. A changeling legend introduces a Swedish folktale (Type 327B).[5]

By including elements from living folk belief, the folktale replaces certain, old, misunderstood motifs with current, more believable ones.

> In various cases borrowings from folk belief and folk legend have already become fixed components of folktales which clearly correspond to a particular tale type. For example, at the start of all complete Norwegian and Swedish versions of "Strong John" (Type 650), a Skogsfru or Huldra appears to the man in the form of his wife. And the Swedish folktale "The Gray Coat" (Type 710) begins with the well-known legend episode of the horses suddenly stopping and the man seeing a troll when he looks through the halter.[6]

These changes which have already become fixed elements of tradition allow the folktale to maintain its claim to belief.

Hans Naumann notes that even Icelandic folktales which "tend toward the rounded form of a novella still follow the archaic practice of fixing the story to specific locales and persona." Icelandic narratives "never shed the names and therefore have not yet acquired a basic feature of our folktales. Icelandic narratives still blur the boundaries between folktale and legend more than our own; most of the stories in this book still have more the tenor of belief than entertainment."[7]

In the remote Rhaeto-Romanic areas of the Grisons Mountains, we find further evidence of active belief in the folktale. Leza Uffer reports that his informant Flori Aloisi Zarn did not want to be called a liar because he considers the contents of his narratives true events that really occurred. Although Zarn's stories are folktales as far as content goes, typologically he is positively a *legend* narrator.[8] This Rhaeto-Romanic narrator assures us that the house in "Master and Servant in the Robbers' House" (which describes how the courageous and cunning servant overpowers the robbers) stood on Coira-Domat Street near Felsberg, and that as a boy he played in the building's ruins.[9]

A Polish folktale reports that Prussian sailors experienced the Polyphemus adventure as late as the Danish War of 1864.[10] Such crosses between folktale and legend, i.e., versions of folktale types presented with the believability associated with the legend, also appear in the volume of Latvian-Lithuanian folktales edited by Franz Specht in the *Märchen der Weltiteratur* series. For example, "How a Witch-Girl Tortured Many Young Men to Death"[11] clearly depicts a witch from folk belief. Clear-cut legend figures such as house ghosts, changelings (*loume*), and even werewolves commonly appear as folktale characters in Latvia and Lithuania. For example, one narrative includes the transformation into a werewolf typical of the legend: While a peasant is tending his horses, the animals suddenly become frightened and run away. He thinks to himself, "What are they afraid of?" But when he looks at himself, he sees that he is a wolf. A belt given to him by an old woman caused the transformation.[12] "Actually all folktales,"

Friedrich von der Leyen observes, "depict people who are afraid of ghosts, witches, and devils."[13]

Experts such as Walter Anderson attest that there are also folktale tellers in Russia who consider their tales historical truth. In any case, elements of living folk belief are well developed in the Russian folktale. However, the resources do not favor precise investigations into this area. Mark Azadovskii[14] names a number of Russian publications containing unaltered folk narratives, but these publications have not yet found their way into any German folklore institutes or libraries.

Most of the Albanian pieces published by Maximilian Lambertz also fall somewhere between legend and folktale. Legendary narratives have folktale endings; narrators imbue versions of known tale types with the tone of a believed report. The older a folktale, the more numinous and monstrous the demonic figures it depicts. Albanian folktales offer some particularly attractive examples. They still take their demons directly from living folk belief: The most important and powerful demon in the Albanian folktale is *Kulshedra*. She is simply *the* monster figure: She plays the role of the wolf in "Little Red Riding-Hood," of the nine-headed monster in "The Dragon-Slayer," of the animal containing the soul of another evil demon, of the evil mother-in-law or witch in "The Magic Flight," and of a monster tricked by a clever lad. Kulshedra is also the most important figure in folk belief in all of Albania. She is a horrible, repulsive figure; her face and entire body are covered with long hair. She is either a giant gray woman with sagging breasts or a dragonlike figure with a long tail and nine tongues who spits fire and whose entire body is covered with red fleece. Kushedra was doubtless originally a weather demon, as Albanian folk belief still reports: When Kulshedra draws near, clouds move in until black clouds accompanied by great thunderstorms fill the sky. Kulshedra's sons, the *Schlige*, evoke small storms.[15]

Likewise, Kulshedra's opponents in "The Dragon-Slayer," the *Drangues*, are not merely fabular heroes of days gone by; no inhabitant of the Albanian mountains doubts that Drangues still live today. As recently as nine years ago, Lambertz reports, no fewer than thirteen Drangues from the Albanian mountain villages gathered in Cermenika, northeast of Elbassan, when a Kulshedra appeared, and they survived the battle with her.[16] Albanian folk belief provides exact descriptions of who is or will be a dragon-slayer hero and how he can be recognized at birth: Drangues enter the world already clad, and they have two or four wings in their armpits. Only mothers and the Lord (!) know which children are Drangues. Later, when the Drangue takes up battle against a Kulshedra, the other Drangues know among themselves he is one of them, but no one else may know, otherwise the Drangue whose identity was revealed dies immediately. Nevertheless there are old shepherds and old women in the mountains who know which local inhabitants are Drangues. In Celza it is said that only people whose mothers are Kulshedras or whose ancestors on both sides of the family committed no adultery for three generations can become Drangues.[17] Thus, in Albania, folk belief and folktale figures have not yet become distinct.

Witches in Albanian folktales also still have positively legendary character; folk belief prescribes the means for protecting oneself from them. For example, during carnival people hang sacks made from goatskin or other materials under the chimney flue; the witches come through the chimney and into the sack and cannot get back out. An Albanian folktale tells of a clever young man who gathers many witches' souls in this manner and earns a living from the ransom.[18]

A male villain in Albanian as well as Greek folktales is the beardless man. The folktale mother warns her son about him before he leaves home. The son must promise to return if he encounters a beardless man along the way. The son returns after the first encounter, but the second time the beardless man joins him on his journey and becomes the boy's evil adversary. Here again living folk belief provides the model: People must be cautious around the beardless man because he has an evil eye and hexes children and livestock. The middle European beardless man is particularly dangerous in Albania; he is not allowed to praise the farmer's livestock or look at small children. Albanian men always have moustaches; even Catholic priests must yield to this folk belief and grow mustaches.[19]

Moses Gaster attests to the belief in the reality of folktales in Rumania:

> This religious belief—I mean this in the broadest sense—is one of the most important aspects of the origin, history, and distribution of the folktale, and folktale scholars have, as yet, systematically neglected it. We need not go far to find the reason for this neglect: European folktales, particularly those in modern collections, have for the most part lost their religious elements; the farther east we go, the more the folktale's religious character stands out. In the West only a few supernatural figures remain, and they are barely tolerated and are waiting for their dismissal. Their environment has disappeared, but in our [Rumanian] folktales, we still encounter figures in their believed forms. The folk mythology of the southern Slavs, Albanians, Greeks, and Rumanians is much richer than that of any Western society; thus their folktales are fuller, richer, more living, and, for me, closer to the original form than any of the corresponding Western traditions.[20]

Greece is also still a rich area for folktales and genuine folk traditions; competition from literature and printed folktale books is not yet too strong.[21] Gypsy narratives frequently contain an equally believing attitude toward the content of folktales. Carl-Herman Tillhagen affirms that "for gypsies the differences between fantasy and reality are much less sharp than for us. In their world almost anything can actually happen. They do not assert the same logical demands we do, nor do they have our need to be able to rationally explain everything. . . . What is valuable knowledge for them, we call, at best, superstition."[22] The gypsies brought this belief in folktales with them from the Balkans, and some of the gypsy folktales recorded by Heinrich von Wlislocki in the Transylvanian Alps have strong legendary character. Mythic figures such as the sun king, the sun mother, the king of the wind, and the king of the moon appear in these tales. The mythical bird of the gypsies also plays a role: He lives for 999 years but will die if he does not nurse from the breast of the same woman every night.[23]

We also occasionally encounter folktales told as "true" in Germany and German-speaking countries. Of course, nineteenth-century collections do not provide a good source here, because the Grimms' methods of reworking the tales influenced almost all collectors. The naive, childish tone put into folktales since romanticism often prevents us from recognizing the narrator's original attitude. Likewise, the effects of other artistic revisions of the folktale had already left their traces: The folktale hero's namelessness, for example, an essential step toward unreal typified tales, has been a stylistic principle of the upper class since Perrault's famous collection of 1697. In any case, most of the printed collections have been so stylized that we can no longer infer the narrator's original subjective attitude toward the reality of the tales from the texts. It usually goes unsaid whether the narrator believes the tale or not; thus we can derive this criterion only from minute details, making the narrators' comments about their folktales all the more important. However, information about narrators has only gradually become important for recent collecting activities.

The folktales in some recent collections are so different from the Grimms' tales and other nineteenth-century collections, people have noted that they don't seem like folktales at all. Some still contain the original belief in the narrative's reality, thus opening new perspectives for the biology of the German folktale. The more a narrative is rooted among the peasantry, the less it is intended for children over adults. The more primitive a folktale is, the closer its connection to folk belief and the more it is a statement of reality. Folktales containing believed wonders are serious narratives because the simple people still have no understanding of purely fictional stories; the idea of fantasy as an end in itself is completely foreign.[24] The degree to which Olrik's epic laws dominate a tale often reveals whether the narrative was composed and reworked into fiction or if it is still true. When the period of belief has been abandoned, the folktale saves itself by becoming an art form.

The adherence to fixed wording indicates a narrative style originally rooted in belief. Collectors have observed this in German-speaking areas as well as for tribal societies,[25] and for narration among children, who constantly demand the same wording.[26] Folktale narrators who do not yet play with fantasy do not interchange folktale motifs, and the need to follow tradition therefore determines their presentation down to the level of single words. Angelika Merkelbach-Pinck notes that it is characteristic that folktales in her collections "repeat previous renderings almost word for word; the audience pays close attention to what the narrator adds or omits."[27] The east Prussian farmworkers in Grudde's collection narrate "word for word, as if they were reciting old ballads." If one woman decided to change the tale on her own, the others would reprimand her for being a liar. "Shut up. That's not how it was!" "Don't lie like that!" The community's beliefs, nothing else, determines how these stories are told. The latent but still real belief in the content of folktales causes the word-for-word maintenance of the texts.[28] The audience demands the truth sanctioned by tradition; it rejects the narrator's authorship. The psychological act of recognizing old and worthy stories is of utmost importance here; every rendering of the folktale reconfirms its reality. At this stage there is still no cause for declaring the tale's truth; this would seem ironic.

Printed collections do not always diminish belief in folktales. Occasionally they even have the opposite effect, because many people trust the printed word more than the spoken one. Adolf Bach describes an old peasant woman who lost her great interest in reading serialized novels when she discovered that the stories were fiction and not "real."[29] She didn't believe the stories because of their content but rather because she trusted anything in print.

We commonly find completely fantastic folktale materials treated as believed legends. In a Silesian narrative, for example, a usurer specifies in his will that anyone who holds a wake at his coffin for three nights will receive the estate. All those who try are found dead the next morning. Then a soldier tries and holds out for two nights, but each night the dead man rises from his coffin between midnight and one. After the third night the soldier is lying strangled next to the usurer's corpse. The soldier's bride receives the inheritance.[30] This tale presents the events we know from the folktale of the princess in the coffin in purely legendary form; the narrative ends with the hero's death.

Some versions of "The Singing Bone" are clearly told as legends about the ordeal of the bier.[31] In a Hessian version of "The Wolf and the Seven Young Kids," a werewolf knocks on the door of the secluded house.[32] The dwarves in a Hungarian-German version of "Snow White" are real underworld figures who live in a cave.[33] Even the motifs of transformation into an animal, the animal bridegroom,[34] the grateful animal,[35] and the Jephthah motif,[36] as well as the introduction to "The Juniper Tree,"[37] are occasionally told as legends. Similarly, "Rumpelstiltskin" has folktale versions as well as a legendary branch of tradition (even today). For example, the Styrian "Hahnengiggerl" ( a local figure in the form of a rooster)[38] still has the numinous features of a legendary demon; whoever conjures him must draw a protective magic circle around himself. The heroine must promise him her soul before receiving his help. This Austrian narrative has other legendary features as well: The queen overhears the Hahnengiggerl's name at the nightly meeting place of all the witches and demons.

The items in Grudde's collection that correspond to the Grimms' "The

Juniper Tree" (KHM 47)[39] are also markedly legendary. The stories focus on the fate of the murdered people who must restlessly fly around as birds. At the close they are not returned to human form; rather, they are merely freed from the torment of having to haunt the living: "The haunting was over; from then on the little bird and his singing never bothered them."

A tale in Kühnau's Silesian collection fixes the familiar material from "The Shroud" (KHM 109) to a particular time and place: "In the spring of 1885 a widow in Kolbnitz lost the last of her children to the measles."[40] The legendary shape of this narrative also rationalizes the folktale: The child himself does not return to his mother as he does in the Grimm tale; instead she dreams about him. "She was inconsolable and could not stop her tears. . . . Then she repeatedly dreamed that the child came to her and looked at her with a sad face. She also dreamed that his little shirt was soaking wet. . . ." The statement added to the end which confirms the mother's experience is also typical of the legend: "Other people had the same dream about the child."

The two legendary reports which follow this tale in Kühnau's collection[41] similarly fix the events in time and place: "Several years ago a twelve-year-old boy, an only child, died near Breslau. . . . " Characteristically, this narrative attempts to make the child's return believable by including realistic details:

> In the middle of the night the servant girl suddenly called out to ask the cook if she had heard something. After receiving a negative response, the girl again asked the cook if she had heard someone filling a cup with water under the bed or the soft, unintelligible murmuring of a child's voice. The girl was very scared. The next day the cook said she didn't hear anything, but she claimed she saw something walk from the foot of the bed to the head of the bed; then it climbed into the air with a soft whisper like a white ray and disappeared halfway to the ceiling.

Amazement in the face of numinous events and rationalizing tendencies indicate that these versions of KHM 109 are still legendary reports of folk belief.

Information about narrators in a few of the German collections is as illuminating as the differing uses of folktale motifs: Matthias Zender's best narrator says the stories he tells "are all true, but I can't guarantee it. I don't lie, but I could tell stories for a week." Zender writes that another narrator prefers "true stories, those that he accepts as true."[42] Merkelbach-Pinck adds that in Lorraine, "the *truthfulness* of the stories is essential to the narrator and audience,"[43] even though the opposition between folktales and true stories does exist. One of her informants confirms this: "This is a true story, not a folktale."[44]

The "dog-girl's" (Romuald Pramberger's most important and most interesting Styrian narrator) unshakable belief in folktale marvels almost seems like a folktale itself. The dog-girl believed a gypsy's tales about the king of a rich land in the Orient who buried the crown the gypsies hope to find one day. When the dog-girl lost her home and began a life of wandering, she actually made a pilgrimage to the holy land, saw the places Christ had been, and looked for the crown. She also journeyed to Salzburg to meet the wonderful people who, according to legend, live under the mountain and to find a magical flower that supposedly made a poor boy rich.[45]

An unpublished collection by H. Schlecht reports that in the Harmersbach Valley in the Black Forest,

> farmers have no understanding of products of fantasy presented for their own sake. The hard life leaves no time to play with idle yarns. If folktale materials appear at all, they maintain a very close relationship to the dominant folk belief; they are embedded in belief and can just as easily appear in legend as in folktale. People who follow folk belief do not depict the make-believe for its own sake; they only consciously include unreal scenarios in the exaggerated episodes of tales of lying and in jest. There is *no* folkloric *distinction* between legend and folktale, both are "little stories"; only jest is distinguished as "funny little stories."[46]

Ulrich Jahn noted early on, in the important introduction to his edition of Pomeranian folktales, how useless the designation "folktale" is among the folk themselves.[47] Where the same expression designates folktales and legends, there do not seem to be conscious generic boundaries.

The designation "folktale," which suggests "untrue," is avoided most strenuously in areas where remnants of belief in folktales still exist. Johann Reinhard Bünker's narrator, for example, calls his folktales "stories." To avoid silencing his informants who associated "folktale" with unreal, Wilhelm Wisser never used the word when soliciting stories.[48] Wisser's informant revealed the tale of the beautiful step-daughter whom the king marries and the evil stepmother changes into a duck only "behind the bushes," "in great secrecy," and with a degree of fear, an indication that this woman believed in the tale's contents.[49]

Hertha Grudde's collection of east Prussian folktales offers the most impressive compilation of believed folktales.[50] No other collection preserves the character of believed folktales so well. Legend and folktale merge, revealing their original proximity quite clearly: We find legendary tales about spooks with the folktale's happy ending when the specter is disenchanted.[51] These specters of death and the devil contradict our usual concept of the central European folktale which has already lost its strong connection to living folk belief. But in east Prussia the folktale was obviously still believed at the time of Grudde's collection. Even clear folktale wonders still have a firm relationship to belief: The folktales in Grudde's collection focus on the supernatural occurrence, not on some hero.[52] Otherworld forces also have a completely different effect and proximity to reality than they do, for example, in the Grimms' tales. The central themes of Grudde's tales are hauntings and disenchantment. Frightful motifs play as large a role here as in the legend. Supernatural, miraculous features have not become fantasy; belief keeps them within relatively narrow bounds. Hertha Grudde herself says that "it was absolutely necessary . . . that I believe in ghosts. Otherwise they would never have told me the tales. They do not tell such things to nonbelievers."[53] The statements Grudde recorded from her narrators support this claim. One woman narrator substantiates her narratives by saying, "It's still that way today." This is characteristic of the conviction that the tales in Grudde's collection are true. The narrators bring all tales into relation with the present; they frequently compare their tales with the way it is in our own time. For example, it is still so "today" that "whatever animal drinks human blood is able to speak at midnight" (no. 33), and it is also still true today that "whoever commits a crime is not able to get within three feet of the altar" (no. 29).

One narrator attests, "It is true because all of the people who believed in it before were no dumber than we are."[54] The women laborers in the east Prussian village of Beisleiden completely reject folktales they cannot believe; "they have no spiritual connection, no inner engagement with the episodes depicted therein."[55] They take only their own folktales seriously; they refer to printed tales as school folktales and reject them along with all other folktales fabricated by the landowners. One of Grudde's informants says, "There are two kinds of folktales: the school folktales and our folktales. I don't think the old women need to tell the young ones the folktales in the books; they can just read them, right?"[56]

Grudde's narrators also clearly distinguish folktales that shouldn't be told to children. Adult folktales are still taken very seriously, particularly all of the frightening numinous episodes, and shouldn't be told with children around because they are far too serious and may upset the little ones.

At first Grudde's collection was fervently greeted and repeatedly used as the basis of further investigations;[57] later it was subjected to extensive criticism. In opposition to Julius Schwietering, Gottfried Henssen considers the tales in Grudde's collection "legends."[58] Will-Erich Peuckert also has the "strongest objections" to Grudde's folktales, which he considers "fictional legends."[59] However, this designation would be more accurate for actual legends that have lost their connection to living folk belief and yet are not folktales, for example, certain dwarf and giant legends.

Henssen went to the same village, Beisleiden, to verify Grudde's work and met a jest and folktale narrator who did not take his narratives for believed reality ("Oh, who believes in that stuff, they're just fairy tales; who knows who made those stories up").[60] But this does not prove that Grudde's informants didn't believe their own stories. And even if we can show that Grudde paid her narrators (other collectors have also done so), and even if it is probable that Grudde's narrators took some of the stories from recent popular fiction, as Friedrich Ranke has shown,[61] the distinguishing features of this collection remain a genuine believing attitude toward the narratives and the legendary depiction of folktale materials. Despite all of the objections, this collection has given us more insight into the psychological development of folk narrative than any other collection because it contains "primitive forms of the folktale"[62] not found in any other modern collections.

We do not draw these conclusions based on Grudde's collection alone: Other east Prussian collections confirm that in this region the folktale still stood in the realm of reality at that time. For example, the genres of folk narrative also merge in the east Prussian texts compiled by Karl Plenzat; there are no stylistic differences, and only minimal differences in how the content is perceived. The believing sentence at the start of the tale about how the suitor frees the black princess by enduring three nights of torture provides a characteristic example: "In the old days anyone who summoned the devil was punished with a black body." The narrative then describes a particular instance which includes legendary failures at disenchantment. Only then comes a three-part folktale about twelve young men; only the last completes the task needed to disenchant the princess.[63] The remarks Plenzat recorded from his informants confirm the actual belief in folktales, even if skepticism has already penetrated the belief and people said folktales were believed only in the "olden days." One of Plenzat's assistants claims, "If asked if they believed their stories, the younger narrators would of course respond, 'It's only a folktale.' The elders, on the other hand, would certainly respond that the narrative events could have occurred anyway, perhaps in the old days; after all, the Bible also tells of ghosts and talking animals. And who can doubt the truth of the Holy Scriptures?"[64]

Finally, as in tribal societies, narration also functions as magic in Europe. In addition to the nature of the narrators' relationships to their narratives, the narrative's function, the context of the narrative situation, and the effect on the audience are important for judging the extent to which a narrative is believed. For example, the degree of reality assigned to a folktale often depends on the time of day. Folktale telling is particularly popular at dusk and at night, when external reality is less important. It is simply not the case that legends are told at night, folktales during the day. The folktale can also use the night to create a different mood toward the tale's reality. The report from Plenzat's assistants is telling:

> The women rarely tell folktales during the light of day; at the most they summarize the contents. Moreover, the summer, during which the material world is so loud and alive, is also not the proper time to tell folktales. A winter night, particularly during the time between Christmas and New Year, when people aren't working and everyday thoughts are eliminated and the gas lamps with their meager light do not illuminate much more than the social circle near the hearth or oven, is the proper time to tell folktales.[65]

An Irish narrator even refused to present her stories during the day because she believed it would bring bad luck.[66] Thus we also find remnants of behavior during narration in Europe that, as we saw, was often closely regulated in tribal societies. Some Albanian closing formulas which banish the folktale and wish the audience good health are still taken very seriously. These formulas impressively demonstrate a magical defense against the demonic, personified power of the folktale: "The folktale to the mountains, health among us!" "The folktale in the brick, health to the men!" "The folktale up to the beams [or the rafters], health to the women!"[67]

Finally, we still find one other magical function of narrative. For example, we need think only of the Merseburg incantations*: A narrative depicting an episode similar to the intended magical effect precedes the incantation and supposedly provides a model for the real outcome. The typical construction of most familiar blessings—including ancient ones as well as modern descendants of the Merseburg incantations—consists of an exemplary introductory narrative plus the actual blessing formula. The narrative's magical reality is particularly clear in cases where the amended blessing is not vital and the narrative itself suffices.[68]

Modern folktale-recording techniques with records or tapes allow new observations of narrators. Gottfried Henssen, who has worked a great deal with the tape recorder, and more recently C. O'Danachair report that good narrators are proud when they are recorded and can hear themselves afterward. In addition, we find even more emotional reactions: Not long ago, tape-recording activities in a newly constructed village for refugees moved German-speaking evacuees from Bohemia and Hungary to tears when they heard their own voices repeat the old traditions through a loudspeaker; a Lithuanian refugee wanted, in all seriousness, to demolish the tape recorder because a devil who had copied his voice was inside.

While recording in Württemberg and Hessia, I have repeatedly had the opportunity to observe how the believing attitude toward the reality of narratives was not to be found among the actual "narrators" but rather among those who remained silent.

---

*Tenth-century Old High German incantations discovered in 1841 and edited by Jacob Grimm a year later. The texts consist of two incantations (one for freeing prisoners, the other to prevent horses from twisting their legs) and the accompanying narratives.—Trans.

# V.

## Paths of Rationalization

### ETHNIC DIFFERENCES

Attempting to extricate the attitudes of a particular ethnic group toward the reality of folktales distributed over the entire globe takes us into a problematic area of research.[1] We must handle these questions with the greatest methodological caution. Even our sources pose a fundamental problem because they may not always be reliable. The volumes of the *Märchen der Weltliteratur*, for example, are not all of equal utility because (1) they are translations, which lose the finer, characteristic features of the original language; (2) some literary or other, not actual folktale, materials have found their way into the volumes; and (3) we must not forget that the editors' subjective preferences influence the selection of items supposedly characteristic of the nation in each volume.

Attempts to draw psychological conclusions about various folk groups on the basis of their folktales must, above all, be independent of national ideologies. The work of Karl Maaß on the German folktale[2] can be taken as a cautionary example here. Maaß finds only "German loyalty," "basic German characters" (*Kerngestalten*), and "ideal forms of a pure Germanic virginity" in the German folktale.

In addition, a further basic methodological question is at issue: Does national character remain constant over time? We can group folktales according to historical phases and shifts in style, as well as ethnic features. What is the relationship between national styles and historical styles? In any case, comparisons of different national styles must be made for only one historical period; for example, we cannot lump Icelandic sagas with modern Icelandic folktales. In addition, we must not generalize from individual narrators' and collectors' contributions to the text. For example, we cannot conclude that Germans, particularly those from Holstein, have exaggerated sexual tendencies on the basis of the folktales collected by Wisser in east Holstein, which are full of blunt, often overly explicit eroticism. This proves only that Wisser had the rare ability to make narrators feel comfortable enough to relax the discretion usually maintained in the presence of educated people. Moreover, Wisser selected mostly men from the lower classes, e.g., servants, as informants. In other words, we can compare only comparable materials. Monographs which trace the ethnic variations of a motif, a folktale group, or a common folktale character over as wide a geographic area as possible provide the best basis for such comparisons.

As soon as an ethnic group adopts the main themes of a tale type, it imbues them with local interests and tastes. Even statistical surveys of tale type distribution found in the tale type indexes now available for many areas can be informative: Entire populations, not only individual narrators, have favorite folktales. For example, Icelandic folktales often depict confrontations between giants and humans, even in international tale types which do not otherwise include this feature.[3]

Individuals and groups adapt and repeat narratives they hear from others according to their own tastes. A folktale can become indigenous to a new culture only once it corresponds to that culture's prevailing expectations. Different people prefer different tales. For example, Jan de Vries has shown that English folktales had little influence on Indian narrative.[4] Likewise, Stith Thompson determined that the English-speaking world had much less influence than Spanish, French, and black folk narratives on the North American Indians.[5]

The Arabian version of "Snow White" recorded by Enno Littmann offers a particularly vivid account of adaptation.[6] Naturally the tale has European, not Oriental, origins, but this makes its assimilation to its new environment all the more interesting. Snow White becomes "Miss Snowey"; her father, Hasan, is the chairman of the merchants' guild. Prayer alone does not help his barren wife bear him a child; natural explanations for their fruitless marriage also cannot be ruled out: "As soon as he and his wife undressed . . . etc." The father bring Miss Snowey to school each day and picks her up again in the evening. Corresponding to the local milieu, the heroine is not led into the forest, but rather is supposed to be pushed into a bottomless well. Miss Snowey also does not end up at the home of dwarves, but rather—far more realistically—at a robber's house. The evil mother doesn't have a magic mirror to update her about her daughter's life and beauty. Moreover, poisoned coffee, not a magic comb, sends Miss Snowey to her apparent death.[7] The marriage to the prince is arranged through a contract signed by both parties. All of these details indicate that the Oriental folktale is realistic and that it has a more rational attitude than our own, not because Oriental people are more rationalistic but because in the Orient the folktale can still make a claim on belief.

Muslims also have a completely different attitude toward the folktale's happy ending than Europeans: Orientals make little attempt to alter given reality; even the folktale hero must endure the hardships of daily life. "If it is written in the stars, it must happen," says the princess in a folktale from Azerbaijan in true Islamic fatalistic fashion.[8]

But let us limit ourselves to the ethnic differences in the attitude toward folktale reality within Europe! We must rely on Löwis of Menar for information on the differences between Russian and German folktales,[9] particularly because the Russian collections, with the exception of Afanas'ev's well-known volume, are not accessible. Russian folktales often depict cruel motifs much more strongly than German folktales. Folktales based on belief in vampires (e.g., "The Princess in the Shroud," Type 307) occur mostly in eastern Europe, where this belief is at home. However, Christian elements also pervade Russian folktales: The heroes are pious and receive special protection from a saint.[10] God himself, or an angel sent by him, frequently appears as the hero's magical helper and adviser in Russian folktales.[11] The hero does not punish the villain himself, as in the legend; rather, these tales explain that God imposes the punishment. The tales also close with didactic statements whenever possible (e.g., "It is clear: The Lord punishes excessive greed").[12] Magical prayers commonly result in miracles. For example, the hero tells his adversary, "I wish, it is God's will, that you, you fiend, turn into a dog!" The curse works, and the hero leads the transformed villain away by the collar.[13] Because of these tendencies, Russian folktales differentiate themselves from humorous narratives more clearly than their German counterparts; the former has not moved toward jest. In general, Russian tales of magic are closer to folk belief than their German parallels. Russian folktale heroes still closely follow typical patterns; in contrast, the German folktale tends to include individual elements.[14] But our lack of recent Russian collections prevents us from making an objective, up-to-date comparison.

We have much better resources for comparing the German folktale with the French folktale. Even borrowed tales seem to retain the character of their land of origin. We still find traces of the French folktale's irony, exaggeration, and pleasure in eating and in pretty clothes in the Grimms' version of "The Wolf and the Seven Young Kids" (KHM 5), "Sleeping Beauty" (KHM 50), and "Little Red Riding-Hood" (KHM 26).[15] And of course, what a difference there is between Perrault and Grimm!

Perrault's realism projects a completely different image of the hero than we are accustomed to from German folktales. His folktale heroes are not untainted, they are realistic and human; they are not a model of virtue, they have their small weaknesses: Sleeping Beauty (la belle au bois dormant), for example, pricks herself with the spindle because she is thoughtless, flighty, and clumsy. People who suffer evil fates in Perrault's folktales are never completely innocent. These small weaknesses make Perrault's characters more human and bring them closer to the listener.[16]

Perrault's French folktales are always rational: The German Sleeping Beauty is as old the day she wakes up as the day she fell asleep; it does not occur to the German narrator to calculate the effect of the magical hundred-year sleep. Perrault's Sleeping Beauty has hard skin because she is 120 years old; "one would be hard pressed to find an animal in the zoo with skin as hard as hers." The musical instruments which wake her play outdated music, and Sleeping Beauty is wearing an old-fashioned dress: "But the prince was careful not to tell her that she was dressed like his grandmother and was wearing a high-necked dress." On the wedding night the princess doesn't sleep much because she is already thoroughly rested.[17]

This French sense of reality corresponds more to the modern knowledge of natural processes than to the German notion of typical folktales. Of course, even the French tale puts up with the typically unreal hundred-year sleep; it rejects as unreal only the idea that time stands still. This "mere recognition" of reality produces Perrault's characteristic irony; there is no such thing as partial reality. The charm of Perrault's folktales lies precisely in this tension between real and unreal events. Perrault never lets us forget that the story takes place in a folktale world, yet he still makes this world as real as possible.[18]

Perrault created the psychological folktale. He wittily uses various, often unnoticeable, connections to reality to move the folktale from an unconscious to a conscious level often bordering on parody. Obviously the lovers are married in the courtly chapel before going off together. Sleeping Beauty's first words reveal that she immediately knows she slept for a hundred years and that she is somewhat late in getting married: " 'Are you my prince? You sure took your time.' He was more ill at ease than she . . . she had plenty of time to contemplate [!] what she would say to him because the good fairy provided her pleasant dreams during this long sleep" (although the story didn't mention this before).

This fairy is always important for the conception of reality in Perrault's folktales: She puts the entire royal household to sleep by touching each person with her magic wand; in the German folktale a simple prick from the spindle produces the magical sleep, even fourteen years after the evil fairy pronounced the spell: Once the spell is cast, the fairy is no longer needed.

The French folktale is teeming with extraoradinary acts by fairies: In the "Cap o'Rushes" tale ("Peau d'âne"), for example, the fairy alone produces the happy ending: She appears as a *deus ex machina* through the hall ceiling in order to tell the princess's story to everyone present and to arrange the extravagant wedding dinner, including the invitations, herself. Similarly, the French "Cinderella" includes neither the tree on the mother's grave nor the bird who magically helps the girl. Cendrillon obtains the clothing she needs to go to the ball from a godmother, "qui etoit fée."[19] Concentrating miraculous events on the fairy alone reduces actual magic to an inevitable occurrence with its own laws. This shifts everything into a new, completely understandable system which almost entirely excludes wonders, except those caused by fairies.

In Perrault's "Riquet á la houppe," a purely psychological approach displaces the supernatural aspects of the fairies. In his subtle analysis of this tale, W. Th. Elwert explains that the fairies play a role here as well, but only as far as they provide the precondition for the plot; then they step back and appear again only at Riquet's banquet in the forest at the end. Otherwise they are excluded. The tale focuses on *people*, Riquet and the princess, and basically abandons the typical folktale tone. Humorous and playful aspects also recede; this is Perrault's most serious folktale. It almost limits irrationality more than a folktale can bear. The princess's declaration of her willingness to marry Riquet does not free him from the spell and transform him back; he merely *appears* to be transformed back to the princess. This is rationalistic, but it also constitutes the narrative's subtlety and depth. . . . Notice that Riquet divulges the miraculous means by which the princess (and not a fairy!) can bestow beauty on him only after the princess has confessed that she adores him. Changing the miracle into a spiritual process disposes of its miraculous aspects and makes it human.[20]

Perrault always tries to provide an explanation: For example, at the beginning of his Thumbling tale ("Le Petit Poucet") he writes, not without irony, "Once upon a time a woodsman and his wife had seven children, a bunch of little rascals. The oldest was just ten years old and the youngest seven. It may seem astonishing that the woodsman had so many children in such a short time, but his wife did the job quickly and never had less than two at a time." Perrault even makes the details psychological: For example, the preceding statement, "after drinking five or six shots," substantially subdues the suddenness with which the king in "Le chat botté" offers his daughter in marriage to the Marquis de Carabas.[21]

It also wouldn't occur to a German folktale narrator that a puss in boots cannot move over the rooftops as well as an ordinary cat. But the French narrator considers the situation more consciously and discovers its grotesqueness: "The tomcat was so frightened when he suddenly saw a lion standing in front of him that in a flash he fled along the edge of the roof, not without effort and danger because his boots were rather unsuited to walking on rooves." With such psychological realism and individualism, it is understandable that Walt Disney's folktale films more commonly rely on Perrault's texts for a model than the Grimms'.[22]

Perrault incorporated the folk speech of his day into the tales,[23] and his moral and satirical allusions are so closely bound to his time that a comparison between Perrault and Grimm does not provide an objective picture of the differences between French and German folktales. We can achieve this goal only by comparing more recent folktales recorded true to their tellers. Elisabeth Koechlin's study has renewed the attention given to this comparative method.[24] By restricting herself to a single narrative type, that of marriage to an animal, Koechlin has shown how much narrators imbue a narrative with national character. Using Koechlin's method, we can deal with the material motif by motif, placing directly comparable materials next to each other so that each statement is based on concrete, objectively verifiable observations. Despite certain generalizations, without which no investigation of national character can proceed, finer and more detailed results emerge than in Löwis of Menar's general comparison.

The modern French folktale is more realistic than its German counterpart. In the former, blank smiles greet magical elements. German and French folktales even have completely different settings: In Germany the hero encounters the animal in the characteristic folktale forest. The French folktale has no forest; instead we find a fair landscape with plentiful nut and fruit trees. Here demonic figures have improbable and grotesque, rather than monstrous, effects.

Marriage to an animal strikes the French narrator as disgraceful: Only the chance of material gain convinces humans to endure such shame. The priest renounces his Christian principles for money; parents abandon their last child only so they can own their rented piece of land. The heroine's sacrifice consists of willingly renouncing human company or its conveniences. Unlike the German folktale, the French does not require the heroine's unconditional devotion to disenchant her animal husband. In fact, her misshapen husband always offends her. In the German folktale the wolf doesn't hesitate to abduct the bride on his shaggy back. In the French folktale, on the other hand, the animal marriage follows the laws of bourgeois society: No marriage occurs without a wedding mass. But the wedding to the wolf receives a comic twist: In southern France the groom is hidden under a mysterious white linen. The priest's blessing often miraculously disenchants him; this corresponds to the power of the heroine's love in the German folktale. It is telling that in most French folktales, the animal husband always appears to his bride in true human form from the wedding day on: Happy coexistence with a demonic figure is unthinkable to the French.

This air of reality also surrounds humans in the French folktale. While only the chosen child has access to wonders in the German folktale, the French folktale binds the miraculous to everyday life: The French heroine is usually a farmer's daughter or a shepherdess, not a princess. In comparison to French folktale characters, German ones have no individual character; they are stylized human types. French tales break the pure type into living individuals: The heroine is a self-confident young lady who knows all of life's tricks and is nobody's fool; she demonstrates her love through boiling emotions at the moment of separation. In the German folktale she proves herself with her unshakable convictions. The German folktale heroine does not belong among ordinary people; she is more than an ideal, she is a model character. In contrast, French narrators create characters more like themselves; they try to depict the thoughts and feelings of their heroines with psychological zeal. A beautiful woman's whim, not a mysterious inner yearning, produces the strange wish for a talking rose. The prospect of riches and a high social position finally overcomes the heroine's doubts about agreeing to marry the animal. The more realistic the folktale, the more it depicts individual characters. Secondary figures become more important when the heroine loses her mark of distinction.

French folktales frequently end tragically because they consider real possibilities. The conciliatory ending is one of the main features of the German folktale. In France, however, reality has completely overtaken the world of magic: Sinister characters become more harmless, essential episodes more coincidental, magic more natural, wonders grotesque. Humorous elements grow stronger, and the tale of magic gradually shifts toward the folk novella. While the German stands enraptured in the face of the wonder, the French seem rather interested in the event which brings the long-known folktale into relationship with the real world; they consider how these events can occur in their personal environment. The French folktale heroine does not confront demonic powers while searching for her lost husband; the real world poses even harsher obstacles.

This ironic dissolution of the folktale's wonders creates a curious duality in French folktale characters which is, for the most part, foreign to the German folktale. The enlightened character rationally evaluates the folktale's wonders, creating an incongruity. Thus the results of Koechlin's study of the tale of marriage to an animal confirm the findings from our comparison of Perrault and Grimm.

Taking Löwis of Menar's and Koechlin's work together, disregarding their differing methods, we can make some important observations on reality in the German folktale. The German perception of folktale reality lies somewhere between western and eastern attitudes. A third investigation may also be necessary because the features that characterize the Russian folktale for Löwis of Menar differentiate the German from the French folktale for Koechlin. In comparison to the Russian material, German folktale narrators always demonstrate a more rational, realistic attitude. Belief in the folktale grows as we move east: The French rationalize, but Germans and, more so, Russians intuitively accept the folktale's relationship to folk belief, even if folktales are no longer "believed" in the rational sense.

Clearly we must still test whether comparisons of other tale types reveal similar characteristics and if other areas of folk tradition confirm Koechlin's findings. For example, can we also establish a similar east-west trend in the degree of reality found in the legend? However, the evidence we have so far does seem usable: Very generally, the French folktale shows a marked development of the individual and a greater tendency toward reality. From the German perspective, French collections frequently contain novellas and jest rather than actual tales of magic; in these texts the French draw the border between humor and seriousness quite differently than the Germans do. For example, the table-be-set is not a serious magical object; instead a piece of a shirt from the hero's beloved's grandmother produces the marvelous meal. The narrator of this tale clearly enjoyed depicting particularly grotesque scenes: The bagpipe which makes everyone dance is inappropriately tested during a funeral procession; even the corpse lifts the cover of the coffin and begins "to jump around and frolic as if he were possessed. . . ."[25]

The French narrator lacks a respectful fear of the folktale. Sarcasm gives the narrative an ironic character: When the cunning smith captures the devil, everyone is satisfied except the lawyers who are put out of business. The good folktale king dies "because he ate and drank too much and excessively amused himself." Sarcasm takes particular aim at women: When the poor hero loses all of his possessions, fate has it that on top of everything else he's still stuck with his wife.[26] The French tale's ironic emphasis of the numskull's awkwardness borders on making him appear mentally deficient, while the German folktale gladly believes that the lowly one actually turns out to be a brilliant hero, and that both his foolishness and his success belong to one and the same person.[27]

Long specialized evolutions have formed and fortified the peculiarities of German and French tradition. Thus it is all the more surprising that similar national psychological differences occur even without the burden of tradition: In a small experiment, the Grimms' version of "Little Red Riding-Hood" (KHM 26) was read to a first-year class at a girls' school consisting of children of German and French civil servants and military officers. After discussing the tale, the children were asked to draw pictures of the story. This experiment offers important methodological possibilities because we can rarely compare national characteristics under completely controlled conditions: All of the girls were the same age, heard the same explanations by the teacher, and saw the same illustrations. All of the German girls drew Little Red Riding-Hood with blond pigtails; the heroine's expression and posture were childishly naive and fearful. They portrayed the wolf as a figure with demonic power. In comparison, the wolf drawn by the ten-year-old French girls seems more like a domesticated dog; he completely lacks demonic traits. Little Red Riding-Hood shows no fear of him; rather, she greets him with a graceful bow. They drew the heroine as a self-confident young lady, not as a child; and naturally Little Red Riding-Hood has black hair under her dainty red cap, which is a coquettish contrast to the childish nightcap of her German counterpart. The children's drawings confirm what we already learned from the folktale collections.

French realism sometimes goes so far that otherwise reliable and precise German translators believe they must suppress overly rationalistic elements so that German readers will still accept the French folktale as a "folktale."[28] The same process occurs more unconsciously among the folk themselves. In migrating to Germany, French folktales sometimes have their rational features changed back into wondrous ones.[29]

The French folktale's deviation from our narrative concept of wonders often strikes us as wanton, unnecessary, or even absurd. The conscious, rational evaluation of miraculous episodes throughout the French folktale is quite the opposite of what we expect from a folktale. Of course, seen from the French perspective, the German folktale seems "undeveloped, childish, uninteresting, and, perhaps worse, humanly impossible."[30] Regardless which type one prefers, the attitude toward reality in the folktale offers a rare glimpse of national expression.

## MAGICAL THOUGHT AND MODERN CIVILIZATION

The folktale's original connection to ancient folk belief has not prevented the modern technological world from entering the story. This is not very surprising because the folk often perceive of technology as a sort of modern wonder. An airplane appears in a folktale collected by Matthias Zender in western Eifel [a region on the northern bank of the Mosel River],[1] and this is by no means an isolated case in the modern folktale. The hero of a Rhaeto-Romanic folktale, for example, moves from Tinizong to the Italian royal court in order to marry the princess, and then must complete two tasks within three days. To show their gratefulness, the dwarves with whom he shares his snack in the forest between Tinizong and Rona offer their help. The hero flies an airplane from Rome to Rona to fetch his helpers from the forest. He lands in the meadow behind the church in Rona, picks up the dwarves, and brings them to Rome, where they complete the difficult tasks for him.[2] The airplane has even found its way into Arabian folk narrative, where it replaces the flying carpet.[3] In a German version of "Bluebeard" the girl escapes in a blimp.[4]

In all of these cases, technology easily replaces older magical wonders because it is received with equal amazement. But more commonly, products of modern civilization enter the narrative completely unconsciously, without the narrator's intent. The folktale's tendency to adapt to the modern world is particularly clear in decorative features where outdated items are weeded out and replaced with modern ones. Technology often provides a basis for comparison: In a Rhaeto-Romanic version of "Six go through the Whole World" (Type 513A), for example, the hero and his supernatural helper arrive in a city; they go into a tavern, where they hear someone say the princess is "faster than a locomotive."[5] In other tales the princess uses a telephone.[6]

We are often told that the hero reads newspapers or books.[7] In a Rumanian folktale the kings make their decrees known in the newspaper.[8] Hinnerch and Binnerch, characters in a Hessian folktale, read in the newspaper that they can meet the princess at the great festival in Ziegenhain.[9] In Holstein a newspaper reports that the princess was stolen.[10]

In modern folktales the revolver supersedes older folktale weapons, such as the sword and the saber.[11] In an Albanian folktale, cannons fire a salute; Russian folktales also contain rifles and cannons (cf. KHM 54 and 70).[12] Ulrich Jahn had already noted at the close of the last century that guns and cannons that reload themselves the second they are fired replace the magical sword in his collection.[13] But by the second half of the twentieth century, even this is no longer considered a wonder.

The juxtaposition of magic and technology often creates anachronisms: For example, in a Silesian dragon-slayer tale, "the coachman lets his horses rest along the way; he puts a pistol to the princess's chest and threatens to shoot her if she does not swear that she will say that *he* killed the *dragon*."[14] In other versions of this tale, coffee[15] and a factory[16] appear along with the dragon.

In a folktale from western Eifel, witches are shot with a revolver; the hero in an Albanian folktale defends himself against the wrath of the *Lugáts* (the living dead) with heavier arms: He finds a bomb in the forest where soldiers had been fighting that morning. He takes it and drops it on the Lugáts: "The bomb went off, and the Lugáts jumped and farted across the field. They cried out: 'What has that human done to us? He has made us bald, blinded us, and tried to kill us!' "[17]

In a folktale recorded by Johann Jegerlehner in Upper Valais [a German-speaking region bordering on French Switzerland at the Rhône], the brave little tailor kills the bears by sitting in a cage in the forest and spraying every bear that comes by with gasoline until they are all dead.[18]

We encounter this mixture of typical folktale elements and modern civilization everywhere. The modern Greek folktale has all the comforts of the modern world, even beer halls and cafés. Women use sewing machines and sharp English scissors and paint their fingernails. Rich men are said to spend like "Americans."[19]

In a tale from Lorraine, the villain is turned over to the police and sentenced: "All of his gold and the furnishings from his robber's den were turned over to the state."[20] The police also investigate a crime in a Russian folktale that otherwise contains ancient motifs from folk belief such as the ordeal of the bier.[21] In a different Russian tale, the employees of a brewery get a good laugh out of the czar's desire to have the most beautiful maiden. Anyone signing a contract has a copy made. We also find the mercantile notion "The more consumption, the greater the profit"—no wonder coffee, matches, soap, and rubber shoes also appear![22]

Narrators replace older aspects of culture they no longer completely understand with modern ones. For example, in some recent tales the insolent princess tells King Thrushbeard that he isn't worthy enough to clean her shoes, instead of saying he can't unstrap them.[23] The modernization process often begins completely unconsciously when narrators reinterpret something they do not understand and introduce new explanations. In a folktale told among the Heanze people in Burgenland [east of Vienna], the king of India's daughter protects herself against the Indian custom of burning widows. But her father categorically explains that "a man needs his wife to cook for him in heaven as well and therefore you too shall be burned."[24]

It is striking how often school and instruction, completely unknown in older folktales, have found their way into the folktale in our age of "mass education." In a Bulgarian tale children go to school and even receive report cards.[25] In Portuguese versions of "The Singing Bones" (Type 780) the teacher inquires about a pupil who was killed by his mother and buried in the garden. The teacher takes the entire class to this garden during recess and a singing flower tells her about the murder.[26]

The hero of a Rhaeto-Romanic folktale "grew up, started school, and demonstrated extraordinary talent. He skipped all the grades. . . . After completing elementary school, he attended secondary schools; here, too, he skipped all the grades. . . . All the teachers, professors, and students adored him. . . ."[27] This model hero then disenchants his three brothers-in-law from their animal form.

A Greek folktale princess studies philosophy and becomes a hypochondriac from all the learning; in an Albanian folktale, instruction in foreign languages is part of a good education.[28] This represents a complete change in the heroic ideal: Brute strength, magic, intuition, and cunning no longer help heroes complete their tasks; knowledge has replaced magic as the ultimate power.

We established above that older folktales contain no written magic because they belong to a preliterate epoch. In newer tales, however, writing plays a large role. Even bureaucracy has found its way into the folktale: The hero who takes part in a race to the well is supposed to bring a certificate from the appropriate authorities to confirm his arrival at the finish line.[29] In a northern German folktale, the contestant must fetch a shepherd boy's baptismal certificate.[30] According to a Styrian tale, a passport is needed to enter hell.[31] Hansel gets the devil to certify in writing that he cannot dance.[32] In a Silesian folktale, the lord of the castle arranges a "nonpartisan commission" to choose who will be sacrificed to the dragon.[33] The tax commission appears in an Austrian narrative: The soldier has just built a castle with the help of a magical stick when the king's tax officer comes and demands the payment of a high property tax. The officials are told to physically enforce their demand if the soldier refuses to pay. However, the castle's owner chases away the king's troops with the help of soldiers he wishes forth. The tale ends by noting that "the owner of the castle paid no taxes from then on."[34]

Although modern technology, particularly the news media (newspaper, film, and radio), is replacing folktale telling and reading, these examples demonstrate that twentieth-century civilization also finds a home within the folktale. The modernization of the folktale, its various means of adapting to current reality, does not necessarily harm the inner belief in folktales. On the contrary, an uninterrupted belief in the folktale requires this external adaptation to modern realities. This process of maintaining belief is quite the opposite of modern rationalizing trends. We must always try to do justice to each folktale's unique references to reality by closely examining how they are used in the folktale.

Often folktales are rationalized not because people no longer believe in them but rather because they want to *continue* believing. H. Schlecht points out that people in the Harmersbach Valley of the Black Forest tell the story of the robber and his murdered women ("Bluebeard," Type 312) so believably that they might still consider it true today. They realistically reinterpret all the magical, unreal motifs. A story about a robber is far more credible than one about a witch or a *Schräcksli*.\* A perfectly normal egg replaces the magical egg or the key from which the girl cannot wipe the blood. The bride must carry the egg wherever she goes, and if she drops it in fright in the horrible chamber, she can no longer show it to the robber and is doomed. The third, smart sister wraps the egg up well so that it won't break if it hits the ground. This does indeed protect the egg, "and she wiped the blood off. . . ." She also does not put her sisters back together to bring them to life; instead she simply packs them in a trunk, which she later shows to the police as evidence. The arrest and execution of the robber at the story's end makes it even more realistic.[35]

We can make the same observations for the Upper Saxon folktales collected by Friedrich Sieber: They tend to be concise, using only the most essential motifs; marvelous episodes are so subdued that the folktale could qualify as a report of experience. The tales even open with pregnant legendary statements: "When I was still in school . . ."; "Some robbers used to live in the mountains behind Holbe"; "In a village between Eisenberg and Naumburg. . . ."[36]

Modern technology has also found its way into believed legends and living folk belief. This modernization does not arrest the existing belief in the narrative, even in the Swabian legend which reports that "after Frau Geiger's father died, she got an electric shock from his funeral wreath, telling her that he had not yet been delivered." A different legend reports that once a "motorcycle stalled . . . but there was nothing wrong with it. . . ." It was possessed. Hermann Bausinger's collection from northeastern Württemberg alone contains three legends which question and explain electric lights suddenly going on or off.[37] I have collected legends about ghost bike riders and the devil driving a car. According to a legend from around Basel, a "railroad demoness" haunts a railroad tunnel.[38]

According to a tale from western Eifel, an electric fire-breathing dragon lived during the time of Napoleon I: "In order to scare the people nearby, they kept a fire-breathing dragon on the mountain. Electricity then slept for 100 years before we got it again."[39] The wild band that roars through the air now uses modern means of flight: "A hot-air balloon containing the wild band flew by."[40] The wild hunt becomes a "truck full of drunks."[41] In these cases technology makes the wonder more real rather than unreal.

We must always turn to the Grimms' tales as a standard by which we judge how much more recent folktale collections have been rationalized,

---

\*A demon which appears in the mountains of southwest Germany.—Trans.

but this is not an absolutely reliable measure, because the rationalization process began in some German folktales in the early nineteenth century. In some cases the Grimms' version is more rational than the original folk versions still in circulation today. In "The Lilting, Leaping Lark" (KHM 88), for example, the sun and moon have realistic astronomical features: They shine at the appropriate time, and the heroine must climb up high into a gusty wind to reach them. In the true folktale, the sun and moon are supernatural demonic creatures who live with their mother in a little house in the forest. The old woman stands at the hearth and greets visitors at the door. She often sits next to the light in the den and spins during the evening. Her sons are often wild cannibals, yet they are easily moved by the heroine's misfortune and gladly provide the help she requests.[42] The Nordic version of "Cinderella" does not contain the tree on the mother's grave found in KHM 21; instead the girl's mother comes out of the grave herself and hands her daughter the marvelous gifts.[43]

The queen bee in KHM 62 can help the hero recognize the true princess only because she had eaten honey. In contrast, the grateful bees in a Styrian folktale help with purely supernatural abilities when they buzz in the hero's ears, "the one in the middle, the one in the middle." The rational use of honey to recognize the correct woman is absent.[44] The hunter in KHM 122 says, "Now that *is* strange; it's just what the little old lady said would happen." In other words, he no longer simply accepts the marvelous events without question.

The German folktale has become increasingly rational in the time since the Grimms' collection. This is quite clear in Ludwig Bechstein's unoriginal, somewhat trite revision of the Grimms' KHM. Bechstein completely rationalizes the magic mirror in "Snow White" (KHM 53): "The mirror didn't flatter; like *all* mirrors it told the truth."[45] Bechstein replaces the end of the Grimms' "Snow White" (where the stepmother must dance to death in red-hot shoes) with a strong image, but a cheap allegory immediately destroys its effectiveness: "A poisonous worm came and ate out the evil queen's heart, and this worm was envy."

We sometimes don't even consciously recognize very early forms of rationalization because we have long since come to take more recent elements of the narratives for granted. The shift from simple acceptance of supernatural events to viewing them as abnormal represents the earliest recognizable rationalization of the folktale. For example, self-transformation by the hero occurs only in a few exceptional European folktales. By limiting self-transformation to sorcerers, trolls, fairies, and witches, narrators seek a rational explanation for this magical ability. The magical helper who plays a role in so many of our folktales became necessary only when the hero could no longer perform magic himself.

The folktale takes a different path of rationalization by giving supernatural beings human form. The post-Grimm evolution of Mother Holle (KHM 24) offers a graphic example of how demons are humanized: Mother Holle becomes a little old lady or a beggar, or an old man appears in her place.[46]

In more recent versions of KHM 14, the three spinners sometimes appear as old women rather than supernatural beings.[47] In many cases the evil stepmother replaces a witch or fairy.[48] The devil's grandmother becomes a proper, completely human grandmother, and "Lord Dragon" occasionally replaces the dragon. Modern narrators freely put robbers in the giants' place. For example, the Grimms' "Brave Little Tailor" (KHM 20) contains giants, while a version from Upper Valais replaces them with robbers, but it still depicts them as giants who can grind rocks to powder during the test of strength.[49] In the same collection, the Griffin (Type 610; also see KHM 165) has become the leader of a gang of robbers.[50] Wilhelm Wisser also reports that one of his informants enjoys changing giants into robbers in an attempt to divest the folktales of their marvelous character.[51] The monster's house in the forest becomes the murderers' den. Energy, bravery, governmental authorities (police or militia), and logic, not supernatural helpers, supernatural powers, or miracles, lead to the apprehension of the robbers as the folktale becomes a crime story.[52]

Serious numinous creatures can become humorous figures; for example, the dumb, outwitted devil has lost his earlier numinous reality. Capturing souls finally becomes mere sport for the devil, and he no longer embodies evil.[53] This evolution into jest is also a type of rationalization, one that changes serious belief into comedy. We can see this process at work in many motifs: The trickster in farcical tales fools people who still believe in the truth of dreams by making up false ones. Even the figures from saints' legends must give way to the rationalistic spirit, and today Old Fritz [King Friedrich II of Prussia] replaces the wandering deities Jesus and St. Peter.[54]

Of course, we can speak of the rationalization of the folktale only when its entire perception of reality has changed and the marvel's magic causality has been completely eliminated. While some intellectuals have now abandoned rationalism, the folk are mostly rationalists today. Skepticism about the supernatural has indeed entered the plots of some recently collected folktales: In a tale about a poor fisherman's son collected in Lorraine,[55] for example, an animal's white beard hairs combined with *thinking about the donor* make a human run so fast that no animal in the world can catch him. The animal hairs alone no longer effect part-for-whole magic.

Modern folk narrators no longer take it for granted that animals can talk. For example, "Franz was quite stunned when he first heard the fox speak. He didn't know whether the fox had been caught and trained [!] or whether it was an enchanted animal."[56] In a folktale collected by Bünker, the transformation of the animal bridegroom back into human form seems astonishing and strange: "I would have never thought that a wolf could become king," says the bride's father when he hears her story.[57] Narrators become skeptical even when depicting animal transformations in more believable legends. Zender provides a fine example:

The narrator of legend 847 in my *Folk Legends of the Westeifel*, who despite his folk beliefs tended toward realism, portrayed every transformation of a

person into an animal as an extraordinarily difficult affair. Even the devil
expends considerable effort to make someone invisible. This narrator saw
a similarity between human transformation and an operation: "The devil
made him invisible by dressing and bandaging him." . . .[58]

In the modern folktale the animal who seeks devoted love to disenchant
him is not the victim of a curse; rather, he suffers from a sort of birth
defect.[59] By promising to pay one of her father's workers a good price if he
disenchants her bear-bridegroom, the miller's daughter, who does not
believe she is capable of doing it herself, completely ignores the central idea
behind disenchantment.[60] A poor boy declares himself ready to stand
watch at the prince's coffin for five hundred marks. Since the undertaking is
very dangerous, he adds the condition that the money will be paid to his
mother in the event of his death. And he keeps checking to see if the
promise is still valid.[61]

In his version of "Cinderella," Henssen's narrator, Egbert Gerrits, limits
the world of marvels to the talking bird; the folktale is almost a folk novella
free of the supernatural.[62] The magic mirror that reveals distant and hidden
things is replaced by a telescope.[63] A pulley block leads down to the
princess in the underworld.[64] A folktale from Lorraine vividly describes a
knight's spooky experiences but resolves everything quite harmlessly in
the end: "He had fallen asleep in front of the castle and *dreamed* it all."[65]

The journey to the water of life eventually becomes a race for mineral
water (!) in a Rhaeto-Romanic folktale: "The king then gave the laborer and
his daughter each a little jar, and they had to walk a hundred kilometers to
fetch mineral water. Whoever arrived first would win."[66] In a humorous
combination of old and new conceptions, the mysterious herb of life turns
out to be an ointment when the doctor fills the prescription tied around the
rabbit's neck.[67]

The combination of magical and rational explanation is always a sign of
uncertainty. In a folktale from the Saar region, the queen who falls in the
water does not come out in the body of a duck (as in KHM 13); instead
pirates pull her out. The narrator of this folktale cannot accept a dead queen
who returns during the night, and therefore doesn't allow her to die. Thus
the living queen returns to the palace at night; she had asked the pirates,
who wanted to keep her, if she could return to her relatives one more time.
But to motivate her to leave the palace each morning, the narrator has her
appear bound in a chain, which the king eventually cuts loose. This
provides a completely rational explanation for the old plot and makes the
motif of magical disenchantment through decapitation completely mean-
ingless.[68]

We have offered a few examples of the general process of rationalization
which frequently plays a role in the folktale's evolution. The last type of
rationalization depicted leads toward the decline of the folktale. But rationalizing also proves the the folktale was not always fictional. On the

contrary, we can be quite sure it was originally believed, because if the folktale originally has been designed for mere entertainment, it would not need to adapt to the changing picture of reality. The folktale's acquisition of modern elements, its adaptation to very recent reality, and the distinction of folk texts from the idealized style of romanticism all show its inner strength and cannot simply be written off as the "decline" of this form of folklore.

# VI.

## The Folktale as a Mirror of the Real World

### THE SIGNIFICANCE OF TIME AND PLACE

Almost every collection offers examples of how specific times and places give folktales a local coloring. Although most of these connections to certain locales and times appear in the folktale's decorative elements, they often reveal a great deal about the narrative's and the narrator's picture of reality.

Even everyday events such as eating and drinking occasionally show unique regional influences: Folktales from the Schild Mountains [a German-speaking region near Budapest] serve up local specialties such as Grundbirn, Nockerl, dicke Fisoln, and Knödel.[1] In Pomerania, folktale characters enjoy "Kliebensuppe" made from fresh flour,[2] and in a Transylvanian folktale the mother gives her real daughter "Eierbriegelchen" for breakfast while the poor stepchild must eat moldy bread and "Paluckes."[3]

Regional character shapes everything from superficial elements, such as eating and drinking, to religion: Several Pomeranian folktales are set in the olden days, "when people were still so dumb they were Catholic." Narrators from Holstein demonstrate their Protestantism by including confirmations and Sunday sermons in their tales. In folktales from Lorraine, in contrast, people go to mass, while in Austrian folktales they pray the rosary, and the Angelus bell rings in the early morning.[4] Albanian folktales depict Muslim, Christian, and Jewish "Dschinn." The Christian ones view the Muslims as evil and vice versa; the Jews are supposedly the most evil.[5]

Folktales also occasionally reflect regional historical and political realities. For example, in the Swabian folktale "The Four Brothers" (Type 513A, "Six go through the Whole World"; cf. KHM 71), the king of Prussia is very sick. The herb of life obtained by the fast runner cures him. The king offers to reward him with as much money as a person can carry. The four brothers put the entire contents of the Prussian king's treasure chamber into a large sack, which strong Michel easily carries. Jörg blows the troops the king sends after them into the sea, where they all die. The Swabian narrator enjoys making a fool of the powerful king of Prussia.[6] The German-speaking devil in Danish folktales is also a political commentary.

In a folktale from western Eifel, giants steal hay from a farmer every night. The lowly hero, who finally gets to keep watch, joins up with the giants, but then leaves them because "the king of Prussia" is holding maneuvers. The hero defeats the princess in three races riding horses the giants gave him, then turns down the prize (marrying her). The king of Prussia makes it known "that all men from the age of fifteen to forty must appear in Bebrich," where the hero is recognized by a scar and is married to the princess. The narrator adapts this folktale to the local milieu so well that even the editor of the collection did not identify it as a variant of the "golden boy" and grouped it with "fictional stories."[7]

Even a collection which has found such a general distribution throughout Germany and beyond, such as the Grimms', shows in strong measure local and regional characteristics of Hesse, particularly in the first volume of the first edition. The unique regional character expresses itself through peculiar words and items such as the "Fretsche" in "The Frog King" (KHM 1) and the "Itsche" in "The Three Feathers" (KHM 63). The three little men in the woods (KHM 13) and the name Kürdchen, i.e., Konrad (KHM 89), are also Hessian. In traditional costume, the Hessian woman braids[8] her hair and puts it in a bun. The princess wears her hair in this manner when she is the goose girl (KHM 89). The devil with the three golden hairs has an authentic Hessian "Ellermutter" (i.e., granny—KHM 29).[9] A Hessian trait in the KHM which cannot be overlooked is the use of *Ei* to begin numerous sentences (cf. KHM 4, 7, 8, 20, 45, 77, 95, 99, 114, 118, 128, 130, and 149).

The local landscape often creates a standard for a region's narratives. Icelandic folktales depict Iceland with its glaciers, cliffs, lava fields, fjords, and alpine pastures.[10] Heath, horse pasture, and forest often provide the earthly and otherworld setting in Wisser's Holstein folktales. Grudde's east Prussian tales take place in the village and in the forest. We find hills dotted with castles in folktales from Lorraine, and in the Alps folktales take place in rocky glens and alpine meadows.[11] In a folktale from Grisons, the fairies' crystal palace stands "on the Julier" [a local mountain].[12]

Of course, not only Germany has forests, yet this landscape has a more essential function in German tradition than in any other folktales. This is certainly not simply an indication that Germany encompasses much forested land. Probably no folktale tellers have a closer relationship to forests than the Indians of the South American tropics, but the forest does not play nearly as large a role there as it does in the German folktale. For South American Indians, the forest is the normal landscape, while for Germans it still represents the wild surroundings of cultivated lands and thus can provide the primary stage for magic and robbers.[13]

Local coloring is particularly important as an index of origin for folktales from cultural border zones. For example, the motif of milking the horse in the folktales collected by Alfred Karasek has Slavic, eastern features. And St. George's salutation to St. Peter in an Albanian tale, "Allah be with you," clearly reveals the text's origin.[14]

Local coloring is even more striking in folktales from lands very different from our own. All French folktales are set in France: When the young man leaves home, he goes on a "tour de France" and ends up in Paris, where the king of France's blond daughter is peering out of the Louvre.[15] The "king" is obviously the king of France, and the king in Russian folktales is always the czar, just as every other land described in Russian folktales is ruled by a czar. Tribal societies adapt their folktales to the local environment just as much: Heroes of African folktales are usually successful hunters and chiefs. In folktales from Oceania, the hero reaches the highest level of the village's secret cult.

The heroes of animal tales also change from country to country: In African tales, tortoise outsmarts elephant in much the same way that the hedgehog does the hare in German folktales (KHM 187; and as the tortoise does the hare in American lore).[16] In southern and parts of central Europe, the donkey corresponds to the northern European horse.[17] The helpful animal in Bantu folktales is a buffalo.[18] In Malaysian folktales, a dwarf deer plays Reineke Fox's role.[19] East Asian folktales change the wolf from European versions of "Little Red Riding-Hood" and "The Seven Young Kids" into a tiger or a panther. The tiger is the primary animal throughout southern Chinese narratives: He is the grateful and the helpful animal, the animal bridegroom as well as the werewolf; in short, he fills all the functions we can expect of an animal in the folktale.[20]

When a folktale moves from one people to another, even the most minute details adopt the new local color: The kind girl in the Indian version of "Mother Holle" must coat the house with cow dung; this corresponds to the Indian concept of menial housework.[21] African folktales reflect the fact that women, not men, tend the fields.[22] A narrative's ethics also depend a great deal on the particular country's values. For example, it would not be appropriate to judge the sexual relations depicted in southern Chinese folktales according to our standards. Nor may we simply label these narratives "jest." Rather, one must know that in southern China people believe that virginity is dangerous. People avoid marrying virgins, and a woman's first child must often be from someone other than her husband.[23]

Modern Oriental folktales provide a particularly precise model of reality; this is already clear in the *Arabian Nights*. Professional public folktale tellers in the Near East, the Turkish Meddâh, prefer to depict scenes from folklife; they do not transplant their listeners to a fabular world, they show them the world as it really is:[24] the Oriental marketplace with its crafts, bazaars, and coffeehouses, business, trade, and small merchants, the slave trade, life in the harem, caravans through the desert—all of this plays a role and is depicted realistically.[25]

The folktales in the *Arabian Nights* and modern Oriental folktales are incomprehensible without a knowledge of Oriental practices and Arabian folklife: Childless parents wish for a child "even if it is only a girl,"[26] because people really desire only male descendants. Out of sorrow over the loss of his beloved, the hero puts on a leather gown and roves about as a dervish.[27] The princess "lies back and falls asleep" in the very spot she ate dinner, just like the narrator himself, who has only a den and no beds.[28]

Josef Henninger has investigated the milieu of the *Arabian Nights* and how it reflects the practices of various cultural groups.[29] He finds that this collection frequently depicts urban environments: The heroes almost always come from the city; if they are not princes, they are usually rich merchants or sons of merchants. Trade, business trips, and profit dominate their thoughts. The tales usually depict the position of women as it was in medieval Islamic cities, and in many cases as it actually was until very recently. For example, the father's complete, independent power over his daughter's marriage indicates the female's subordinate position.[30]

We also find traces of an older nomadic past, particularly in regard to family law, in these tales. For example, they have a predilection for marriage to relatives, particularly marriage to cousins, which is frequently presented as normal. This corresponds to racial pride and the specifically Bedouin concern for maintaining pure blood; thus it has nothing to do with the urban milieu of the harem. Recommendations of monogamy found in individual narratives, although the Koran allows four legitimate wives and an unlimited number of slaves, also contrast with urban ideas.[31] Moreover, a betrayed man's right to kill his untrue wife in certain tales is an old Bedouin right based on ancient tribal practices.[32] Henninger also identifies the importance of the clan, vendettas, the father's brother's special role, and other elements as part of this older cultural layer in the *Arabian Nights*.

In contrast to the Oriental folktale's deliberate emphasis on realistic elements, European narrators usually add local coloring unconsciously. Of course, some of our folktale collections do include conscious localizations, making the generalization "The folktale takes place everywhere and nowhere" inapplicable. Even a few of the Grimms' tales mention specific locations, such as east India (KHM 137), Farther Pomerania (KHM 152), Bremen (KHM 27), Hohenfurt (KHM 82), Keuterberg (KHM 96), and Mosel (KHM 119). The Swabian folktales collected by Ernst Meier, an Orientalist from Tübingen, around the middle of the nineteenth century also prefer connections to specific places, much like the historical legend. The tale about the boy who served in hell for ten years begins: "In the village of Bodelshausen, which lies on the road between Rottenburg and Hechingen, there was once a man whose wife died and left him six ill-bred children. . . ."[33] A Swabian "table-be-set" tale begins, "In the old days a miller who lived a few hours from Stuttgart, near the place where Hohenheim lies today, could not get anywhere with his mill. . . ."[34]

Unfortunately, older collections are not exact transcriptions and usually lack the narrator's characteristic comments; thus we cannot determine whether these localizations suggest that the folktale and legend were once more closely related or whether editors simply added this feature. More recent narrators, however, employ localizations to bring their folktales more into line with the demands audiences generally place on a narrative these days. Thus even purely fantastic stories are often adapted to the modern sense of time and place, much as memorates are: Husum, Bergen auf Rügen, Kolberg, Nordhausen, Danzig, Königsberg, Leipe bei Löwen (Lausitz), Breslau, and other cities are named.[35] In a Silesian folktale, lion and fox live "in the forest near Beneschau," and the lion fishes with his tail in the Prezehima pond.[36] In one version of "The Clever Peasant Girl" (Type 875; cf. KHM 94), the dramatis personae are Old Fritz in Berlin, master painter Schulte's laborer in Haselünne, and his daughter Marie.[37]

Localizations are particularly common in the folktales collected in Lorraine by Merkelbach-Pinck. For example, the witch-queen is brought to Ohlich.[38] In a tale set in the city of Namur and its surroundings, the sorcerer's apprentice who is changed into a dove flies over the Bischwald pond on his way to Bitscherland.[39] French words, names, and salutations round off the local milieu of Lorraine. These tales also set distant kingdoms in concrete geographic locations: One tale ends in Paris;[40] another starts in Hamburg and then shifts to Berlin.[41] Nepal and America are also mentioned. Moreover, the tales include strikingly exact distances and dates: In one instance a church is ten kilometers away from the palace; the servant is twenty meters behind his master;[42] the prince meets the forest fairy after exactly eight days;[43] and a war begins on June 23rd.[44]

The modern sense of reality also takes hold of our folktale with exact statements of time; in recent collections, specific times are not uncommon. Gottfried Henssen's narrator Gerrits has his brave little tailor fight against the Russians at Sevastopol,[45] and another narrative begins, "It was 1812, after the Battle of Leipzig."[46]

Austrian folktales contain similar designations of time, although they are still sometimes formulaic. For example, in a narrative about a grateful dead man, the king's oldest son rode for about seven months; one year passes before the king makes his next decree; it also takes the next son seven months to reach his goal, and a second year passes before the youngest son comes forward. He needs only six months to travel the same route that his brothers followed two years earlier. The hero then rides on for several weeks. He helps a dead man finally rest in peace and then rides again for fourteen days; he is also underway for a couple of weeks on his next adventure. The time required for the following episodes is also always calculated in weeks and months.[47]

A version of this tale type recorded by Bünker in Carinthia contains similar statements of time: The older sons have been gone for three years when the youngest sets out after them; he meets a wild man whose wife had died six weeks earlier and begins working for him; three weeks later the wild man must go on a journey for one day in order to take care of some business; the hero is allowed to stay in hell for only three minutes; the hero is supposed to live with a hermit in the forest for seven years, but "the time passed frightfully slowly; a day seemed longer than a week to him."[48]

Familiar Grimms' tales (e.g., "Sleeping Beauty") often simply ignore long periods of time; they seem to lack the dimension of time.[49] But modern, living folktales do not necessarily abide by such artistic laws or by the literary norm of a "genre" as found in reworked collections.

The folktale has also never been afraid to seize upon actual *historical figures*. As the historical facts fade from the folk's memory, the folktales depicting them become more fantastic. Our only sources for discovering how classical and medieval folktales treated history are literary works (Alexander, Dietrich of Bern, Artus, *Gesta Romanorum*), but modern, living folk narratives offer us almost the same picture:[50] For example, Emperor Trajan plays the king with an animal's ears in Greece, where he lives on in folk tradition as "King Trojan with the Goat Ears."[51] In the Near East we find folktale-like narratives about Solomon and Alexander the Great, and in Turkestan narratives Alexander continues his conquest of the water of life today.[52] Solomon and King David appear in Arabian-influenced African Swahili folktales.[53]

A knowledge of historical details is sometimes a prerequisite for recognizing historical figures in the folktale: For example, 'Alî ez-Zaibak, the hero of the Arabian rogue and robber stories, was the actual leader of the rogues of Bagdad in 1052/53.[54] The name of Albanian folktale giants, the "Difs," comes from the notorious Catalonian mercenaries whom Emperor Andronikos II summoned for help in 1302 and whom the emperor employed to fight against the Turks in Asia Minor (1305–1307). They continued to battle and murder on their own, terrorizing Thracia, Macedonia, and Tessalonia, and finally became pirates on Greek shores and islands during the fourteenth and fifteenth centuries. The Albanian folktale figure can thus be dated as far back as six hundred years.[55]

The magical viking Járnhauss, who often appears as a wild ruffian and sorcerer in ancient Icelandic literature (e.g., the saga of Flóamanna, ch. 15), lives on as a three-headed giant in modern Icelandic folktales.[56] Another typical figure in Icelandic folktales has a kernel of historical truth, namely, the "Utilegumenn," the marginal outlaws in "outcast" tales. The once-real outlaws have gradually become demonic figures: They can cause bad weather, fog, and snow, they can tell the future, and, like trolls, they steal women and livestock.[57]

Various historical personalities have been suggested as the source of Charles Perrault's Barbe-bleue. Eugène E. Bossard combed historical sources in an effort to trace the folktale back to the cruel Gilles de Rais.[58] In any case, in Vendée, Anjou, and Brittany, people will still show you the palace and room where Bluebeard murdered his wives.

In the tale "Emperor Maximilian and the Lucky Boy," the emperor opposes the hero according to the tale type's pattern ("The Rich Man and His Son-in-Law"). But the historical echo influences the tale enough that it depicts the adversary sympathetically. Emperor Maximilian provides order in the country, takes action against bandits, and sends the boy to the best school.[59]

Among modern German historical figures, Friedrich the Great is most notable. In folk narratives he becomes the legendary wild hunter and a member of the wild band, a comical figure and a granter of wishes. Theodor Fontane calls him the peasant's Lord, and they speak of him as if he were still alive.[60] Old Fritz appears as King Thrushbeard in a Holstein folktale in Wisser's manuscript collection,[61] and we also find him in a Hessian version of the tale about the good trade (cf. KHM 7).[62] In an Austrian version of KHM 97, he is the youngest of the three brothers and is called Prince Fritz of Prussia; his brothers are named Prince Johann and Prince Josef—in other words, this tale is so well adapted to the Austrian milieu that it names members of the Hapsburg family.[63]

A figure such as Friedrich the Great whom folk narrative includes in such a variety of roles makes it clear that reality can vary a great deal from tale to tale. Naming historical personalities makes even folktale wonders more believable. Regarding folktales about Old Fritz collected in the border region between North-Rhine and Westphalia known as the Bergisches Land, Gottfried Henssen notes that "many narrators consider their content, no matter how fantastic it occasionally is, to be within the realm of possibility."[64] Geographic and historical statements can, however, also be conscious inventions by the narrator designed to use the audience's existing belief to increase the narrative's effectiveness.

Thus the folktale's statements of place and time also fluctuate between reality and fiction. The external historical world seems to originally have entered the folktale as a believed reality. The pseudohistorical folktale developed secondarily. In each individual case we must pose the question anew: Does the real world elevate the folktale's believability, or does it, in contrast, underscore the narrative fiction? We still find both types of thought in modern folk tradition.


## THE SOCIAL MILIEU

In the course of the nineteenth and twentieth centuries, not only the folktale itself but also the social stratification of its bearers went through critical changes. Collectors once spent most of their time in rural spinning dens, but according to recent collectors, the modern folktale teller is rarely a landed farmer. Craftsmen are represented in greater numbers today,[1] but we find most folktales among the lowest classes of the population. It is fascinating to search the most important recent collections for information pertaining to the narrators' occupations and social classes; this background information is also essential if we are to consider the social reality depicted in folktales.

Wisser found his Holstein stories predominantly among *Katenleute,* i.e., the lowest workers on a farm who live in the stall, as well as among day laborers and their widows, fishermen, basket weavers, night watchmen, weavers, hired servants, woodsmen, cowhands, and highway workers; less commonly skilled laborers, masons, cobblers, and tailors told the tales, and other informants include a boilerman, a beer carrier, pensioners, gardeners, factory workers, rock pounders, a half-blind former cabinetmaker, people from the poorhouse, and bell ringers. Wisser rarely met people who could tell folktales among actual farmers as well as among the "educated."[2] The preceding generation of collectors had similar experiences in Low Germany: Day laborers and servants, not farmers, told Jahn's folktales published in 1891.[3] Innkeepers and quarrymen, as well as small farmers, factory workers, railroadmen, merchants, hunters, shoemakers, masons, lowly agricultural workers who protect the crops from animals, carpenters, and low-level civil servants, are the narrators in Dittmaier's collection from the lower Sieg River.[4]

In eastern and southern Germany the picture is essentially the same: Peuckert's informants for his Silesian folktales were farmhands and female laborers.[5] Karl Storch's texts from Egerland were told by retired people, street sweepers, and widows of miners and poormen.[6] A worker in a knitwear factory, an embroiderer, a railroad linesman, a herdsman, a retired steelworker, factory workers, day laborers, stonecutters, bricklayers, odd-jobbers, woodcutters, and a soldier, among others, narrate the folktales collected by Merkelbach-Pinck in the German Lorraine. The narrators frequently practice itinerant trades (tailors, potters, and tinkers); one informant was a peddler.[7]

H. Schlect's collection mentioned above confirms that on large, rich farms, people rarely tell tales anymore. The modern large farmer does not want anything to do with folktales, and there are also few narrators among factory workers. Most narrators on the farm are small farmers and day laborers. However, most folktale bearers do not live on the farm; they are people who are often on the road and come into contact with others: mailmen, people who deliver wedding invitations, town criers, and craftsmen with a clientele that wants to be entertained or who do work on the farm, e.g., carpenters, masons, and cabinetmakers. Shoemakers, tailors, basketmakers, and kegmakers also enjoy narrating. Among women, midwives, seamstresses, and knitters are the primary narrators.[8]

Ernst Meier obtained numerous items in his Swabian collection from a blind man from Bühn, near Tübingen.[9] Invalid soldiers, traveling journeymen, elderly day laborers, bricklayers, basket weavers, sextons, and women who gather wood are the narrators of the Styrian folktales collected by Father Pramberger. Pramberger recorded his most beautiful texts from a sixty-year-old woman beggar, the "dog-girl," who wandered through the upper Murg Valley dressed in rags, accompanied by three or four small dogs, seeking alms from farmers. Other narrators include Winkler the beggar, the "blind shepherd," and "crooked Alois," the son of a maid who toiled through life mending shoes.[10] Viktor von Geramb identifies, among others, woodsmen, umbrella makers, and peddlers, women who gather berries, herders, apprentices, and beggars as narrators.[11] Tobias Kern, a street sweeper from Ödenburg who is completely illiterate, narrates all 122 entries in Bünker's collection from Burgenland (Austria).[12]

The landowning class of farmers thus no longer bears folktales; instead the lower social classes, the toilsome and burdened little people, the village's poor, tell folktales. Little attention has been paid to these socio-psychological questions,[13] even though the narrators' status and occupation are the primary determinants of the folktale's social reality.

The advent of published folktales seems to have sped the confinement of the circle of narrators to the lower classes, and the shift in the social milieu in the narratives themselves clearly corresponds to this development. Even certain elements of the Grimms' tales seem to have already pointed in this direction: "Hans in Luck" (KHM 83) and "The Twelve Lazy Servants" (KHM 151a) are clearly servants' tales. The milieu of journeymen provides the basis for "The Two Traveling Companions" (KHM 107); KHM 131 depicts a broommaker's courtship. "Clever Gretel" (KHM 77) is a tale about a cook. The heroes of many other tales are wandering journeymen (KHM 106, 120), servants (KHM 60), or the children of broommakers and woodsmen (KHM 15, 99, and 169). Kitchen boys and shepherds are favorite heroes (KHM 152), and in general every "youngest child" and "numskull" is a socially oppressed person. The heroines are often poor servant girls (KHM 123) and foundlings (KHM 51). Cinderella (KHM 21) and many other figures mirror the narrators themselves. Courtship of a girl from a higher or lower social class and other problems caused by unequal birth are constantly recurring themes in the Grimms' tales.

In more recent collections, the folktale's picture of this social reality becomes even sharper. The narrator's unconscious adaptation of the reality in which he lives, not a conscious effort to make the tales more realistic, usually accounts for this reflection of reality. For example, in the folktales narrated by peasants, the princess regains her prince's love by hiring herself out as a maid in the palace and being subjected to lowly work; but in the narrative told by Bünker's street sweeper, which takes place in an urban environment, she works as a household maid.[14]

In eighteen of the twenty-one folktales told by a rural Hessian shoe-maker, the heroes are the children of peasants or craftsmen.[15] Traveling journeymen and musicians, drivers, and sons of day laborers disenchant in Grudde's collection from east Prussia. A poor girl in a Styrian folktale, whose father died suddenly, leaving her in great need, goes to a woman in the forest and asks her if she knows an enchanted prince whom she could disenchant.[16]

It is no coincidence that people from the lower classes, the boys who pave streets and "hen-girls,"[17] acquire kingdoms, or at least a rich step-father, in folktales. The social climb is the essential element of these tales; the hero of a folktale from Burgenland emphasizes this as a postscript: "Instead of millers we're royalty now, and we'll stay that way."[18]

Democratic elements have also recently found their way into folktales which were previously completely monarchic. In a modern Greek folktale, a prince demands that the pasha's daughter eat at his table; he is liberal and wants to live like a European. In a Bulgarian folktale a hussar officer plays the czar's role.[19] According to an east Prussian tale, the owl flies only at night because it is "communist" and can't show itself during the day. The owl opposes the election of a king of the birds: "No, no, we don't want a king!"[20] Bausinger recorded a Swabian folktale from an eight-year-old boy about "the president of Germany" who "drives around the world in his diesel Mercedes Benz".[21] But republican titles and offices rarely outweigh the glitter of folktale kingdoms.

Folktale characters do not always wish for the social climb into royalty; folktales often remain within a lower social milieu and depict this culture very accurately. Fantastic and real folktale situations reflect the limited physical and intellectual environment within which simple people live. For example, Henssen's narrator Gerrits replaces the prince in "Cinderella" with a rich miller's son.[22] An oral version of "The Frog King" recorded in southern Egerland dialect (in Sudetenland) transfers the events to the milieu of poor people: A day laborer's daughter, not a princess, must take the frog to bed with her.[23] In another tale from southern Egerland, Iron Hans (called "the wild man" here) is not captured by a king and his retinue and put in a cage in the palace's courtyard; a hunter catches him and "locks him in the cellar at home. The hunter planned on showing him to the others on Sunday."[24] The Styrian Sleeping Beauty is a child from the village, and during her magical sleep a steer walks around the house and doesn't let anyone in. Fearing a magical prophecy, the peasant has "all spinning wheels brought to the woodshed and destroyed." The child pricks herself on a nanny's spindle, and a simple lad awakes and disenchants her.[25] The narrators are often so needy that they cannot use their own life as a model for folktale happiness. In a tale from a collection of German folktales since Grimm, a "wedding is celebrated as loudly and joyously as it is in eternity."[26]

Folktales often depict great poverty and need. The journeyman tailor in KHM 115 was so poverty-stricken "that he didn't have a single penny for food." A poor cobbler goes into the forest to hang himself because he can't feed his eight children.[27] When not the typical number of three, folktale characters, like the poor, usually have quite a few children: "Poor people always have many children," reports an east Prussian folktale (cf. KHM 42).[28] In KHM 44 the hero's parents are so poor they can't find a godfather for the child. Not only Hansel and Gretel (KHM 15) don't have their daily bread: People often dream of eating white bread.[29] Indeed, bread is so precious that the hungry tailor in KHM 107 trades both of his eyes for a piece of it. Narrators of southern Italian and Sicilian folktales sometimes try to soothe the audience's envy when they hear about the food at a wedding celebration.[30]

The folktale's depictions of eating and drinking, clothing, and other manners and customs complete the picture of an extremely simple social reality. In an east Prussian folktale the king declares: "Today I want to eat some soup, and I'll punch anyone in the face who disturbs me. . . ."[31] In KHM 65 the king enjoys "bread soup" so much, he repeatedly has it prepared. Even though every wish has come true so far, Dumb Hans wishes for "a bowl filled to the brim with potatoes," causing the princess to turn up her nose (KHM 54a). Another poor boy wishes for a magnificent meal, by his standards, from the sorcerer, namely, potatoes with herring. To top it off he asks for fried potatoes with bacon the next day.[32] The heroine in the fairy palace wishes for the most wonderful things she can imagine, all of which are simple peasant dishes, with some beer, of course.[33] The broommaker's wife considers herself lucky because she has three good things every day: bread soup, mush, and baked mushrooms.[34] It is quite extraordinary that the poor girl in Mother Holle's kingdom receives "boiled meat or roast meat every day" (KHM 24).

Folktales strongly emphasize social differences. They commonly pit large and small farmers, or farmers and workers, against each other. For example, in tales from around Münster, the farmers are grouped as large farmers, cottagers, and hired laborers.[35] Farmers by no means form a closed social whole in the folktale. Farmer Little with his one ox must succeed amid competition from the wealthy farmers (KHM 61).[36] The people in the folktale, particularly the heroes, come either from the lowest social class or from the highest royalty. This royal class of counts and kings is strongly contrasted with the lower classes: The Swabian miller's son passes all the tests, but since he is not aristocratic enough to marry into royalty, he is paid off with money.[37] In "Faithful Johannes" the princess of the golden roof would rather die than "fall into the hands of a merchant." The princess is comforted only when the merchant reveals that he is a king; "her heart spoke in his favor, and she gladly consented to become his wife" (KHM 6). The princess's love for her husband in a Pomeranian folktale is also aroused only when she hears that he is of royal lineage and not a beggar.[38] The princess regrets having rejected King Thrushbeard (KHM 52) only when she walks with the "beggar" through the meadows and forests that belong to the king.[39] The young queen in "The Brave Little Tailor" absolutely cannot accept being married to a former tailor (KHM 20). The first edition of the KHM in 1812 addresses this point even more clearly than the later, reworked editions: The king is in great despair because his daughter must marry an unknown man. "Had he known that he was a tailor, he would sooner have given him the rope than his daughter." And although the tale doesn't make it sound too drastic, the king and his daughter decide to murder the little tailor after he divulges his origins in his sleep.

Folktale kings frequently use any means available to prevent poor boys from entering their families and, hence, their social class. The king sends the boy to war to get rid of him, and he always finds new tasks, demands, and conditions before giving permission for the marriage. Characteristically, narrators critically evaluate such behavior by the royal father-in-law.[40]

The vehement social critique that frequently appears in the folktale also derives from the simple man's point of view. The Grimms' "Eve's Unequal Children" (KHM 180), which explains the origin of professions, already speaks a clear language. A Pomeranian version of this tale type expresses this point of view even more adamantly:

> After creating the world, God created many emperors, kings, princes, electors, counts and lords, and the entire clergy. Only then did he say: "Let us make a man in our image!" And he created Adam and Eve. Later, when the commandments were given, they applied only to Adam's children. Thus the great lords follow no laws and can wage wars and raise troops for fights and battles and let men be killed. . . . But when an ordinary person kills someone, he is put on the gallows in broad daylight.[41]

In KHM 180, Eve accepts the inequality among occupations when she finally understands that the world must have an order. KHM 44 ("Godfather Death") displays a very different attitude when the poor man lets even the good Lord simply stand there and rejects him as a potential godfather: "You give to the rich and let the poor go hungry." In later editions the brothers Grimm attempted to subdue this statement by adding, "The man said this because he didn't know how wisely God distributes wealth and poverty." The 1812 edition of the KHM contains the critique of the existing social order in its unexcused, accusing form.[42]

In the folktale the poor man is almost always ethical, in contrast to the evil wealthy man. The idea behind KHM 167 is that a rich person is admitted to heaven once in a hundred years. Tales about helpful animals often express the idea that even animals demonstrate more compassion than humans. And folktales frequently speak of unjust treatment. A folktale from Lorraine names the parties responsible for creating a horrifying spook which kills the watchman each night: "The wife of the king, and the wives of lots of high ministers and civil servants."[43]

The east Prussian women laborers who narrate the tales in Grudde's collection also express a thorough social critique in their folktales. They severely reproach the aristocracy with pronounced accusations. We find speculations about the aristocracy's wickedness and crimes throughout these tales: A count fails to seduce a servant girl and then carries her into his palace and immures her in the cellar.[44] A girl's father in another tale protests against the count's actions and yells: "What, you want my hard-earned money? No, little count, no way you'll get it. You just squander my money, and when you're done, my daughter isn't good enough for you; then you remember that she was only a farmgirl and send her back to me with a child in her arms. No, little count, find someone dumber!"[45]

The east Prussian tales also imbue transformation and disenchantment with a socio-psychological tone. The narrators seem to believe that fate will punish those who unjustly persecute and oppress the poor. One tale in Grudde's collection uses social criticism to explain why palaces are so often haunted: "It's no wonder it's haunted. It's no wonder because the people did bad things there. And it's no wonder rich people are possessed by the devil: They have nothing to do but eat, and that can only lead to trouble."[46]

The rich are considered evil from the start in these tales; even a wealthy farmer is "a real beast."[47] "Yes, the world is unjust. The good man's piece of bread falls out of his pocket, and the good Lord bestows gifts upon the counts, and the devil gives them even more."[48] The east Prussian critique attacks rich farmers as well as aristocracy. The servants of the rich, who are viewed as their master's accomplices, are subject to equal disdain: Instead of having her servant disenchant her, a princess chooses to continue "playing ghost." "Do you really think I'm going to let myself be disenchanted by a servant and then marry him? A poor man, or even a journeyman for all I care, but never, ever a servant! I'd rather be a ghost!"[49]

Sympathy belongs exclusively to those who are collectively labeled "poor people." "Poor people" is the generic term for wandering and settled farmworkers and craftsmen, discharged soldiers and beggars. Such biases are not surprising considering that the east Prussian tales sometimes still depict the conditions of serfdom. Lords even thrash their servants with their own hands. Insurbordination and indolence against royal orders are quickly punished with a slap in the face.[50] It is thus no surprise that the socially oppressed enjoy being superior to the lord just once. A Pomeranian version of "Strong Hans" published by Otto Knoop embodies this attitude: The hero hires himself out in exchange for his meals and three blows to his master at the end of the year's service. The landowner dies from the blows, but the servant tells the workers, "He has oppressed you long enough, I have freed you; now divide the wealth amongst yourselves and be sensible, things will go better for you" (cf. KHM 90).[51] A faithless king is forced to abandon his land forever and become a barefoot journeyman.[52] Many narratives end by emphasizing the superiority of those who were oppressed at the beginning: The hungry discharged soldier in KHM 100 ("The Devil's Grimy Brother") puts extra wood under the kettles containing his former military superiors. The apprentice outdoes his master (KHM 68); "Emperor and Abbot" (Type 922) is essentially about a servant who knows more than his lord (cf. KHM 152): The hero of this tale is the lord's herdsman, Miller, or cook, i.e., a common man, who answers the apparently insoluble questions, proving that his intelligence and mother wit are superior to his master's.[53]

The folktale's characterization of thieves also represents social criticism. Theft is a craft one learns like any other (KHM 129, "The Four Artful Brothers"). The folktale does not morally condemn theft; on the contrary, the thief corrects social inequities and deserves the audience's sympathy. The master thief in KHM 192 declares, "You mustn't take me for a common thief, I steal only rich people's excesses. The poor have nothing to fear from me; I prefer to give to them than to take." Incidentally, this clearly contrasts with the depiction of robbers (e.g., KHM 27, 40): The robber is an asocial pest; the thief corrects social injustices by taking only what "lawfully" belongs to him and all other poor people.[54]

The folktale soldier is also often a vehicle for severe social criticism. The soldier at his post doesn't have a dime and devotes himself to the devil out of need.[55] Even after giving the hussar twenty-five lashes, the captain tries to get rid of him by assigning him to a dangerous post where a hundred men have already lost their lives.[56] Another soldier is wounded during his long service to the king; when the war is over, he must become a beggar because cripples receive neither work nor a pension.[57] The king mercilessly tells the loyal discharged soldier who can no longer serve because of his wounds, "You can go home, I don't need you anymore. You won't be getting any more money, because when I pay wages, I expect something in return." The discharged soldier learns his lesson: "I served the king faithfully, but he sent me away and let me go hungry. Now I'm going to take revenge!" (KHM 116; cf. KHM 133).

As a central theme of the folktale, the desire for happiness seems largely due to the social conditions under which folktale bearers live; narrators may occasionally find an alternative to the prosaic realities of their life in the folktale's fiction.[58] Their conceptions of happiness are often modest and full of social inhibitions. The folktale's minor features are quite fascinating and often reveal the little man's joy in having possessions. For example, an apprentice in a Swabian folktale wishes that his pipe were constantly full of tobacco and burned by itself. Only with his third wish does he ask for "eternal salvation."[59] In a folktale from the Saarland, the farmer who becomes a prince presents himself in his Sunday best: "He wore a light suit with a belt and a buckle and low shoes. And a pair of pants that looked like knickers."[60] The merchant's only daughter in a Hungarian-German animal bridegroom tale asks her father to bring "a beautiful necklace" back from his travels.[61] The woman in an Icelandic version of "The Fisherman and His Wife" does not want to become pope; rather, her wishes are clearly the sort we would expect from a peasant: a cow that gives a quarter-keg of milk every time and a barrel of meal for cooking grits.[62]

Folktale tellers enjoy ending a narrative by describing the extraordinary wealth that the hero or heroine has gained, but happiness is not necessarily the result of becoming royalty or acquiring immeasurable wealth. Having modest material possessions without having to work and owning one's own property are often enough. The tales from Grudde's collection and the rewards they promise the hero for disenchanting someone are again characteristic. The reward may consist of "a lot of money," a "good" or "proper" "basket full." The money is commonly used to buy a piece of land: "You disenchanted us, and I'll give you something so that you can buy a plot of land." Poor laborers couldn't wish for anything more than a piece of farmland.[63] These wishes contain a degree of realistic materialism, occasionally hidden but sometimes quite obvious. For example, when "The Two Women" who haunt a farmer's land in Grudde's east Prussian collection are disenchanted, there is rejoicing, but the main agricultural realism comes at the end: "The farmer," who disenchanted his two sisters who were transformed many years ago and hadn't been seen since, "was happy that he now had two strong young sisters to do some work";[64] i.e., the most important aspect of the disenchantment is the recovery of two workers!

In a folktale from east Holstein, the two older brothers receive leave from military service to attend the youngest brother's confirmation. They also use this opportunity to discuss their inheritance with their father.[65] In another tale recorded by Wisser, the hero unwittingly makes a deal with the devil because he thinks about his livestock before his wife: "Musche Urjan" (the devil) demands that whatever is born in the farmer's house that evening be delivered to him in fifteen years. The farmer, who knows he has a pregnant cow, makes the promise without concern: "He figured if the cow gave birth to a calf he could milk it. And if it was a bull he could use it for stud during that time. He didn't even think of his pregnant wife."[66] Concern over valid currency is surprisingly real in a Pomeranian folktale: The hero takes a sack of gold coins to his parents, who live over a thousand miles away, "because gold is valued according to its weight throughout the world."[67] Jolly Ferdinand's principle, which he even writes on the king's doors in a Swabian folktale, is "Money makes the world go 'round."[68]

As marvelous as some elements of the folktale may be, the depiction of social life is never far from the truth. Reality underpins even fantasy; not even fantasy is independent of the social conditions in the narrator's real life. Narrators use their own environment as a model for heaven and hell; they do not question the assumption that the earthly way of life continues in the next world. The hard-working kind girl in "Mother Holle" (KHM 24) is as industrious in Mother Holle's world as she is at home: She shakes the beds, harvests the apples, and bakes bread.[69] In KHM 100 ("The Devil's Grimy Brother") the hero must keep house in hell, carry the sweepings out the back door, and generally keep things in order. In KHM 29 ("The Devil with Three Golden Hairs") the devil's grandmother sits in a big armchair; in a tale recorded by Ignaz Zingerle she is home alone eating her morning soup when the hero arrives. She puts her bowl aside, limps annoyedly to the gate, and yells, "Who's there?" when the hero knocks.[70] In a Transylvanian folktale, the devil's son comes home from traveling abroad,[71] and yet another narrative noted by Haltrich reports that the devil "was working in the woods" when the hero arrived in hell. Only the old grandmother is at home. She looks through the window and has a nice chat with the hero, who says, "God [!] bless you, old grandmother" when he leaves.[72]

The narrator's environmental reality applies even to God and the saints. The angels thresh oats in heaven (KHM 112). In gypsy folktales a girl delouses God, incense cures his toothache, and he wanders through the world like a gypsy himself. The Lord enjoys vagabonds and good-for-nothings, has unlimited patience and even helps some gypsies who don't always tell the whole truth.[73]

The narrator's real world is particularly noticeable when the narrative is set in some distant land. This is clear in the folktale's depiction of kings, emperors, and court society: Folktale kings certainly do not correspond to historical kings, even if illustrated books picture them with Barbarossa's beard, Karl the Great's coat, and a Merovingian crown. Simple people just do not know about court affairs. Thus the king wears his golden crown to bed and while hunting (KHM 11), but he must take it off to scratch his head.[74] The queen packs her husband's uniform and crown in his suitcase as he prepares to go on a trip.[75]

The folktale palace is not surrounded by pomp: When the princess looks out the window, Fuldôwat is walking down the street on his way home from the butcher: "As Fuldôwat went past the palace, the king's daughter happened to be looking out the window. 'Fuldôwat,' she called, 'can't you wipe your nose, you old snot?' 'Oh, girl,' he said, 'it's none of your business! I hope you have a baby, you whore!' "[76]

Hans deliberates whether he should enter his father's house and greet the princess: "Oh, what the hell! Go on in as you are!" He then appears before the princess wearing "boots with shit on them, . . . takes his hand out of his pocket, and wipes his nose with his fingers. He then extends his hand and says: 'Good day, girl, what can I do for you?' "[77]

The princess who laughs so hard her stomach shakes and she falls on her back also lacks ceremonial poise.[78] The princess lets the swineherd sleep with her chambermaid twice and then sleeps with him herself in exchange for a dancing piglet which she finds so entertaining.[79] The princess rides through all of the towns and cities on Whitsunday searching for her runaway groom.[80]

The emperor in a gypsy folktale hears that the empress has borne him a son: "In his joy he went to the pub and drank until he was completely bombed."[81] Another tale makes it clear that a gypsy doesn't really want to become king; "he would rather eat gooseberries and semolina pudding and fight with his wife."[82]

In the east Prussian folktales collected by Grudde, kings are replaced by aristocratic landowners, "counts," "knights," or the lord "who owns every-thing, including the village church."[83] The famous count also appears in place of the king in folktales from around Münster.[84] But in most other collections, members of the petty bourgeoisie or small farmers play the king's role. The king's main attribute is his wealth, but it is measured by the standards of the unpropertied: A Silesian folktale merely states that the king has many sheep.[85] Another adds that he stands counting his sheep each evening as the shepherd brings them back to the large farm which is, by implication, the royal residence.[86] The king is also only a large land-owner in folktales from east Holstein: The rooster crows from his roof, and his cowhand is on intimate terms with the princess. Each morning the king strolls into his garden and delights over the apple trees he planted.[87] Another king counts the apples in his orchard and has his sons guard them (KHM 57). He offers a linen skirt and a pair of wooden shoes as a reward for the capture of the thief.[88]

Folktale kings have neighbors across the field just like other farmers. The princess in KHM 89 ("The Goose Girl") is "betrothed to a prince who lives way across the field." The king in a modern Icelandic folktale "owns herds just like his subjects; he too has his favorite animal, and his new wife often makes the royal children tend the herd. . . ." Kings take part in the slaughtering of their livestock. They have their own smithy to do the most necessary work on the palace themselves; they fell their own wood in the forest or arrange a woodchopping contest between their minister and a winter guest."[89] The king retires to the part of the farm reserved for the elderly after he has turned over "the business" to his successor.[90]

The queen is depicted as "a decent, neat wife who is also functional,"[91] and the king's daughters are measured by the same standards. One daugh-ter "wasn't one for running a household. Spinning and working were not for her."[92] In the true folktale it is only natural that the princess also speaks Low German (KHM 198) or that she learns about her enchanted brother's existence on the day of the "big wash" (KHM 9). At their fathers' request, the king's daughters take the watering can to the meadow and bleach the wash.[93] The king's daughter wears a kerchief and slippers (KHM 111), and once she even has lice (KHM 212). And not only simple girls and women wear their aprons to work and for ornamentation; princesses, queens, empresses—even nixies, the Virgin Mary, and God do as well.[94]

One king goes to the yearly market fair to do some shopping and asks his daughters what he should bring them.[95] A different folktale king angrily orders his stubborn daughter to move into the chicken coop.[96] The princess who marries the blind servant against her father's will moves with him into the washhouse behind the palace;[97] and even folktale princesses occasionally give birth to illegitimate children (e.g., KHM 54a).[98]

Likewise, princes follow the normal life course of an ordinary man. The kings in many folktales have their sons learn a trade when they are old enough.[99] For example, they learn to weave baskets and to carve wood;[100]

one becomes a silversmith, another a cabinetmaker.[101] In another case they go into the world, serve an old witch, and work "like horses."[102] According to rural tradition, the prince and his friends are allowed to ride horses to the tavern on his fourteenth birthday.[103] A different prince drives a wagon into the forest to chop wood.[104]

In the folktale king's court we again find a village environment. Palaces also have cow stalls (KHM 19), and there is flax lying on the floor of the queen's chamber (KHM 14). When the master thief approaches to steal the countess's ring, the count says to his wife, "Give me the ring so it doesn't fall in the straw [on which they were sleeping]!"[105] The Hessian folktale "How Hans Got the Princess" frames the story with the daily activities on the farm: feeding the animals, drinking coffee, reading the paper, etc.[106] In the evening the king and his wife lie "under the window" like leisurely citizens of a small city,[107] and when the king and the queen are out, the palace is empty (KHM 50). A boy seeking work in the palace must deal with the maid because the king is off with the troops. He asks her, "Isn't the king's wife home?" The maid answers, "Yes, she is here," so he says, "Go get her for me." The queen, who had already talked to her husband about the boy, gladly lets him in. "When the king entered the kitchen [!], the smith's apprentice was sitting there. He stood up, put his hand out to the king, and asked him for work. The king hired him."[108]

Our folktale palaces are clearly not designed by inhabitants of actual palaces. These narrators rely more on the model of their own surroundings than invention to describe the royal residence: A king who is completely impoverished after his palace burns down twice moves into the forest, where he keeps a modest household with his wife; while he collects firewood, she cooks the soup.[109] An Irish folktale king hides his sons from their stepmother because, like an impoverished tenant farmer, he fears his family may seem too big to the young woman.[110] In a Russian folktale the dishwater is thrown onto the czar's court,[111] and the czarina must do the wash on the riverbank.[112] Greek folktales do not contain wash basins; people wash by having water from a pitcher poured over their hands.[113]

Thus the depiction of the milieu often shows rather wretched and impoverished conditions. The poor millboy even lets his goose sleep "behind the oven" when he stays in the "beautiful big house."[114] In order to indicate the splendor and enormity of the royal premises, one narrator mentions that the king has eleven rooms.[115] Because there is no other place for him, the foundling farmboy sleeps with the princess.[116] The royal residence doesn't own enough plates for the baptismal feast, and the king finds himself in a predicament trying to accommodate a thirteenth guest (KHM 50).

Since the folktale depicts courtship and weddings so often, the narrator's social reality occasionally shows itself with unusual clarity and vividness during these events. Recent folktale recordings (in contrast to the Grimms' collection) clearly reveal the family's strong patriarchal order. In

Grudde's east Prussian tales, for example, fathers initiate plans for marriage. The suitor always addresses the marriageable girl's father first.
Grudde's tale no. 80 reports in detail the suitor-devil's conversation with
the count: "The devil dressed as finely as a lord and asked for the count's
daughter, but he said: 'Everyone can come here, what makes you so
special? You think you can just jump in a warm nest. No! First say who you
are!' The devil thought and said, 'I have a nice castle. You think I'm good
enough, huh?' Now they were satisfied, and they all said that she should
marry him."[117]

Economic considerations are the most important motivation for marriage. Husbands benefit from their wives' essential contributions around
the house. The king who wants to pass on his holdings endeavors to marry
off his sons, because without a competent housewife the household cannot
survive. In order to give his sons a choice, he arranges a celebration, but he
invites only people he "considers proper."[118] The folktale father who offers
to give his property to the son who brings home the most competent and
thrifty woman (particularly in animal bride tales) follows actual peasant
practices. Similarly, the king promises his daughter to anyone who can
herd his rabbits (KHM 165). A Hessian farmer prefers to give his land to the
son who succeeds in at least doubling his portion of the inheritance.[119]

The conditions for marriage in the folktale accurately reflect real social
needs. Men demand that a wife be able to weave, spin, bake, etc. The king
in a Hessian folktale likes nothing more than spinning; before going on a
trip, he gives his daughters a large crate full of flax to spin by the time he
returns.[120] The ability to spin as a condition for the folktale marriage clearly
corresponds to actual rural demands (KHM 14, 55; cf. KHM 156). Thus a
golden or silver spindle, as a wish or a gift, is one of the most important
folktale objects: Even the prince dressed as a merchant offers to sell the
princess spindles and distaffs.[121]

It is no coincidence that folktale characters insist upon having industrious wives: The country household depends on the wife's collaboration.
The heroes of genuine, unstylized folktales look for the most competent as
well as the most beautiful women.[122] Disenchanting a beautiful but incom-
petent princess is a luxury the simple man cannot afford. A folktale from
Lorraine expresses the social doubts a peasant has about performing a
disenchantment: "Poof! A beautiful princess stood before him. She began
to weep with joy and hugged and kissed him and said, 'You have released
me. I have been under the spell for six hundred years. Now I want to marry
you.' But Pipet said, 'I'm too old for you' and told her to look for someone
else, an aristocrat or a prince."[123]

Royal courtship is carried out in an unconventional, simple manner
without courtly ceremony. Let us take Cinderella at the king's ball as a
characteristic situation. Wisser's "Ruchklas" depicts it as a Holstein peasants' ball: "When she arrived at the ball, all the others stood up. They all
wanted to dance with her and get her. Finally the king danced with her,
and he didn't let her go."[124]

A Hungarian-German version displays exactly the same behavior in this scene: The ball which Cinderella attends despite all the obstacles is an authentic saloon affair. The count gets hooked on the lovely girl and never leaves her side.[125]

Tobias Kern, the street sweeper from Ödenburg, describes an even more casual event in a tale collected by Bünker: The prince is looking for a wife, "and he arrives in a big city. So he walks around in the city for three days and looks in the windows. She was as beautiful as he had always wished a woman to be. He immediately complimented her as he was looking at her and said, 'Can I talk to you?' She said, 'Hardly!' "

The second encounter is more successful: "Today he went up to her room. Today he said, 'I'm a prince and I want to marry you.'

'Yes,' she said, 'my mother is a sorceress, and I have little money,' said the girl. He said, 'I don't need any money, I love you.' 'So,' she said, 'good, I'm satisfied.' "[126] The narrator may have met his wife the same way.

In a gypsy folktale the courtship proceeds differently: "He took her by the hair and began to hit her."[127]

The folktale does not depict the wedding itself as a fantasy ball with fairy-tale splendor, fireworks, magnificent wardrobes, and untold delicacies; rather, it occasionally depicts true folk festivals where "everything goes," or everyone sits down to a nice cup of coffee, tells stories (cf. KHM 40), and recites old toasts. Everything is depicted in detail: The bride's sisters are her bridesmaids.

With great splendor and music they went to church; after mass and after the couple was united, the celebration began. During the meal they drank to health and happiness. Someone yelled:

"Gute Gsundheit in Ehrn,
auf der Hochzeit bin i gern."

[Good health and honor,
I am glad to be at the wedding.]

Someone else yelled:

"Gute Gsundheit übern Tisch,
mei Kranzmadl is auch ka Flederwisch!"

[Good health over the table,
my girl is also no slouch!]

And a third yelled:

"Gute Gsundheit! Hier hab ich ein Glas Wein,
das schenk ich mit Freudn ein
dem Bräutigam und der Braut zu Ehrn.
Den Wein trink ich gern."

[Good health! I have a glass of wine,
that I gladly fill
in honor of the groom and bride.
I'll gladly drink the wine.]

and quickly drank it.

There were pastries you can only dream of. I also danced with the bride.[128]

A narrative recorded by Alfred Karasek expresses quite plainly what happens after the wedding at the end of the folktale: "Then the queen and king rode home to the palace, and they continued to run the house."[129]

# VII.

## The Folktale's Inner Reality

### THE NARRATOR'S EGO

Nineteenth- and twentieth-century printed collections rarely reveal the individual narrator's original stamp on the tales because the editors usually considered the text itself more important than its creator. However, the significance of individual folktale bearers, of creative individuals, has increasingly become the focus of folktale scholarship over the past twenty years.[1] Indeed, the *Volksmund* (voice of the people) does not narrate; not everyone can render a story, let alone invent one. In any case, an anonymous "primitive community"* does not bear folktales, individuals do.

This new consideration of individual members of the folk has important bearing on our question as well: The various nuances that differentiate one narrator from the next are largely responsible for determining the folktale's relationship to reality. We occasionally even find folktales that report experiences in the first person. A Danish brickmaker uses this mode to tell a tale about transformation into a dog, a falcon, and a lion, and about the monster's soul hidden in an egg.[2] Another Dane[3] claims he acquired ten tons of gold and married a Prussian princess while serving a troll; then he began wandering about because all kings must learn a trade, but after the War of 1864 he didn't want to return to his father-in-law. One Flemish narrator reports his adventure with a cannibal, another his journey with five extraordinary companions.[4] This reminds us of the traveling scholar who boasted to Archbishop Heriger in the tenth century that he experienced the story of the stolen liver himself,[5] of similar reports about visits to the beyond that Berthold of Regensburg mentions in the thirteenth century,[6] and of the traveling humanist Samuel Karoch, who recited one of Boccaccio's novellas as his own adventure.[7]

More recent collections contain more of the same. Recordings faithful to the original oral rendering, in particular, frequently include first-person narratives. One of Gustav Friedrich Meyer's Low German folktales opens,

*An allusion to Hans Naumann's concept of *"primitive Gemeinschaft."*—Trans.

"When I was young I was supposed to go visit them, and my father went with me"; this is followed by a version of the "golden boy" tale type (Type 314). One narrator begins a version of "Simeli Mountain" (Type 676, "Open Sesame") by saying, "My brother had a farm and was castellan in the village, and I had to work as a servant there. . . ."[8] Telling a tale about the animal brothers-in-law, an Austrian informant recounts, "There was once a count who had three daughters—cute girls, I know it; I went out with one of them, I liked her—and the poor guy also had too much to drink" (i.e., like the narrator himself).[9]

In an effort to increase a tale's effect, some narrators use their artistic control over the material to turn it into their own experience. In printed collections we cannot always differentiate believed memorates from purely fictitious first-person narratives at first glance. Using the form of a fictional memorate either increases a narrative's suspense and believability by giving it a stronger, albeit merely alleged, connection to reality, or turns the folktale into a marked tale of lying. At any rate, only skilled narrators can lie with false honesty.

The best narrator in Dittmaier's collection from the lower Sieg, for example, constantly narrates in the first person and renders explicit tales of lying.[10] "I went through a forest," a Breton sailor begins, "where there was no wood, through a stream in which there was no water, through a village in which there wasn't a single house; I knocked on the door and everyone answered. The more I tell, the more I lie; I don't get anything for telling you the truth."[11] Similarly, a Holstein version of "The Jew in the Brambles" (Type 592) opens, "Back in the old days we didn't have so much money, and I hired myself out. . . ."[12] But here, too, it sounds improbable that the narrator experienced everything himself. We are equally skeptical about narrators who claim to have been the heroes in "The Animals in Night Quarters" ("Bremen City Musicians," Type 130; cf. KHM 10) or the cunning fox who deceived the evil wolf.[13]

The fictional first-person mode has retained a practical material function only in the well-known Russian closing formulas with which the narrator assures the audience he was at the folktale wedding:

> I was there too,
> I drank mead and wine.
> It spilled over my mustache,
> nothing went into my mouth.[14]

The narrator hopes to improve his tips by saying he didn't get anything to drink at the wedding.

Narrators may use the first person merely to invent superficial connections to reality, but sometimes in the passion of narration they develop a deeper attachment to the story: Tradition becomes their own experiences. This annexation process is highly illuminating for psychological interpretations: Emotional narrators experience the tale themselves; they express their inner attachment to the story and its characters. Henssen's narrator Gerrits is sometimes "so captivated by the experience that he completely forgets reality; by suddenly switching from the third to the first person, he becomes the hero of the story himself."[15]

The Swedish gypsy Taikon also suddenly identifies himself with the heroes of his tales and switches from the third person into the first: "And the witch was so devilish! She is ugly, she is insidious, she has an aura of evil, she's as cold as a cellar! Ah, if only I had her here! I'd like to show her a thing or two! God knows, you damn witch, you . . . ! But, where did I leave off?" Only then does he return to the actual folktale.[16]

The inner folktale experience is fed by sympathy with the hero; the narrator frequently "becomes the hero" at the narrative's climax. When the hero finally finds the palace he longs for, after going astray for so long, Taikon says, "and finally, what does he see?" (And then the sudden switch to the first person:) "Truly, my friends! What do I see? A palace so wonderfully beautiful, unlike any I have ever seen; I have never heard anything so beautiful described in words, so beautiful that I have never even had the privilege of seeing something like it my dreams. . . ."[17]

An inner attachment to the materials even allows the good narrator to occasionally become an *actor*; his or her performance transfers the folktale into reality. Wilhelm Busch reports that "when the tale became very dramatic," one of his best informants, a normally taciturn man, "would stand up and switch places according to which person was speaking, causing his nightcap, which normally bowed quietly forward, to swing all around."[18] During the humorous saint's legend "Why St. Peter Is Bald," Gerrits took his cap off as if he were St. Peter himself and demonstrated how the apostle hid the pancake on his head.[19]

Merkelbach-Pinck reports that her informant Adolf Walther from Götzenbrück in Lorraine "becomes an actor while narrating; . . . he performs his folktales."[20] Dittmaier says one of his narrators "could not remain seated for five minutes. He played the part of all the characters in his narrative with a mobility one would not expect from an eighty-one-year-old."[21]

The gypsy Taikon, whom we have repeatedly mentioned, describes his own experiences:

> Now and then four or five of us told folktales together. One of us was the wolf, another the prince, a third the giant, the caliph, or whatever was necessary. It was a real show, understand? It could happen while we were working. Someone would start. The others naturally kept working, but soon, when the tale became more suspenseful, they couldn't care less about everything else, and they didn't do anything but listen or wait for their turn. Because as the tale develops, more new characters appear. For example, someone was supposed to be the judge and has such and such to

say, and he immediately sat down, crossed his legs, twisted his beard,
made a solemn face, and judged and talked like mad. And the accused
stood there and bowed deeply and was afraid. And then there were guards
and people, and lord knows what else. Oh dear, that was fun, that was
fun!"[22]

Narrators are therefore often literally involved with "body and soul"; they
want to impart themselves to the audience. Like ingenious actors, they
transform themselves into the characters they play.

In folktale telling among tribal societies, the performance's reality often
comes out even more clearly: "The 'visual rendering,' " writes Leo Frobenius, "was more important to good narrators than what they said. The
importance of this duality became particularly clear one day when I repeated a story I had heard a few minutes earlier, and the narrator plainly
denied having told it. A thorough investigation revealed that the visual
enactment differed fundamentally from the mere words alone. I learned
then that a literal translation lacks the life and the soul of the original."[23]

Narrators bring their personal experiences as well as social environment
into the folktale. A folktale can be a very personal reality; unique personal
experiences can supply a narrator with a lifelong stock of motifs and give
his or her narratives their unique stamp. Military service is one such
formative experience. This was often the only time in the elderly narrator's
life when he escaped his mundane job, had his own "adventures," and
heard about others' experiences.[24]

Even the brothers Grimm "gave an old sergeant of dragoons some old
clothes in exchange for some entirely characteristic soldier tales."[25]
"Bearskin" (KHM 101), "The Blue Light" (KHM 116), "The Shoes That Were
Danced Through" (KHM 133), "The Drummer" (KHM 193) and "The Buffalo-hide Boots" (KHM 199) are explicit soldier tales. The devil's grimy
brother is a discharged soldier who finds temporary employment heating
the kettles in hell (KHM 100). The old knapsack which produces a large
army when slapped, turning the little hat which brings forth artillery, and
the little horn which blows down walls seem like a soldier's wishful dream
to be general (KHM 54).

More recent collections contain folktales about discharged soldiers told
by invalid soldiers themselves. Father Pramberger's collection from Styria
includes some tales of this sort, and Leza Uffer also found an old narrator
who assured her that he told his comrades stories while in the army. This
former corporal gladly recalls his military service and derives particular
pleasure from the soldiers in his tales. The hero of one of his tales receives a
pipe which helps him herd goats; when he blows on it, he can put his goats
through military exercises: "Since he was used to the military, he figured
he'd try out some drills on his goats. And truly, he called his goats together
on a flat plane, blew a short toot, and began to give militaristic orders. . . .
He gradually divided the goats into lines of four, one behind the other, the
big ones in front and the kids in back. . . ."[26]

Military service repeatedly plays an essential role in Wisser's texts: "There once was a peasant who had two sons. When they got out of school the father said to them: 'Well, boys, what do you want to learn now?' 'Father,' they said, 'we don't want to learn anything, we want to join the army.' So they applied and were accepted." Even the disenchantment of the kingdom turned to stone has a militaristic air in this Holstein folktale: "There's a loud bang, as if a thousand cannons fired at once. And the stone man stood there, he had changed into a young king; in front of him stood servants and then an army." When the hero enters the palace with his princess, "a guard called out: 'Alert!' from his post, and the entire guard force came out and presented themselves to the couple."[27]

A Westphalian folktale applies the law of threes to military ranks: "First a corporal volunteered, took some cartridges, and started on his journey, but didn't come back. Then a private—he didn't come back either. And then a very, very dumb recruit."[28] Bünker's street sweeper from Ödenburg apparently still remembers the military maneuvers that once took place in the Balkans: "There was a hussar, a private, who received twenty or twenty-five lashes every now and then because he didn't return on time."[29]

Jahn provides a striking example of the influence of the individual's personality on folktales. A young man from Ückermark [eastern Pomerania] would start his story only after someone paid him the respect due a red hussar. All the good soldiers in his tales are red hussars; even all the princes and kings wear the red hussar's uniform.[30] In all of these cases reality and fantasy are seen exclusively from the perspective of military experiences.

Countless folktales are autobiographical. In contrast to legend narrators, however, folktale narrators are usually not conscious that they are depicting their own experiences. But individual narrators do freely choose what to include in their repertoires of tales, and in many cases a narrator's individuality even affects composition and selection on the subtale level. From the perspective of individual psychology, contamination or mixing of motifs is not coincidental. Even absurdities tell us something about the individual; they correspond to "slips" in psychology. Folktale motifs are thus not shaken together like objects inside a kaleidoscope; every new combination of motifs has a basis in individual psychology, i.e., a version of a folktale is not defined by the sum of its motifs alone, but also by the interrelationship of the motifs.

A traditional tale must suit the individual's subjective inner willingness to accept the text if it is to survive. A folktale must please the narrator in some way if it is to be retained and told again.[31] A favorite tale says a lot about a narrator and what he or she likes in a tale. We can say much the same for the audience: They are most interested in tales with heroes who experience conflicts similar to their own.

Thus the folktale often becomes a concealed or even open statement about the narrator and reflects his or her personality throughout. Merkelbach-Pinck aptly says, "The folktale accurately reflects the narrator's

hidden emotions, his minor and sublime, kind, touching, and ugly features. He can present himself as he is in the folktale, without being shy and
without pretense."[32]

Literature repeatedly employs the folktale's real autobiographical content as an artistic device. For example, in Ibsen's *The Feast at Solhaug*, Margit
tells folktales which conceal her own fate,[33] and not coincidentally,
Gretchen sings the verse from "The Juniper Tree" while in prison in *Faust*:
"My mother the whore / who killed me . . . !"

In tribal societies, autobiographical folktales deviate little from actual
experiences. For example, Frobenius describes an old African woman in
Bena Lulua who was sad because ugly gossip had recently dashed her last
hope of spending the final days of her life with an old man. Thereafter she
told a folktale that depicted her fate almost exactly as it really occurred.[34]
Frobenius observed how this purely individual tale was on everybody's
tongue only a few months later. Frobenius also reports that an old native
disguised his agony over the death of his sons in a narrative.[35]

A folktale narrator lives within the text; thus a morphological approach
must always ask how a folktale grew in its narrator's mind, as well as
historically. Psychological analyses of narrators reveal that informants almost always prefer certain themes and rarely go beyond the bounds of their
personality.[36] Although tradition provides the materials and the plot, the
folktale nonetheless allows for individual differentiation. Wilhelm Grimm
expresses this unique combination in a beautiful metaphor: The folktale is
like a well whose depth we do not know, but from which everyone draws
according to his or her need.[37] Because every rendering of a folktale is the
individual property of its narrator, it cannot be transferred unchanged. An
inner feeling of appropriateness tells the narrator "that no one else tells his
stories precisely the same, i.e., as *he* is able to tell them."[38]

The folktale's strikingly egocentric attitude should also be mentioned
here: The entire plot revolves around a single person, the hero; only he or
she connects the various episodes. The attachment between two lovers is,
as a rule, seen only from the perspective of one of them and is usually of
interest only as long as the lovers are apart; as soon as they come together,
the folktale ends. It is also striking that the folktale almost exclusively
depicts individual problems (e.g., birth, maturation, marriage, death);
community (e.g., nation, farm, or village) problems are absent. Sympathy
and antipathy apply exclusively to an individual hero. All this facilitates the
tacit analogy between the folktale hero and the narrator. Narrators consider
the hero's adversaries their own as well and depict everything that happens
to the folktale hero as if they are going through it themselves.

We occasionally can even find traces of the narrator's personal relationship to the folktale in printed collections.[39] For example, a narrator
from Lorraine grew so fond of a folktale that she would tell it to only one
person at a time.[40] Sometimes narrators are moved to tears by their own
tales, even if they do not consider them historical reality at all.[41] At one

point during her rendering of "The Girl Whose Hands Were Chopped Off" (a version of KHM 31 from Burgenland, the easternmost state in Austria), Haiding's informant Miazi-Moam said, "I'm not doing too well myself," and tears began to well in her eyes.[42] One of my Hessian informants broke into tears at the end of her story and said sobbingly: "I can't tell that—because I always end up bawling!"

These examples clearly show that the folktale is a real experience. It is an experiential narrative and not "mere entertainment." Clearly the folktale experience lies on a different plane of reality today than the legend experience. The folktale concerns the inner human world; the experience is not external numinous fright. While the legend shows us a numinous other-world reality, the folktale mirrors the unconscious reality of our own existence. And this inner folktale world affects modern people as much as "primitives."

The close inner connection between narrators and their texts leads us to difficult questions regarding the folktale's relationship to dreams. Comparisons have often been made between folktales and dreams, although folklore alone can make only groping attempts at such research.[43] Both folktales and dreams freely mix real and unreal events; dreams often contradict experiential reality as much as folktales. The two often play with reality similarly: Wish fulfillment found in such folktale motifs as "Schlaraffenland" (cf. Type 1930), the fountain of youth, the helpful dwarves, or other spirits who help the hero, resembles wishful dreams. The motif about magically transporting one's beloved into the bedroom and sending her back the same way (KHM 116, "The Blue Light") appears to have originated in a dream.[44] Forgetting that one is engaged is a motif that occurs in dreams *and* folktales (e.g., KHM 56, 186, 193).[45] There are also striking parallels between impossible tasks and the longing for an apparently unattainable object in dreams and folktales: The fruits which recede whenever a hand grasps at them (KHM 130), restricted movement (KHM 69), the bloodstains which cannot be removed (KHM 46), the task of sorting various types of grains (KHM 21), solving riddles to save one's neck (KHM 191), futile attempts at climbing the glass mountain (KHM 93, 193, 196), and other difficult tasks could just as easily occur in dreams, just as the reverse of these motifs, i.e., the accomplishment of a difficult job, could. Finally, all varieties of transformation in dreams are equally possible in folktales. Like the folktale, dreams usually revolve around a single person, a single problem, or a single characteristic. Dreamers can be the object of their own dreams even if the characters do not resemble them.

The bed that rolls away while the person is still sleeping and marvelous journeys through the air[46] are well-known dream motifs. It is no coincidence that the bed serves primarily as a magical vehicle or airplane in the folktale: In "The Boy Who Left Home to Find Out About the Shivers" (KHM 4) and, incidentally, in Wolfram von Eschenbach's *Parzival*, the hero lies down in a bed that begins to move by itself and rolls around the entire palace. In an Icelandic folktale, the hero lies down with the maiden on the giantess's bed, which flies away when he says the magic words: "Run, run, my bed, wherever I want!" In a Baluchistan version of "The Four Artful Brothers," the bride is fetched in a flying bed.[47] The origin and meaning of these motifs seem quite clear: The wonder occurs in a dream, i.e., in bed, and therefore the bed itself becomes the object of this wonder. In complete correspondence to the respective civilization's milieu, carpet takes over the function of the moving or flying bed in Arabian folktales, as do grass, straw, or willow mats in African tales.

There are even isolated folktales that emphatically claim to be based on dreams. One such narrative begins, "I dreamed something, and this is how the story goes. . . ."[48] The narrator of a Siberian folktale confesses, "I cannot say whether I really experienced it or if it was a dream."[49] The introduction to the Japanese folktales in the *Märchen der Weltliteratur* series notes that the Ainu (in northeast Japan) claim that folktales are dreams.[50]

The volume of Lithuanian folktales in the *Märchen der Weltliteratur* tells of an old man whose guest told him folktales one night until they discovered they had transformed into a wolf and a bear. After several (dream) adventures, one of them suddenly fell from his bench, and they realized that it was all a dream.[51] "Da kam eine Frau mit Lichte, / und aus war die Geschichte" (And then a woman came with a light, and the story was over) is a well-known closing formula; folktales that end with the rooster crowing may point in the same direction: "Cock-a-doodle-doo, the tale is told, cock-a-doodle-doo!" The French version is "le coq chanta, il était jour, et mon conte est fini."[52] Like sleep and dreaming, these folktales end with the rooster's first cry.

There is no lack of folklorists who infer the folktale's direct dependence on dreams on the basis of these correspondences and transitional forms.[53] But a narrated dream is not a folktale merely because it has the same motifs; and despite all the similarities, we cannot overlook the distinctions: Despite its doubtless connection to the unconscious, folktale narration is indeed a conscious art. We oversimplify matters if we assume that folktales simply derive from dreams. It is also of little use for folkloristic folktale research to interpret folktales with dreams, particularly those of neurotics or psychotics, using psychoanalytic and deep psychological theories.[54] This overlooks an obvious question which proceeds from the folktale itself, namely, how does the folktale itself handle the dream?

Although folktales and dreams are equally unreal to the modern westerner's developed consciousness, they could be equally real to a primeval, tribal consciousness. Dreams, like folktales, are commonly reported as real experiences in tribal societies.[55] Our European folktale seems to have preserved a remnant of this idea when it views dreams as reality.

In the folktale, dreams have the character of reality. Their content does not merely mean something; instead their concrete realization occurs just as the events were dreamed. In "The Nixie of the Pond" (KHM 181), for example, the woman whose husband disappeared into the pond dreams what really happens the next day. Likewise, in "Jorinda and Joringel" (KHM 69) a dream is realized immediately after Joringel wakes up. A shepherd boy's dream that he is king of Spain[56] also becomes reality in a folktale. This narrative type about dreamed prophecies that the dreamer doesn't reveal to anyone, and is therefore thrown in jail, is widely distributed.[57] The prophetic dream is always taken for concrete fact. In one of Afanas'ev's Russian folktales, for example, a father tells his sons: "Children, tell me tomorrow morning what you dream tonight. If you conceal your dreams from me I will have you killed." The younger son who dreams about the future does not dare confess the dream's contents and is disowned by his father.[58] A dream also reveals reality in the well-known motif "the dream of the treasure on the bridge."[59]

Some folktales reverse this motif's logic; i.e., reality produces a dream. In "The Devil with the Three Golden Hairs" (KHM 29), the devil's grandmother presents facts (poisoned well, etc.) to the devil as dreams. The princess, whom the helpful spirit carries to a soldier for whom she must slave until dawn, believes that it was only a dream (KHM 116, "The Blue Light"). On her wedding day the robber's bride describes her real experiences in the murderer's den as a dream (KHM 40, "The Robber Bridegroom"). In other folktales the hero describes his real odyssey as an evil dream after he returns home. His adversaries respond by thinking of punishments for the dream adversaries; of course, they really pronounce their own sentences. An Armenian folktale, in which a cowherd sells a shepherd his dream and therewith its prophetic meaning, shows most clearly how materially real a dream can be.[60]

## THE FOLKTALE'S THEMES

Some narrators underline the modern folktale's characteristic fluctuation between reality and fiction with the apt formula "It did and didn't happen."[1] Despite the story's many miraculous events, this emphasizes that folktales do indeed have meaning. Even the folktale's markedly fictional elements say something about reality. Max Lüthi is right when he says folktales do not show how the world should or could be, but rather what this world is really like. The folktale is not, as André Jolles unilaterally declared, poetry which contrasts with the real world; on the contrary, "it conveys the essence of the real world."[2]

Although these thoughts seem new to us, the romantics actually had similar ideas: Wilhelm Grimm spoke of the folktale's "truth,"[3] and the introduction to one of the first true German folktale collections, the *Kindermärchen aus mündlichen Erzählungen gesammelt* (Erfurt, 1787), states that "the love of folktales is to be explained by the love of truth. The general propensity for marvels grows from the love of truth."[4]

Although the folktale's memorable miraculous motifs provide an important emic criterion for defining the genre today, the tale's underlying ideas are even more important for its inner reality and poetic effect. In general, a folktale contains a marvelous supernatural motif here and there, but its *theme* is not of this sort.[5] Simply interpreting folktales as "wishful fiction" does not help us understand their essence: Human wishes and their fulfillment are in no way the folktale's only "theme." On the contrary, almost every folktale contains serious conflicts which are as much a part of the folktale's normal pattern as the, often very superficial, happy ending: children are abandoned; the groom is separated from his true bride; a monster captures a maiden, etc. The confrontation with dragons, giants, cannibals, sorcerers, and witches is always a battle of life and death. Tasks and tests must truly seem impossible to the hero at first. The suitor's head is at stake when he engages in riddling. Narrators take the hero's becoming an orphan, his poverty, hunger, and other needs seriously. The violation of interdictions puts the hero in extremely critical, life-threatening situations.

The generation gap, conflicts between parents and children, plays a large role in many folktales, as do other familiar problems such as disloyal spouses and ungratefulness (KHM 16 and 38). The child must overcome extraordinarily severe obstacles and dangers created by the evil stepmother or malevolent siblings. The folktale ending is stereotypical: lovers are united; the poor become rich. The conflict situations, on the other hand, vary much more; and since actual general human predicaments cause the conflicts, they are more true than the resolutions.

Folktales usually begin with a conflict at hand. The object of confrontation does not even need to be named; it is often latent, and only the psychologist can recognize it: The daughter who does not want to leave her father, the king who does not want to part with his daughter,[6] the girl who is locked and hidden in a tower until she reaches a certain age,[7] and the virago who tries to defeat her suitors in physical tests or riddling contests are all common human types whose conflict folktales repeatedly depict. The king or princess who cannot laugh also has a psychic disorder. The narrators themselves consider such figures completely abnormal. An east Prussian informant formulates it aptly: "There was once a princess who was so proud she didn't know what to do, and she always thought, 'Oh no, oh no, you are too precious for all the men!' And so she made it known that she would never marry," until one day the king declared: "It can't go on this way; she must marry the next suitor who comes along, otherwise she'll be too old to find a husband, and the children will stick their tongues out at her because she's an old maid."[8]

Childlessness is commonly the abnormal situation depicted at the start of the folktale. An east Prussian folktale expresses this quite clearly: "There once was a forester who had a pretty wife but no children. That displeased him, and he thought: 'Everyone has children, only you don't have any; no, it's no good to always be alone with my old woman in the woods."[9] The hero's birth is special because it occurs after the parents' long period of childlessness. The hero's fate is sealed from the start if, for example, the parents use magic to become fertile, if they promise him to a demon, or if he is cursed to be born in the form of an animal.

As a rule the folktale depicts the surmounting of obstacles, the harmonious solution of all problems, and the restoration of the natural order. The folktale's "true" happiness comes from mastering the art of life, not merely from the hero's superficial social climb: Defeating demonic adversaries and overcoming danger provides a new and lasting feeling of security, even in such simple tales as "Little Red Riding-Hood" (KHM 26), "The Wolf and the Seven Young Kids" (KHM 5), and "Hansel and Gretel" (KHM 15).

Inconspicuous, but not unimportant, motifs often depict how the hero restores the world to its natural order: The ripe apples in Mother Holle's garden must be harvested; the bread must be taken from the oven so it will not burn (KHM 24). The right "bride" who fits Cinderella's lost shoe must be found before the wedding can take place (KHM 21). The monsters from the magical world clear the path for the hero's last, decisive step only when he arranges their food so that each receives his proper meal.

Perhaps we could speak of basic *motifs of rectification* which restore order. Even though the rectifying tasks are sometimes quite inconspicuous, they produce the hero's deepest success: At the end of the folktale the conflict is overcome and "true" order restored. Folktales which humble greed, arrogance, and pride (the hubris theme, e.g., KHM 19 and 52) belong to the same thematic category. In some versions of KHM 191, the riddling princess symbolically expresses the elimination of her superiority by destroying her magical mirror herself.[10]

In addition to minor motifs of rectification, we find grandiose motifs of wandering; the hero's search often takes him "to the end of the world." The ordering principle of these themes lies in the hero's hidden leadership, provided he is "on the right path": "Just keep going your way," the hero in KHM 122 is advised, and this is completely characteristic of folktales because the hero's way is the right way.

Wonders are not actually a folktale "theme"; nothing could be more natural and real in the hero's story. Wonders always occur by chance; someone stumbles upon them: For example, the queen in KHM 55 learns Rumpelstiltskin's name through one such coincidence; in KHM 122 ("The Donkey Lettuce") the hero coincidentally finds the lettuce which transforms people into donkeys and back into human form; and in KHM 116 ("The Blue Light") a helpful spirit suddenly appears when the soldier happens to light his pipe with the blue light. Snow White's pallbearers happen to stumble, thus shaking the "poisoned apple core" from the heroine's throat so that she comes back to life (KHM 53). The prince in KHM 21 never doubts he can recognize his bride with the shoe; it doesn't occur to him that numerous people have the same shoe size: In the folktale the shoe fits only one person, and, vice versa, whomever the shoe fits is the person he's looking for.[11]

Folktales treat the oddest connections between episodes and the strangest encounters as everyday events. A helpful demon or a good fairy appears at the critical moment and tells the hero what he faces if he tries to win the princess and how he can master these difficulties. Clearly "blind" chance is not at work here; rather, a latent belief in fate lies behind the events in which the worthy succeed and the unworthy fail. Fate works imperceptibly: The chosen hero reaches his goal while his adversaries are still wandering about; the third brother executes the task after both of his brothers try unsuccessfully. This is all predetermined by fate's hidden control.[12] Therefore, only the hero chosen by fate can go out "to make his fortune." Anyone else who deliberately tries to do so without a pure heart is ruined. For example, when evil people try to repeat the good person's lucky adventure, they are punished or meet their downfall. Many folktales have this notion in common (e.g., KHM 13, 24, 87, 107).[13]

The question of happiness is a central idea in the folktale, and Wundt's expression *Glücksmärchen* is appropriate for modern European tradition. Of course, the hero is not always born a "lucky one" who inevitably succeeds (as in KHM 29, "The Devil with the Three Golden Hairs"). The theme of "happiness" means that there is always unhappiness in the folktale as well: Heroes do not succeed without effort; they must pass a test which engages all their resources. Most reach happiness only through suffering.

The theme of realizing happiness, the fulfillment of the search for happiness, makes the folktale a delightful narrative. This pursuit of happiness may sometimes seem superficial because happiness is measured monetarily, but much of the folktale's inner reality is to be found here. Riches and a long life are merely the superficial conclusion of the folktale; inner gratification comes from settling the conflict. In any case, contentment is as much a part of folktale happiness as love and wealth. Thus folktales often end with "They lived happily and content."

Folktale happiness often means liberation in the broadest sense: liberation from the dragon, giant, sorcerer, or witch, liberation from imprisonment, from the brambles, from marriage to the monster; liberation from the enchanted body of an animal, liberation from superior adversaries, and liberation from an overly strong parental bond.

The polar oppositions between characters, their contrasting attributes, give the folktale the clarity that makes its inner reality so distinct. There are no mixed characters, and every figure represents only one trait: There is only good and bad, beautiful and ugly, poor and rich, just and unjust, faithful and faithless. Animal tales are no different: Cat and mouse (KHM 2), wolf and goat (KHM 5), eagle and wren (KHM 17) all have opposing characteristics.

As we have seen, one of the most important areas of tension lies in the social realm: the poor hero or heroine marries into money; the unrefined cinder-boy evolves into the hero; the poor street urchin becomes a prince.[14] The last become the first, and the youngest son, neglected in the will, gains the greatest wealth in the end. Rich become poor and poor become rich; the folktale often rectifies social injustice in this way.

The theme of the hero who climbs from his humble beginnings does not mark the folktale as a narrative purely about wish fulfillment. Differences in wealth are not only a sociological phenomenon in the folktale, they also build an element of tension; i.e., they are an artistic necessity for advancing the plot. These differences also reveal an inner reality because in the folktale everything material simultaneously stands for something spiritual. Conversely, the folktale depicts inner fulfillment and maturation through concrete processes. Folktales are clearly about something very different from superficial wealth, and they often make this evident, although not always as grotesquely as in the farcical tale "Hans in Luck" (KHM 83), where the simple-minded boy is pleased to be freed from the burden of possessions. But the folktale speaks a deep truth when it says even the poor can gain true wealth. Not only saints' legend–folktales depict examples of Christian charity as a means for gaining true happiness (e.g., KHM 153); the folktale always puts its hero through the social test of giving until he is poor himself. Only then is he ready for wealth.

Dumbness and laziness are also common folktale themes. There are stories about dumb men with smart wives (e.g., KHM 94), and some (particularly farcical tales) about men with very dumb wives (e.g., KHM 34, 59, 104). The irony is particularly clear when even the title assures us of the dumb person's "intelligence," e.g., "Clever Hans" (KHM 32), "Clever Else" (KHM 34), "Clever Gretel" (KHM 77), "The Wise Servant" (KHM 162), and "Wise Folk" (KHM 104). The depiction of all sorts of successful ruses poses a contrasting theme. Here we find clever women who cause and motivate all of their husbands' successes, and negative motifs about cunning women who render all men defenseless. Naturally all of the folktale's successful riddle-solvers are smart, or at least cunning. The weak outsmarting the strong is one of the most beloved folktale themes: It is the maxim behind most devil and giant tales, and is part of the animal tale's permanent stock of motifs, for example, when the slow animal outsmarts the fast one and wins the race (e.g., KHM 187). Many other animal tales depict the opposition between the strong, dumb animal and the weak, sly one.[15] In the Grimms' "The Kinglet and the Bear," the birds cunningly defeat the much stronger four-legged animals and send them running (KHM 102; cf. KHM 171). In "The Musicians of Bremen" (KHM 27), intelligent animals even defeat robbers who have a guilty conscience. The theme that intelligence is worth more than strength recurs particularly often in European as well as tribal animal tales.

The numskull is an entirely different matter. He is taken to be dumb even though he really is not. The folktale treats him as it does the poor: In the end he gains wealth because of his disposition. "Truly" dumb people always remain dumb, and they finally fail because of their stupidity. In contrast, the numskull is, "in reality," wise: The third and youngest tailor, "a useless little dunderhead who didn't even know his trade properly," solves the princess's riddle (KHM 114). Similarly, the count's son (KHM 33), "who was dumb and couldn't learn anything," is sent out into strange lands, where he learns the various animal languages. His father sees this as the pinnacle of all stupidity and throws his son out of the house. But the boy's knowledge of animal languages soon helps him to achieve distinction. A true folktale numskull is not actually dumb, only naive; but his heart's naiveté is the basis for his later success.

All successes in the folktale are connected to tests of worth. All sorts of tests appear in folktales around the world: tests of obedience, patience, skill, courage, strength, intelligence, and acumen. The hero's fate can even rest on an apparently trivial and seemingly harmless task. In some cases no more is demanded than refraining from opening a door (KHM 3), taking bread out of the oven on time, harvesting a ripe apple tree (KHM 24), or guarding a well from impurities (KHM 136). The princess must scratch the humpbacks of three mysterious men in the woods, cut their nails, and clean their noses.[16]

But the folktale often poses seemingly insolvable tasks: killing a four-headed monster, emptying a sea in one night, climbing a glass mountain, picking the bad peas out of an enormous supply, not speaking for seven years, solving a completely inexplicable riddle—these are the heroic or humiliating tasks that the folktale poses. Of course, the hero rarely accomplishes the task without supernatural help: A helpful bird enables the hero to climb the glass mountain; the lover who is a sorcerer's daughter helps the hero break her father's power. The birds help Cinderella sort out the bad lentils. Rumpelstiltskin helps the unhappy queen spin straw into gold. The hero is able to solve the riddle with the help of an otherworld being who makes him invisible.

But isolated motifs of tasks and tests alone are not what is crucial for the folktale's inner reality; they must be seen in connection with the goals which they hinder. Above all other tasks stand the suitors' tests: Man and woman must prove themselves to each other. The isolated test motif is not what is crucial here, but rather the total question of worth posed by the tests. The folktale demands an all-out effort from people; only those who are ready to lose their lives can secure it. The proximity to defeat, facing death, precedes success.

Often a small element of the test remains unfulfilled, making the ensuing happiness incomplete. The youngest brother who has been changed back into human form still has a swan's wing instead of one arm (KHM 49). The murdered person's bones must be laid in place to successfully bring him or her back to life, but the little finger or toe is missing, and the living person also lacks this part (cf. KHM 25). The hero loses a piece of his heel as he slips through the gate at the last second (KHM 97). These motifs of "barely," "almost," and "minimal harm" curtail the central characters' happiness so that their luck does not become limitless and they do not become models of virtue like the saint's legend figure. This also makes their lot more realistic and believable. The same is true when the hero does not pass the test of worth on his or her first try. Moreover, it seems that most interdictions are imposed only so the hero can violate them. The prohibition of curiosity is almost always broken. Of course, the hero's goal is still reached in the end. But the folktale depicts limitations on human abilities and supernatural possibilities; the folktale does this so that it does not leave reality too far behind, and to create more tension.

One of the hero's most important qualities which the folktale puts to the test is fearlessness. This is by no means a test of bodily strength; courage is far more important: Nothing can happen to the hero who "knows no fear" and "is not even afraid of the devil." For example, "The Boy Who Left Home to Find Out About the Shivers" (KHM 4), "Brother Scamp" (KHM 81), and "Hans the Gambler" (KHM 82) depict this carefree, courageous hero type. But even the folktale's tests of pure courage differ from bravery in heroic legends. In the folktale, heroes *are tested;* they don't test themselves. Human refinement and maturation is a central theme in the folktale, and refinement through pain and sorrow is essential. Folktales do not only depict daredevils and boasters; physical heroic ruggedness also requires a strong heart: The hero and heroine must muster patience and a sense of sacrifice. Rather than proving themselves through heroism, heroes may be required to perform tests of everyday work and daily duties which try the quiet heroism of patience and obedience. Heroes who humble themselves qualify for their climb in life. Even the king's son must serve Iron Hans (KHM 136) and work in another king's palace until he acquires his own kingdom. But more commonly women must undauntingly endure such fate: The princess is degraded to a goose girl (KHM 89), and the king's daughter must sweep up the ashes in the kitchen (KHM 65). The ridiculed bride in "Bearskin" "was quiet, and nothing they said could ruffle her" (KHM 101). Acquiring the ability to wait is—as in real life—one of the most important preconditions for future success. The test of worth is often intensified by a ban on talking; silence is also a form of self-sacrifice. Silence plays its most striking role as a means of disenchantment in "The Twelve Brothers" (KHM 9).

The folktale demands an unselfish willingness to sacrifice from the hero. "The Twelve Brothers" (KHM 9) makes this clear: The young queen could save herself from the fiery death if she only would speak in her own defense. But disenchanting her brothers is more important to her than her own life. Faithful Johannes (KHM 6) also sacrifices himself, and the king must sacrifice his own children to bring his loyal servant back to life. The superficial sacrifice of an object never suffices in the folktale; rather, heroes must always give of themselves. The frog king does not want clothes, pearls, jewels, or the princess's golden crown, only the girl's devotion.

The folktale contrasts the willingness to sacrifice with selfishness, as in "Cinderella" (KHM 21) and "Mother Holle" (KHM 24), or with the egotistic

princess in "The Three Snake-Leaves" (KHM 16), who accepts her husband's promise to be buried alive with her if she should die first and later
throws him into the sea while he is sleeping. Numerous folktales contain
tests of friendship based on the theme "How far does the willingness to
sacrifice go among friends?" (e.g., KHM 6, 60, 107). Egotism is always
punished in the folktale; willingness to help is rewarded. Only those who
unselfishly help others find help themselves. Unselfishness and compassion are important motivating powers in the folktale; they are even demanded in encounters with the dead and animals, i.e., figures from whom
the hero cannot expect gratefulness or something in return.

These are the primary reasons we get a feeling of inner satisfaction from
folktales. The tale's equalizing judgment of proper and improper behavior
adds to this satisfaction. Our emotions can comprehend the events as inner
needs. The folktale's inner reality even touches on religious questions in
many places. Of course, concepts such as "heaven" and "hell" often appear
completely secularized, and the beyond is usually thought of in earthly
terms (cf. pp. 192–93), but a certain religiosity is nevertheless part of the
folktale's general tone. The tales deal with general religious ideas rather
than specifically Christian ones when they raise ethical questions, and
particularly when good is rewarded and evil punished. The awareness that
people are dependent on otherworld powers[17] and knowing we cannot
escape the presence of supernatural beings also represent basic religious
thoughts. The fruits of the tree of life and the water of life have Biblical and
mythical parallels. Likewise, the concept of release—the release of good
figures from evil powers and the necessity of releasing love—is also a basic
concept in high religions. An important lesson of many folktales is that
only those who can sacrifice themselves earn the right to live. Thus it is not
surprising that folktale wonders and sacred wonders are similar in many
ways. The folktale is religious in the broadest sense, and it is no coincidence that collectors frequently claim that the guardians of folk tradition
are also usually pious people.

Again and again we see how important a comprehensive view of the
folktale is and how inquiring about motifs does not suffice. Although many
isolated episodes are unreal, the folktale raises actual problems of general
human significance. The folktale concerns everyone because it presents
everyone's reality. Although the formula "once upon a time" projects the
events onto an indefinite past, the deeper reason for the folktale's spread
lies in its everyday actuality, its references to everyday life. The folktale
touches all of our personal relationships, those between parents and children, siblings, husband and wife, master and servant. Everything in the
story relates to people; thus folktales do not depict the landscape and
nature. When animals appear in the folktale, and even when only animals
appear (e.g., KHM 38), the tale is nonetheless "really" about human affairs.

"The Cat and the Mouse Set Up Housekeeping" (KHM 2) illustrates
"might over right." In "The Nightingale and the Blindworm" (KHM 6a),

good nature and the willingness to help are poorly rewarded. In contrast, "The Dog and the Sparrow" (KHM 58) shows how the small and weak are indeed in a position to avenge the wrongs done by the strong.[18] Human fate is the theme everywhere, even if the events are completely fantastic, as in a Russian folktale that takes place "in a czardom the size of a sieve."[19] Even if a straw, a coal, and a bean (KHM 18), a sausage (KHM 23), or a spindle, shuttle, and needle (KHM 188) are the protagonists, we still experience human modes of thought and feeling from the tale. The folktale's content is always a general reality, timeless events that everyone has experienced or can experience.

We have traversed the folktale's superficial and inner realities; we have sketched the historical course of attitudes toward reality from the magical to the rational; and we have therefore arrived at the end of our investigation. The multiplicity of problems the question of reality poses for folktale research does not allow us to summarize the results in the form of a single thesis statement. Each section sets forth the results for particular issues. Some of the results are negative: On the question of how the genres of folk narrative are to be divided, we saw that the question "real or unreal?" does not provide a distinct border between the folktale and the legend or other genres of folk narrative. The concept of "folktale" is not constant; its meaning continually changes so that even marvels, i.e., the most characteristic aspect of the folktale, are replaced by real elements (for example, the robber replaces the giant). Similarly, the question of reality has not simplified the other problems; on the contrary, it has complicated them: Where the folktale seemed most unreal, we found remnants of the oldest human views of reality (e.g., with cutting someone up and bringing him or her back to life). Where the folktale seemed to depict facts, they sometimes turned out to be pictures of inner psychic states, concrete representations of a spiritual, mental state. Conversely, the folktale treats inner spiritual events, such as the dream, as reality.

We were able to trace many aspects of the folktale's historical evolution. We found that the circle of narrators changes with the narratives, that narrative forms transform, motifs receive new meanings and content, or they make room for others and are forgotten. The folktale did not begin changing in the modern technological world; "folktales" have always, at all times, adapted to the current picture of reality, and they assimilated to the present reality even after centuries of development. The relationship between folktales and realtiy is therefore different in every historical epoch; it takes new shape again and again, and must be interpreted anew as well.

# Notes

## I. INTRODUCTION

1. BP IV, 4; Wilhelm Wundt, "Märchen, Sage und Legende als Entwicklungsformen des Mythus," *Archiv für Religionswissenschaft* 11 (1908), 206; Johannes Bolte, *Name und Merkmale des Märchens*, FFC no. 36 (Helsinki: Suomalainen Tiedeakatemia, 1920), p. 38; Friedrich Ranke, *Volkssagenforschung*, Deutschkundliche Arbeiten, Allgemeine Reihe, vol. 4 (Breslau: Maruschke & Berendt, 1935), p. 83; Friedrich Panzer, "Märchen," in *Deutsche Volkskunde*, ed. John Meier (Berlin and Leipzig: W. de Gruyter, 1926), pp. 219f.; Stith Thompson, *The Folktale*, 2nd ed. (New York: Holt, Rinehart & Winston, 1951), p. 8; Adolf Bach, *Deutsche Volkskunde* (Leipzig: S. Hirzel, 1937), p. 365.

2. For example, Gerhard Kahlo, *Die Wahrheit des Märchens* (Halle: M. Niemeyer, 1954); Wilhelm Giese, "Sind Märchen Lügen?" *Cahiers Sextil Puscariu. Linguistique, philologie, littérature Roumaines* 1 (1952), 137–50; Lalita Gollwitzer, "Sind die Märchen Wahr?" *Die neue Schau*, January 1951, 19–20; Maxim Gorki, *Märchen der Wirklichkeit* (Berlin: Malik, 1952); Friedrich Rieck, *Das volkhafte Erzählen im Lichte organischer Wirklichkeitspädagogik*, Habilitationsschrift Frankfurt, 1942; or the essay by H. Hieber, "Märchen und Wirklichkeit," special supplement to *Staatsanzeigers für Württemberg* 11 (1927), 281–92, which considers only the realism in Wilhelm Hauff's *Kunstmärchen*.

3. For example, Wilhelm Jürgens, *Der Wirklichkeitsgehalt des Märchens*, Diss. Kiel, 1937 (Kiel: Schmidt & Klaunig, 1937); Josef Prestel, *Märchen als Lebensdichtung* (Munich: Max Hueber, 1938).

4. For example, Anneliese Dymke, *Die wirkliche Welt im deutschen Zaubermärchen. Studien zum Märchengepräge*, Diss. Würzburg, 1951.

5. For example, Richard Winter, "Die geschichtliche Wirklichkeit im deutschen Volksmärchen," *Euphorion* 25 (1924), 194–225.

6. Antonie Töpfer, *Der König im deutschen Volksmärchen*, Diss. Jena, 1930.

7. Matthes Ziegler, *Die Frau im Märchen* (Leipzig: Koehler, 1937); also see Irmgard Greif, *Die Frau in der deutschen Volkssage*, Diss. Göttingen, 1947.

8. Marianne Isenberg, *Geburt und Tod im deutschen Volksmärchen*, Diss. Bonn, 1948; Vera Ludwig, *Leben, Tod und Unsterblichkeit im deutschen Volksmärchen*, Diss. Erlangen, 1946.

9. Marie Luise Becker, *Die Liebe im deutschen Volksmärchen* (Leipzig: H. Seemann Nachfolger, 1901); Marie-Elisabeth Rosenbaum, *Liebe und Ehe im deutschen Volksmärchen*, Diss. Jena, 1929.

10. E. Wulffen, "Das Kriminelle im deutschen Volksmärchen," *Archiv für Kriminalanthropologie und Kriminalistik* 38 (1910), 340ff.; Karl Friedrichs, "Das Recht in den Kinder- und Hausmärchen," *Mitteilungen der Schlesischen Gesellschaft für Volkskunde* 22 (1920), 16–43; Otto Ludwig, *Richter und Gericht im deutschen Märchen*, Bausteine zur Volkskunde und Religionswissenschaft (Bühl), vol. 12 (Bühl: Konkordia, 1935); H. Fehr, "Das Recht im Bündner Märchen," *Zeitschrift für schweizerisches Recht* 54 (1935), 219–39; Siegfried Anger, *Das Recht in den Sagen, Legenden und Märchen Schleswig-Holsteins*, Diss. Kiel, 1947.

11. Alfred Usteri, *Die Pflanzenwelt in der Sage und im Märchen* (Basel: R. Geering, 1947).

12. Othenio Abel, *Die vorweltlichen Tiere in Märchen, Sage und Aberglauben* (Karlsruhe: G. Braun, 1923); Hildegard Hendricks, *Die beseelten Tiergestalten des deutschen Volksmärchens und ihre Entsprechung im Volksglauben*, Diss. Bonn, 1952.

13. Dore Rebholz, *Der Wald im deutschen Märchen*, Diss. Heidelberg, 1944; cf. Wolfgang Baumgart, *Der Wald in der deutschen Dichtung* (Berlin and Leipzig: Walter de Gruyter, 1936).

14. Here we must add a word to the notion of "reality" itself: It is striking that the discussion of the problem of reality currently pervades all disciplines (cf. Eduard Spranger, *Urschichten des Wirklichkeitsbewußtseins*, Sitzungsberichte der Berliner Akademie der Wissenschaft, Philosophische-historische Klasse [Berlin, 1934]; Carl Gustav Jung, *Die Wirklichkeit der Seele* [Zurich: Rascher, 1934]; E. Weinhandl, "Der Begriff der Wirklichkeit," *Forschungen und Fortschritte* 13 [1937], 61ff.; Nicolai Hartmann, *Möglichkeit und Wirklichkeit* [Berlin: W. de Gruyter, 1938]; M. Bense, "Philosophie im Zeitalter der Technik," in *Die neue Weltschau, Internationale Aussprache über den Anbruch eines neuen aperspektivischen Zeitalters* [Stuttgart: Deutsche Verlags-Anstalt, 1952], pp. 119–44; Ernst Cassirer, *Philosophie der symbolischen Formen*, vol. 2: *Das mythische Denken*, 2nd ed. [Berlin: B. Cassirer, 1953]; Jonas Cohn, *Wirklichkeit als Aufgabe* [Stuttgart: W. Kohlhammer, 1955]). The concept does not recur merely because it is no longer obvious and unequivocal, but also because it is quite clearly in the midst of a reevaluation. For example, art and literature offer us a new concept of reality almost annually: objectivity and neo-objectivity, surrealism and surnaturalism, metaphysical realism, neo-realism, neo-verism, novels as reports, three-dimensional films, abstract art—all claim to express a high degree of reality. Every direction in art and every current in literature assures us that it has taken the decisive step toward the comprehension of "true reality." We mention only the latest works on this problem here: Clemens Lugowski, *Wirklichkeit und Dichtung* (Frankfurt: Moritz Diesterweg, 1936); Erich Ruprecht, "Dichtung—Wahrheit oder Spiel?" *Wirkendes Wort* 1 (1950–51), 257–64; Frank Thiess, *Dichtung und Wirklichkeit*, Abhandlungen der Klasse der Literatur, no. 1 (Mainz: Akademie der Wissenschaften und der Literatur, 1952); Frank Thiess, *Die Wirklichkeit des Unwirklichen. Untersuchungen über die Realität der Dichtung* (Hamburg: P. Zsolnay, 1954); Gerhard Storz, "Über die Wirklichkeit von Dichtung," *Wirkendes Wort*, 1st special vol. (1953), 94–103; A. Weis, "Der Surrealismus und das Problem der Wirklichkeit," *Hochland* 45 (1953), 426–37; Alexander Abusch, *Literatur und Wirklichkeit* (Berlin: Aufbau, 1953).

The word *reality* has undergone decisive changes in meaning: *real (wirklich)* was originally "that which has an effect" *(wirkt)*, *reality* the result of this effect. In late medieval mysticism, where our word first appears, "reality" is the translation of the Latin *operatio*, which means activity, productivity. But what people recognize as effective or productive changes over time and ranges from material to supernatural processes. For rational thought, reality is only that which is visible, that which we can conceive with the senses. But intangible concepts can also be "effective." God is "real" to those for whom he has an effect. Sometimes something only spiritually existent is labeled "real." "Reality" can also mean the essence of a thing, i.e., its ontological truth.

The tribal world-view recognizes things which are unreal in the rational sense (e.g., magic of all sorts) as effective. Moreover, our division of material and supernatural reality is somewhat of a historical product: The prevailing world-view determines what counts as reality. Thus there are only relative, historically conditioned concepts of reality, and every conception of reality has its limits in the face of illusion, make-believe, and error. Reality is by no means an objective constant, and K. Jaspers is right when he speaks of "reality's lack of finality" (Karl Jaspers, *Allgemeine Psychopathologie*, 5th ed. [Berlin: Springer, 1948], p. 271; also see Adolf Ellegard Jensen, *Hainuwele Volkserzählungen von der Molukkeninsel Ceram* [Frankfurt: V. Klostermann, 1939], pp. 3f; also Adolf Ellegard Jensen, *Das religiöse Weltbild einer frühen Kultur* [Stuttgart: A. Schröder, 1948], p. 73.) Completely different conceptions of reality reign in systems of thought separated by history and geography.

We need not turn to tribal societies to reach such conclusions; we need only consider foreign "high" cultures closely. According to Lao-tse's teachings, which continue to play a large role in Chinese thought, vital reality exists in a vacuum. The reality of a room, for example, can be found only in the empty room that is surrounded by the ceiling and walls, and not in the ceiling and walls themselves. The empty room is all-powerful because it is universal. According to the teachings of Chinese Taoists, the true master of the art of life enters the life of dreams at birth and wakes to "reality" only at death (cited from Kakuzo Okakura, *Das Buch vom Tee* [Wiesbaden, 1952]).

Here one of the most difficult problems in the scientific study of culture becomes clear. Namely, to what extent is it possible for the researcher to comprehend pictures of reality in other cultures? Earlier times and distant peoples may also have valid, correct, and true things to say without knowing, or even imagining, the physical, factual reality of our modern world-view. Every culture has its own conception of reality that is necessarily one-sided, and for which other realities fall into oblivion. Even the modern material conception of reality is historically conditioned and relative, and certainly much of what seems objective to us will be viewed as an antiquated world-view which does not correspond to "reality" in future centuries. A countercurrent has already appeared. For example, Martin Heidegger rejects the subject-object relationship: Everything is real because there is no measure for objective reality. Who is to say that inner reality is less real then external, tangible reality? Existential truth is "more real" than rational, factual reality. Roughly speaking, this is how Heidegger makes what was previously only a "poetic truth," i.e., basically a nonreality, a reality. (Cf. Heidegger's interpretations of Hölderlin's poems: "Andenken," in *Hölderlein-Gedenkschrift zu seinem 100. Todestag 7. Juni 1943,* 2nd ed. [Tübingen: Mohr, 1944], pp. 267ff., particularly pp. 292f.; also Martin Heidegger, "Der Ursprung des Kunstwerkes," *Holzwege,* 2nd ed. [Frankfurt, 1952], pp. 7–68, esp. 38ff.) Like the historically changing consciousness of reality, science's concept of reality is also relative and subject to historical change.

15. There are other types of folktales besides the novella that do not entail wonders: For example, "The Old Man and His Grandson" (KHM 78) contains nothing typical of the folktale, but it is also not a legend. It is more of a realistic exemplum, a moralistic tale for well-behaved children and those who want to be.

16. Cf. Kurt Wagner, "Formen der Volkserzählung," in *Volkskundliche Ernte, Hugo Hepding dargebracht am 7. September 1938 von seinen Freunden,* Gießener Beiträge zur deutschen Philologie 60 (Gießen, 1938), 254.

17. Novalis writes: "Wonders vary with natural laws: The two mutually limit each other, and together they make a whole. They unify by neutralizing each other. No wonders without a natural event and vice versa" (Novalis, *Fragmente,* ed. Ernst Kamnitzer [Dresden: Wolfgang Jess, 1929], no. 64).

18. In a short essay on the folk legend (in 1839), Friedrich Hebbel says the task of folk legend research is to set up an "alphabet of ideas."

19. Cf. Hans Honti, "Märchenmorphologie und Märchentypologie," *Folk-Liv* 3 (1939), 308.

20. Cf. Mark Asadowskij, *Eine sibirische Märchenerzählerin,* FFC no. 68 (Helsinki: Suomalainen Tiedeakatemia, 1926)—English translation: Mark Azadovskii, *A Siberian Tale Teller,* James R. Dow, trans., Monograph Series no. 2 (Austin: Univ. of Texas Center for Intercultural Studies in Folklore and Ethnomusicology, 1974); Gottfried Henssen, *Überlieferung und Persönlichkeit; die Erzählungen und Lieder des Egbert Gerrits* (Münster: Aschendorff, 1951); Lutz Röhrich, "Die Märchenforschung seit dem Jahre 1945," *Deutsches Jahrbuch für Volkskunde* 1 (1955), 279–96, and 2 (1956).

21. Cf. Lutz Röhrich, "Märchen und Psychiatrie," in *Bericht über den Allgemeinen volkskundlichen Kongreß des Verbandes deutscher Vereine für Volkskunde in Jugenheim an der Bergstraße* (Stuttgart, 1952), pp. 44f.

22. Cf. Max Lüthi, ed., *Europäische Volksmärchen* (Zurich: Manesse, 1951), pp. 560f., as well as Max Lüthi, *Die Gabe im Märchen und in der Sage*, Diss. Bern, 1943 (Bern: Francke, 1943); and Max Lüthi, *Das europäische Volksmärchen* (Bern: Francke, 1947), pp. 112ff. [This work, hereafter *Volksmärchen*, has been translated as *The European Folktale*, John D. Niles, trans. (Bloomington: Indiana Univ. Press, 1986).— Trans.]

## II. THE GENRES OF FOLK NARRATIVE AND THEIR RELATIONSHIP TO REALITY
### Folktale and Legend

1. From the introduction to the *German Legends* in 1816. Jacob Grimm's illustrative comparison also emphasizes this point: "Folktales are like flowers, these legends like fresh herbs and shrubs, often of unique scent and aura" (H. Schneider, ed., *Die deutschen Sagen der Brüder Grimm* [Berlin and Leipzig o. J., 1916], p. xxii. [Translated as *The German Legends of the Brothers Grimm*, 2 vols., trans. and ed. Donald Ward (Philadelphia: Institute for the Study of Human Issues, 1981). I cite the work in English when item numbers, rather than page numbers, are given.— Trans.]

2. From *Volkssagenforschung*, pp. 11–25; also see Heinrich Burkhardt, *Zur Psychologie der Erlebnissage*, Diss. Zurich, 1951.

3. "By nature the legend demands belief, from the narrator as well as the audience; it depicts reality, things that really happened. The folktale does not make this claim; it demands no belief, at least no more belief than any other product of conscious fiction" (F. Ranke, *Volkssagenforschung*, p. 73).

4. BP IV, 36; Bolte, *Name und Merkmale*, p. 38. Likewise, Hans Naumann adopted the conventional definition when he stated: "We call less realistic primitive narratives 'folktales'; those whose realism is stronger because of the fixing of place, time, and historical figures we call 'legends'" (Hans Naumann, *Primitive Gemeinschaftskultur* [Jena: Diederichs, 1921], p. 62). Friedrich Panzer expresses a similar view: "The legend begins with, and aims at, the reality of the human world. It does not hang in the air like the folktale's plot. Rather, it is tied to a particular place or thing of any sort, an object, an appearance, a process in the real world . . ." (Panzer, "Märchen," p. 235). In his important essay "Die Volkssage als Kunstwerk," *Norddeutsche Zeitschrift für Volkskunde* 7 (1929), 143, Friedrich Wilhelm Schmidt says: "It is a feature of the true legend that it presents reality, even if the content is unbelievable and fantastic."

5. Cf. Gottfried Henssen, "Volkstümliche Erzählerkunst," *Westdeutsche Zeitschrift für Volkskunde* 32 (1935), 14.

6. In Schambach and Müller's collection (1854), 34 folktales and farcical tales are outnumbered by 261 legends. Johann Jegerlehner also collected many more legends than folktales. The ratio disfavors the folktale more and more in the twentieth century. In W. Bodens's collection (*Sage, Märchen und Schwank am Niederrhein* [Bonn: L Röhrscheid, 1937]) there are 1,066 legends to only 17 folktales, and Gottfried Henssen writes: "While the folk on the periphery of the Bergisches Land [North-Rhine-Westphalia] still know many legends, we hear relatively few folktales among them today. The interest of most narrators in legendary events is great; they have, in general, little understanding of stories 'in which nothing is true'" (Gottfried Henssen, "Bergische Märchen," *Zeitschrift des Vereins für rheinische und westfällische Volkskunde* 25 [1928], 41). Georg Graber's collection from Carinthia also contains only 17 folktales alongside hundreds of legends (Georg Graber, *Sagen und Märchen aus Kärnten* [Graz: Leykam, 1935]). The ratio is 400 to 9 among the nar-

ratives compiled by M. Sooder in Haslital (cf. Melchoir Sooder, *Zelleni us em Haslital. Märchen, Sagen und Schwänke der Hasler aus mündlicher Überlieferung aufgezeichnet* [Basel: Helbing & Lichtenhahn, 1943], p. 8).

7. Cf. Ranke, *Volkssagenforschung*, pp. 17f.

8. Carl Wilhelm von Sydow tried to replace the inexact concepts "legend" and "folktale" with more precise scientific terms such as *memorat* (report of experience in the first person), *fabulat* (invented, fantastic report), *chimerat* (tale of magic in which the magic is no longer believed), *novellat* (the Semitic folktale), and *fikt* (humorous fiction) (Carl Wilhelm von Sydow, "Kategorien der Prosavolksdichtung," in *Volkskundliche Gaben, J. Meier zum 70. Geburtstag dargebracht* [Berlin and Leipzig: W. de Gruyter, 1934], pp. 257ff.; also in Carl Wilhelm von Sydow, *Selected Papers on Folklore* [Copenhagen: Rosenkilde & Bagger, 1948], pp. 6off. and pp. 106ff.). But these expressions have not taken hold. As abstract concepts they do not do justice to the multiplicity of forms human ideas may take.

The concept "Märlein," which Albert Wesselski places between the basic report and the artistic novella-like folktale, has also not found general validity (Albert Wesselski, *Versuch einer Theorie des Märchens*, Prager deutsche Studien, no. 45 [Reichenberg: B. F. Kraus, 1931], p. 99. Also see Wagner, "Formen der Volkserzählung," pp. 253f). Robert Petsch, in yet another definition, wanted to use the concept *Märlein* to designate narratives of the type in Grudde's collection and suggested, in all seriousness, a division between the two concepts "Märlein P" and "Märlein W"! (Robert Petsch, "Wesen und innere Form des Volksmärchens," *Norddeutsche Zeitschrift für Volkskunde* 15 [1937], p. 3).

9. See Hermann Bausinger, *Lebendiges Erzählen. Studien über das Leben volkstümlichen Erzählgutes auf Grund von Untersuchungen im nordöstlichen. Württemberg*, Diss. Tübingen, 1952, p. 144.

10. "It is sad," says an informant from Lorraine, "that in the enlightened twentieth century there are still Catholics who understand their religion so poorly that they can doubt the existence of witches. . . . Every holy mass read by a priest, every consecration with holy water is an indication that there are witches" (Angelika Merkelbach-Pinck, *Lothringer erzählen*, vol. 2: *Sagen, Schwänke, etc.* [Saarbrücken: Saarbrücker Druckerei und Verlag, 1936], p. 23). Johann Kruse, *Hexen unter uns? Magie und Zauberglauben in unserer Zeit* (Hamburg: Hamburgische Bücherei, 1951), contains ample evidence of living belief in witches today. Regarding belief in witches in a single village, see Gertrud Emrich, *Formen und Grundlagen gegenwärtigen Hexenglaubens*, Diss. Mainz, 1953.

11. Where we have recordings true to the original, the gradual shifts in belief are still demonstrable. R. Boell compiled oral versions of the legend of the dwarves' passage found in Marburg's Central Archives of German Folk Narrative for his exams in 1952. Experiential, legendary elements are still clearly traceable: Some narratives are brought into relation to the narrator's family; for example, one narrator's own grandfather ferried the dwarves across the river.

In other cases the legend of the crossing is transferred to other demonic figures, e.g., the devil, in whom belief is still current; or the figures are human—for example, smugglers want to get across. This maintains the motif's experiential, legendary tone. But as a rule it has long since become a fabulat-legend which is no longer considered true, and sometimes, with the addition of various decorative ingredients, it becomes a work of narrative art.

12. Sydow, "Kategorien," p. 262; cf. Schmidt, "Die Volkssage als Kunstwerk."

13. Scholars often err on this point, and folktale collections often contain a few legends. Even the Grimms' KHM includes items which, according to their relationship to reality, are clearly legends: KHM 42 ("The Godfather") is a devil legend without a happy folktale ending. "The man" (this label is also typical of legends)

saves himself only by suddenly fleeing from the strange house when he sees the "godfather's" two long horns. This atypical "folktale" ends by noting, "who knows what the godfather would have done to him otherwise." "Frau Trude" (KHM 43) is a legend witch, not a folktale witch, and the tale includes the typical legend motif of courting the devil. The entire narrative, which ends with the transformation and death of the disobedient child, is much closer to a legend than a folktale.

The three narratives about "The Elves" (KHM 39 I-III) contain typical legend elements in the motifs of "rewarding the elves," "godmother to the elves," and the "changeling" which we find in no other folktales. "The Gifts of the Little Folk" (KHM 182) also uses motifs from dwarf legends.

The growth of the hand from the grave and all other features of "The Naughty Child" (KHM 117) have legendary character. "The Ungrateful Son" (KHM 145), who does not give his father any of the good food, is harassed by a demonic toad for his entire life: He must constantly feed it; otherwise it eats from his face. This is clearly not a folktale punishment, but rather one typical of the legend.

14. Friedrich Ranke also emphasized the relativity of the differences between the genres in his definition: "The plots of legends are *more* realistic . . . ; the characters as well as the narrated events of the folktale are *more* poetic, while also being more colorless and typical" (Ranke, *Volkssagenforschung*, p. 16; also see Kurt Wagner, "Zu den Grundlagen und Formen des Stils der Volksdichtung und ihrer Nachbargebiete," *Hessische Blätter für Volkskunde* 31 [1932], p. 199).

15. Cf. Lüthi, *Die Gabe*, p. 5ff.

16. KHM 192—*The German Legends of the Brothers Grimm*, no. 335.

17. KHM 99. Legends often report that ghosts can be magically compelled into a container (commonly a measuring can) and thus made harmless ("bottle-ghost"); e.g., Anton Birlinger, *Volkstümliches aus Schwaben*, 2 vols. (Freiburg: Herder, 1861–62), vol. 1, p. 295; Karl August Reiser, *Sagen, Gebräuche und Sprichwörter des Allgäus*, 2 vols. (Kempten: J. Kösel, 1895–1902), vol. 1, p. 80; cf. the "spiritus familiaris," "the bottle imp," the "Teufel im Glase" (in Grimmelshausen, *Der seltsame Springinsfeld*, ch. 13); cf. "Geist im Glas," HdM II, 449ff. (by Schulte-Kemminghausen), and BP II, 414ff.

18. KHM 28—Graber, *Sagen und Märchen aus Kärnten*, pp. 29f. and 46.

19. Cf. the article "Lenore," in HdA V, 1209ff. (by Mengis); Adolf Friedrich, *Afrikanische Priestertümer; Vorstudien zu einer Untersuchung*, Studien zur Kulturkunde, A. E. Jensen ed., vol. 6 (Stuttgart: Strecker and Schröder, 1939), p. 282, contains examples from tribal societies. For examples from folktales, see pp. 22 and 207, note 65.

20. KHM 110—*German Legends*, no. 245.

21. Cf. conjuring demons in the legend. In the folktale the helpful otherworld figure says, "If you're in trouble, come to the edge of the forest and shout: 'Iron Hans!' Then I'll come and help you" (KHM 136). Rumpelstiltskin is related.

22. In the legend the co-walker spirit follows someone like a shadow; in the folktale we find the motif of the magic flight.

23. Cf. BP II, 349ff.

24. KHM 17—*German Legends*, no. 240; cf. Johannes Künzig, "Der im Fischbauch wiedergefundene Ring in Sage, Legende, Märchen und Lied," in *Volkskundliche Gaben*, pp. 85ff.

25. Cf. Friedrich von der Leyen and Valerie Höttges, eds., *Lesebuch der deutschen Volkssage* (Berlin: Junker & Dünnhaupt, 1933), no. 42, pp. 89ff. and 173.

26. The legend of sacrifice: for example, a human sacrifice to placate river demons. In the folktale the princess must be turned over to a dragon or some other monster (e.g., KHM 60; cf. KHM 33).

27. Rumpelstiltskin (KHM 55) or the three spinners (KHM 14) fulfill the motif of supernatural help with spinning in the folktale; various demons do so in the legend.

28. *Württemburgische Jahrbücher* 1904, pp. 92ff.; also see Ernst Meier, *Deutsche Sagen, Sitten und Gebräuche aus Schwaben* (Stuttgart: J. B. Metzler, 1852), no. 150, p. 134.

29. K. Müller-Lisowski, ed., *Irische Volksmärchen*, MdW (Jena: Diederichs, 1923), no. 26, pp. 204ff.

30. For example, Graber, *Sagen und Märchen aus Kärnten*, p. 85; Birlinger, *Volkstümliches aus Schwaben*, vol. 1, pp. 133f.; cf. Lutz Röhrich, "Die Grausamkeit im Märchen. Ihre kulturhistorischen, rechtsgeschichtlichen und psychologischen Grundlagen," *Rheinisches Jahrbuch für Volkskunde* 6 (1956), 148ff.

31. "Jephthah motif"; cf. Judges 2:29–40; also consider the tales about Isaac or Iphigenia, in which the willingness to sacrifice satisfies the god, who allows the victim to live; cf. F. Ranke, *Volkssagenforschung*, pp. 20f.

32. For example, Paul Zaunert, ed., *Deutsche Märchen aus dem Donaulande*, in collaboration with Viktor v. Geramb, J. R. Bünker, Romuald Pramberger, Siegfried Troll, and Adolf Schullerus, MdW (Jena: Diederichs, 1926).

33. *German Legends*, no. 337; cf. W. Baumgartner, "Israelitisch-griechische Sagenbeziehungen," *Schweizerisches Archiv für Volkskunde* 41 (1944), 6ff. Inger Margrethe Boberg, *Baumeistersagen*, FFC no. 151 (Helsinki: Suomalainen Tiedeakatemia, 1955).

34. Items which deviate from this rule are notable. In Bodens's collection from the lower Rhine we find a markedly gruesome "legend" with a happy ending: A skeleton rises from the ashes and points toward a large treasure that makes the owner of the house rich (no. 1076, pp. 265f.). The editor groups the narrative with the folktales, apparently because of its positive ending, but its horror and its one-stranded plot which lacks episodes make it a legend. In a story published by Gottfried Henssen, the treasure is raised after an initial attempt fails. The frightful moments are completely legendary (the devil owns the treasure). But the narrative is not short like a legend; rather, it is spun like a folktale, and it has a happy ending. Both of the treasure-diggers (a farmer and his hand) are never in poverty again (Gottfried Henssen, *Volksmärchen aus Rheinland und Westfalen* [Wuppertal-Elberfeld: A. Martini & Grüttefien, 1932], no. 25, pp. 127ff.).

35. Cf. Lüthi, *Die Gabe*, p. 129, as well as "Verwandlung," HdA VIII, 1637 (by K. Beth).

36. Cf. Johannes Malthaner, *Die Erlösung im Märchen*, Diss. Heidelberg, 1934, p. 91.

37. Cf. pp. 79–92.

38. Cf. Lüthi, *Die Gabe*, p. 82.

39. Cf. F. Ranke, *Volkssagenforschung*, p. 107; also Hans Naumann, *Grundzüge der deutschen Volkskunde* (Leipzig: Quelle & Meyer, 1922), p. 152.

40. Cf. Lüthi, *Die Gabe*, p. 134.

41. Cf. pp. 76–80.

42. For example: "My grandfather experienced it himself," or "This happened in my father's village."

43. Cf. Lüthi, *Volksmärchen*, p. 49; Max Lüthi, "Märchen und Sage," *Deutsche Vierteljahresschrift für Literaturwissenschaft und Geistesgeschichte* 25 (1951), 172ff. Jean Cocteau discovered the stylistic feature of isolation back in 1930: "True realism strips things of their normal connections and isolates their strange essence. Our name seems absurd and spooky when called out by a mailman in the morning in a lonely hotel corridor. We are taken aback by a Louis XVI chair when it is chained to the

front of an antique store. What a droll find! It's a Louis XVI chair. In a store we would not have noticed it." Jean Cocteau, *Neue Rundschau* 1930, p. 412. Clemens Lugowski writes: "That which is isolated is truly real!" (*Wirklichkeit und Dichtung*, p. 89).

44. Other demonic figures are less common in the folktale than in the legend, or they appear in both genres only in particular regions. The wild man, for example, depicted as "Iron Hans" in KHM 136, is a demon who otherwise belongs in the legend. It is also uncommon that nixies find their way into folktales (KHM 79 and 181). Werewolves appear in some Livonian folktales (August von Löwis of Menar, ed., *Finnische und estnische Volksmärchen*, MdW [Jena: Diederichs, 1922], no. 84, pp. 279ff.), and in Latvian-Lithuanian folktales (Maximilian Boehm and F. Specht, eds., *Lettisch-litauische Volksmärchen*, MdW [Jena: Diederichs, 1924], no. 12, p. 99) as the hero's demonic adversary, but as a figure of living folk belief the werewolf appears only in the legend.

45. Cf. Friedrich Ranke, "Aufgaben volkskundlicher Märchenforschung," *Zeitschrift des Vereins für Volkskunde*, new series 4 (1933), 209.

46. For example, witches who bake their victims in the oven and then devour them appear in Russian folktales (Aleksandr Nikolaevich Aphanassjew [Afanas'ev], *Russische Volksmärchen*, translated into German by Friedrich Hildebrand, 2 vols [Leipzig o. J.] vol. 1, no. 8, p. 1. English translation by Norbert Guterman, *Russian Fairy Tales* [New York: Pantheon Books, 1945]).

47. The stepmother witch in folktales is more closely related to the legend witch and is certainly influenced by this figure as well as historical witch trials. Thus she is burned in the folktale as well. Cf. Will-Erich Peuckert, *Deutsches Volkstum in Märchen und Sage, Schwank und Rätsel* (Berlin: Walter de Gruyter, 1938), pp. 109f. The HdM does not contain an article on the witch, but see "Hexe," HdA III, 1835ff. (by Weiser-Aall), as well as Alfred Wittmann, *Die Gestalt der Hexe in der deutschen Sage*, Diss. Heidelberg, 1933; H. Vordemfelde, "Die Hexe im deutschen Volksmärchen," *Festschrift Eugen Mogk* (Halle: M. Niemeyer, 1924), pp. 558ff.; Arne Runeberg, "Witches, Demons and Fertility Magic," *Societas Scientarum Fennica, Commentationes Humanarum Litterarum* 14:4 (Helsingfors, 1947); cf. note 10 in this chapter.

48. Cf. Walter Anderson's review of Thompson's *The Folktale, Schweizerisches Archiv für Volkskunde* 65 (1948), 224.

49. Rich material in Rudolf Drinkuth, "Die drei Frauen in Deutschland als Gestalten der Sage, des Märchens und des christlichen Kultes," *Hessische Blätter für Volkskunde* 32 (1933), 109–54, and 33 (1934), 1–77.

50. HdM II, 216ff.; cf. BP I, 207ff.

51. Cf. Prestel, p. 19. Legend and folktale demons have other mutual names in various European motif complexes. The "Dschinn" in Maximilian Lambertz's collection indicate that the same is true in Albania.

52. Cf. the article "Dienst beim elbischen Wesen" (service to a supernatural being), HdM I, 396ff (by Heiligendorff).

53. Cf. F. Ranke, "Aufgaben," p. 209; A. Genzel, *Die Helfer und Schädiger des Helden im deutschen Volksmärchen*, Diss. Leipzig, 1922, p. 98.

54. Cf. BP I, 148ff.; also see John R. Broderius, *The Giant in Germanic Tradition*, Diss. Chicago, 1932.

55. Cf. E. Hartmann, *Die Trollvorstellungen in den Sagen und Märchen der skandinavischen Völker*, Tübinger germanistische Arbeiten, H. Schneider, ed., vol. 23 (Stuttgart: W. Kohlhammer, 1936), p. 143.

56. E.g., Henssen, "Bergische Märchen," p. 44.

57. Angelika Merkelbach-Pinck, *Lothringer Volksmärchen* (Kassel: Bärenreiter, 1940), p. 274.

58. Josef Haltrich, *Deutsche Volksmärchen aus dem Sachsenlande in Siebenbürgen*, 3rd ed. (Vienna: C. Graeser, 1882), no. 26.

59. Cf. Franz Brietzmann, *Die böse Frau in der deutschen Literatur des Mittelalters* (Berlin: Mayer & Müller, 1912).

60. Cf. Waltraud Woeller, *Der soziale Gehalt und die soziale Funktion der deutschen Volksmärchen*, Habilitationsschrift Berlin, 1955, pp. 181f.

61. Karl Josef Simrock, *Deutsche Märchen* (Stuttgart: J. G. Cotta, 1864), no. 24 ("Des Teufels Schürenbrand").

62. Cf. Woeller, pp. 181f.

63. For example, Viktor von Geramb, *Kinder- und Hausmärchen aus Steiermark*, 3rd ed. (Graz and Vienna: Leykam, 1948), pp. 82ff.; cf. Oswald Adolf Erich, *Die Darstellung des Teufels in der christlichen Kunst* (Berlin: Deutscher Kunstverlag, 1931); Isenberg, p. 72; Thompson, *The Folktale*, pp. 42f.

64. Klara Stroebe, trans., *Nordische Volksmärchen*, MdW, 2 vols. (Jena: Diederichs, 1922), vol. 1, no. 6, 30ff.; cf. the article "Aschenputtel," HdM I, 125f. (by S. Singer); Lutz Röhrich, "Das Todesproblem im Spiegel der Sage," *Blätter für Pfälzische Kirchengeschichte und religiöse Volkskunde* 17 (1950), 90ff.

65. Carl Herman Tillhagen, *Taikon erzählt, Zigeunermärchen und -geschichten* (Zurich: Artemis, 1948), pp. 183ff., also see p. 289. A different gypsy narrative tells of a woman whose dead husband returns to her nightly and pursues his trade as a coppersmith just as he did when he was alive. His wife takes the orders for his work. The relationship is discovered only after her dead husband impregnates her (!) (Tillhagen, p. 289).

66. Johann Georg von Hahn, *Griechische und albanesische Märchen*, 2nd ed., Paul Ernst, ed. (Munich and Berlin: G. Müller, 1918), no. 40, p. 217 ("Die versteckte Königstochter"); cf. Ingrid Hartmann-Ströhm, *Das Meerhäschen. Eine vergleichende Märchenuntersuchung*, Diss. Göttingen, 1953, pp. 126f.

67. Cf. Lüthi, *Volksmärchen*, pp. 11ff.; Max Lüthi, "Gattungsstile," *Wirkendes Wort* 4 (1953/54), 321ff.

68. Cf. Lüthi, *Europäische Volksmärchen*, p. 570.

69. Max Lüthi correctly speaks of the folktale's "one-dimensionality" (*Volksmärchen*, pp. 16f. and 23; *Gabe*, p. 97; and "Märchen und Sage," p. 164). "The encounter with the otherworld is there, but the experience of the otherworld is lacking" (*Volksmärchen*, p. 83).

70. Bausinger, *Lebendiges Erzählen*, p. 103.

71. Cf. Lüthi, *Gabe*, p. 33.

72. Max Lüthi, from whom most of these examples are taken, speaks of the "diminution of magical power in the folktale."

73. For example, cutting down a forest, bailing out a pond, and building a palace, each within a few hours (KHM 113, 186, and 193), or spinning black yarn white, sorting rye and wheat, etc.

74. For example, the "green hunter" in Swabian legend "digs with a shovel and hoe but doesn't move a speck of dust." The "stone-sharpener" must sharpen a boundary stone without it becoming smaller. The "case-boy" must count the cases at the wine press but never gets past ninety-nine, and the "basket-laden woman" is disenchanted only when she has worn through the iron soles of her shoes. A herdsman who treated his stock poorly must, as a ghost, carry a cow up the mountain, but as soon as he reaches the top the cow falls down again.

The legend depicts completely useless Tantalus tortures and Sisyphean and Danaiden tasks; the folktale, on the other hand, depicts the performance of herculean deeds (cf. Lutz Röhrich, *Die dämonischen Gestalten der schwäbischen Volksüberlieferung*, Diss. Tübingen, 1949, pp. 173f.; Ludwig Laistner, *Nebelsagen* [Stuttgart: W. Spemann, 1879], pp. 33ff. [the chapter "Sisyphus in Deutschland"] contains other examples; also see Albert Camus, *Der Mythos von Sisyphus*).

75. The heroic legend and the historical legend are not considered here.

76. Only a few exceptions occur in the Grimms' tales (confirming the rule), e.g.,

"Iron Hans" (KHM 136), which belongs to the "Golden Boy" tale type, and "Rumpelstiltskin" (KHM 55), which is actually an ancient legend. "Mother Holle" is also a legend figure.

77. Cf. Will-Erich Peuckert, *Wiedergeburt; Gespräche in Hörsälen und unterwegs* (Berlin: Weidmann, 1949) (the section "Die Ordnung der Welt und das Fehlende"), pp. 129f.; cf. HdM I, 102f.; BP II, 275ff.

78. "Where it can, the folktale replaces inner emotions with external impulses" (Lüthi, *Volksmärchen*, p. 23). "With surprising consequences the folktale projects the contents of various realms onto the same plane (ibid., p. 31).

79. Karl Spiess, *Das deutsche Volksmärchen* (Leipzig and Berlin: B. G. Teubner, 1917), p. 17.

## The Aetiological Narrative

1. The labels for aetiological narratives vary: The English-speaking world speaks of the "explanatory tale"; in Germany the concept of "nature legend" (*Natursage*) or "nature-interpreting legend" has caught on, but this veils the folktale character these narratives often have.

2. Oskar Dähnhardt, *Natursagen* (Leipzig and Berlin: B. G. Teubner, 1907–11), esp. vols. III–IV.

3. Vols. 2ff (Paris, 1887ff.).

4. Adolf Ellegard Jensen, *Mythos und Kult bei Naturvölkern* (Wiesbaden: F. Steiner, 1951).

5. Hermann Baumann, *Schöpfung und Urzeit des Menschen im Mythus der afrikanischen Völker* (Berlin: Dietrich Reimer, 1936).

6. Robert Lehmann-Nitsche, *Studien zur südamerikanischen Mythologie. Die ätiologischen Motive* (Hamburg: Friederichsen, De Gruyter, 1939).

7. Georg Christoph Lichtenberg has called man a "seeker of causes." *Aphorismen* (Berlin: B. Behr, 1908), vol. 4, I, 1279.

8. Cf. Carl Gustav Jung and Karl Kerényi, *Einführung in das Wesen der Mythologie* (Zurich: Rascher, 1941), p. 16.

9. Cf. F. Dornseiff, "Antikes zum Alten Testament 1. Genesis," *Zeitschrift für das alttestamentliche Wissenschaft und die Kunde des nachbiblischen Judentums*, new series 11 (Gießen, 1934), 57–75; also Lehmann-Nitsche, pp. vf.; also see H. Gunkel's article "Mythus" II, RGG IV, 381ff.

10. Regarding the aetiological principle in the historical legend, see Lutz Röhrich, "Eine antike Grenzsage und ihre neuzeitlichen Parallelen," *Würzburger Jahrbücher* (1949/50), no. 2, pp. 339ff.

11. BP III, 542f., and II, 543ff.; also see the explanation of the name "Snow White" in KHM 53.

12. Walter Arthur Berendsohn, *Grundformen volkstümlicher Erzählerkunst in den Kinder- und Hausmärchen der Brüder Grimm* (Hamburg: W. Gente, 1921); cf. Lüthi, "Märchen und Sage," pp. 160f.

13. For example, in the Oceanian folktales in Paul Hambruch, ed., *Südseemärchen*, MdW (Jena: Diederichs, 1927).

14. The earth created from the bottom of the sea is a motif distributed around the world. Water covers the earth at the start of Genesis in the Old Testament as well (Genesis 1:2ff.).

15. Cf. Antti Aarne, *Verzeichnis der finnischen Ursprungssagen und ihrer Varianten*, FFC no. 8 (Hamina: Suomalaisen Tiedakatemian Kustantama, 1912), pp. 3ff.

16. Merkelback-Pinck, *Lothringer Volksmärchen*, p. 31.

17. J. R. W. Sinninghe, *Katalog der niederländischen Märchen-, Ursprungssagen-, Sagen- und Legendenvarianten*, FFC no. 132 (Helsinki: Suomalainen Tiedeakatemia, 1943), p. 47.

18. MdW, *Deutsche Märchen aus dem Donaulande*, p. 198.
19. Ibid., p. 199.
20. Dähnhardt, *Natursagen*, vol. 2, pp. 107, 247; vol. 1, pp. 171f.; cf. Wesselski, *Theorie*, p. 41.
21. Cf. Bausinger, *Lebendiges Erzählen*, p. 130.
22. Lehmann-Nitsche, p. ix.
23. Friedrich von der Leyen, *Die Welt der Märchen*, 2 vols. (Düsseldorf: E. Diederich, 1953/54), vol. 2, p. 85.
24. The explanatory tale lives on in children's stories which explain animal voices.
25. These examples are chosen from Lehmann-Nitsche's particularly rich collection.
26. Aarne, *Ursprungssagen*, pp. 10ff.
27. Leyen, *Welt*, vol. 1, p. 235.
28. Ibid., p. 247.
29. Cf. Wilhelm Wundt, *Völkerpsychologie*, vols. 4 and 5: *Mythus und Religion* (Leipzig: W. Engelmann, 1910 and 1914), vol. 4, p. 362.
30. Dähnhardt, *Natursagen*, vol. 3, p. 269.
31. For example, Carl Meinhof, ed., *Afrikanische Märchen*, MdW (Jena: Diederichs, 1921), pp. 65f.
32. MdW, *Südseemärchen*, no. 24, p. 75.
33. Atlantis, vol. XI, *Volksdichtungen aus Oberguinea, Fabuleien dreier Völker* (Jena: Diederichs, 1924), no. 20, pp. 118f.
34. Ibid., no. 14, pp. 104ff.; even modern fact-oriented ethnology is increasingly concerned with mythology and folktales. Hermann Baumann says, "It seems that the natives capture and depict much more factual information about the course of their cultural development in their 'legends' than we have previously admitted" (Baumann, p. 334).
35. Atlantis, vol. IX, *Volkserzählungen aus dem Zentralsudan* (Jena: Diederichs, 1924), p. 30; also see p. 270.
36. Atlantis, vol. X, *Die atlantische Götterlehre* (Jena: Diederichs, 1926), p. 274.
37. Cf. Wundt, *Völkerpsychologie*, vol. 5, p. 350.
38. Aarne, *Ursprungssagen*, pp. 7ff.
39. Peuckert, *Deutsches Volkstum*, pp. 85f.
40. Aarne, *Ursprungssagen*, pp. 10ff.
41. Jensen, *Hainuwele*, no. 242, pp. 278f.
42. Paul Hambruch, ed., *Malaiische Märchen aus Madagaskar und Insulinde*, MdW (Jena: Diederichs, 1927), no. 25, pp. 93f.; cf. p. 320. This narrative depicts a special case of how a boy became a monkey.
43. Lehmann-Nitsche, pp. vii, 137ff.
44. Cf. Jensen, *Mythos*, pp. 91f.; Jensen labels this group of narratives explanatory or aetiological myths, in contrast to true myths.
45. Jensen, *Hainuwele*, p. 113.
46. Atlantis, vol. IX (Zentralsudan), p. 287 ("The Dragon-Slayer"). Such narratives are also common in the material compiled by Diedrich Westermann (*Die Kpelle, ein Negerstamm in Liberia*, Quellen der Religionsgeschichte, vol. 9 [Göttingen: Vandenhoeck & Ruprecht, 1921]); also see Westermann's notes on pp. 362 and 371.
47. Atlantis, vol. VIII, *Erzählungen aus dem Westsudan* (Jena: Diederichs, 1922), no. 120, p. 274.
48. Dähnhardt, pp. 277f.
49. Cf. Westermann, *Kpelle*, p. 362.
50. Aetiological thought can also occur in narratives that explain a proverb, such as many collected by Leo Frobenius in Upper Guinea (Atlantis, vol. XI).

## Saint's Legend and Folksong

1. The label *Legende* indicates how scientific categories of genre can be problematic: English and French authors use *legend* for the German *Sage*. In German folkloristics *Legende* designates, almost exclusively, legends about Christian saints. But in ethnology *Legende* usually indicates narratives which have lost their original mythic belief; these range from tribal and heroic legends to folktales. Anthropologists use *Legende* as an overarching concept for legend and folktale, particularly where a clear classification is not possible.

2. Quoted from Heinrich Schauerte, *Die volkstümliche Heiligenverehrung* (Münster: Aschendorff, 1948), pp. 15ff.; cf. Georg Schreiber, *Das Weltkonzil von Trient. Sein Werden und Wirken* (Freiburg: Herder, 1951); Helmut Thielicke, *Das Wunder, eine theologische Untersuchung über den Begriff des Wunders* (Tübingen, 1938); Gustav Mensching, *Das Wunder im Völkerglauben* (Amsterdam: Pantheon Akademische Verlagsanstalt, 1942).

3. Regarding the staff miracle see BP III, 463ff., and "Grabpflanzen," HdM II, 659 (by Kahlo).

4. Merkelbach-Pinck, *Lothringer Volksmärchen*, p. 142.

5. Heinrich Dittmaier, *Sagen, Märchen und Schwänke von der unteren Sieg* (Bonn: L. Röhrscheid, 1950), no. 404, p. 145.

6. Matthias Zender, *Volkssagen der Westeifel* (Bonn: L. Röhrscheid, 1935), no. 329, p. 87.

7. As no. 67, as well as *German Legends*, no. 330; cf. BP, no. 157a, vol. III, pp. 241ff.; and the article "Kümmernis," HdA V, 807ff. (by Wrede).

8. Compilation of other motifs in Heinrich Günter, *Psychologie der Legende* (Freiburg: Herder, 1949), pp. 94ff.

9. Examples in ibid., p. 186.

10. Examples in ibid., pp. 85f.

11. Cf. BP III, 457f.

12. Cf. ibid., 308–21, and Günter, pp. 7f.

13. Cf. BP I, 322ff.

14. Cf. "Christliche Motive im deutschen Volksmärchen," HdM I, 362ff. (by Ittenbach).

15. Laura Gonzenbach, *Sicilianische Märchen* (Leipzig: W. Engelmann, 1870), no. 20; cf. BP I, 18.

16. Cf. Moses' procession through the Red Sea in Exodus 14.

17. Cf. BP I, 296; "Tränen," HdA VIII, 1106f. (by Seligmann).

18. Ernst Meier, *Deutsche Volksmärchen aus Schwaben* (Stuttgart: C. P. Scheitlin, 1852), no. 36.

19. Cf. BP I, 14ff.; also see Johann Reinhard Bünker, *Schwänke, Sagen und Märchen in heanzischer Mundart* (Leipzig: Deutsche Verlagsactiengesellschaft, 1906), no. 54.

20. Hans Schmidt and Paul Kahle, *Volkserzählungen aus Palästina*, 2 vols. (Göttingen: Vandenhoeck & Ruprecht, 1918 and 1930), vol. 2, pp. 187f.

21. Paul Kretschmer, ed., *Neugriechische Märchen*, MdW (Jena: Diederichs, 1941), no. 13, pp. 48ff.

22. Cf. Leyen, *Welt*, vol. II, pp. 132f.; Ernst Tegethoff, ed., *Französische Volksmärchen*, 2 vols., MdW (Jena: Diederichs, 1923), vol. 2, pp. if., 332.

23. Harri Meier, ed., *Spanische und portugiesische Märchen*, MdW (Jena: Diederichs, 1940), no. 25, pp. 121ff.; cf. note p. 326.

24. Cf. BP I, 99ff.

25. Cf. HdM II, 220.

26. Ignaz and Josef Zingerle, *Kinder- und Hausmärchen aus Süddeutschland*, 2 vols. (Regensburg: F. Pustet, 1854), p. 88 ("Der Hirtenknabe").

27. Woeller, *Der soziale Gehalt*, pp. 122ff.

28. For example, KHM 35 in the 1812 edition ("The Sparrow and His Four Children").

29. Albert Wesselski, *Märchen des Mittelalters* (Berlin: H. Stubenrauch, 1925), p. 168.

30. MdW, *Donauland*, pp. 104ff.

31. Ulrich Jahn, *Volksmärchen aus Pommern und Rügen* (Norden and Leipzig: Soltau, 1891), p. 135 ("Der Bärensohn").

32. August Ey, *Harzmärchenbuch* (Stade: F. Steudel, 1862), p. 9 ("Die Königstochter ein Schmetterling"); cf. Dymke, pp. 114f.

33. Paul Zaunert, ed., *Deutsche Märchen seit Grimm*, 2 vols., MdW (Jena: Diederichs, 1912 and 1923), vol. I, pp. 164ff.

34. MdW, *Donauland*, no. 1, pp. 1ff.

35. Cf. Elfriede Rath, *Studien zur Quellenkunde und Motivik obersteirischer Volksmärchen aus der Sammlung Pramberger*, Diss. Vienna, 1949, p. 75.

36. *Deutsche Volkslieder mit ihren Melodien*, ed. das deutsche Volksliedarchiv, ballad section, under the direction of John Meier (Berlin: W. de Gruyter, 1935ff.) (hereafter Meier): "Graf Friedrich," no. 48; "Die entführte Graserin," no. 45.

37. "Der Tannhäuser" (Meier no. 15).

38. "Wegwarte," no. 91, and "Das versteinerte Brot," no. 106, in John Meier, ed., *Deutsche Literatur in Entwicklungsreihen, Sammlung literarischen Kunst- und Kulturdenkmäler. Reihe 10: Das deutsche Volkslied, Abteilung Balladen.*

39. "Der edle Moringer" (Meier no. 12).

40. "Der Markgraf von Backenweil" (Meier no. 13).

41. "Der Spielmannssohn" (*Deutsche Literatur in Entwicklungsreihen*, no. 12, version B).

42. "Edelmann and Schäfer" (*Deutsche Literatur in Entwicklungsreihen*, no. 55); "Die Rabenmutter" (no. 96 in same) is similar.

43. "Raumensattel" (Meier no. 27); "Das Schloß in Österreich" (Meier no. 24); "Alter Mann und Schüler" (Meier no. 25); "Herr und Schildknecht" (Meier no. 33); and "Die unschuldige Dienstmagd" (*Deutsche Literatur in Entwicklungsreihen*, no. 105) have similar features.

44. Merkelbach-Pinck, *Lothringer Volksmärchen*, pp. 146f.; cf. note, p. 381. Further examples of poems which have become prose can be found in Samuel Singer, *Schweizer Märchen. Anfang eines Kommentars*, Untersuchungen zur neueren Sprach- und Literaturgeschichte, no. 3 (Bern: A. Francke, 1903), vol. I, pp. 1ff.

45. Franz Magnus Böhme, *Deutsches Kinderlied und Kinderspiel* (Leipzig: Breitkopf & Härtel, 1897), book 2, nos. 123–59, pp. 459ff.

46. Ibid., pp. 552f.

47. Cf. BP III, 489.

48. Cf. Thompson, *The Folktale*, p. 19.

49. Cf. Hartmann, *Trollvorstellungen*, pp. 182ff.

50. Lutz Mackensen, *Der singende Knochen*, FFC no. 49 (Helsinki: Suomalainen Tiedeakatemia, 1923), p. 14; also see the Swedish folk ballad "The Two Sisters" (*Nordische Volkslieder*, Max Kuckei, ed. [Wedel: C. Brauns, 1944], pp. 176ff.).

51. *Nordische Volkslieder*, pp. 12ff.

52. Ibid., pp. 63ff.

53. Ibid., pp. 53f.; pp. 133ff. are similar.

54. Maximilian Lambertz, *Albanische Märchen*, Akademie der Wissenschaften in Wien: Schriften der Balkankommission, Linguistische Abteilung, vol. 12 (Vienna: A. Hölder, 1922), pp. 65ff.

55. Cf. *Zeitschrift für Volkskunde*, new series 8 ( =46) (1936/37), 87ff.

56. Cf. pp. 57–59.

57. Francis J. Child, *English and Scottish Pouplar Ballads* (Boston and New York:

Houghton, Mifflin & Co., 1904), vol. 1, no. 44, p. 339 ("The Two Magicians"); this volume also contains the French ballad mentioned above; also see *Schweizerisches Archiv für Volkskunde* 30 (1930), pp. 107ff.

58. Ludwig Erk and Franz M. Böhme, *Deutscher Liederhort*, 3 vols. (Leipzig: Breitkopf & Härtel, 1893–94), vol. III, nos. 1081ff.

## Folktales without the Happy Ending

1. On the concept of the folktale's "conflict situation," see pp. 208–14.
2. Joseph Lefftz, ed., *Märchen der Brüder Grimm. Urfassung nach der Originalhandschrift der Abtei Oelenberg im Elsaß*, Schriften der Elsaß-Lothringer wissenschaftlichen Gesellschaft, Reihe C, vol. 1 (Heidelberg: C. Winter, 1927), pp. 6off. ("Die zwei Schornsteinfegers Jungen").
3. Ibid., pp. 105f. ("Goldner Hirsch").
4. Maximilian Lambertz, *Die geflügelte Schwester und die Dunklen der Erde. Albanische Volksmärchen* (Eisenach: E. Röth, 1952), pp. 134ff. ("Die kleine Schöne der Erde").
5. Otto Sutermeister, *Kinder- und Hausmärchen aus der Schweiz*, 2nd ed. (Aarau: H. R. Sauerländer, 1873), no. 50.
6. *Tradiçáo, revista mensal d'enthnographia portugueza* 1 (1899), Piçarra and Dias, eds., p. 28.
7. Alfred Hermann and Martin Schwind, *Die Prinzessin von Samarkand. Märchen aus Aserbeidschan und Armenien* (Cologne: Greven, 1951), no. 12, pp. 127ff. ("Der Wolfsmensch").
8. Cf. Lutz Röhrich, *Erzählungen des späten Mittelalters und ihr Weiterleben in Literatur und Volksdichtung bis zur Gegenwart* (Bern and Munich: Francke, 1962), vol. I, pp. 62ff.
9. Cf. Warren E. Roberts, *The Tale of the Kind and the Unkind Girls*, Fabula, supplemental series B, Untersuchungen no. 1 (Berlin: de Gruyter, 1958).
10. Rudolf Kapff, *Schwäbische Sagen* (Jena: Diederichs, 1926), pp. 31f. ("Das Vöglein auf der Eiche").
11. Hertha Grudde, *Plattdeutsche Volksmärchen aus Ostpreußen* (Königsberg: Gräfe & Unzen, 1931), no. 27, pp. 47ff. ("Steefmuttä"), and no. 44, pp. 83ff. ("Vogelke").
12. Cf. Hans Ulrich Sareyko, *Das Weltbild eines ostpreußischen Volkserzählers*, Diss. Marburg, 1954.
13. Cf. BP I, 57; Robert Petsch, *Formelhafte Schlüsse im Volksmärchen* (Berlin: Weidmann, 1900), pp. 10f.
14. Cf. the compilation ch. II, "Folktale and Legend," note 13.
15. MdW, *Finnische und estnische Volksmärchen*, no. 52, pp. 179f.
16. E.g., in those by Schönwerth, Jahn, Kühnau, Peuckert, and others; cf. Kurt Ranke, *Schleswig-Holsteinische Volksmärchen*, vol. I (Kiel: F. Hirt, 1955), pp. 272f.
17. As in KHM 43 and Will-Erich Peuckert, *Schlesische Sagen* (Jena: Diederichs, 1924), pp. 103f.
18. Paul Delarue, *Le conte populaire Français*, vol. 1 (Paris: Érasme, 1957), pp. 373ff.; Marianne Rumpf, *Rotkäppchen. Eine vergleichende Märchenuntersuchung*, Diss. Göttingen, 1951.
19. Petsch, *Formelhafte Schlüsse*, p. 12.
20. Cf. K. Ranke, *Schleswig-Holsteinische Volksmärchen*, vol. 1, pp. 270ff.; HdM II, pp. 227f.
21. Marianne Rumpf, "Caterinella. Ein italienisches Warnmärchen," *Fabula* 1 (1957), 76ff.
22. Gottfried Henssen, "Deutsche Schreckmärchen und ihre europäischen Anverwandten," *Zeitschrift für Volkskunde* 50 (1953), 84ff.
23. Cf. Marianne Rumpf, *Ursprung und Entstehung von Warn- und Schreckmärchen*, FFC no. 160 (Helsinki: Suomalainen Tiedeakatemia, 1955), pp. 5ff.

24. MdW, *Nordische Volksmärchen*, no. 54, pp. 305ff. ("Die Historie vom Pfann-kuchen").

25. Cf. "The Aetiological Narrative."

26. Bertha Kössler-Ilg, ed., *Indianermärchen aus den Kordilleren*, MdW (Düsseldorf and Cologne: Diederichs, 1956), e.g., no. 28, pp. 97ff.; no. 42, pp. 159ff.; no. 61, pp. 242ff.

27. Hugo Kunike, ed., *Märchen aus Siberien*, MdW (Jena: Diederichs, 1940), e.g., no. 2, pp. 13ff.; no. 9, pp. 48ff.; no. 23, pp. 90ff.

28. Ibid., no. 26, p. 104.

29. Knud Rasmussen, *Die Gabe des Adlers. Eskimoische Märchen aus Alaska* (Frankfurt: Societas, 1937), p. 135.

30. MdW, *Afrikanische Märchen*, p. 78.

31. Hans Stumme, *Märchen und Geschichten aus der Stadt Tripolis* (Leipzig: J. C. Hinrich, 1898), p. 120.

32. Atlantis, vol. VII, *Dämonen des Sudan* (Jena: Diederichs, 1924), no. 3, p. 273.

33. MdW, *Südseemärchen*, no. 30, p. 92.

34. Personal communication from Wolfram Eberhard during a lecture at the University of Mainz.

35. Cf. pp. 12–27.

36. E. Meier, *Deutsche Volksmärchen aus Schwaben*, p. 174; cf. Dymke, *Die wirkliche Welt*, p. 111.

37. Elisabeth Koechlin, *Wesenzüge des deutschen und des französischen Volks-märchens*, Basler Studien zur deutschen Sprache und Literatur, vol. 4 (Basel: B. Schwabe & Co., 1945).

## Jest

1. Wagner, "Formen der Volkserzählung," p. 251; cf. Wagner, "Zu den Grundlagen und Formen," p. 196; BP II, 149ff. and 163ff.

2. Ludwig Felix Weber, *Märchen und Schwank*, Diss. Kiel, 1904.

3. Wagner, "Formen der Volkserzählung," p. 252.

4. Matthias Zender, *Volksmärchen und Schwänke aus der Westeifel* (Bonn: L. Röhrscheid, 1935), p. VII.

5. Henssen, "Bergische Märchen," p. 41.

6. Ibid., p. 44.

7. Wulffen, "Das Kriminelle," p. 349; HdA VIII, 1029f.

8. Gustav Friedrich Meyer, *Plattdeutsche Volksmärchen und Schwänke* (Neumünster: K. Wachholtz, 1925), no. 208.

9. Dittmaier, no. 477, p. 175.

10. Ibid., no. 483, p. 177.

11. Even Sooder's collection from Haslital in Switzerland confirms the observation that all humorous stories are more alive today than folktales and legends (cf. M. Sooder, p. 9).

12. Cf. BP IV, 130; Peuckert, *Deutsches Volkstum*, pp. 158f.; Kurt Ranke, "Schwank und Witz als Schwundstufe," in *Festschrift für Will-Erich Peuckert* (Berlin: E. Schmidt, 1955), pp. 41ff.

13. For example, see Hugo Hepding, "Ein Schwank über das Segensprechen," *Hessische Blätter für Volkskunde* 33 (1934), 78–89.

14. Dittmaier, no. 490, p. 179.

15. Will-Erich Peuckert, *Schlesiens deutsche Märchen* (Breslau: Ostdeutsche Verlagsanstalt, 1932), no. 166, p. 389; cf. H. Schauerte, "Des Volks Scherz und Spiel mit heiligen Dingen," *Theologie und Glaube* 40 (1950).

16. Walther Aichele, ed., *Zigeunermärchen*, MdW (Jena: Diederichs, 1926), no. 14, p. 61.

17. Tillhagen, *Taikon*, pp. 115ff.

18. MdW, *Donauland*, pp. 276ff.

19. MdW, *Lettisch-litauische Volksmärchen*, p. 239.

20. Ibid., p. 134.

21. Peuckert, *Schlesiens deutsche Märchen*, no. 166, p. 389. When Jesus and St. Peter spend the night at a Swabian farmer's, they hear the following in the morning: "Up, to work! There's threshing to be done!" And when they don't react: "Dammit! You're not out of bed yet, you lazy dogs, you! Did I let you stay here so you could loaf around? For God's sake, do I have to yell all day?" (E. Meier, no. 11, p. 50). Also see Thompson, *The Folktale*, pp. 150f.

22. BP III, 538ff.

23. Cf. ibid., 542, and Johannes Bolte, "Ein dänisches Märchen von Petrus und dem Ursprunge der bösen Weiber," *Zeitschrift des Vereins für Volkskunde* 11 (1901), 252–62.

24. Examples in BP II, 189.

25. Cf. ibid., 149ff. and 163ff.

26. See the relevant items in Merkelbach-Pinck, *Lothringer Volksmärchen*, e.g., pp. 103, 126, 135, 149, 352, etc.; also Dittmaier, nos. 384ff.; pp. 137ff.; Leza Uffer, *Rätoromanische Märchen und ihre Erzähler*, Schriften der Schweizerischen Gesellschaft für Volkskunde 29 (Basel: G. Krebs, 1945), nos. 13ff., pp. 194ff.

27. Cf. BP III, 189.

28. Examples in ibid., 451.

29. Cf. BP II, 149ff.

30. Cf. Wagner, "Formen der Volkserzählung," p. 251.

31. Max Wehrli, *Allgemeine Literaturwissenschaft*, Wissenschaftliche Forschungsberichte, geisteswissenschaftliche Reihe, vol. 3 (Bern: A. Francke, 1951), p. 86; cf. P. von Tieghem, "La question des genres littéraires," *Helicon* 1 (1939), 95; J. Schwarz, "Der Lebenssinn der Dichtungsgattungen," *Dichtung und Volkstum* 42 (1942), 93ff.; P. Böckmann, "Die Lehre von Wesen und Formen der Dichtung," in Fritz Martin, ed., *Vom Geist der Dichtung. Gedächtnisschrift für Robert Petsch* (Hamburg: Hoffmann & Compe, 1949).

32. Cf. James G. Frazer, *Folklore in the Old Testament*, 3 vols. (London: Macmillan & Co., 1918); Hermann Gunkel, *Das Märchen im Alten Testament*, Religionsgeschichtliche Volksbücher, II. Reihe, vols. 23–25 (Tübingen: Mohr, 1921).

33. Cf. O. Weinreich, "Das Märchen von Amor und Psyche und andere Volksmärchen im Altertum," in Ludwig Friedländer, *Darstellungen aus der Sittengeschichte Roms*, 9th and 10th eds., vol. 4 (Leipzig: S. Hirzel, 1921), pp. 89–132.

34. Cf. Friedrich von der Leyen, *Das Märchen in den Götterliedern der Edda* (Berlin: G. Reimer, 1899).

35. Cf. Andreas Heusler, *Die Anfänge der isländischen Saga*, Abhandlungen der königlichen preußischen Akademie der Wissenschaften, 1913, philosophische-historische Klasse, no. 9 (Berlin: G. Reimer, 1914); Jan de Vries, *Betrachtungen zum Märchen, besonders in seinem Verhältnis zu Heldensage und Mythos*, FFC no. 150 (Helsinki: Suomalainen Tiedeakatemia, 1954).

36. Cf. Jensen, *Mythos*.

37. Cf. BP IV, 41ff. (the section "Zeugnisse zur Geschichte der Märchen").

## III. THE FOLKTALE AND THE REALITY OF
## THE MAGICAL WORLD-VIEW

### Magic

1. The article "Similia Similibus," promised for the supplement in HdA I, 38, and VIII, 4, did not appear.

2. Antti Aarne counted a total of 760 narratives of "The Magic Flight" among 43 different peoples (Antti Aarne, *Die magische Flucht*, FFC no. 92 [Helsinki:

Suomalainen Tiedeakatemia, 1930]), and a considerable number of versions have been compiled since. Because the motif of the magic flight is well suited to depict the hero's escape from the power of a demon or sorcerer, it is added as a closing motif to numerous folktales; for example, we find it in versions of the following tales: "Rapunzel" (cf. BP I, 97), "Hansel and Gretel" (cf. BP I, 115), "Fledgling" (cf. BP I, 443), "The Water Nixie" (cf. BP II, 140ff.), "The Prince and the Princess" (cf. BP II, 526f.), "Iron Hans" (cf. BP III, 136), and "The Drummer" (cf. BP III, 93).

In addition to the numerous versions compiled by Aarne and Bolte and Polivka, we should also mention that the magic flight appears in ancient American tradition (Walter Krickeberg, ed., *Märchen der Azteken und Inkaperuaner, Maya und Muisca,* MdW [Jena: Diederichs, 1928], p. xii.) There are also African versions in Omdurman (southern Egypt; Atlantis, vol. IV, *Märchen aus Kordofan* [Jena: Diederichs, 1923], no. 19, pp. 216ff.), as well as in west Sudan (Atlantis, vol. VIII, no. 68, pp. 132ff.).

Prestel, p. 59, also contains numerous instances of the magic flight; also see Sydow, *Selected Papers on Folklore,* pp. 232ff.; "magische Flucht," HdM II, 158ff. (by Aly); HdA V, 1128 ("magische Flucht im Totenkult"); Marie His, "Die magische Flucht und das Wettverwandeln," *Schweizerisches Archiv für Volkskunde* 30 (1930), 107–29; K. Ranke, *Schleswig-Holsteinische Volksmärchen,* vol. 1, pp. 150ff.

3. Examples in BP II, 140, note 1.

4. Ovid, *Metamorphoses* 10, 664, "Atalante motif"; cf. Wilhelm Roscher, *Ausführliches Lexikon der griechischen und römischen Mythologie* (Leipzig: B. G. Teubner, 1884–86), vol. 1, pp. 664ff.

5. Ovid, *Metamorphoses* 7, 54; cf. Roscher, *Lexikon,* vol. 1, p. 3, and Aarne, *Magische Flucht,* pp. 16f.

6. *Sammlung Thule,* 2nd series, vol. 21 (Jena: Diederichs, 1923), pp. 221ff.

7. Prestel, p. 59; the HdA lacks an article on "zurückwerfen" (throwing back); the article "Rücken" promised for the supplement did not appear, but see the entries listed under "rückwärts" in the index, as well as Hugo Hepding, "Hintersichwerfen als Kultritus," in *Festgabe für K. Helm* (1951), pp. 219ff., and Hugo Hepding, "Hintersichwerfen in Orakelbrauch," *Hessische Blätter für Volkskunde* 64 (1953), 110.

8. *American Anthropologist* 4 (1902), 626; cf. Naumann, *Primitive Gemeinschaftskultur,* pp. 26 and 62; W. Muster, *Der Schamanismus und seine Spuren in der Saga, im deutschen Brauch, Märchen und Glauben,* Diss. Graz, 1947, p. 146.

9. Cf. HdA III, pp. 1239ff.; the HdM still lacks an article on "Haare" (hair). The king and freemen wear their hair unshorn, in contrast to the slaves, who are property controlled by others.

10. Karl Bartsch, *Sagen, Märchen und Gebräuche aus Mecklenburg* (Vienna: W. Braumüller, 1879/80), vol. 2, p. 137.

11. BP I, 282; in the final version of KHM 29 this sentence is missing.

12. Saxo Grammaticus, 8th book; additional examples in BP I, 282, 289; IV, 111.

13. Cf. Roscher, *Mythologisches Lexikon,* III, 2, pp. 3261ff. The modern Greek folktale of Zakynthos also belongs here: "Captain Thirteen's" wife betrays him by cutting off his three chest hairs which contain his strength (Bernhard Schmidt, *Griechische Märchen, Sagen und Volkslieder* [Leipzig: B. G. Teubner], pp. 91ff.; cf. Hahn, *Griechische und albanesische Märchen,* vol. 2, p. 282).

14. Judges 16:17ff.; cf. Gunkel, p. 109.

15. Some versions of KHM 113 contain similar episodes; cf. BP I, 501, and II, 526.

16. Cf. BP I, 235; also Rumpf, *Rotkäppchen;* Paul Delarue, "Les contes merveilleux de Perrault et la tradition populaire," *Bulletin folklorique d'Ile de France,* new series 13 (1951).

17. Cf. "Blut," HdM I, 278ff. (by Heckscher), and, "Blut," HdA I, 1434ff. (by Stemplinger); for further instances see BP II, 274, 526, and IV, 107.

18. Cf. Adelbert Erler, "Der Ursprung der Gottesurteile," *Paideuma* 8 (1941), 44–

65; HdA III, 1050 and 1054; the "ordeal of the bier" also occurs in the folktale: The murdered person's bones turn red in the murderer's hand (MdW, *Lettisch-litauische Märchen*, no. 49, p. 317). The events in "The Singing Bone" (KHM 28) are also a sort of intensified ordeal of the bier.

19. Cf. the origin of the ritual Jewish slaughter: "Only be sure that you do not eat the blood; for the blood is the life, and you shall not eat the life with the flesh. You shall not eat it; you shall pour it upon the earth like water" (Deuteronomy 12:23f.).

20. Saliva, semen, urine, blood, hair, etc., can also represent the person from whom they originate.

21. Robert Hamilton Mathews, *Ethnological Notes on the Aboriginal Tribes of New-South Wales and Victoria* (Sydney: F. W. White, 1905), p. 157. A related phenomenon is the burglar who leaves his droppings at the scene of the crime. Hans Gross (Handbuch für Untersuchungsrichter, 6th ed. [Munich: J. Schweltzer, 1914], vol. 1, pp. 531f.) says, "It commonly occurs that the perpetrator leaves some belonging at the scene of the crime because he believes this will prevent his deed, or at least its perpetrator, from being discovered. . . . Even in recent years robbers' excrement is almost regularly found after robberies in large jewelery stores in Berlin."

22. Vladimir Germanovich Bogoraz, *Chukchee Mythology*, Publications of the Jesup North Pacific Expedition, vol. 8, pt. 1 (Leiden: E. J. Brill, and New York: G. E. Stechert, 1910), pp. 282f.

23. Vladimir Iokel'son, *The Koryak*, Publications of the Jesup North Pacific Expedition, vol. 6 (1905), p. 316; cf. Geza Roheim, "Das Selbst," *Imago* 7 (1921), pp. 160ff.

24. Cf. the ordeal of the bier. Conversely, the whole demands its parts: The hanged man who had his liver or loin cut out by a hungry man comes from the gallows and demands the return of his bodily parts (KHM 211; cf. BP III, 478ff., and HdM II, 304).

25. In the Spanish folktales collected by Aurelio Macedonia Espinosa, a flower sings on the murdered man's grave when someone blows on it, thus revealing the crime (*Spanische Märchen*, MdW [Jena: Diederichs, 1961], p. 331).

26. Cf. BP I, 26off.

27. Theodor Vernaleken, *Österreichische Kinder- und Hausmärchen* (Vienna, 1864), no. 59.

28. August von Löwis of Menar, *Russische Volksmärchen*, MdW [Jena: Diederichs, 1921), no. 28, pp. 158f.

29. *German Legends*, no. 62.

30. For further parallels in folktales, legends, and myths, see BP I, 422f.; cf. "Knochen," HdA V, 6–14 (by Bächtold-Stäubli); E. Benninger, "Die Leichenzerstückelung als vor- und frühgeschichtliche Bestattungssitte," *Anthropos* 26 (1931), 769ff. (The section "Knochenkultus" in Ernst Ludwig Rochholz, *Deutscher Unsterblichkeitsglaube* [Berlin: F. Dümmler, 1867], pp. 219ff., contains numerous examples of reincarnation from bones.)

31. Cf. Roscher, *Mythologisches Lexikon*, vol. 3, p. 2.

32. *Die jüngere Edda*, Sammlung Thule, vol. 20 (Jena: Diederichs, 1925), pp. 91f.; cf. Jan de Vries, *Altgermanische Religionsgeschichte*, vol. 2 (Berlin: W. de Gruyter, 1937), pp. 117 and 188.

33. The history of symbols contains other such transformations into opposite meanings. For example, today Justice with the blindfold is a symbol of judgment "without looking at the individual," but it originally stood for the blind, dumb justice to whom people frequently lied.

34. Adolf Friedrich, "Knochen und Skelett in der Vorstellungswelt Nordasiens," *Wiener Beiträge zur Kulturgeschichte und Linguistik* 5 (1943), 196; cf. Uno Harva, *Die religiösen Vorstellungen der altaischen Völker*, FFC no. 125 (Helsinki: Suomalainen Tiedeakatemia, 1938).

35. Friedrich, "Knochen"; cf. Karl Meuli, "Griechische Opferbräche," in Olaf Gigon, ed., *Phyllobolia für Peter von der Mühll* (Basel: B. Schwabe, 1946), pp. 185–288.

36. Friedrich, "Knochen," pp. 193f.

37. MdW, *Märchen aus Siberien*, no. 17, pp. 74ff.; cf. Adolf Friedrich and Georg Budrus, *Schamanengeschichten aus Siberien* (Munich: O. W. Barth, 1955). Narrative no. 57 in MdW, *Siberien*, pp. 228–36, reports similar events; cf. Friedrich, "Knochen," pp. 204f. and notes 36–37.

38. Vladimir Germanovich Bogoraz, "Tales of Yukaghir, Lamut, and Russianized Natives of Eastern Siberia," *Anthropological Papers of the American Museum of Natural History* 20:1 (New York: The Trustees of the American Museum of Natural History, 1918), 44; cf. MdW, *Siberien*, p. 307, the annotation to no. 17.

39. Friedrich, "Knochen," p. 207, contains numerous examples; cf. Muster, *Schamanismus*, p. 151; T. Lehtisalo, "Der Tod und die Wiedergeburt des künftigen Schamanen," *Journal de la Societé Finno-Ougrienne* 48 (1937); H. Nachtigall, "Die kulturhistorische Wurzel der Schamanenskelettierung," *Zeitschrift für Ethnologie* 77 (1952), 188–97.

40. Compilation of the examples from Friedrich, "Knochen," note 37, pp. 240f.; Friedrich, *Priestertümer*, pp. 184f., contains African examples.

41. Reinhold Köhler, *Kleinere Schriften zur Märchenforschung*, ed. Johannes Bolte (Weimar: E. Fulber, 1898), pp. 258f.

42. Atlantis, vol. II, *Volksmärchen der Kabylen* (Jena: Diederichs, 1922), pp. 36f.

43. Jeremiah Curtin, *Myths and Folklore of Ireland* (Boston: Little, Brown & Co., 1890), p. 32, quoted from Leopold Schmidt, "Pelops und die Haselhexe," *Laos* 1 (Stockholm, 1951), 69f.

44. Johann Adolf Heyl, *Volkssagen, Bräuche und Meinungen aus Tirol* (Brixen: Verlag der Buchhandlung des kath.-Pol.-Pressvereins, 1897), pp. 435f., no. 125, quoted from Schmidt, "Pelops," p. 68; additional examples compiled from legends from the Alps in Leopold Schmidt, "Der 'Herr der Tiere' in einigen Sagenlandschaften Europas und Eurasiens," *Anthropos* 47 (1952), 509–38.

45. *German Legends*, no. 62.

46. Examples in Muster, p. 151.

47. MdW, *Siberien*, no. 55, pp. 221ff.

48. Gavriil Vasil'evich Ksenofontov, *Legenden und Erzählungen von den Schamanen bei Jakuten, Burjaten und Tungusen* (Moscow, 1930), pp. 74f., quoted from Nachtigall, p. 193.

49. Georg Sverdrup, *Die Hausurnen und die Heiligkeit des Hauses* (Oslo, 1947), p. 30; Max Scheler, *Wesen und Formen der Sympathie*, 5th ed. (Frankfurt: G. Schulte-Bulmke, 1948).

50. Adolf Wuttke, *Der deutsche Volksaberglaube der Gegenwart*, 3rd ed. (Berlin: Wiegandt & Grieben, 1900), p. 126; cf. R. Bilz, "Tiertöter-Skrupulantismus. Betrachtungen über das Tier als Entelechial-Doppelgänger des Menschen," *Jahrbuch für Psychologie und Psychotherapie* 3 (1955), 266ff.

51. Rochholz, *Deutscher Unsterblichkeitsglaube*, p. 146.

52. Merkelbach-Pinck, *Lothringer Volksmärchen*, pp. 127ff.; cf. Hendricks, pp. 126f.

53. Heinrich von Wlislocki, *Märchen und Sagen der transsilvanischen Zigeuner* (Berlin: R. Stricker, 1886), p. 335; cf. BP III, 442; also see BP's compilation of versions of "Friendly Animals: Three Tales" II, 459ff.

54. Cf. HdA VIII, 807f.; Hendricks, p. 7.

55. Motifs of "the separable soul" and "the ogre's heart in the egg"; e.g. Merkelbach-Pinck, *Lothringer Volksmärchen*, pp. 212ff.; cf. KHM 197 ("The Crystal Ball"), although this tale does not preserve the pure tale type; cf. BP III, 434–40; I, 134; II, 340; III, 92 and 425; also see the article "Ei," HdM I, 457ff. (by Bargheer); Maria Lioba Lechner, *Das Ei in Volksglauben und Brauch. Beiträge zur Volkskunde*, Diss. Freiburg/Switzerland, 1953; cf. Wilhelm Hauff's tale "Das kalte Herz."

56. Carl Wilhelm von Sydow points out that geese and ducks, not chickens, are usually the domesticated birds in this tale. Sydow thus concludes that the tale type

"The Monster with His Heart in the Egg" must be older than the introduction of the domesticated chicken to Europe. Legends, which are not as old, speak of chickens, not ducks. The folktale appears to have stood still and maintained its older elements, while the legend must incorporate newer developments in order to survive as a believed form. Thus in the legend, as in reality, the chicken has superseded the duck. Carl Wilhelm von Sydow, *Vära Folksagor*, Natur och Kultur, vol. 146 (Stockholm: Natur och Kultur, 1941), pp. 118ff.; cf. Thompson, *The Folktale*, p. 35.

57. James Mooney, *Myths of the Cherokee*, 19th annual report, American Ethnological Bureau (Washington: Government Printing Office, n.d.), p. 394; cf. Vries, *Betrachtungen*, pp. 50ff.

58. Atlantis, vol. II (Kabylen), p. 99; see also p. 110.

59. Vladimir Iokhel'son, *Religion and Myths of the Koryak*, Publications of the Jesup North Pacific Expedition (Leiden: E. J. Brill, and New York: G. E. Stechert, 1905), no. 62 = MdW, *Siberien*, no. 57, pp. 228ff.; cf. Adolf Friedrich, "Die Forschung über das frühzeitliche Jägertum," *Paideuma* 2 (1941), 37. In an Eskimo tale, a chief skilled in magic is injurable only on his big toe, which contains his heart (Rasmussen, *Die Gabe des Adlers*, p. 170).

60. MdW, *Siberien*, p. 30.

61. BP III, 434 ff.; cf. James Frazer, *The External Soul in Folktales* (London, 1913); Friedrich von der Leyen, "Zur Entstehung des Märchens," *Archiv für das Studium der neueren Sprachen und Literaturen*, vols. 113–16, years 58–60 (1904–1906), vol. 115, p. 6; Thompson, *The Folktale*, pp. 35 and 76; Isenberg, p. 107.

62. For example, MdW, *Nordische Volksmärchen*, II, 119ff. (from Norway).

63. Cf. Sydow, *Vära Folksagor*, pp. 118ff.

64. Jacob Grimm, *Deutsche Mythologie*, unchanged reprint of the 4th edition, Elard Hugo Meyer, ed. (Basel: B. Schwabe, 1953), vol. 2, pp. 697f.; cf. Karlis Straubergs, *Lettisk Folktro om de Döda* (Stockholm: Nordiska museets, 1949).

65. *Danske Studier* 25 (1928) and the HdM article "Glasbergritt," II, 627ff.

66. Vries, *Betrachtungen*, p. 63; cf. Peuckert, *Deutsches Volkstum*, pp. 49ff.

67. Examples and variants: BP II, 46, and I, 442; see also Panzer in John Meier, *Volkskunde*, pp. 232f.; Gerhard Kahlo, *Die Verse in den Sagen und Märchen* (Leipzig: Noske, 1919).

68. Cf. BP III, 199.

69. Cf. Goethe's "Sorcerer's Apprentice" or Hauff's "Kalif Storch."

70. Only folktales in the *Arabian Nights* contain written magic; cf. Sydow, *Vära Folksagor*, pp. 92ff.; Alfred Bertholet, *Die Macht der Schrift in Glauben und Aberglauben*, Abhandlungen der deutschen Akademie der Wissenschaften zu Berlin; philosophisch-historische Klasse, 1949, no. 1 (Berlin: Akademie-Verlag, 1949). In "The Seven Ravens" (KHM 25), the heroine does not think of *writing down* that she is innocent. The motif of being forbidden from speaking thus presupposes a nonliterate epoch. We must remember that illiteracy lasted into the nineteenth century, and in other countries even into the twentieth.

71. The spell also takes effect immediately in many versions of "The Six Swans" (KHM 49); cf. BP I, 430; also see KHM 119a (cf. BP II, 560f.) and KHM 219 (cf. BP III, 531ff.).

72. Rasmussen, p. 158.

73. Panzer in John Meier, *Volkskunde*, pp. 250f.; cf. Isaiah 43:1: "I have called you by name, you are mine . . . ;" cf. "Namen," HdA VI, 950ff. (by Aly); Hellmut Rosenfeld, "Die Magie des Namens," *Bayerisches Jahrbuch für Volkskunde* (1950), 94–98; Lutz Röhrich, "Der Dämon und sein Name," *Beiträge zur Geschichte der deutschen Sprache und Literatur* 73 (1951), 456–68; Inger Boberg, *Baumeistersagen*, FFC no. 151 (Helsinki: Suomalainen Tiedeakatemia, 1955), pp. 7ff.

74. For example, when someone asked a shepherd boy in Wiesental what his name was, he answered: "My name is what it is," and finally wrote his name in the

air (HdA. VI, 950).

75. Cf. BP I, 490ff.; cf. Sydow, *Våra Folksagor*, pp. 138ff.; Edward Clodd, *Tom-Tit-Tot: An Essay on Savage Philosophy in Folk-tale* (London: Duckworth & Co., 1898); Carl Wilhelm von Sydow, *Två Spinn sagor* (Stockholm, 1909); Jan de Vries, *Die Märchen von klugen Rätsellösern*, FFC no. 73 (Helsinki: Suomalainen Tiedeakatemia, 1928); also see the Liungman-Sydow debate in *Rig* 1941 and 1943.

76. Compilation of versions in BP I, 497.

77. Song of Alwis; Edda (Sammlung Thule), vol. 2, no. 14, pp. 100ff.

78. Atlantis, vol. I (Kabylen), pp. 280ff.

79. Cf. Leopold Schmidt, "Kulturgeschichtliche Gedanken zur Musik im Märchen," *Muzikerziehung* 3:3 (Vienna, 1950).

80. MdW, *Siberien*, p. 66, no. 15.

81. Rasmussen, pp. 107ff.; cf. Dagobert Frey, *Dämonie des Blickes*, Akademie der Wissenschaft und der Literatur; Abhandlungen der geistes-und sozial-wissenschaftlichen Klasse (1953), no. 6 (Wiesbaden: Verlag der Akademie der Wissenschaften und der Literatur, 1954).

82. MdW, *Irische Volksmärchen*, p. 14, no. 4.

83. Ibid., p. 69, no. 12, and p. 37, no. 7.

84. Leyen, *Die Welt der Märchen*, vol. 2, p. 153.

85. Atlantis, vol. II (Kabylen), p. 31; Theodor Storm's novella "Die Regentrude" contains a similar motif.

86. Plutarch, *De Iside* XVI.

87. Cf. Robert Douglas Scott, *The Thumb of Knowledge in Legends of Finn, Sigurd and Taliesin* (New York: Institute of French Studies, 1930); HdA II, 1489, and "Finger," HdM II, 121ff. (by Archer Taylor).

88. Cf. U. Holmberg, "Über die Jagdriten der nördlichen Völker Asiens und Europas," *Journal de la Société Finno-Ougrienne* 41 (1925); Meuli, *Opferbräuche*, pp. 224ff. We also encounter the motif of the dragon's tongues in Wolfdietrich, in the Greek heroic legend, and in Indian narratives. There are numerous parallels in folktales and heroic legends: BP I, 547ff.; cf. Rath, p. 28.

89. BP I, 88; cf. W. Blasius, "Krankheit und Heilung im Märchen," *Materia Medica Nordmark* VI, 12 (1954), 448ff.

90. Cf. "Blut," HdM I, 278ff. (by Heckscher).

91. Cf. "Galgen," HdA. III, 258ff. (by Müller-Bergström), particularly no. 4, "Galgenamulette"; also see Gross, *Handbuch für den Untersuchungsrichter*, pp. 528ff.

92. Ludwig Strackerjahn, *Aberglauben und Sagen aus dem Herzogtum Oldenburg* (Oldenburg: G. Stalling, 1909), vol. 2, p. 172; cf. Hendricks, p. 125.

93. Wuttke, p. 117; cf. Hendricks, pp. 131f.; also see Wilhelm Wisser, ed., *Plattdeutsche Volksmärchen* (Ausgabe für Erwachsene), MdW (Jena: Diederichs, 1922), vol. 1, pp. 42ff., vol. 2, pp. 270ff.

94. Alois John, *Sitte und Brauch im deutschen Westböhmen* (Prague: J. Koch, 1905); cf. Wuttke, p. 314; Hendricks, p. 133.

95. Also see MdW, *Donauland*, pp. 8off., and MdW, *Plattdeutsche Märchen*, vol. 1, pp. 1ff.

96. Wlislocki, no. 21, pp. 55ff.

97. Schmidt and Kahle, *Palästina*, pp. 165ff.

98. BP I, 289.

99. Atlantis, vol. IV (Kordofan), pp. 31ff.

100. MdW, *Südseemärchen*, no. 48, 206.

101. Cf. Otto Spies, *Türkische Volksbücher. Ein Beitrag zur vergleichenden Märchenkunde*, Form und Geist 12 (Leipzig: Hermann Eichblatt, 1929), p. 29.

102. MdW, *Zigeunermärchen*, no. 23, pp. 91ff.; cf. no. 14, p. 61.

103. The change in the classical Mediterranean view of reality took place very early. We have evidence from ancient Greece which demonstrates that folktales

were considered nursemaids' tales only for children (cf. Weinreich, "Das Märchen von Amor und Psyche," in Friedländer, *Darstellungen aus der Sittengeschichte Roms;* BP IV, 42.

### Man and Animal—Transformation and Disenchantment

1. The 1819 edition of KHM, no. 104; cf. BP II, 451ff.; I, 134; and V, 299. Grateful animals also appear in some versions of KHM 24 ("Mother Holle"), cf. BP I, 227. Versions of this motif complex still circulate among tribal societies. For example, helpful animals do valuable service for their benefactors in Kpelle folktales from Africa: Cat, goshawk, porcupine, dog, and otter help the lad who took care of them. A mongoose, cat, rat, and snake save the boy who helped them. The fish rewards the man for sparing his life. The eagle bestows gifts upon the poor. Other examples in Westermann, *Die Kpelle*, p. 368.

2. MdW, *Irische Volksmärchen*, no. 28, pp. 224ff.; cf. no. 35, pp. 294ff.; cf. Lutz Röhrich, "Hund, Pferd, Kröte und Schlange als symbolische Leitgestalten in Volksglauben und Sage," *Zeitschrift für Religions- und Geistesgeschichte* 3 (1951), 69ff.

3. Vernaleken, *Österreichsche Kinder- und Hausmärchen*, no. 9.

4. Merkelbach-Pinck, *Lothringer Volksmärchen*, pp. 308ff.; cf. Woeller, pp. 206f.

5. For example, Adolf Friedrich compiled African instances of this motif (*Priestertümer*, pp. 18off.); cf. Hendricks, p. 121; also see Lutz Röhrich, "Mensch und Tier im Märchen," *Schweizer Archiv für Volkskunde* 49 (1953), 165–93; the main findings of this chapter were published in this article.

6. Haltrich, no. 40, p. 170; cf. A. Genzel, p. 137.

7. Sigmund Freud, *Totem und Tabu: einige Übereinstimmungen im Seelenleben der Wilden und der Neurotiker* (Leipzig and Vienna: H. Heller, 1913).

8. Baumann, p. 375.

9. Cf. Baumann, p. 379; also Hermann Baumann, "Das Tier als alter ego in Afrika," *Paideuma* 5 (1952), 167–88.

10. Franz Boas, "The Central Eskimo," *Ethnological Reports* 6 (1888), 638f., quoted from Wundt, *Völkerpsychologie*, vol. 5, p. 167.

11. For example, Jahn, *Volksmärchen aus Pommern und Rügen*, no. 21, p. 135; MdW, *Russische Volksmärchen*, pp. 214f.; cf. "Bärensohn," HdM I, 172ff. (by W. Golther); Lily Weiser-Aall, *Altgermanische Jünglingsweihen und Männerbünde*, Bausteine zur Volkskunde und Religionswissenschaft, no. 1 (Bühl: Konkordia, 1927), pp. 53ff. Pertev Naili Borotav, *Les histoires d'ours en Anatolie*, FFC no. 152 (Helsinki: Suomalainen Tiedeakatemia, 1955), addresses bear stories which claim to report true events; also see Werner Bergengruen's story "Die Bärenbraut."

12. Romulus and Remus; cf. Panzer in John Meier, ed., *Deutsche Volkskunde*, p. 252. Baumann also suspects a totemic basis for African folktales which depict "child raising by animals" (Baumann, *Schöpfung und Urzeit*, p. 374).

13. Cf. Wesselski, *Märchen des Mittelalters*, p. 247.

14. MdW, *Irische Volksmärchen*, no. 16, pp. 75ff.; cf. KHM 66.

15. Arnold van Gennep, *Mythes et légendes d'Australie* (Paris: E. Guilmoto, 1906), cited from Wesselski, *Versuch einer Theorie des Märchens*, p. 38.

16. R. Lewinsohn, *Eine Geschichte der Tiere, ihr Einfluß auf Zivilistion und Kultur* (Hamburg: Rowohlt, 1952), p. 103.

17. Aarne, *Ursprungssagen*, no. 112.

18. Cf. James G. Frazer, *Totemism and Exogamy* (London: Macmillan & Co., 1910); Cornelius François Visser, *Über den Ursprung der Vorstellungen von tierischen Menschenahnen bei den Eingeborenen Zentralaustraliens*, Diss. Leipzig, 1913; M. Pancritius, "Europäischer Totemismus," *Anthropos* 12/13 (1917–18); Arnold van Gennep, *L'état actuel du problème totémique* (Paris: E. Leroux, 1920); Wilhelm Koppers, "Der Totemismus als menschheitsgeschichtliches Problem," *Anthropos* 31 (1936), 159–76; Wilhelm Schmidt, *Handbuch der Methode der kulturhistorischen Ethnologie* (Münster:

Aschendorff, 1937); "Animals," in *Encyclopaedia of Religion and Ethics* (Edinburgh: T. & T. Clark, 1908), vol. 1, p. 484; "Totemismus," HdA VIII, 1034–46 (by K. Beth); "Tiergestalt," HdA VIII, 819–42 (by Riegler).

19. Cf. HdM II, 59. This is the approach we still find in Brehm's "Tierleben," when the great natural scientist calls his animals "cruel," "noble," "grateful," and "untrue."

20. Cf. Karl von Amira, "Tierstrafen und Tierprozesse," *Mitteilungen des österrichischen Institutes für Geschichtsforschung* 4 (1891), 545ff.; also see Exodus 21:28ff.

21. Wesselski, *Märchen des Mittelalters*, pp. 247ff.

22. Cf. Melchoir Sooder, *Bienen und Bienenhalten in der Schweiz*, Schriften der Schweizerischen Gesellschaft für Volkskunde (Basel: G. Krebs, 1952), pp. 196ff.; "Biene," HdA I, 1231; Hendricks, pp. 6f.

23. Jensen, *Mythos und Kult*, p. 165.

24. Aphanassjew [Afanas'ev], *Russische Volksmärchen*, vol. 1, no. 9, p. 73.

25. Cf. Antti Aarne, *Der tiersprachenkundige Mann und seine neugierige Frau*, FFC no 15 (Hamina: Suomalaisen Tiedeakatemian Kustantama, 1914); Theodor Benfey, *Kleinere Schriften zur Märchenforschung* (Berlin: Reuther & Reichard, 1894), vol. 2, pp. 19ff.; Friedrich von der Leyen, *Das Märchen*, 3rd ed. (Leipzig: Quelle & Meyer, 1925), pp. 116f.

26. MdW, *Afrikanische Märchen*, p. 12.

27. Cf. Édourd Délebecque, *Le cheval dans l'iliade* (Paris: C. Klincksieck, 1951). We also find the talking horse that warns its owner about potential harm in Kordofan: Atlantis, vol. IV (*Märchen aus Kordofan*), p. 165; also see Georg Siegmund, "Tiersprache und Menschensprache," *Stimmen der Zeit* 156:7 (1955), 6ff.

28. Cf. HdM II, 429ff., and BP III, 283.

29. Atlantis, vol. I, *Volksmärchen der Kabylen*, vol. 1, "Weisheit" (Jena: Diederichs, 1921), p. 76.

30. Rasmussen, p. 52.

31. In a Caucasian folktale a pig changes itself into a beautiful maiden and marries a king. The jealous vizier marries a real pig, but it remains a pig (Leyen, *Die Welt der Märchen*, vol. 2, pp. 7ff.).

32. For example, MdW, *Nordische Volksmärchen*, vol. 1, no. 1, pp. 3ff.

33. Cf. "Geburt," HdA III, 406–19; "Schwangerschaft," HdA VII, 1406–27 (both by Kummer); Sydow, *Våra Folksagor*, pp. 53ff.

34. Wisser, vol. 1, p. 202; also see Johann Wilhelm Wolf, *Deutsche Hausmärchen* (Göttingen: Dieterich, 1851), p. 112, no. 23, as well as BP I, 536. The same motif also occurs in some versions of KHM 62 ("The Queen Bee"); cf. BP II, 22; KHM 181 ("The Nixie of the Pond"), BP III, 322; and KHM 197 ("The Crystal Sphere"), BP III, 434.

35. Rasmussen, p. 169.

36. Adam Mischlich, *Neue Märchen aus Afrika*, Veröffentlichungen des staatlichen sächsischen Forschungsinstitutes für Völkerkunde, vol. 9 (Leipzig: R. Voigtländer, 1929), p. 152; cf. Helmut Straube, *Die Tierverkleidungen der afrikanischen Naturvölker*, Studien zur Kulturkunde 13 (Wiesbaden: F. Steiner, 1955).

37. Rasmussen, p. 52.

38. Ibid., p. 142.

39. Ibid., pp. 374f.

40. Baumann, *Schopfung and Urzeit*, p. 375.

41. Franz Boas, *Indianische Sagen*, pp. 90ff., cited from Wundt, *Völkerpsychologie*, vol. 5, pp. 192f.; cf. MdW, *Südseemärchen*, no. 26, p. 82.

42. Cf. BP II, 68f. The pursued person's self-transformation also appears in legends: When a poacher is surprised by a hunter, he changes himself into a hazel bush. The hunter breaks a bud off the bush when he goes by, and he thus pulls out some of the poacher's hair (Anton Birlinger, *Aus Schwaben* [Wiesbaden: H. Killinger, 1874], vol. 1, p. 315). In other cases the poacher turns himself into a stump on which

the hunter takes his noon rest (Karl Reiser, *Sagen, Gebräuche und Sprichwörter des Allgäus* [Kempten: J. Kösel, 1895–1902], vol. 1, p. 210). The article "Verwandlung," HdA VIII, 1629ff. (by K. Beth), includes additional examples.

43. Cf. BP II, 61ff. For additional parallels to the transformation contest, see MdW, *Siberien*, no. 1, pp. 11ff.; Aphanassjew [Afanas'ev], *Russische Volksmärchen*, vol. 1, no. 12, pp. 93ff.

44. Cf. Wesselski, *Versuch einer Theorie des Märchens*, pp. 30f.; Aarne, *Die magische Flucht*; Robert Wildhaber, "Kirke und die Schweine," *Schweizerisches Archiv für Volkskunde* 47 (1951), 236, note 13; Sydow, *Vära Folksagor*, pp. 92ff. The motif of the transformation contest appears in an ancient Greek legend about the demon Gelu, who steals children, and it is still part of folk belief in this case (cf. Roscher, *Mythologisches Lexikon*, vol. 1, p. 1610). Also, when Themis is pursued by Zeus, he continually changes himself into new animal forms (cf. Roscher, *Lexikon*, vol. 5, pp. 570ff.).

45. Steinen, *Unter den Naturvölkern Zentralbrasiliens*, p. 350, cited from Wundt, *Völkerpsychologie*, vol. 5, p. 109.

46. Atlantis, vol. IX (Zentralsudan), p. 141.

47. Leo Frobenius, *Kulturgeschichte Afrikas* (Zurich: Phaidon, 1933), p. 257; also see Friedrich, *Priestertümer*, pp. 183f.; as well as Friedrich, *Die Forschung über das frühzeitliche Jägertum*, pp. 27ff. and 35ff.

48. Theodor Benfey, *Pantschatantra, fünf Bücher indischer Fabeln, Märchen und Erzählungen*, 2 vols. (Leipzig: F. A. Brockhaus, 1859), vol. 1, pp. 216 and 415; cf. HdM II, 267ff.

49. This process must have entered Europe very early, because the sorceress Circe uses degrading black magic to transform Ulysses' companions into pigs in the *Odyssey* (cf. Wildhaber, "Kirke und die Schweine," p. 234).

50. Cf. BP II, 229–73; the chapter "Animal Wives and Husbands" in Thompson, *The Folktale*, pp. 353ff.; "La belle et la Bête," HdM I, 237 (by E. Tegethoff); and Jan Öjvind Swahn, *The Tale of Cupid and Psyche* (Lund: C. W. K. Gleerup, 1955).

51. Cf. Ziegler, *Die Frau im Märchen*, pp. 80f.

52. The word *Löweneckerchen* in the German title of this tale means "lark" and corresponds to the Westphalian *Lauberken* and the Lower Saxon *Leverken* (BP II, 229).

53. MdW, *Siberien*, p. 170.

54. Cf. HdM II, 286.

55. Atlantis, vol. XI (Oberguinea), no. 24, pp. 128ff. In southwest African folktales, the contest is between hyena and jackal; jackal is the luckier suitor in the end (MdW, *Afrikanische Märchen*, no. 30, pp. 138f.).

56. Atlantis, vol. X (Die atlantische Götterlehre), p. 280.

57. MdW, *Afrikanische Märchen*, no. 38, pp. 177ff.

58. Atlantis, vol. X (Die atlantische Götterlehre), p. 280.

59. Atlantis, vol. VIII (Westsudan), no. 113, pp. 263ff.

60. MdW, *Malaiische Märchen*, no. 60, pp. 288ff.; cf. note 60, pp. 324f.

61. George Amos Dorsey, *The Pawnee* (Washington, D.C.: Carnegie Institution, 1906), vol. 1 *(Mythology)*, p. 487, as well as another version of the same narrative on p. 686; cited from Wundt, *Völkerpsychologie*, vol. 5, pp. 172f.

62. Atlantis, vol. X (Götterlehre), pp. 241f.

63. Jensen, *Hainuwele*, no. 251, pp. 288ff.

64. Ibid., no. 217, p. 256; the same occurs in no. 228, pp. 266f. The animal spouse can also be the wife. For example, a Chinese folktale tells of a marriage between a peasant and a she-bear (Wolfram Eberhard, *Volksmärchen aus Südostchina*, FFC no. 128 [Helsinki: Suomalainen Tiedeakatemia, 1941], no. 80, p. 138). In a Siberian folktale a man catches a fish-girl (MdW, *Siberien*, pp. 84f.). We also find this tale type in Germany: In KHM 63 ("The Three Feathers") the bride is a toad. The poor miller's servant in KHM 106 finally wins the princess, who, as a cat, first demands he serve her. In east Prussian and Masurian versions we find a frog-

princess who leads Dumb Hans home instead of the frog-king (Karl Plenzat, *Die ost- und westpreußischen Märchen und Schwänke nach Typen geordnet*, Veröffentlichungen des volkskundlichen Archivs der pädagogischen Akademie Elbing, vol. 1 [Elbing: Verlag des volkskundlichen Archivs, 1927], p. 25; cf. HdM II, 267).

What is said for the animal husband obviously applies to the animal wife, too. We find all developmental forms for the bride as well. Among tribal societies there are narratives that perceive human-animal bonds without any negative ethical evaluation. For example, a South American narrative states, "A woman loved a sloth. Every time she went into the field or the woods, she took food and drink with her. Then she called out 'How! How!' The sloth climbed down from the tree, and they fondled each other like two lovers" (Theodor Koch-Grünberg, ed., *Indianermärchen aus Südamerika*, MdW [Jena: Diederichs, 1927], no. 22, p. 69). Temporary transformations into a woman also occur in tribal narratives: An African folktale from Kordofan tells of a wife who is a beautiful woman during the day, but at night she becomes a lioness (Atlantis, vol. IV [Märchen aus Kordofan], p. 297). In a narrative from the Moluccan island of Ceram, a man has a snake for a wife: During the day she is a snake; at night she changes herself into a woman (Jensen, *Hainuwele*, no. 227, p. 266).

65. MdW, *Neugriechische Märchen*, no. 26, p. 84.

66. Reider Th. Christiansen, *The Norwegian Fairytales*, FFC no. 46 (Helsinki: Suomalainen Tiedeakatemia, 1922), pp. 23f.

67. Aphanassjew [Afanas'ev], *Russische Volksmärchen*, vol. 2, pp. 22f.

68. Peuckert, *Schlesiens deutsche Märchen*, no. 5, p. 5.

69. The article "Werwolf" planned for the supplement to HdA IX, 503, did not appear; but see Wilhelm Hertz, *Der Werwolf. Beitrag zur Sagengeschichte* (Stuttgart: A. Kröner, 1862); Otto Höfler, *Kultische Geheimbünde der Germanen*, vol. 1 (Frankfurt: M. Diesterweg, 1934); and Otto Höfler, "Über germanische Verwandlungskulte," *Zeitschrift für deutsche Altertum* 73 (1936), 109ff.

70. Charlotte Oberfeld, *Beiträge zum Leben und der Bedeutung des Märchens in der Gegenwart*, Diss. Marburg, 1943, pp. 70f.

71. *Zeitschrift für Ethnologie* 1 (1869), 53f., cited from HdA VIII, 830.

72. Stith Thompson, *Tales of the North American Indians* (Cambridge: Harvard University Press, 1929), p. 91.

73. MdW, *Südseemärchen*, no. 38, p. 161.

74. Diamond Jenness, *Myths and Traditions from North-Alaska: The Mackenzie Delta and Coronation Gulf, Report of the Canadian Arctic Expedition, 1913–1918*, vol. 12, Eskimo Folklore, 57A, cited from "Verwandlung," HdA VIII, 1639.

75. "Death is transformation. Disenchantment is the return to life" (Naumann, *Primitive Gemeinschaftskultur*, p. 22). Cf. Naumann, *Grundzüge der deutschen Volkskunde*, p. 152; "Erlösung," HdA II, 925–39 (by F. Ranke).

76. For more details on burned animal coats, see the references in BP V, 299, and particularly the versions of "The Lilting, Leaping Lark" listed in BP II, 235ff. "No transformation is absolute; there is always something that remains constant while the form changes" (von der Leeuw, "Verwandlung," in RGG V, 1576).

77. Elli Zenker-Starzacher, *Eine deutsche Märchenerzählerin aus Ungarn* (Munich: Hoheneichen, 1941), p. 67.

78. For numerous examples of disenchantment through decapitation, see HdM II, 395f.; also see the article "Fuchs," HdM II, 286f. (by Peuckert); in addition see the references to release and disenchantment through decapitation in BP V, 271 (Erlösung und Entzauberung durch Enthauptung).

79. For example, KHM 193; cf. BP III, 406ff.; Thompson, *The Folktale*, pp. 87f.

80. Atlantis, vol. XII (Dichtkunst der Kassaiden), p. 90.

81. Atlantis, vol. XIII (Westsudan), no. 86, p. 160.

82. The double article "Erlösung" in HdM I, 578–90, by Ittenbach and Diewerge, tells us nothing about the history of the conception of disenchantment; cf. Heiligen-

dorff's article "Entzauberung," HdM I, 56off. Also, in the index to BP we find only references to particular instances under the entry "Entzauberung." In contrast, the article "Erlösung" in HdA II, 925–39, by Friedrich Ranke is very important, as well as the article "Erlösung" by J. Wach in RGG II, 279ff., and the article "Verwandlung" by v. d. Leeuw in RGG V, 1576f. The article "Verwünschung" planned for the supplement to HdA VIII, 1660, did not appear. See Stith Thompson, *Motif-Index of Folk-Literature*, FFC no. 16off. (Helsinki: Suomalainen Tiedeakatemia, 1932–36), DO-D799, for the range of individual motifs.

In addition, see Joachim Wach, *Der Erlösungsgedanke und seine Deutung* (Leipzig: Forschungsinstitut für vergleichende Religionsgeschichte, 1922); Hilde Boesebeck, *Verwünschung und Erlösung des Menschen in der deutschen Volkssage der Gegenwart. Ein Beitrag zur Untersuchung der Verwandlungsvorstellung im deutschen Volksglauben*, Diss. Frankfurt, 1926; Emma Frank, *Der Schlangenkuß. Die Geschichte eines Erlösungsmotivs in deutscher Volksdichtung*, Form und Geist 9 (Leipzig: H. Eichblatt, 1928), pp. 110ff.; Walter Hegar, "Die Verwandlung im Märchen," *Hessische Blätter für Volkskunde* 28 (1929), 110–40; Johannes Malthaner, *Die Erlösung im Märchen*, Diss. Heidelberg, 1934; *Eranosjahrbuch* 1936 (Zurich, 1937), special issue on "The Idea of Release in the East and West"; Traut Anacker, *Verzauberung und Erlösung im deutschen Volksmärchen*, Schriften der Albertus-Universität, Geisteswissenschaftliche Reihe, vol. 32 (Königsberg: Ost-Europa, 1941); Isenberg, *Geburt und Tod*; Wilfried Daim, *Tiefenpsychologie und Erlösung* (Vienna: Herold, 1954).

83. Peuckert, *Schlesiens deutsche Märchen*, no. 51, pp. 87f.
84. Jahn, *Volksmärchen aus Pommern und Rügen*, no. 2, pp. 12ff.
85. For example, disenchantment through a kiss in "Sleeping Beauty" (KHM 50); see the references under "Entzauberung durch Kuß" in BP V, 271.
86. Lefftz, *Märchen der Brüder Grimm, Urfassung*, p. 54.
87. Examples in BP I, 1ff., and Ziegler, *Die Frau im Märchen*, p. 104.
88. Grudde, *Plattdeutsche Volksmärchen aus Ostpreußen*, no. 30, p. 55.
89. Wisser, vol. 1, p. 160.
90. A. Karasek, "Drei Märchen aus Hedwig (Deutschprobener Volksinsel)," *Schlessische Blätter für Volkskunde* 3 (1941), 134.
91. "Erlösung," HdA II, 929 (by F. Ranke). Disenchantment through nightly torture also occurs in some versions of KHM 63 ("The Three Feathers"); cf. BP II, 37. Sexual intercourse also disenchants; for example, Grudde, *Plattdeutsche Volksmärchen*, no. 13, pp. 13ff.
92. Friedrich Giese, *Türkische Märchen*, MdW (Jena: Diederichs, 1925), no. 24, pp. 193ff.; MdW, *Russische Volksmärchen*, no. 14, is similar; cf. Roscher, *Mythologisches Lexikon*, vol. 3, pp. 3317ff. (on Ovid, *Met.* 10:243ff.).
93. Cf. Anacker, p. 109.
94. Regarding motifs of unsuccessful release in the legend, see Friedrich Ranke's article "Erlösung," HdA II, 931.
95. Naturally there are also transitional and mixed forms. For example, it is legendary when the woodsman asks the hero to cut off his head and then flies away as a white dove in a Bohemian version of "Golden Boy" (Type 314) (cf. Rath, p. 117).
96. Cf. Gustav Mensching, *Das Wunder im Völkerglauben* (Amsterdam: Pantheon, 1942). It is interesting that in the Old Testament, disenchantment is still conceived of as being completely of this world: Yahweh "released" his people from slavery to the Egyptians. Israel's entire history consists of Yahweh releasing others. Release (or disenchantment) in the Old Testament means release from external suffering (disease, temptation) in the individual's life as well; cf. RGG II, 269f.

### Manners and Customs

1. Prestel, *Märchen als Lebensdichtung*, p. 48.
2. Cf. the controversy between Waldemar Liungman ("Till folksago-forskningens metodik," *Rig* 24 [1941], 89–108) and Carl Wilhelm von Sydow ("Finsk

metod och modern sagoforskning," *Rig* 26 [1943], 1–23), as well as the compilation of the versions of KHM 55 in BP I, 490ff.

3. Naumann, *Grundzüge der deutschen Volkskunde*, p. 150; cf. BP I, 289ff.

4. Cf. Woeller, pp. 42 and 58.

5. Cf. Ruth Klein, *Lexikon der Mode* (Baden-Baden: W. Klein, 1950), pp. 223ff.; Olga Šroňková, *Die Mode der gotischen Frau* (Prague: Artia, 1954).

6. Cf. "Wege zur Altersbestimmung," HdM I, 58ff. (by Kahlo); also see Friedrich von der Leyen's attempt at classifying the Grimms' folktales according to their relative age in his edition of the tales in the *Märchen der Weltliteratur* series (Jena: Diederichs, 1942).

7. P. Saintyves (pseudonym of Emile Nourry), *Les contes de Perrault et les récits parallèles* (Paris: E. Nourry, 1923); cf. Erich Sielaff, "Bemerkungen zur kritischen Aneignung der deutschen Volksmärchen," *Wissenschaftliche Zeitschrift der Universität Rostock* 2 (1952–53), 261; Lutz Röhrich, "Sage und Brauch," *Forschungen und Fortschritte* 25 (1949), 251ff.

8. Cf. BP II, 37f.; Töpfer, p. 43; Kurt Schmidt, *Die Entwicklung der Grimmschen Kinder- und Hausmärchen seit der Urhandschrift*, Hermaea 10 (Halle: Max Niemeyer, 1932), p. 27.

9. MdW, *Neugriechische Märchen*, no. 39, p. 155.

10. This is particularly clear where cannibalism is only simulated, for example, when the heroine's evil adversaries take her child away, smear blood around her mouth, and accuse her of cannibalistic desires. This atrocity can be punished only with death; cf. Woeller, pp. 12ff.; Lutz Röhrich, "Die Grausamkeit im Märchen. Ihre kulturhistorischen, rechtsgeschichtlichen und psychologischen Grundlagen," *Rheinisches Jahrbuch für Volkskunde* 6 (1956), 187ff.

11. For example, Grudde, *Plattdeutsche Volksmärchen*, no. 73, pp. 134ff.

12. Cf. BP I, 115ff.; HdM I, 61; Rumpf, *Ursprung und Entstehung von Warn- und Schreckmärchen*. Moreover, the abandonment of children is an international epic motif, as the stories of the childhoods of Moses (Exodus 2:3–10), Oedipus (Sophocles), Romulus and Remus (Livius I, 3f.), and Perseus (Apollodor 2, 2, 1 and 4, 1, 4) adequately indicate.

13. BP offer no information on this motif complex's basis in reality under the entries "Liebe" (love), "Ehe" (marriage), "Verlobung" (engagement), and "Hochzeit" (wedding); but see Paul Sartori, *Sitte und Brauch*, pt. 1: "Die Hauptstufen des Menschendaseins," Handbücher zur Volkskunde, vol. 5 (Leipzig: Heims, 1910); Ferdinand von Reitzenstein, *Urgeschichte der Ehe* (Stuttgart: Franckh'sche Verlagshandlung, 1908); Arnold von Gennep, *Les rites de passage* (Paris: E. Nourry, 1909); Ferdinand von Reitzenstein, "Eheschließungs- und Hochzeitsgebräuche," in Max Marcuse, *Handwörterbuch der Sexualwissenschaften*, 2nd ed. (Bonn: Marcus & Weber, 1926); Alfred Reginald Radcliffe-Brown and Daryll Forde, *African Systems of Kinship and Marriage* (Oxford: Oxford University Press, 1950); "Hochzeit," HdA IV, 148ff. (by Kummer); "Ehe," HdM I, 452 (by Kahlo); "Braut und Bräutigam," HdM I, 302ff. (by Heiligendorff); "Brautschau," HdM I, 314ff.; and "Brautwerbungsmärchen," HdM I, 316ff. (both by L. Mackensen); Becker, *Die Liebe im deutschen Märchen*; Rosenbaum, *Liebe und Ehe im deutschen Volksmärchen*; Karl Robert Villehad Wikman, *Die Einleitung der Ehe* (Åbo: Åbo Akademi, 1937).

14. August von Löwis of Menar, *Der Held im deutschen und russischen Märchen* (Jena: Diederichs, 1922), p. 58.

15. MdW, *Russische Volksmärchen*, no. 3, p. 8.

16. Cf. BP I, 99.

17. Sydow (*Våra Folksagor*, pp. 73ff.) justifies this position on the basis of the versions in the Scandinavian archives. This conclusion cannot be confirmed with certainty on the basis of the abbreviated contents of the versions of KHM 6 provided by BP I, 45ff., and of KHM 135 (BP III, 85ff.).

18. Cf. Woeller, pp. 191ff.

19. Karl Victor Müllenhoff, *Sagen, Märchen und Lieder der Herzogtümer Schleswig-Holstein und Lauenburg* (Kiel: Schwersche Buchhandlung, 1845), no. 7 ("Vom Mann ohne Herz").

20. Cf. Rosenbaum, pp. 40f.

21. Cf. BP II, 59.

22. Jacob Grimm, *Deutsche Rechtsaltertümer*, 4th ed., A. Heusler and R. Hübner, eds., 2 vols. (Leipzig: Dieterich, 1899), vol. 1, p. 214; cf. BP I, 187.

23. Examples in Jungbauer's article "Schuh," HdA VII, 1327f.; consider the German saying "jemand steckt noch in den Kindershuhen." The Romance wedding practices depicted are related to ancient Roman customs.

24. Cf. Peuckert, *Deutsches Volkstum*, p. 21; Will-Erich Peuckert and Otto Lauffer, *Volkskunde, Quellen und Forschungen seit 1930* (Bern: Francke, 1951); Woeller, pp. 41f.; Vries, *Betrachtungen*, pp. 30f.

25. Westerman, *Die Kpelle*, p. 370.

26. MdW, *Indianermärchen aus Südamerika*, no. 3, pp. 7ff.

27. As, for example, in the folktales from Kordofan, Atlantis, vol. IV, p. 113, or MdW, *Indianermärchen aus Südamerika*, no. 3, pp. 7ff.; regarding the Germanic parallels see Richard Schröder and Eberhard von Künssberg, *Lehrbuch der deutschen Rechtsgeschichte*, 7th ed. (Berlin: W. de Gruyter, 1932), pp. 75ff. and 328ff.

28. Cf. Winter, p. 229; Rosenbaum, pp. 35f.; "Entführung," HdM I, 541ff. (by Goebel).

29. Dmitrij Zelenin, "The Genesis of the Fairy Tale," *Ethnos* (1940), 54–59; cf. G. Gessmann, *Die Pangwe*, 2 vols. (Berlin, 1913); Ewald Volhard, *Kannibalismus*, Studien zur Kulturkunde, A. E. Jensen, ed., vol. 5 (Stuttgart: Strecker & Schröder, 1939), pp. 448f.

30. Cf. Sydow, *Våra Folksagor*, pp. 63ff. O. Höfler recently compiled considerable evidence from ancient Germanic sources for the isolated rearing of boys during initiation. Höfler draws parallels to the folktale: The upbringing in the wilds of the forest in KHM 136, the golden hairs which the boy acquires while serving the wild man, the subsequent test in battle—in these episodes the author sees the "ideal story of the young initiate . . . essentially as it 'really' occurred" (Otto Höfler, *Germanisches Sakralkönigtum*, vol. 1: *Der Runenstein von Rök und die germanische Individualweihe* [Tübingen, Münster, and Cologne: M. Niemeyer, 1952], pp. 208ff.).

31. For example, see Jung's psychological interpretations of the helpful old man in the folktale, Carl Gustav Jung, *Symbolik des Geistes* (Zurich: Rascher, 1948); and Marguerite Loeffler-Delachaux, *Le symbolisme des contes des fées* (Paris: Arche, 1949).

32. For example, Peuckert, *Deutsches Volkstum*, pp. 19f.; Zelenin, "Genesis"; I. Hanika, "Die schwarzen Prinzessinnen. Beziehungen eines Märchenmotivs zum Brauchtum," *Rheinisches Jahrbuch für Volkskunde* 2 (1951), 39–47; also see Preben Nodermann, *Folksagorna, en Orientiering*, 2 vols. (Lund: Sydsvenska bok-och musik-förlaget, 1928/29), and Johannes Bolte's review in *Hessische Blätter für Volkskunde* 27 (1928), 205f.; also see the criticism of this thesis by de Vries, *Betrachtungen*, pp. 32ff.

33. Cf. MdW, *Irische Volksmärchen*, no. 4, pp. 14f.; MdW, *Zigeunermärchen*, p. 265. Some of our believed legends also warn women about going out in the open, but here it is always new mothers who are not immediately accepted back into the church after their purification.

34. Cf. Sydow, *Våra Folksagor*, pp. 63ff.

35. Zelenin, "Genesis."

36. Cf. Max Hippe, "Hochzeitsrätsel des 17. Jahrhunderts," in Walter Steller, ed., *Festschrift Theodor Siebs*, Germanische Abhandlungen, vol. 67 (Breslau: M. & H. Marcus, 1933), pp. 421ff. Archer Taylor, *English Riddles from Oral Tradition* (Berkeley and Los Angeles: University of California Press, 1951).

37. Cf. BP I, 200.

38. Cf. BP I, 188ff., with various riddles.

39. Also see the examples in BP IV, 138f.

40. Tillhagen, *Taikon*, pp. 158ff.

41. The 1856 edition, p. 267; cf. BP III, 438ff.; see the entry "Lausfell erraten" in BP V, 284; "Erraten des Lausfells," HdM I, 599f. (by Archer Taylor).

42. Cf. BP III, 42f.

43. [There is some question regarding the proper translation of *Meerhäschen* in the title of the Grimms' version. Ralph Mannheim chooses "mongoose," while Jack Zipes prefers "hamster."—Trans.] In any case, this cute decorative element in this text clearly does not belong to the tale's basic form. Cf. Hartmann-Ströhm, *Das Meerhäschen. Eine vergleichende Märchenuntersuchung*, pp. 3f.

44. BP III, 365ff.; hiding from the maiden also occurs in some versions of "The Queen Bee" (KHM 62); cf. BP II, 23.

45. Cf. BP III, 21; also see MdW, *Donauland*, pp. 297ff. ("Die versteckte Königstochter"); Hahn, *Griechische und albanesische Märchen*, no. 40, p. 217; Va'clav Tille, *Verzeichnis der böhmischen Märchen*, FFC no. 34 (Helsinki: Suomalainen Tiedeakatemia, 1929), p. 244; cf. Hartmann-Ströhm, pp. 126ff.

46. The hero must find the king (!) three times in addition to hiding three times (MdW, *Irische Volksmärchen*, no. 28, pp. 224ff.); cf. Hartmann-Ströhm, pp. 36f. and 121f.

47. Cf. the section "Suchen im Hochzeitsbrauch" in P. Sartori's article "Suchen," HdA VIII, 578; other examples in Sartori, *Sitte und Brauch*, pp. 74ff.

48. A compilation of numerous examples can be found in BP II, 28f.

49. Johannes Hoops, ed., *Reallexikon der Germanischen Altertumskunde* (Strasbourg: K. J. Trübner, 1911–19), vol. 4, pp. 185f.

50. Examples in BP II, 29, and "Suchen," HdA VIII, 586ff.; cf. Sartori, *Sitte und Brauch*, pp. 74f.

51. Sartori, *Sitte und Brauch*, p. 75, contains numerous examples of this custom. H. Usener also provides numerous examples: "A playful wedding practice frequently occurs among the southern Slavs: When the groom or his representative, the starashin, comes to the wedding house in the festive procession to pick up the bride, the bride is withheld at first and they try to give him an ugly old woman instead" (H. Usener, "Italienische Mythen," *Rheinisches Museum für Philologie* [1875], 182–229). In addition: Felix Liebrecht, *Zur Volkskunde* (Heilbronn: Gebr. Henninger, 1879), p. 408; cf. P. Arfert, *Das Motiv von der unterschobenen Braut in der internationalen Erzählungsliteratur*, Diss. Rostock, 1897; Hanns Bächtold-Stäubli "Die falsche Braut," *Schweizer Volkskunde* 1 (1911), 3.

52. Armin Ehrenzweig, "Die Scheinehe in europäischen Hochzeitsbräuchen," *Zeitschrift für vergleichende Rechtswissenschaft* 21 (1908), 267ff.

53. Cf. BP I, 85, and III, 443ff.

54. Examples in BP II, 234ff.

55. Versions compiled in BP III, 449; cf. Arfert, pp. 39ff.; Sydow, *Vâra Folksagor*, pp. 77ff; "Die untergeschobene Braut," HdM I, 307ff. (by Golther); Paul Geiger, *Deutsches Volkstum in Sitte und Brauch* (Berlin and Leipzig: W. de Gruyter, 1936), pp. 120f.

56. Cf. BP III, 515.

57. Examples in Sartori, *Sitte und Brauch*, pp. 72ff.

58. On the forbiddance of speech in folk belief, see Jungwirth's article "Schweigen," HdA VII, 1460ff.

59. Cf. the numerous versions compiled under the entry "Braut, vergessen" in BP V, 268; in addition, see Liljeblad's article "Die vergessene Braut," HdM I, 311ff.; Ittenbach's "Lethe-Trank," HdA V, 1224f.; and Karle's "Kuß," HdA V, 842ff.

60. Sartori, *Sitte und Brauch*, pp. 110ff., provides references.

61. Cf. BP II, 335ff.

62. MdW, *Deutsche Märchen seit Grimm*, vol. 1, pp. 101ff.; cf. "Keusches Beilager,"

HdM I, 230, and "Keuschheit," HdA IV, 1291ff. (both by Fehrle), and "Geschlechtsverkehr," HdA III, 735ff. (by Kummer).

63. Cf. BP II, 229 (variants of KHM 88).

64. Cf. Jacob Grimm, *Rechtsaltertümer,* vol. 1, p. 232; Sartori, *Sitte und Brauch,* pp. 110ff.; Sydow, *Våra Folksagor,* pp. 88ff.; examples from poetry and heroic legend in "Dichtung und Heldensage," BP I, 554f.

65. Examples in Sartori, *Sitte und Brauch,* pp. 109ff.; cf. Tob. 6:19.

66. Olaus Magnus, *Historia de gentibus septentrionalibus* (History of the Nordic Peoples), book 15, ch. 35ff. (Romae: Johannes Maria de Viottis, 1555), p. 527; cf. Sartori, *Sitte und Brauch,* p. 67; Sydow, *Våra Folksagor,* pp. 84ff.; Alfred Martin, *Deutsches Badewesen in vergangen Tagen* (Jena: E. Diederichs, 1906), pp. 184ff.; "Rein— Reinheit," HdA VII, 630ff. (by Pfister).

67. Numerous versions in BP III, 83f.

68. References in ibid.

69. MdW, *Nordische Volksmärchen,* vol. 2, no. 7, pp. 25ff.

70. Ibid., vol. 1, no. 1, pp. 3ff.

71. Examples in BP III, 33; cf "Milch," HdA VI, 243ff. (by Eckstein).

72. Cf. BP I, 490ff.

73. Regarding the distribution of this motif in this tale type, see variant group in BP I, 302ff.

74. Cf. the compilation of various variant groups in BP I, 13ff.

75. Variant group A3 in BP III, 97ff.

76. Cf. BP II, 516ff.

77. Cf. BP III, 465.

78. Cf. "Wechselbalg," HdA IX (supplement), 835ff. (by Piaschewski).

79. Höfler, *Germanisches Sakralkönigtum,* vol. 1.

80. Synopsis from ibid., pp. 154f.; cf. BP I, 98f.

81. In his book noted above, Höfler calls attention to a number of other cases. For example, the Eddic "Lay of Hyndla" tells of the Danish king Harald Wartooth and his clan:

> Harald Wartooth
> was to Hroerek born,
> the sower of rings:
> he was the son of Auth . . .
>
> *were given to gods,*
> these godlly men.

(Hyndlalied, Str. 30, *Edda,* rendered in High German by Felix Genzmer, Sammlung Thule, vol. 2, p. 99.) Harald Wartooth was also born with Odin's help after his mother's initial infertility. (An extensive prose version can be found in Saxo Grammaticus's *Gesta Danorum,* books VII and VIII, J. Olrik and H. Raeder, eds. [Copenhagen: Hauniae, Levin & Munksgaard, 1931], vol. 1, pp. 374ff.; cf. Höfler, *Germanisches Sakralkönigtum,* vol. 1, pp. 89ff.; and the article "Haraldr Hilditannr" in Hoops, ed., *Reallexikon der Germanischen Altertumskunde,* pp. 449f.)

82. From Höfler, pp. 213ff.

83. Svend Grundtvig, *Danmarks gamle Folkeviser* 33:2 (Copenhagen: Samfundet til den danske literatuis fremme, 1856), pp. 1–13; synopsis from Höfler, pp. 177ff.; cf. BP I, 98f.

84. From Höfler's (p. 243) rendering of the French novel's content; cf. BP III, 107f.

85. Examples in Ludwig Uhland, *Schriften zur Geschichte der Dichtung und Sage,*

W. L. Holland et al., eds. (Stuttgart: Cotta, 1865–73), vol. 7, pp. 656ff.; cf. Höfler, pp. 243ff., and BP III, 107f.

86. Höfler, pp. 87, 205ff., 257; cf. Weiser-Aall, *Altgermanische Jünglingsweihen und Männerbünde*, pp. 34ff.

87. Even before Höfler's book appeared, scholars warned about one-sided interpretations of this practice. Most notably, Walter Baetke and his students demonstrated how many aspects of these ancient Germanic pagan customs are the product of Christian interpretations and how medieval Christian thought shades Eddic depictions of sacrifices to Odin and devoting souls to Thor. Cf. Walter Baetke, *Christliches Lehngut in der Sagareligion*, Berichte über die Verhandlungen der Sächsischen Akademie der Wissenschaft zu Leipzig, Philosophische-historische Klasse, 98:6 (Berlin: Akademie, 1952), pp. 11ff.; Ekkehart Vesper, *Christen und Christentum in der Darstellung der isländischen Sagas*, Diss. Leipzig, 1950.

88. Cf. "Nasiräer," RGG, 2nd ed., vol. 4, 416ff. (by Alt); v. Orilli, "Nasiräat," in Johann Jakob Herzog, ed., *Realencyklopädie für protestantische Theologie und Kirche*, 3rd ed., vol. 13 (Leipzig: J. C. Hinrichs, 1903), pp. 653ff.; and the article "Nazirite" in *The Westminster Dictionary of the Bible* (Philadelphia: Westminster Press, 1944), p. 421. All animals' first births also belong to the Lord (Exodus 22:29; Numbers 8:17; Deuteronomy 15:19).

89. Our necessary limitation to Germanic and Jewish cultures here should not imply that devotions in exchange for procreativity did not exist in other societies. Here we might mention an African example: "It happens that many spirits importune a woman, one after the other, so that the children she has will be consecrated to them. 'Chief' Mazanza's first wife was supposedly possessed eight times. Next to her hut she erected eight different little houses; these were consecrated to eight different spirits. She bore four children, four spirits were satisfied; the others are still waiting" (R. P. Colle, *Les Baluba*, Collection de Monographies ethnographiques, Cyrille van Overbergh, ed. [Brussels: A. Dewit, 1913], vol. 2, pp. 437f., cited from Friedrich, *Priestertümer*, p. 283). God as a help in procreation seems to presuppose a high religion, one more developed than the stage in which God himself, or a demon, actually procreates.

90. Gunkel, *Das Märchen im Alten Testament*; Peuckert, *Deutsches Volkstum*, pp. 36ff.; Sydow, *Selected Papers on Folklore*; Baumgartner, *Israelitisch-griechische Sagenbeziehungen*. Similar features are found in the story of Jephthah, who, in exchange for victory, promises the Lord the first thing that comes his way when he returns home. It is his daughter who is sacrificed in fulfillment of the pledge (Judges 11:31–39). Here we do not have the Nazirite consecration, but it is evidence that similar motifs seem to have come to us from the Near East.

### Cruelty in the Folktale

1. Cited from the 7th ed. of Otto Apelt's translation, Phil. Bibl., vol. 80 (Leipzig: F. Meiner, 1920). Cf. E. Heimpel, "Gedanken über das Märchen," *Die Sammlung* 4 (1949), 718ff.

2. Cf. Kant's works (ed. by the königliche preußische Akademie der Wissenschaften, vol. 2, p. 215): "The fairy tales of French folly are the most horrible masks that have ever been carved."

3. Georg Biedenkamp, *Was erzähle ich meinen Sechsjährigen* (Jena: Constenoble, 1903), Introduction.

4. Cf. Hermann Hamann, *Die literarischen Vorlagen der Kinder- und Hausmärchen und ihre Bearbeitung durch die Brüder Grimm*, Palaestra 47 (Berlin: Mayer & Müller, 1906), 15.

5. For example, see the report from the first meeting of the International Library for Youth in Munich (*Neue Zeitung* 1951, no. 274, p. 4).

6. "German Educational Reconstruction," Allgemeine deutsche Nachrichten-dienst bulletin from July–August 1948; cf. Kahlo, *Die Wahrheit des Märchens*, p. 13.

7. Peuckert and Lauffer, *Volkskunde. Quellen und Forschungen seit 1930*, p. 271; cf. Peuckert, *Wiedergeburt. Gespräche in Hörsälen und unterwegs*, p. 107.

8. Cf. L. Tetzner, "Probleme der Kinder- und Jugendliteratur," *Schola* 5 (1947).

9. HdM II, 669ff.

10. HdA VIII, 938ff.

11. MdW, *Französische Volksmärchen*, vol. 2, pp. 259ff., no. 51.

12. Rumpf, *Rotkäppchen. Eine vergleichende Märchenuntersuchung*, pp. 51ff.

13. Cited from Paul Delarue, "Les contes merveilleux de Perrault."

14. Rumpf, *Rotkäppchen*, pp. 94ff.

15. Also see Gottfried Henssen, "Deutsche Schreckmärchen und ihre europäischen Anverwandten," 84ff. Such "warning tales" also clearly exist in tribal societies. A folktale recorded by Leo Frobenius in central Sudan closes with the drastic words: "If a mother throws her child on the dung heap, we can be sure that the kid wasn't good for anything else" (Atlantis, vol. IX [*Volkserzählungen und Volksdichtungen aus dem Zentralsudan*], p. 241).

16. Heinrich Böll's novel *Haus ohne Hüter* (Cologne: Kiepenheuer & Witsch, 1954), for example, shows how children can develop cannibalistic complexes from such narratives.

17. According to Rumpf, *Ursprung und Entstehung von Warn- und Schreckmärchen*, pp. 4ff.

18. From the folktale comedy "Die Schöne im Walde" by Jules Supervielle.

19. Cf. BP I, 398ff.; HdM I, 268; John Meier et al., eds., *Deutsche Volkslieder mit ihren Melodien*, vol. 2, p. 96; also see Friedrich Holz, *Die Mädchenräuberballade*, Diss. Heidelberg, 1929, and Holger Olof Nygard, *The Ballad of Heer Halewijn*, FFC no. 169 (Helsinki: Suumalainen Tiedeakatemia, 1958).

20. Naumann, *Primitive Gemeinschaftskultur*, p. 84.

21. Ernst Tegethoff, "Die Dämonen im deutschen und französischen Märchen," *Scweizerisches Archiv für Volkskunde* 24 (1923), 151ff.

22. Cf. J. Meier et al., eds., *Deutsche Volkslieder*, p. 97. Marie Ramondt, "Heer Hallewyn en Blauwbaard," Miscellanea J. Gessler, vol. 2 (Leuwen, 1948), pp. 1030–43.

23. Cf. Baumgartner, "Israelitisch-griechische Sagenbeziehungen."

24. Also see the literary use of this motif in Heinrich Böll's *Haus ohne Hüter*, pp. 161ff.

25. Graber, *Sagen und Märchen aus Kärnten*, p. 85.

26. Regarding live burial as a magical protection of borders, see Lutz Röhrich, "Eine antike Grenzsage und ihre neuzeitlichen Parallelen," *Würzburger Jahrbücher für die Altertumswissenschaft* (1949/50), 339–69, particularly pp. 349ff.

27. Wlislocki, *Märchen und Sagen der transsilvanischen Zigeuner*, no. 52, pp. 121ff.

28. Cf. Ulrich Jahn, "Die deutschen Opferbräuche bei Ackerbau und Viehzucht," in K. Weinhold, ed., *Germanistische Abhandlungen*, vol. 3 (Breslau, 1884); human sacrifice in particular on pp. 62ff.

29. Cf. Eugen Mogk, *Die Menschenopfer bei den Germanen*, Abhandlungen der Philosophisch-historischen Klasse der königlichen Sächsischen Gesellschaft der Wissenschaft, vol. 27 (Leipzig: B. G. Teubner, 1909), pp. 625ff.; also Berndt Götz, *Die Bedeutung des Opfers bei den Völkern*, Sociologus, supp. 3 (Leipzig: C. L. Hirschfeld, 1933); and Freidrich Schwenn, *Die Menschenopfer bei den Griechen und Römern* (Gießen: A. Topelmann, 1915). Lechner, *Das Ei im deutschen Brauchtum*, pp. 2ff. (of the partial printing), contains a compilation of cases of human sacrifice as a building sacrifice. Günther Schmitt, *Das Menschenopfer in der Spätüberlieferung der deutschen Volksdichtung*, Diss. Mainz, 1959; Lutz Röhrich, "Die Volksballade von 'Herrn Peters

Seefahrt' und die Menschenopfersagen," in Hugo Kuhn and Kurt Schier, eds., *Märchen, Mythos, Dichtung, Festschrift zum 90. Geburtstag Friedrich von der Leyens* (Munich: Beck, 1963), pp. 177–212.

30. E. Volhard, *Kannibalismus*, Studien zur Kulturkunde (series ed. A. E. Jensen), vol. 5 (Stuttgart: Strecker & Schroeder, 1939), pp. 394ff.

31. Cf. ibid., p. 405.

32. Volhard speaks of "profane cannibalism" wherever no identifiable differentiation is made between human flesh and some other form of nourishment (ibid., pp. 374ff.).

33. MdW, *Russische Märchen*, no. 3, pp. 4ff. (a variant of "The Juniper Tree" in which need, rather than evil, motivates the parents to consume human flesh. Nevertheless, the parents are executed at the end).

34. Merkelbach-Pinck, *Lothringer Volksmärchen*, p. 140.

35. E. Meier, *Deutsche Sagen, Sitten und Gebräuche aus Schwaben*, no. 135, p. 121.

36. For example, see Emrich, *Formen und Grundlagen gegenwärtigen Hexenglaubens*.

37. Lefftz, *Märchen der Brüder Grimm. Urfassung*, pp. 121 and 125f.

38. Lambertz, *Albanische Märchen*, p. 114.

39. Anders Allardt, *Sagor i Urval*, Finlands svenska Folkdiktning (Helsinki: Tidnings och Tryckeri-Aktiebolagts, 1917), no. 103, p. 165.

40. MdW, *Neugriechische Märchen*, p. 7, no. 2.

41. BP I, 88; cf. "Blut," HdM I, 278 (by Heckscher).

42. Ulrich Jahn, "Zauber mit Menschenblut und anderen Teilen des menschlichen Körpers," *Verhandlungen der Berliner Gesellschaft für Anthropologie, Ethnologie und Urgeschichte* (Berlin, 1888), p. 135.

43. Jahn, ibid., p. 135; also see Albert Hellwig, *Verbrechen und Aberglaube* (Leipzig: B. G. Teubner, 1908), pp. 63ff.; and the article "Hingerichteter," 2nd section: "Zauberkraft der Leichenteile," HdA IV, 43ff.

44. Wilhelm Schoof, *Briefe der Brüder Grimm an Savigny* (Berlin: E. Schmidt, 1953), p. 430.

45. *Historia Francorum* 9, c. 34.

46. Sammlung Thule, vol. 1 (Jena: Diederichs, 1913), pp. 20ff.; cf. BP I, 422, and Adeline Rittershaus, *Die neu-isländischen Volksmärchen* (Halle: S. M. Niemeyer, 1902), pp. 35 and 129.

47. Sammlung Thule, vol. 1, pp. 49ff.

48. Roscher, *Mythologisches Lexikon*, vol. 1, pp. 712ff.

49. This sometimes occurs in other, related contexts. For example, in a Nyiha folktale the evil mother rips apart her daughter's child, cooks him in vegetables, and serves him to his mother (Tr. Bachmann, "Nyiha-Märchen," *Zeitschrift für Kolonialsprachen* 6 [1915/16], 93; Atlantis, vol. X [Die atlantische Götterlehre], pp. 217ff., contains different episodes).

50. KHM 46, 47, 81; *German Legends*, no. 62; cf. BP I, 422ff.

51. Cf. L. Schmidt, "Pelops und die Haselhexe."

52. An exact parallel to the reincarnation of a sheep, also by placing the bones into the sheepskin, can be found in MdW, *Deutsche Märchen aus dem Donaulande*, pp. 305ff.

53. Cf. the extensive documentation in Friedrich, "Die Forschung über das frühzeitliche Jägertum."

54. For example, some Siberian narratives depict these customs: MdW, *Märchen aus Siberien*, no. 17, pp. 74ff., and no. 57, pp. 228ff.; above all, p. 307, annotation to no. 17.

55. Cf. Muster, *Der Schamanismus*. Nachtigall, "Die kulturhistorische Wurzel der Schamanenskelettierung."

56. Cf. pp. 63–64.

57. As, for example, in Walter Tomann, *Dynamik der Motive* (Frankfurt and Vienna: Humboldt, 1954).

58. Zenker-Starzacher, *Eine deutsche Märchenerzählerin aus Ungarn*, p. 67. Numerous examples of disenchantment through decapitation can be found in HdM II, 395f., as well as BP V, 271.

59. Zingerle, *Kinder- und Hausmärchen aus Tirol*, p. 43.

60. Karl Plenzat, "Ostpreußische Märchen," *Niederdeutsche Zeitschrift für Volkskunde* 4 (1926), no. 6, p. 56; also see Bilz, "Tiertöter-Skrupulantismus."

61. Cf. pp. 79–82.

62. Jennes, *Myths and Traditions from North-Alaska*, p. 57.

63. MdW, *Finnische und estnische Volksmärchen*, no. 37, p. 113, and Jensen, *Hainuwele*, no. 354, pp. 370f., depict similar tales about fathers cruelly plotting to kill their sons. Also see BP I, 70ff.

64. Friedrich Panzer, ed., *Die Kinder- und Hausmärchen der Brüder Grimm in ihrer Urgestalt* (Hamburg: Stromverlag, 1948), vol. 1, no. 9, p. 24; cf. Lefftz, *Märchen der Brüder Grimm, Urfassung*, p. 74.

65. MdW, *Neugriechische Märchen*, no. 35, p. 412.

66. Cf. BP I, 70ff.

67. Josephine Bilz, *Menschliche Reifung im Sinnbild, eine psychologische Untersuchung über Wandlungsmetaphern des Traumes, des Wahns und des Märchens* (Leipzig: S. Hirzel, 1943), p. 62.

68. For example, Woeller, *Der soziale Gehalt*, pp. 61ff.

69. Jacob Grimm, *Kleinere Schriften*, vol. 2, "Abhandlungen zur Mythologie und Sittenkunde" (Berlin: F. Dümmler, 1865), pp. 258f.

70. Paul Sartori, "Die Sitte der Alten- und Krankentötung," *Globus* 67 (1895), 107ff.

71. Adalbert Kuhn, *Märkische Sagen und Märchen*, reprint (Berlin: F. A. Herbig, 1937), p. 335.

72. Cf. BP II, 1ff.; Josef Müller, *Das Märchen von Unibos* (Jena: Diederichs, 1934).

73. Also see "Der große und der kleine Peter" (MdW, *Nordische Volksmärchen*, vol. 2, no. 40, pp. 233ff.).

74. For examples of more recent versions of "Unibos" without the killing of the grandmother, see H. Nevermann, *Die Reiskugel. Sagen und Göttergeschichten, Märchen, Fabeln und Schwänke aus Vietnam* (Eisenach: E. Röth, 1952), pp. 66ff.; and H. Kähler, *Die Insel der schönen Si Melu. Indonesische Dämonengeschichten, Märchen und Sagen aus Simalur* (Eisenach: E. Röth, 1952), pp. 179ff.

75. In other versions the princess can almost build a tower with the heads of the unlucky suitors (e.g., MdW, *Neugriechische Märchen*, no. 25, p. 76). Punishment of unsuccessful attempts at courtship also occurs in KHM 22, 133, and 134.

76. Here I am largely following Hartmann's treatise, *Das Meerhäschen. Eine vergleichende Märchenuntersuchung*, pp. 75f.

77. Arthur Schott, *Walachische Märchen* (Stuttgart and Tübingen: J. G. Cotta, 1845), no. 13, pp. 153ff.: "Die Prinzessin und der Schweinehirt."

78. Cf. Jacob Grimm, *Deutsche Rechtsaltertümer*, vol. 2, p. 265.

79. August von Löwis of Menar, *Die Brünhildsaga in Rußland*, Palaestra 142 (Leipzig: Mayer & Müller, 1923), p. 82.

80. According to Arthur Amelung and Oscar Jänicke, *Ortnit und die Wolfdietriche*, Deutsches Heldenbuch, vol. 3 (Berlin, 1871), p. xxix, note 1.

81. Adolf Friedrich von Schack, *Poesie und Kunst der Araber in Spanien und Sizilien* (Berlin: W. Hertz, 1865), vol. 1, pp. 250ff.

82. Welcker, "Die griechische Tragödie," *Rheinisches Museum für Philologie* (1839), 364.

83. References from Hartmann, p. 105.

84. Amelung and Jänicke, vol. 1, Ortnit, I, pp. 19f.

85. Amelung and Jänicke, vol. 2, Wolfdietrich D, VI, pp. 13f.

86. Wlislocki, *Märchen und Sagen der transsilvanischen Zigeuner*, no. 47, pp. 111ff.

87. Christoph Friedrich von Stälin, *Wirtembergische Geschichte*, vol. 1 (Stuttgart and Tübingen: J. G. Cotta, 1841), p. 509, contains an example from the eleventh century.

88. Johannes Heinrich Schultz, *Organstörungen und Perversionen im Liebesleben* (Munich: E. Reinhardt, 1952).

89. Georg Schambach and Wilhelm Müller, *Niedersächsische Sagen und Märchen*, reprint (Stuttgart: W. Kohlhammer, 1948), no. 25, pp. 296f.

90. KHM 21 and 107; for additional examples see the article "Blendung," HdMI, 270ff.

91. MdW, *Deutsche Märchen seit Grimm*, vol. 1, p. 249; *Nordische Volksmärchen*, vol. 2, no. 7.

92. MdW, *Deutsche Märchen aus dem Donauland*, p. 129.

93. Josef Haltrich, *Deutsche Volksmärchen aus dem Sachsenland in Siebenbürgen*, 3rd ed. (Vienna: C. Graeser, 1882), no. 25, p. 106. Dragging to death also occurs in the Ulinger-ballad, e.g., version 5 in Meier.

94. The same occurs in KHM 135; MdW, *Nordische Volksmärchen*, vol. 1, no. 1, p. 9, and vol. 1, no. 4, pp. 27f.; for additional examples see BP I, 108f. The nail-lined barrel also appears in ballads and saints' legends.

95. Cf. MdW, *Finnische und estnische Volksmärchen*, no. 28. For parallels in poetry and legal history, see Grimm, *Rechtsaltertümer*, vol. 2, pp. 285f.

96. *Rechtsaltertümer*, vol. 2, pp. 291ff.

97. Ibid., pp. 295ff.; additional examples in "Blendung," HdM 1, 270ff.

98. *Rechtsaltertümer*, vol. 2, p. 272.

99. *Rechtsaltertümer*, vol. 1, pp. 272f.; cf. Karl von Amira, *Die germanischen Todesstrafen. Untersuchungen zur Rechts- und Religionsgeschichte*. Abhandlungen der Bayerischen Akademie der Wissenschaft, Philosophisch-historische Klasse, vol. 31, sec. 3 (Munich: Bayerischen Akademie der Wissenschaften, 1922), pp. 131ff.

100. *Rechtsaltertümer*, vol. 2, p. 278; also see Franz Heinemann, *Der Richter und die Rechtspflege in der deutschen Vergangenheit*, 2nd ed. (Jena: E. Diederich, 1924), p. 111.

101. Grudde, *Plattdeutsche Volksmärchen aus Ostpreußen*, no. 50, p. 98.

102. MdW, *Deutsche Märchen seit Grimm*, vol. 1, pp. 142 and 145.

103. *Rechtsaltertümer*, vol. 2, pp. 274f.

104. Cf. Agnes Bernauer; *Rechtsaltertümer*, vol. 2, pp. 278ff.; Heinemann, p. 111, Kahlo, *Die Wahrheit des Märchens*, p. 29.

105. *Rechtsaltertümer*, vol. 2, pp. 264f.; cf. Eberhard Freiherr von Künssberg, *Rechtliche Volkskunde*, Reihe "Volk," K. Wagner, gen. ed., vol. 3 (Halle: M. Niemeyer, 1936), p. 29; Siegfried Anger, *Das Recht in den Sagen, Legenden und Märchen Schleswig-Holsteins*, Diss. Kiel, 1947.

106. Cf. Andreas Heusler, *Das Strafecht der Isländersagas* (Leipzig: Duncker & Humblot, 1911).

107. Amira, *Die germanischen Todesstrafen*.

108. Cf. Berhard Rehfeldt, *Todesstrafen und Bekehrungsgeschichte. Zur Rechts- und Religionsgeschichte der germanischen Hinrichtungsbräuche* (Berlin: Duncker & Humblot, 1942), pp. 129 and 158f.; Hans Fehr, "Altes Strafrecht im Glauben des Volkes," *Deutsches Jahrbuch für Volkskunde* 1 (1955), 149ff.; Hans Fehr, *Das Recht in den Sagen der Schweiz* (Frauenfeld: Huber, 1959).

109. Cf. *Rechtsaltertümer*, vol. 2, pp. 272f.

110. Carl Wesle, ed., *Das Rolandslied des Pfaffen Konrad* (Bonn: F. Klopp, 1928), p. 316, v. 9009ff.

111. Cf. Hans Fehr, "Das Recht im Bündner Märchen," *Zeitschrift für schweizerisches Recht* 54 (1935), 228f.

112. Cf. BP I, 109.
113. Amira, *Todesstrafen*, pp. 138ff.; cf. BP I, 108f.; Eleanor Susan Page, "The 'Nageltonne': Its Uses in History and Folklore," *Journal of American Folklore* 59 (1945), 20–24.
114. KHM 135; cf. HdM II, 669.
115. MdW, *Nordische Volksmärchen*, vol. 2, no. 21, p. 114.
116. Gonzenbach, *Sicilianische Märchen*, no. 49; cf. BP I, 87.
117. Cf. Bronislaw Malinowski, *Crime and Custom in Savage Society* (London: Routledge & Kegan Paul, 1955); Hermann Trimborn, *Auffassung und Formen der Strafe auf den einzelnen Kulturstufen* (Berlin and Bonn: F. Dümmler, 1931), pp. 5ff.
118. MdW, *Märchen seit Grimm*, vol. 1, p. 145.
119. E.g., KHM 13, 89, 111, 135; Haltrich, no. 25, p. 106; MdW, *Donauland*, p. 129.
120. Peuckert, *Schlesiens deutsche Märchen*, no. 40, p. 41.
121. M. Lambertz, *Albanische Märchen*, p. 117.
122. Cf. W. Schadewald, "Furcht und Mitleid," *Hermes* 83 (1955), 129–71.
123. "Grausamkeit," HdM II, 670 (by Groth). The abandonment of children in KHM 15 and 201 offers cases in point.
124. Gerhard Gesemann, *Heroische Lebensform* (Berlin: Wiking, 1943), pp. 134f.
125. Cf. Friedrichs's compilation of such cases in "Das Recht in den Kinder- und Hausmärchen," p. 36.
126. In other versions, particularly the oldest ones, it is a monk; cf. Johannes Bolte, "Das Märchen vom Tanze des Mönches im Dornbusch," *Festschrift . . . Neuphilologentag* (Berlin, 1892), pp. 1–76; BP II, 490ff.
127. Schambach and Müller, no. 15, pp. 276ff.
128. MdW, *Lettisch-litauische Volksmärchen*, no. 9, pp. 81f.
129. MdW, *Zigeunermärchen*, no. 36, pp. 151ff.
130. Atlantis, vol. I (Volksmärchen der Kabylen), pp. 120ff.
131. MdW, *Indianermärchen aus Südamerika*, no. 7, p. 27.
132. Antonin Perbosc, *Contes de Gascogne*, Contes merveilleux des Provinces de France, P. Delarue, gen. ed., vol. 3 (Paris: Editions Erasme, 1954), no. 1, pp. 1ff.
133. Peuckert, *Wiedergeburt. Gespräche in Hörsälen und unterwegs*, pp. 113ff.
134. "Cruel and thoughtless,—indeed cruelty always comes from thoughtlessness" (Thomas Mann, *Dr. Faustus* [Frankfurt: S. Fischer, 1948], p. 690).
135. Cf. Wilhelm Hansen, *Die Entwicklung des kindlichen Weltbildes*, 2nd ed. (Munich: Kösel, 1949), p. 455; Sebald Rudolf Steinmetz, *Ethnologische Studien zur ersten Entwicklung der Strafe nebst einer psychologischen Abhandlung über Grausamkeit und Rachsucht*, 2nd ed., 2 vols. (Groningen: P. Noordhoff, 1928), vol. 1, p. 8; Jean Piaget, *Das moralische Urteil beim Kinde* (Zurich: Rascher, 1954), p. 277, among others; cf. the masterful depiction of this phenomenon in the prize-winning film "Jeux Interdits," where children kill animals just so they can bury them in their game.
136. Cf. BP I, 202ff.: Eberhard Freiherr von Künssberg, *Rechtsbrauch und Kinderspiel*, 2nd ed. (Heidelberg: C. Winter, 1952), § 33, pp. 28f.; the *Mainzer Allgemeine Zeitung* of Nov. 19, 1955, noted a real parallel to the "game of slaughter" under the headline "Children Played 'Hanging.'"
137. Jahn, *Volksmärchen aus Pommern und Rügen*, no. 7, pp. 43f.
138. Jahn, no. 37; cf. HdM II, 670.
139. Zenker-Starzacher, pp. 62f.
140. Grudde, no. 44, p. 86.
141. Grudde, no. 108, pp. 206ff.
142. Grudde, no. 55, p. 107.
143. Grudde, no. 38, pp. 71ff.
144. Grudde, no. 61, p. 120; cf. Sareyko, *Das Weltbild eines ostpreußischen Volkserzählers*, p. 35.
145. Cf. Gottfried Henssen, "Sammlung und Auswertung volkstümlichen

Erzählgutes," *Hessische Blätter für Volkskunde* 43 (1952), 26; Sareyko, p. 14, and the section "Rache und Vergeltung," pp. 100ff.

146. Grudde, no. 27, pp. 47ff., and no. 44, pp. 83ff.

147. H. Schlecht, "Die Volkserzählung im Harmersbachtal," ms., Staatsexamenarbeit Mainz, 1951, p. 74.

148. E.g., the end of Kafka's "The Trial" or his "In the Penal Colony."

149. Cf. Dieter Wyss, *Der Surrealismus* (Heidelberg: L. Schneider, 1950), e.g., pp. 17ff., 22f.; Joachim Ringelnatz's ghastly, grotesque poem "Das Terrbarium" gives this an ironic tone.

150. John Boynton Priestley, *Das jüngste Gericht;* cf. G. Hensel, "Über das Vergnügen an kriminellen Gegenständen," *Neue literarische Welt* (1952), no. 23, p. 4.

151. E.g., "Panique," "Rom offene Stadt," "Die Faust im Nacken."

## IV. THE MODERN FOLKTALE AS BELIEVED REALITY
### Tribal Narratives

1. Only an article on "ethnological folktale *interpretation*" (vol. 1, pp. 603ff.). Kurt Ranke is presently preparing for the publication of an international folktale handbook. [To date, the *Enzyklopädie des Märchens*, based in Göttingen, has reached the letter *G.*—Trans.]

2. Lucien Lévy-Bruhl, *La Mentalité primitive* (Paris: Felix Alcan, 1912); *L'Ame primitive* (Paris: Felix Alcan, 1927).

3. *Les "Carnets" de Lucien Lévy-Bruhl,* preface by M. Leenhardt (Paris: Presses Universitaires de France, 1949); cf. E. F. Podach, "Zum Abschluß von Lévy-Bruhls Theorie über die Mentalität der Primitiven," *Zeitschrift für Ethnologie* 76 (1951), 42–49; Jensen, *Mythos und Kult,* p. 37. Konrad Zucker, *Psychologie des Aberglaubens* (Heidelberg: Scherer, 1948), p. 18; Jean Gebser, *Ursprung und Gegenwart,* vols. 1 and 2 (Stuttgart: Deutsche Verlagsanstalt, 1949 and 1953); Paul Radin, *Die religiöse Erfahrung der Naturvölker* (Zurich: Rhein, 1951).

4. The twelve volumes of the Atlantis series published by Leo Frobenius contain numerous examples of tribal and heroic legends that greatly resemble folktales. Regarding stories that are told as tribal legends among one group and as "folktales" among others, see Atlantis, vol. IV (Kordofan), pp. 273ff.

5. Cited from Peuckert, *Deutsches Volkstum,* p. 24; cf. Woeller, pp. 28f.

6. As, for example, in the totemic folktales of the African Kpelle in Westermann, *Die Kpelle;* cf. Baumann, p. 376.

7. Schmidt and Kahle, *Palästina,* p. 21.

8. Rasmussen, pp. 177ff. As late as 1870, the festive burial of the dead on the island of Timor—which was often postponed for up to a year because of its complexity and cost—was forbidden until all of the dead person's debts were paid (Gramberg, in *Verhandelingen van het Bataviaasch Genootschap* 36, 212; Huet, *Revue des traditions populaires* 24 [1909], 307; cited from BP III, 512).

9. Atlantis, vol. VI (Spielmannsgeschichten der Sahel), p. 332; in India the master thief has become an incarnation of Buddha (cf. BP III, 403ff.).

10. Westermann, *Die Kpelle,* pp. 212 and 363.

11. Thompson, *The Folktale,* p. 68.

12. Alphonse Riesenfeld, *The Megalithic Culture of Melanesia* (Leiden: Brill, 1950), p. 273.

13. This and various other examples (e.g., magical conceptions of the airplane, of modern guns, etc.) can be found in Andreas Lommel, "Traum und Bild bei den Primitiven in Nordwest-Australien," *Psyche* 5 (1951), 205.

14. Wundt, *Völkerpsychologie,* vol. 1, p. 583, and vol. 5, p. 110.

15. Rasmussen, p. 7.

16. Westermann, *Die Kpelle*, p. 379, note 287.
17. MdW, *Südseemärchen*, pp. xiiff. Other scholars who reach the same conclusion on the basis of different materials include Wundt, *Völkerpsychologie*, vol. 5, p. 270; Konrad Preuss, *Die geistige Kultur der Naturvölker* (Leipzig and Berlin: B. G. Teubner, 1914), pp. 99f.; Atlantis, vol. IX (Zentralsudan), pp.8f.; Westermann, *Die Kpelle*, p. 358; Bronislaw Malinowski, *Myth in Primitive Psychology* (London: K. Paul, Trench, Trubner & Co., 1926), pp. 21, 43, and 124; G. von der Leeuw, "Urzeit und Endzeit," *Eranos-Jahrbuch* 17 (1949), 11ff.; Peuckert, *Deutsches Volkstum*, pp. 11ff.
18. Cf. Archer Taylor's article "Formelmärchen," HdM II, 165.
19. MdW, *Märchen der Azteken und Inkaperuaner*, pp. ixf.
20. MdW, *Südseemärchen*, p. vii.
21. George Amos Dorsey, *The Pawnee: Mythology*, pp. 437 and 503ff., cited from Wundt, *Völkerpsychologie*, vol. 5, pp. 109f.
22. Alex F. Chamberlain, "Taboos of Tale-Telling," *Journal of American Folklore* 13 (1900), 146–47, cited from Paul Sartori, "Erzählen als Zauber," *Zeitschrift für Volkskunde* 40 (1930), 43f.
23. Atlantis, vol. I (Volksmärchen der Kabylen), pt. 1 ("Weisheit"), pp. 49ff.; cf. Vries, *Betrachtungen*, p. 170.
24. Cf. BP IV, 5.
25. Preuss (*Globus* 87, p. 396); Sartori, "Erzählen," p. 42.
26. Cf. Sartori, "Erzählen," p. 42.
27. *Archiv für Religiöse Wissenschaft* 26 (1928), 415; cf. Sartori, "Erzählen," p. 42.
28. Westermann, *Die Kpelle*, p. 360.
29. Ibid.
30. Jensen, *Hainuwele*, p. 368.
31. Ibid., p. 2.
32. For example, MdW, *Siberien*, no. 12. In contrast, Russian folktales have been influenced more from the West than from the East. Western Russia belongs to the European sphere of tradition, and the folktales in Afanas'ev's collection are closely related to middle European tales.
33. Baumann, p. 227; cf. Wundt, *Völkerpsychologie*, vol. 5, p. 301.
34. Baumann, pp. 221f., contains a compilation of the motifs of birth from the leg or knee.
35. Richard Wilhelm, ed. and trans., *Chinesische Märchen*, MdW (Düsseldorf: Diedrichs, 1952), no. 7, pp. 13ff.; cf. p. 387.
36. Baumann, p. 34.
37. Atlantis, vol. X (Götterlehre), pp. 199ff.
38. Baumann, p. 9.
39. Jensen, *Hainuwele*, p. 324.
40. Cf. Friedrich, *Priestertümer*, p. 183.
41. For example, MdW, *Siberien*, pp. 115ff.
42. For example, the "Iwaquille" among the Bascari in Upper Guinea: The limbs on one side are long and powerful, on the other side short and atrophied (Atlantis, vol. XI [Oberguinea], no. 2, p. 70).
43. Jensen, *Mythos*, pp. 390f.
44. E.g., Jensen, *Hainuwele*, pp. 371f.
45. Gunnar Landtmann, *The Folk-tales of the Kiwai Papuans*, Acta Societatis scientiarum Fennicae, vol. 47 (Helsingfors: Finnish Society of Literature, 1917); cf. Jensen, *Mythos*, p. 289.
46. MdW, *Siberien*, p. 81.
47. Ibid., no. 5, pp. 34ff.
48. Westermann, *Die Kpelle*, p. 363.
49. Cf. Wundt, *Völkerpsychologie*, vol. 5, p. 211.
50. Johannes Hertel, ed., *Indische Märchen*, MdW (Düsseldorf: Diederichs,

1954), "Nachwort," pp. 390f.; cf. Else Lüders, ed. and trans., *Buddhistische Märchen aus dem alten Indien*, MdW (Jena: Diederichs, 1921); Elisabeth Kutzer, "Das indische Märchen," in BP IV, pp. 286–314; Benfey, *Pantschatantra*; Walter Ruben, *Ozean der Märchenströme*, FFC no. 133 (Helsinki: Suomalainen Tiedeakatemia, 1944); Helmut von Glasenapp, *Die Literaturen Indiens von ihren Anfängen bis zur Gegenwart*, Handbuch der Literaturwissenschaft, vol. 15 (Potsdam: Akademie, 1929); Walter Ruben, *Über die Literatur der vorarischen Stämme Indiens*, Deutsche Akademie der Wissenschaften zu Berlin; Institut für Orientforschung, vol. 15 (Berlin: Akademie, 1952).

## European Narratives

1. Heinrich Zimmer, "Keltische Beiträge," *Zeitschrift für deutsche Altertum* 33 (1889), 150ff.

2. Cf. Martin Ninck, *Älteste Märchen von Europa* (Basel: B. Schwabe & Co., 1945), pp. 78ff.; cf. Wagner, *Wirklichkeit und Schicksal*, pp. 161ff.

3. Cf. Julius Pokorny, "Einleitung," MdW, *Irische Märchen*, p. II.

4. MdW, *Irische Märchen*, no. 17, pp.86f.; cf. Leyen, *Die Welt der Märchen*, vol. 2, p. 147. In his introduction to the Irish folktales (MdW) Pokorny says the tales are "storehouses" of ancient Irish culture "in modern form." The research on Irish folktales is just beginning. The enormously rich material is still mostly scattered in archives waiting to be published. Linguistic difficulties contribute to the problem, since few folklorists are also Celticists. Perhaps, as Will-Erich Peuckert says, "a new period of folktale research will dawn" (*Volkskunde*, p. 151) when the wealth of Irish folktales becomes accessible.

Cf. Thomas Crofton Croker, *Irische Elfenmärchen*, first translated by the brothers Grimm, newly edited by Will-Erich Peuckert (Berlin: Weidman, 1948); Douglas Hyde, *Irische Volksmärchen*, K. Müller, trans. (Berlin: E. Rowohlt, 1920); J. M. Eirwen, *Folktales of Ireland* (Oxford, 1949); also see the article "Celtic Folklore," in Maria Leach, ed., *Standard Dictionary of Folklore, Mythology and Legend*, 2 vols. (New York: Funk & Wagnalls, 1949/50), vol. 1, pp. 200ff.

5. Hartmann, *Trollvorstellungen*, pp. 141f.

6. Ibid; also see Hartmann's other examples.

7. Hans Naumann, ed., *Isländische Volksmärchen*, MdW (Jena: Diederichs, 1923), pp. vif.

8. "Zarn is convinced of the truth of the narratives. He treats his narratives as others treat legends" (Uffer, *Rätoromanische Märchen und ihre Erzähler*, pp. 65ff. and 14).

9. Uffer, pp. 189ff. and 289ff.

10. A. Szulczewski, "Polnische Märchen aus der Provinz Posen," *Mitteilungen der Schlesischen Gesellschaft für Volkskunde* 7:14 (1905), no. 1, pp. 6off.

11. MdW, *Lettisch-litauische Volksmärchen*, no. 14, pp. 205ff.

12. Ibid., no. 40, pp. 295ff.

13. Leyen, *Die Welt der Märchen*, vol. 2, p. 68.

14. Azadovskii, *A Siberian Tale Teller*, Introduction.

15. Lambertz, *Albanische Märchen*, pp. 9 and 15. Also see Lambertz's more recent collection, *Die geflügelte Schwester. Albanische Volksmärchen* (Eisenach: E. Röth, 1952).

16. Lambertz, *Albanische Märchen*, pp. 11f.

17. Ibid., pp. 11f. and 101ff.

18. Ibid., p. 18.

19. Ibid., pp. 51f. Cf. G. Megas, *Der Bartlose im neugriechischen Märchen*, FFC no. 157 (Helsinki: Suomalainen Tiedeakatemia, 1955).

20. Moses Gaster, "Fairy Tales from Inedited Hebrew Mss. of the Ninth and Twelfth Centuries," *Folklore* 7 (1896), 218f., cited from Wesselski, *Theorie*, pp. 218f.

21. Cf. MdW, *Neugriechische Märchen*, p. I. Also see Richard McGillivray

Dawkins, *Modern Greek Folktales* (Oxford: Clarendon, 1953); and Dawkins, *More Greek Folktales* (Oxford: Clarendon, 1955).

22. Tillhagen, *Taikon*, p. 273.

23. Wlislocki, *Märchen und Sagen der transsilvanischen Zigeuner.*

24. Bach, *Volkskunde*, p. 366. "For the most part the folk has little respect for the narrator's creativity and often equates composition with lies; since the audience demands that what the narrator reports as having happened did indeed take place, tale tellers often find themselves in a predicament with adult audiences" (BP IV, p. 17).

25. For example, Westermann reports that a Kpelle audience "immediately protests and corrects inaccuracies, and if the narrator repeats his mistakes they mercilessly jeer him; weak narrators are easily discouraged and retire early" (Westermann, *Die Kpelle*, p. 361). Leo Frobenius also witnesses this for Africa: "The material . . . followed tradition word for word; if a narrator added any new, i.e., false, elements, the audience often corrected him. Thus exact repetitions play an important role" (Frobenius, *Paideuma; Umrisse einer Kultur- und Seelenlehre* [Munich: Beck, 1921], p. 21). It is said that "as a rule Hausa folktales are so well known that even if some unimportant expression is changed during the presentation, someone quickly corrects the narrator" (Mischlich, *Neue Märchen aus Afrika*, p. 15).

26. Cf. Ch. Bühler, *Das Märchen und die Phantasie des Kindes*, Beihefte zur Zeitschrift für angewandte Psychologie no. 17 (Leipzig: J. A. Barth, 1918).

27. Angelika Merkelbach-Pinck, "Wanderung der Märchen im deutschsprachigen Lothringen," *Folk-Liv* 2 (1939), 224.

28. Hertha Grudde, *Wie ich meine "Plattdeutschen Volksmärchen aus Ostpreußen" aufschrieb*, FFC no. 102 (Helsinki: Suomalainen Tiedeakatemia, 1932). Otto Brinkmann, *Das Erzählen in einer Dorfgemeinschaft* (Münster: Aschendorff, 1933), p. 1, and Gottfried Henssen, *Volk erzählt. Münsterländische Sagen, Märchen und Schwänke*, 2nd ed. (Münster: Aschendorff, 1954), depict similar cases; cf. Dymke, p. 36.

29. Bach, *Deutsche Volkskunde*, p. 366.

30. Peuckert, *Schlesiens deutsche Märchen*, no. 54, pp. 91ff.

31. Cf. BP I, 26off., and Mackensen, *Der singende Knochen*.

32. Hermann von Pfister, *Sagen und Aberglaube aus Hessen und Naussau* (Marburg: R. G. Elwert, 1885), p. 58. The same occurs in numerous French versions of this folktale; cf. Rumpf, *Ursprung und Entstehung von Warn- und Schreckmärchen*; BP I, 37.

33. Zenker-Starzacher, *Eine deutsche Märchenerzählerin aus Ungarn*, p. 56.

34. Zender, *Volkssagen der Westeifel*, no. 762.

35. Karl Heinrich Henschke, *Pommerische Sagengestalten*, Veröffentlichungen des volkskundlichen Archivs für Pommern, vol. 2 (Greifswald: L. Bamberg, 1926), pp. 54f.

36. Götz, *Mährisch-Weißkirchen*, no. 68, cited from Peuckert, *Deutsches Volkstum*, p. 111, note 1.

37. Edmund Schneeweis, *Slavische Sagen aus der Čechoslovakischen Republik* (Prague: Staatische Verlagsanstalt, 1935), no. 47. Examples from Peuckert, *Deutsches Volkstum*, p. 111, note 1.

38. Geramb, *Kinder- und Hausmärchen aus der Steiermark*, pp. 41ff.

39. Grudde, *Plattdeutsche Volksmärchen aus Ostpreußen*, no. 27 ("De Steefmuttä") and 44 ("Vogelke"); cf. Anacker, pp. 125f. Rudolf Kapff, *Schwäbische Sagen*, Deutscher Sagenschatz (Jena and Stuttgart: Diederichs, 1926), pp. 31f., contains a similar legend using the contents of "The Juniper Tree."

40. Richard Kühnau, *Schlesische Sagen* (Leipzig: G. B. Teubner, 1910), vol. 1, no. 584.

41. Ibid., nos. 585 and 586.

42. Zender, *Volksmärchen*, p. 152; cf. p. xvii.

43. Merkelbach-Pinck, *Lothringer erzählen*, vol. 1: *Märchen*, p. 39; also see p. 33. Fox's statement about folklore in the Saarland is somewhat unclear, but in any case it applies to the folktale: "Legends, tales, and stories overlap in various forms. Today there are many people on the Saar River . . . who believingly listen to all folktales and ghost stories and whose belief in magic books and interpretations of dreams is stronger than their belief in the Holy Scripture." Nikolaus Fox, *Saarländische Volkskunde* (Bonn: Klopp, 1927), p. 163.

44. Cf. Karl Heinz Langstroff, *Lothringer Volksart. Untersuchung zur deutsch-lothringischen Volkserzählung an Hand der Sammlungen von Angelika Merkelbach-Pinck* (Marburg: N. G. Elwert, 1953), p. 76.

45. Rath, p. 13.

46. Schlecht, *Die Volkserzählung im Harmersbachtal*, p. 75; other sections reiterate this observation.

47. Jahn, *Volksmärchen aus Pommern und Rügen*, p. xii. Uffer also notes that the Rhaeto-Romanic concept corresponding to the German "Märchen" (folktale), i.e., "parevlas" or other terms, is absent among the narrators themselves, although published collections have recently introduced it in some places. Uffer asserts that "the folk and the narrator call legends, folktales, jest, in short all narratives, 'istorjias' or 'historias.' I have not drawn this conclusion only for the Rhaeto-Romanic area, but also in the city and surroundings of St. Gallen. In general all folk narratives are called 'stories.' If children or adults differentiate folktales from legends anywhere, this can surely be traced to the influence of schooling and books" (Uffer, p. 18).

48. Wilhelm Wisser, *Auf der Märchensuche* (Hamburg and Berlin o. J.: Hanseatische Verlagsanstalt, n.d.), p. 32.

49. Ibid., pp. 35f.

50. Grudde, *Plattdeutsche Volksmärchen*.

51. E.g., nos. 10ff.

52. "The supernatural events in these folktales, which derive from belief, do not occur in a fantasy world but rather in the laborers' real surroundings" (Julius Schwietering, "Volksmärchen und Volksglaube," *Dichtung und Volkstum*, new series 36 [1935], 74; cf. Mechtilda Brachetti, *Studien zur Lebensform des deutschen Volksmärchens* [Bühl: Konkordia, 1935], pp. 53ff.).

53. Grudde, FFC no. 102, p. 12.

54. Ibid.

55. Personal communication from Hertha Grudde; Brachetti, p. 54.

56. Grudde, FFC no. 102, pp. 9 and 16. Also see Schwietering, "Volksmärchen und Volksglaube," p. 73.

57. By J. Schwietering, M. Brachetti, E. Goetz-Rötzel, E. v. Königslöw, A. Krause-Siebert, H. U. Sareyko, and others.

58. Cf. Henssen, "Volkstümliche Erzählerkunst," p. 15. Sareyko, *Das Weltbild eines ostpreußischen Volkserzählers*.

59. Peuckert and Lauffer, *Volkskunde*, p. 184; Will-Erich Peuckert, "Erdichtete Sage," *Niederdeutsche Zeitschrift für Volkskunde* 21 (1943), 14.

60. Gottfried Henssen, "Sammlung und Auswertung volkstümlichen Erzählgutes," *Hessische Blätter für Volkskunde* 43 (1952), 10ff.

61. Friedrich Ranke, "Kunstmärchen im Volksmund," *Zeitschrift für Volkskunde* 46 (1936–37), 123–33.

62. Karl Plenzat, *Niederdeutsche Zeitschrift für Volkskunde* 9 (1931), 242f., and Friedrich Ranke, "Märchenforschung. Ein Literaturbericht (1920–1934)," *Deutsche Vierteljahrsschrift für Literaturwissenschaft und Geistesgeschichte* 14 (1936), 254. The term *primitive* is used in a psychological sense here, not in the philological sense of an

"ancient folktale" (*Urmärchen*).

63. Karl Plenzat, "Ostpreußische Märchen," *Niederdeutsche Zeitschrift für Volkskunde* 4 (1926), no. 2 and 3, pp. 50ff.

64. Ibid., p. 48; cf. Wagner, "Zu den Grundlagen," p. 197.

65. Plenzat, "Ostpreußische Märchen," p. 48.

66. BP IV, 5. Wilhelm Hauff depicts an invented, fictional narrative situation, yet one which is very illustrative, in the frames of his tales, particularly for the cycle "Das Wirtshaus im Spessart." Above all it is very clear here how *fear* can lead to the telling of folktales.

67. Cf. Giese, "Sind Märchen Lügen?" pp. 143f.

68. Cf. Sartori, "Erzählen als Zauber," pp. 41f.; further examples can be found here.

## V. PATHS OF RATIONALIZATION

### Ethnic Differences

1. E. Spranger's treatise "Wie erfaßt man einen Volkscharakter?" stands out among the recent theoretical statements on the problem of folk character; also see R. Thurnwald, "Grundprobleme der vergleichenden Völkerpsychologie," *Zeitschrift für die Gesamte Staatswissenschaft* 87:2. In folklore the volume edited by Martin Wähler, *Der deutsche Volkscharakter* (Jena: Diederichs, 1937), provides the groundwork; also see Martin Wähler, "Der deutsche Volkscharakter," in Adolf Spamer, *Die deutsche Volkskunde*, 2nd ed., vol. 1, pp. 600–22. In addition, see the last chapter, "Staat, Recht und Volkscharakter," in Richard Weiss, *Volkskunde der Schweiz* (Zurich: E. Rentsch, 1946), and A. Helbok, "Zur Methodik der Volkscharakterkunde," *Festschrift zu Ehren Hermann Wopfners*, pt. 2 (Innsbruck: Wagner, 1948), pp. 101–18, and Willy Hellpach, *Der deutsche Charakter* (Bonn: Athenäum, 1954).

Among psychological studies of a people through their folktales, the work of Löwis of Menar, *Der Held im deutschen und russischen Märchen*, and Koechlin, *Wesenszüge des deutschen und französischen Volksmärchens*, should be noted in particular; also see Friedrich Ranke, "Volksmärchen und Volksart," *Schweizerisches Archiv für Volkskunde* 43 (1946), 439ff.; Ernst Tegethoff, "Die Dämonen im deutschen und französischen Märchen," *Schweizerisches Archiv für Volkskunde* 24 (1923), 137–66; Ralph Boggs, *A Comparative Survey of the Folktales of Ten Peoples*, FFC no. 93 (Helsinki: Suomalainen Tiedeakatemia, 1930); Anna Krause-Siebert, *Der ostpreußische Volkscharakter, wie er sich in ostpreußischen Volksmärchen widerspiegelt*, Diss. Kiel, 1947.

2. Karl Maaß, *Das deutsche Märchen* (Hamburg: J. F. Richter, 1886).

3. Cf. Rittershaus, *Die neuisländischen Volksmärchen*, p. xvii.

4. Jan de Vries, *Volksverhalen uit Oost-Indie*, 2 vols. (Zutphen: W. J. Thieme & cie., 1925 and 1928).

5. Stith Thompson, *The Tales of the North American Indians* (Cambridge: Harvard University Press, 1929); cf. Thompson, *The Folktale*, the section "The Folktale in a Primitive Culture," pp. 297ff.

6. Enno Littmann, *Arabsiche Märchen* (Leipzig o. J.: Insel, 1935), pp. 332ff. and 458; cf. Enno Littmann, "Sneewittchen in Jerusalem," *Festschrift für Georg Jacob* (Leipzig: Otto Harrassowitz, 1932), pp. 165–73.

7. The "dead" Snow White is awakened with a certain matter-of-factness when the princess's mother washes the corpse with warm water. But in the Orient, Littmann tells us, people are so accustomed to the waking of the dead in Christian and Islamic saints' legends that it is not surprising when it occurs in the folktale (Littmann, "Sneewittchen," pp. 171ff.).

8. Hermann and Schwind, *Die Prinzessin von Samarkand*, no. 3, cf. pp. 145ff.; cf.

Wolfram Eberhard and Pertev Naili Borotav, *Typen türkischer Volksmärchen* (Wiesbaden: F. Steiner, 1953).

9. Löwis of Menar, *Der Held;* cf. Nikolaĭ Gogol, "Wesen und Eigenart der russischen Poesie," in Otto Buek, ed., *Gogols sämtliche Werke* in 5 vols. (Berlin o. J.: Propyläen, 1923), vol. 5, pp. 294f.

10. Cf. Löwis of Menar, *Der Held,* p. 132.

11. E.g., Aphanassjew [Afanas'ev], vol. 2, p. 22.

12. Ibid., p. 61.

13. Ibid., pp. 8of.

14. Cf. Löwis of Menar, *Der Held,* pp. 126ff.

15. Cf. MdW, KHM, p. xxiii.

16. Cf. Theodor Pletscher, *Die Märchen Charles Perrault's,* Diss. Zurich, 1905, p. 30. H. V. Velten, "The Influence of Charles Perrault's Contes de Ma Mèrè L'Oie on German Folklore," *Germanic Review* 5 (1930), pp. 4ff.; Agnes Nordick, *Der Stil der Märchen Perraults,* Diss. Münster, 1934; Rolf Hagen, *Der Einfluß der Perraultschen Contes auf das volkstümliche deutsche Erzählgut und besonders auf die KHM der Brüder Grimm,* Diss. Göttingen, 1954; Rolf Hagen, "Perraults Märchen und die Brüder Grimm," *Zeitschrift für deutsche Philologie* 74 (1955), 392ff.

17. W. Th. Elwert notes that Perrault expresses everything so properly that "it all seems quite clear and correctly motivated to a child who hears the story; yet for adults the style has an ironic, almost frivolous effect. The 'ésprit gaulois' shines through here" (W. Th. Elwert, "Charles Perrault und seine Märchen," *Archiv für das Studium der neueren Sprachen* 188 [1951], 93). Also see W. Kröber, *Charakteristik der Märchen Perraults,* Diss. Leipzig, 1915, and two studies on the relationship of Perrault to oral tradition: Delarue, "Les contes merveilleux de Perrault et la tradition populaire," and Rumpf, *Rotkäppchen.*

18. Elwert, p. 91.

19. Richard Benz, *Märchendichtung der Romantiker* (Gotha: F. A. Perthes, 1908), p. 16.

20. Elwert, pp. 96f.; cf. Carl Wilhelm von Sydow, "Ein Märchen von Perrault und seine Urform. Riquet à la houppe," *Schweizerisches Archiv für Volkskunde* 20 (1916), 441ff.

21. Cf. Pletscher, p. 29.

22. The German folktale has strong emotional power. Germans can only half-heartedly accept an animated folktale film, such as Disney's *Snow White,* as an effective work of art because they are too familiar with Snow White through tradition and custom; she has become an almost sacrosanct figure. For the German, the dwarves playing jazz is not only an anachronism but also almost a sacrilegious desecration of the folktale.

23. Pletscher, pp. 28 and 42.

24. Koechlin. The following remarks rely exclusively on this study.

25. W. Klee, *Bretonische Volksmärchen* (Munich, 1948), pp. 6ff.

26. MdW, *Französische Volksmärchen,* vol. 2, p. iii.

27. Tegethoff, "Dämonen."

28. E.g., Klee, pp. 245ff.

29. Cf. Matthias Zender, "Quellen und Träger der deutschen Volkserzählung," *Rheinische Vierteljahrsblätter* 7 (1937), 32.

30. Friedrich Ranke, "Volksmärchen und Volksart," p. 444. Houston Stewart Chamberlain exaggerates a bit when he says, "I believe that the Grimms' folktales are a richer record of the German world-view than all the academic writings of German philosophers taken together" (*Rasse und Persönlichkeit* [Munich: F. Bruckmann, 1937]).

## Magical Thought and Modern Civilization

1. Cf. Zender, *Volksmärchen*, p. xxvi.
2. Uffer, p. 79.
3. Littmann, *Arabische Märchen*, p. 456. During World War I it was said that the banned Chediwe returned to his palace in Cairo each night from Constantinople in a blimp or plane (Littman, *Tausendundeine Nacht in der arabischen Literatur, Philosophie und Geschichte*, vol. 2 [Tübingen: J. C. B. Mohr, 1923], p. 21).
4. Emil Heckmann, *Blaubart, ein Beitrag zur vergleichenden Märchenforschung*, Diss. Heidelberg, 1930, p. 16.
5. Uffer, p. 119.
6. Karasek, pp. 131ff.
7. Löwis of Menar, *Der Held*, p. 53; E. Meier, *Volksmärchen aus Schwaben*, p. 143. A narrator from the lower Rhine begins, "So—the king had it put in the paper: Whoever defeats the giant will get my daughter" (Bodens, no. 1068, p. 257).
8. Leyen, *Die Welt der Märchen*, vol. 2, p. 107.
9. Oberfeld, pp. 79ff.
10. K. Ranke, *Schleswig-Holsteinische Volksmärchen*, pp. 98f.
11. Merkelbach-Pinck, *Lothringer erzählen*, p. 52.
12. Leyen, *Die Welt der Märchen*, vol. 2, p. 24.
13. Jahn, *Volksmärchen aus Pommern und Rügen*, p. xiii.
14. Peuckert, *Schlesiens deutsche Märchen*, no. 34, p. 41.
15. MdW, *Plattdeutsche Märchen*, vol. 1, p. 204.
16. MdW, *Russische Volksmärchen*, no. 35; cf. HdM I, 57f.
17. Lambertz, *Albanische Märchen*, p. 132.
18. Johann Jegerlehner, *Sagen und Märchen aus dem Oberwallis*, Schriften der Schweizerischen Gesellschaft für Volkskunde, vol. 9 (Basel: Schweizerische Gesellschaft für Volkskunde, 1913), no. 144, p. 122.
19. Cf. Leyen, *Die Welt der Märchen*, vol. 2, p. 97. In a Swabian legend from my unpublished collection, "a beautiful American woman" is a supernatural figure.
20. Merkelbach-Pinck, *Lothringer Volksmärchen*, p. 339; also see Langstroff, p. 140.
21. MdW, *Lettisch-litauische Märchen*, no. 49, p. 317.
22. Leyen, *Die Welt der Märchen*, vol. 2, pp. 24f.
23. Bach, *Deutsche Volkskunde*, p. 390.
24. Bünker, no. 73, p. 193.
25. Leyen, *Die Welt der Märchen*, vol. 2, p. 85. School even plays a role in "The Spirit in the Bottle" (KHM 99).
26. Cf. Dymke, p. 187.
27. Uffer, p. 171.
28. Leyen, *Die Welt der Märchen*, vol. 2, pp. 97 and 90.
29. Merkelbach-Pinck, *Lothringer Volksmärchen*, pp. 257f.
30. Schambach and Müller, *Niedersächsische Sagen und Märchen*, p. 282.
31. Geramb, *Kinder- und Hausmärchen aus der Steiermark*, p. 84.
32. Johannes Mattias Firmenich, *Germaniens Völkerstimmen* (Berlin: Friedberg & Mode, 1846–54), vol. 3, p. 400.
33. Peuckert, *Schlesiens deutsche Märchen*, p. 37.
34. MdW, *Donauland*, pp. 47f.; cf. Woeller, pp. 362ff.
35. Schlecht, *Die Volkserzählungen im Harmersbachtal*, p. 73.
36. F. Sieber, "Obersächsische Volksmärchen," *Mitteldeutsche Blätter für Volkskunde* 10:5 (1935), 138.
37. Bausinger, pp. 131 and 135.
38. G. Müller and P. Suter, *Sagen aus Baselland* (Basel: Landschaftler, 1938), p. 123.

39. Zender, *Volkssagen*, no. 30.
40. Ibid., no. 1000.
41. R. Weber, "Oberpfälzische Sagen," *Die Nachbarn. Jahrbuch für vergleichende Volkskunde* 2 (1954), p. 148, no. 23.
42. As in the collections by Wisser, Jahn, Müllenhoff, and Bünker; cf. Koechlin, pp. 75ff., and Dymke, pp. 197ff.
43. MdW, *Nordische Volksmärchen*, vol. 1, p. 31; cf. R. Hünnerkopf, "Volkssage und Märchen," *Oberdeutsche Zeitschrift für Volkskunde* 3 (1929), 6. No one "cries pearls instead of tears" anymore; even the narrator of KHM 179 believes that "the poor would soon become rich" if this happened.
44. Geramb, *Kinder- und Hausmärchen aus der Steiermark*, pp. 119ff; cf. Hendricks, pp. 137f.
45. Cf. Franz Heyden, *Volksmärchen und volksmärchenerzähler* (Hamburg: Hanseatische Verlagsanstalt, 1922), pp. 58f.
46. Examples in HdM II, 220.
47. BP I, 109ff; cf. Carl Wilhelm von Sydow, *Två spinnsagor. En studie i jämförande folksagoforskning* (Stockholm, 1909).
48. Cf. the references under "Hexe" and "Steifmutter" in BP V, 278 and 297.
49. Jegerlehner, no. 144, p. 122.
50. Jegerlehner, no. 79, p. 62.
51. Wisser, *Auf der Märchensuche*, p. 8; also see Jegerlehner, no. 65, p. 43 ("Aus Räuberhand gerettet").
52. Cf. Woeller, pp. 379 and 112.
53. Cf. MdW, *Französische Volksmärchen*, vol. 2, p. v.
54. Peuckert, *Schlesiens deutsche Märchen*, pp. xf.
55. Cf. Hendricks, p. 59.
56. MdW, *Donauland*, pp. 120ff. ("Die weiße Amsel").
57. Bünker, p. 248 ("Ta' waissi Wulf"); cf. Dymke, p. 201.
58. Zender, "Quellen," p. 36.
59. MdW, *Deutsche Märchen seit Grimm*, vol. 1, pp. 164ff. ("Die Schlange").
60. Merkelbach-Pinck, *Lothringer Volksmärchen*, pp. 163ff. ("Das verwunschene Schloß"); cf. Dymke, pp. 112f.
61. Henssen, *Volk Erzählt*, no. 176, pp. 237ff.
62. Henssen, *Überlieferung und Persönlichkeit*, appendix no. 5; cf. p. 39.
63. In some versions of KHM 191; cf. Hartmann-Ströhm, *Das Meerhäschen*, pp. 78ff.
64. K. Ranke, *Schleswig-Holsteinische Volksmärchen*, pp. 98ff.
65. Merkelbach-Pinck, *Lothringer Volksmärchen*, pp. 45f.
66. Uffer, p. 119.
67. Unpublished tale from Wossidlo's collection in the Wossidlo Archive in Rostock, cited from Woeller, p. 377.
68. *Volksmärchen in den Landschaften der Westmark*, 3rd ed. (Saarlautern, 1941) ("Ringelfest"); cf. Isenberg, p. 97.

## VI. THE FOLKTALE AS A MIRROR OF THE REAL WORLD
### The Significance of Time and Place

1. Zenker-Starzacher, *Eine deutsche Märchenerzählerin aus Ungarn*.
2. Jahn, *Volksmärchen aus Pommern und Rügen*, p. 107 ("Das Wolfskind").
3. Haltrich, p. 168 ("Die Geschenke der Schönen"); cf. Dymke, pp. 79 and 93f. In order to understand a Swabian folktale in which the beadle summons the entire city council from heaven by saying, "Pst! Pst! Gentlemen! there's a wine sale in

Haußen," you have to know that in Württemberg the village council is allowed to drink *for free* at wine sales (E. Meier, *Volksmärchen aus Schwaben*, no. 18, pp. 66f.).

4. Cf. Dymke, p. 119.

5. Lambertz, pp. 27ff.

6. E. Meier, *Volksmärchen aus Schwaben*, "Die vier Brüder"; cf. Hans Lucke, *Der Einfluß der Brüder Grimm auf die Märchensammler des 19. Jahrhunderts*, Diss. Greifswald, 1933, p. 55.

7. Zender, *Volksmärchen*, no. 190, pp. 138ff. (also see p. 169); cf. Henssen, "Volkstümliche Erzählerkunst," p. 6, note 9. The Upper Styrian text of the same tale type, "Vom senner, der König wurde," in Karl Haiding's collection also has strong local coloring (Haiding, *Österreichs Märchenschatz* [Vienna: Pro Domo, 1953], pp. 7ff). Of course, the illustrations which show the prince wearing the festive Styrian costume and fairies dressed in Bavarian *Dirndln* exaggerate the localization.

8. This is called *schnatzen*, which means the hair is braided; a "Schnatz" is the braid. The bride goes to church wearing braids; cf. BP II, 274.

9. Cf. Konrad Tönges, *Lebenserscheinungen und Verbreitung des deutschen Märchens*, Gießener Beiträge zur deutschen Philologie 56 (Gießen: von Münchowsche Üniversitätsdruckerei, 1937), 52ff.; also see the purely Hessian illustrations by the famous illustrator of the Grimms' tales, Otto Ubbelohde.

10. Cf. MdW, *Isländische Volksmärchen*, p. II.

11. Cf. Dymke, p. 118; Tönges, *Lebenserscheinungen*, the section "Die Ergiebigkeit der deutschen Landschaften für das echte Märchen," pp. 84ff.

12. Cf. Peuckert, *Volkskunde*, p. 150.

13. Cf. Baumgart, p. 34.

14. Lambertz, *Albanische Märchen*, p. 189.

15. MdW, *Französische Volksmärchen*, vol. 2, p. vii.

16. MdW, *Afrikanische Märchen*, no. 17, pp. 93ff.

17. Cf. Aarne, *Leitfaden*, p. 36.

18. MdW, *Afrikanische Märchen*, no. 20, pp. 100ff.

19. MdW, *Malaiische Märchen*, pp. 33–63.

20. Cf. Wolfram Eberhard, *Volksmärchen aus Südostchina*, FFC no. 128 (Helsinki: Suomalainen Tiedeakatemia, 1941).

21. Reinhard Wagner, "Einige vorder- und hinterindische Fassungen des Märchens von der Frau Holle (Goldmarie und Pechmarie)," *Zeitschrift für Volkskunde* 42 (1933), 163.

22. MdW, *Afrikanische Märchen*, p. 81.

23. Cf. Eberhard, *Südostchina*, pp. 215f.

24. Cf. Georg Jacob, *Märchen und Traum* (Hannover: H. Lafaire, 1923), pp. 13f.

25. Cf. Leyen, *Die Welt der Märchen*, vol. 1, pp. 276ff. J. Oestrup, "Alf laila wa-laila" ("The Arabian Nights"), in *Enzyklopädie des Islam. Geographisches, ethnographisches und biographisches Wörterbuch der mohammedanischen Völker*, Th. Houtsma, ed. (Leiden: E. J. Brill, 1913–36), vol. 1, pp. 265ff., and D. B. MacDonald, "Hikáya," ("Narrative"), vol. 2, pp. 321ff.; BP IV, 364–418 (essay on the Arabian folktale by Bernhard Heller); Enno Littman, *Die Erzählungen aus den tausandundein Nächten*, complete edition in 6 vols. from the original Arabic text, 2nd ed. (Wiesbaden: Insel, 1953). Littmann, *Tausandundeine Nacht in der arabischen Literatur, Philosophie und Geschichte*, vol. 2 (Tübingen: J. C. B. Mohr, 1923).

26. Cf. Littmann, "Sneewittchen," p. 171.

27. Littmann, *Arabische Märchen*, pp. 332ff. and 458; cf. Littmann, "Sneewittchen."

28. Schmidt and Kahle, *Volkserzählungen aus Palästina*, vol. 1, p. 213; cf. p. 34.

29. Josef Henninger, "Über die völkerkundliche Bedeutung von 1001 Nacht," *Schweizerisches Archiv für Volkskunde* 44 (1947), 35–65. The following remarks rely on this article.

30. Ibid., pp. 59f.

31. Ibid., pp. 35ff. and 46ff.
32. Ibid., pp. 57ff.
33. E. Meier, *Volksmärchen aus Schwaben*, no. 74, p. 257.
34. Ibid., no. 22, p. 76; similar localization can be found in nos. 16 ("Das Märchen vom Räuber Matthes"), 59 ("Der langnasige Riese und der Schlossergesell"), and 61 ("Das Nebelmännle"); cf. p. viii.
35. References in Erna Andersen, *Die Eingänge im deutschen Märchen. Ein Beitrag zur Stilkunde der Volkserzählung*, Diss. Jena, 1937, p. 65.
36. Peuckert, *Schlesiens deutsche Märchen*, no. 1, p. 1.
37. Henssen, *Überlieferung und Persönlichkeit*, no. 29, pp. 106ff.
38. Merkelbach-Pinck, *Lothringer erzählen*, no. 1, p. 53; cf. the review by Kurt Ranke, *Niederdeutsche Zeitschrift für Volkskunde* 15 (1937), 238.
39. Merkelbach-Pinck, *Lothringer erzählen*, pp. 66ff. and 72.
40. Ibid., pp. 122ff.
41. Ibid., pp. 195ff.
42. Ibid., p. 82.
43. Ibid., p. 83.
44. Ibid., p. 211. The Bavarian folktales in E. Stemplinger's collection also reveal precise knowledge of the local environment. During his journey, the Bavarian "Thumbling" encounters the rural mailman at his station outside Schliersee. The foundling in "The Devil with the Three Golden Hairs" floats down the Amper (river) "in a melba toast [a common Bavarian food] box" but gets stuck on the watergate outside Dachau. "The little old lady" in another tale lives in Munich, and the queen in "Sleeping Beauty" bathes in Lake Schlier. "Hans in Luck" worked for seven years "for the Woazinger brewery in Miesbach" (E. Stemlinger, *Oberbayrische Märchen*, Bücher der Heimat, vols. 1 and 10, 1st and 2nd series [Altötting, 1924 and 1926]). However, these are not original tales but polished renderings of Grimm tales that the editor changed into High Bavarian himself (according to a letter from the author, Sept. 26, 1952).
45. Henssen, *Überlieferung und Persönlichkeit*, no. 33, pp. 115ff.
46. Henssen, *Volk erzählt*, p. 163.
47. MdW, *Donauland*, p. 57 ("Die Vögel Phoenus und Floribunda").
48. MdW, *Donauland*, pp. 118ff. ("Die weiße Amsel"); cf. Dymke, pp. 68f.
49. André Jolles speaks of the folktale being "always," in contrast to the novella, which occurs "once" (Jolles, *Einfache Formen*, Sächsische Forschungsinstitute in Leipzig, Forschungsinstitut für neuere Philologie, II. Neugermanistische Abteilung," vol. 2 [Halle: M. Niemeyer, 1930], pp. 218ff.); cf. Lüthi, "Märchen und Sage," p. 169; Dymke, p. 78; Günther Müller, *Die Bedeutung der Zeit in der Erzählkunst* (Bonn: Universitäts-Verlag, 1946).
50. Historical personalities and historical events play a role even in the ancient Egyptian folktale (cf. Alfred Wiedemann, *Altägyptische Sagen und Märchen* [Leipzig: Deutsche Verlagsactiengesellschaft, 1906]) and in tales from ancient American civilizations: MdW, *Märchen der Azteken und Inkaperuaner*, p. vii.
51. Cf. Max Vasmer, "König Trojan mit den Ziegenohren," *Zeitschrift für Volkskunde* 46 (1936), 184–88.
52. Gustav Jungbauer, ed., *Märchen aus Turkestan und Tibet*, MdW (Jena: Diederichs, 1923), no. 19, pp. 196ff.
53. MdW, *Afrikanische Märchen*, p. 4.
54. Cf. Littmann, *Arabische Märchen*, pp. 435f.
55. Lambertz, *Albanische Märchen*, p. 45; cf. Georgiji Ostrogorski, *Geschichte des Byzantinischen Staates*, 2nd ed. (Munich: Beck, 1952), pp. 391ff.
56. Ritterhaus, *Die neuisländischen Volksmärchen*, p. xxxvi.
57. MdW, *Isländische Volksmärchen*, nos. 5, 8, 11–14, 20, 32, 46, 47, 62; cf. pp. vii and xiff.
58. Eugène Bossard, *Gilles de Rais, maréchal de France, dit Barbe-Bleue (1404–1440)*

(Paris: H. Champion, 1885); cf. "Blaubart," HdM I, 266ff. (by Voretzsch); Raimond, "Heer Hallewyn"; Pletscher, *Die Märchen Charles Perraults*.

59. G. F. Meyer, *Ik will di wat vertelln* (Garding: H. Lühr & Dircks, 1916), p 32. Woeller, p. 209.

60. "Friedrich der Große," HdM II, 230ff. (by Kügler), contains a compilation of motifs; cf. Heinz Diewerge, *Der alte Fritz im Volksmund* (Munich: Albert Langer & Georg Müller, 1937).

61. Wisser's manuscript no. 12, 3rd text, cited from Andersen, p. 78.

62. Oberfeld, p. 184a.

63. *Zeitschrift für österreichische Volkskunde* 2 (1896), 213.

64. Henssen, "Bergische Märchen," p. 41.

## The Social Milieu

1. Particularly in Zender's and Uffer's collections.

2. MdW, *Plattdeutsche Volksmärchen*, vol. 1, p. xvi; Wisser, *Auf der Märchensuche*, p. 46; cf. Leyen, *Die Welt der Märchen*, vol. 2, p. 253.

3. Jahn, *Volksmärchen aus Pommern und Rügen*. In contrast to these collectors, Gottfried Henssen emphasizes that he obtained valuable items from large farmers and property owners as well as from day laborers. However, his best narrators were craftsmen (Gottfried Henssen, *Volk erzählt*, pp. 3f., and Henssen, *Überlieferung und Persönlichkeit*, p. 40). Drivers, woodcutters, rural innkeepers, and silk weavers are also among the narrators of his "Bergische Märchen." Masons, cobblers, handymen, and cowherds narrate his other collections (Henssen, *Volk erzählt*, p. 20). His narrator Gerrits was a temporary laborer.

Matthias Zender, for whom farmers compose the largest group of narrators, clearly emphasizes that this is unusual. But even among a population consisting mostly of farmers, the large farmers do not make up half of the informants. Zender still obtained 20.5 percent of his material from workers, day laborers, and small farmers, and 17.5 percent from craftsmen (cf. Zender, *Volksmärchen*, pp. xxiif.; Zender, "Quellen," p. 40).

4. Dittmaier, *Sagen, Märchen und Schwänke von der unteren Sieg*.

5. For example, a Jewish draper's delivery boy (Peuckert, *Schlesiens deutsche Märchen*, nos. 114, 130, 157, 214).

6. Karl Storch, *Märchen aus dem Südostegerlande* (Plan, 1940).

7. Merkelbach-Pinck, *Lothringer Volksmärchen*, pp. 375ff.; Merkelbach-Pinck, *Wanderung*, p. 230.

8. Cf. Schlecht, *Die Volkserzählung im Harmersbachtal*.

9. E. Meier, *Volksmärchen aus Schwaben*, Introduction.

10. Romuald Pramberger, *Märchen aus Steiermark*, 2nd ed. (Seckau: Benediktinerabtei, 1946); MdW, *Donauland*, pp. viff.; cf. Rath, pp. 14f. Elfriede Rath writes that Pramberger's narrators "are characteristically outsiders to the bourgeois farming community, because of either a bodily defect or their social position. The narratives are not cultivated in houses or villages, such as in Brinkmann's home town in Westphalia; rather, they are more commonly brought in from the outside" (Rath, p. 17).

11. Geramb, *Kinder- und Hausmärchen aus der Steiermark*, p. 2; MdW, *Donauland*, p. vi.

12. Bünker, *Schwänke, Sagen und Märchen in heanzischer Mundart*. Non-German-speaking narrators belong to the same social groups: Asbjörnson's narrators are, among other things, men hired to keep birds or deer out of the crops, sailors, fishermen, gravediggers, adolescent boys, and soldiers on leave (cf. Leyen, *Die Welt der Märchen*, vol. 2, pp. 192f.). According to the information provided by collectors, French tale tellers belong to the same lower classes as the German-speaking narrators: Here we find barkeepers, maids, rural telegram carriers, and traveling

people of all sorts, e.g., tinkers, rag pickers, mole trappers, and the like. (For example, see Klee, pp. 242ff.; cf. F. Ranke, "Volksmärchen und Volksart.")

A gardener narrates the Polish folktales collected by Szulczewski. The narrators of the recent Russian collections which are available to us are journeymen and beggars; in the northern parts of the country, fishermen and sailors also tell tales (Lutz Mackensen, "Zur Märchenforschung," *Zeitschrift für deutsche Bildung* [1930], 368). According to Mark Azadovskii, exiles and vagabonds are Siberia's most important folktale bearers. Narration often serves as a means of livelihood for them (Mark Azadovskii, *A Siberian Tale Teller*).

Some of the modern Greek narratives in the *Märchen der Weltliteratur* volume were recorded from laborers, and Moses Gaster names the "nursemaid from Hungary and the housewife from Wallachia, the Albanian with his sweetmeats, and the peasant with his fowls and eggs, pilgrims returned from the holy land, the hawker, and the gipsy" as Rumania's most important tale tellers ("Fairy Tales," *Folklore* 7 [1898], 218f.).

13. Cf. Dymke; "häusliche Arbeit," HdM I, 108ff. (by Kahlo); "Bauer," HdM I, 184ff. (by Herold); and "Gestalten und Umwelt im Märchen," HdM II, 606ff. (by R. Petsch); also see Woeller, *Der soziale Gehalt*.

14. Bünker, no. 56, pp. 128ff.

15. Specifically, the narrator Heinrich L.; cf. Oberfeld, pp. 178ff.

16. Geramb, *Kinder- und Hausmärchen aus der Steiermark*, pp. 41ff.

17. E.g., in MdW, *Donauland*.

18. Bünker, p. 256.

19. Cf. Leyen, *Die Welt der Märchen*, vol. 2, pp. 86ff.

20. Grudde, *Plattdeutsche Volksmärchen*, no. 7, p. 5.

21. Bausinger, pp. 111ff.

22. Henssen, *Überlieferung und Persönlichkeit*, no. 29, p. 39.

23. Storch, pp. 15f.

24. Ibid., p. 47.

25. Pramberger, pp. 40ff. ("Der lange Schlaf").

26. MdW, *Deutsche Märchen seit Grimm*, vol. 1, pp. 164ff.

27. Zingerle and Zingerle, *Kinder- und Hausmärchen*, vol. 1, no. 13.

28. Grudde, *Plattdeutsche Volksmärchen*, no. 40.

29. Pramberger, pp. 114ff.; cf. Rath, p. 82.

30. Cf. Giese, p. 144.

31. Grudde, *Plattdeutsche Volksmärchen*, no. 49, p. 94.

32. Otto Knoop, *Sagen und Märchen aus dem östlichen Hinterpommern* (Posen: J. Jolowicz, 1885), no. 11.

33. Firmenich, vol. 2, p. 322.

34. Adalbert Kuhn, *Märkische Sagen und Märchen*, reprint (Berlin: F. A. Herbig, 1937), no. 2, p. 267.

35. Henssen, "Volkstümliche Erzählerkunst," p. 22.

36. Cf. Müller, *Das Märchen vom Unibos*.

37. E. Meier, *Volksmärchen aus Schwaben*, p. 31 ("Das Schiff, das zu Wasser und zu Land fährt").

38. Ulrich Jahn, *Schwänke und Schnurren aus Bauern Mund* (Berlin o. J.: Mayer & Müller, 1890), p. 87.

39. Cf. Woeller, pp. 212, 220, and 422.

40. Cf. ibid., pp. 219 and 251f.

41. Jahn, *Schwänke und Schnurren*, p. 45; cf. Woeller, pp. 222f.

42. Cf. Johannes Bolte, "Das Märchen vom Gevatter Tod," *Zeitschrift des Vereins für Volkskunde* 4 (1894), 34ff.; Alexander Krappe, "Über die Erzählung vom Gevatter Tod," *Schlesische Blätter für Volkskunde* 2 (1940), 12ff.

43. Merkelbach-Pinck, *Lothringer Volksmärchen*, p. 140.

44. Grudde, *Plattdeutsche Volksmärchen*, no. 108, pp. 206ff. ("De injemuuäde Merjell").

45. Ibid., no. 20, pp. 31ff. ("Vom Ferstä").

46. Ibid., no. 60, pp. 116ff.; cf. Sareyko, p. 169.

47. Grudde, no. 69, p. 126.

48. Ibid., no. 45, p. 89.

49. Ibid., no. 39, p. 75; cf. Henssen, *Sammlung und Auswertung*, p. 26.

50. Grudde, no. 14, pp. 15ff.; cf. Sareyko, pp. 32, 64, and 172.

51. Knoop, *Volkssagen, Erzählungen;* cf. Wolfgang Steinitz, "Aufgaben und Ziele der volkskundlichen Arbeit in der Deutschen Demokratischen Republik," *Wissenschaftliche Annalen* 2 (1953), 4. In a version from southeast Egerland, "Strong Michael" offers to work for the farmer free of charge, "under the condition that at the end he could box the farmer's ears. At first the farmer didn't accept; he said he already had two servants and didn't need a third. But his wife convinced him. 'Don't be dumb,' she said, 'you should be glad to get a cheap hand; you'll survive the slap!' He then hired him" (Storch, p. 11).

52. E. Meier, *Volksmärchen aus Schwaben*, p. 75.

53. Cf. Walter Anderson, *Kaiser und Abt. Die Geschichte eines Schwankes*, FFC no. 42 (Helsinki: Suomalainen Tiedeakatemia, 1923); cf. Woeller, pp. 238f.

54. Cf. Woeller, pp. 16ff.

55. MdW, *Plattdeutsche Volksmärchen*, vol. 1, p. 189 ("De Suldat und de Düwel").

56. Bünker, no. 61, pp. 140ff.

57. Ey, *Harzmärchenbuch*, p. 122 ("Der eiserne Mann"); cf. Woeller, pp. 354ff.

58. For an early analysis of the social-psychological function of folk narratives and folk literature, see Friedrich Engels, "Die deutsche Volksbücher," in the *historische kritische Gesamtausgabe* (of his works), vol. 2, pt. 1, p. 49.

59. E. Meier, *Volksmärchen aus Schwaben*, no. 78, p. 270.

60. Nikolaus Fox, *Volksmärchen* (Saarlautern: Hausen, 1943), Introduction; cf. Woeller, p. 274.

61. Zenker-Starzacher, p. 63.

62. MdW, *Isländische Volksmärchen*, no. 28, pp. 124ff.

63. Grudde, *Plattdeutsche Volksmärchen*, nos. 31, 32, 53; nos. 14 and 54 are similar; cf. Anacker, pp. 126f.

64. Grudde, *Plattdeutsche Volksmärchen*, no. 58, pp. 113ff.; cf. Krause-Siebert.

65. MdW, *Plattdeutsche Volksmärchen*, vol. 2, p. 215.

66. Ibid., vol. 1, p. 171.

67. Jahn, *Volksmärchen aus Pommern und Rügen*, p. 281; cf. Dymke, pp. 104, 72, and 90.

68. E. Meier, *Volksmärchen aus Schwaben*, p. 54; cf. Woeller, p. 365.

69. Cf. Isenberg, pp. 66f.

70. Zingerle and Zingerle, *Kinder- und Hausmärchen*, vol. 1, p. 5.

71. Haltrich, no. 27.

72. Ibid., no. 29; cf. Genzel, p. 113.

73. Leyen, *Die Welt der Märchen*, vol. 2, p. 105.

74. MdW, *Nordische Volksmärchen*, no. 2, p. 188 (from Sweden).

75. Woeller, p. 144.

76. MdW, *Plattdeutsche Volksmärchen*, vol. 1, p. 193.

77. Ibid., vol. 1, p. 240.

78. Jahn, *Volksmärchen aus Pommern und Rügen*, p. 43 ("Wie Dummhans für ein Gerstenkorn ein Königreich bekam").

79. Wilhelm Busch, *Ut öler Welt* (Munich: L. Joachim, 1910), p. 39 ("Der Schweinejunge und die Prinzessin").

80. Emil Sommer, *Sagen, Märchen und Gebräuche aus Sachsen und Thüringen* (Halle: E. Anton, 1846), no. 4 ("Der dumme Wirrschkopf"); cf. Woeller, p. 140.

81. MdW, *Zigeunermärchen*, no. 23, p. 92.
82. Tillhagen, *Taikon*.
83. Grudde, *Plattdeutsche Volksmärchen*, no. 107; cf. Dymke, p. 19; Brachetti, p. 18.
84. Henssen, "Volkstümliche Erzählerkunst," p. 19.
85. Peuckert, *Schlesiens deutsche Märchen*, no. 20, p. 26.
86. Bünker, no. 71, pp. 171ff.
87. Brachetti, p. 29.
88. Sommer, no. 4.
89. Rittershaus, pp. xxiiif.
90. Grudde, *Plattdeutsche Volksmärchen*, no. 24, p. 41, and no. 51, pp. 98ff.
91. Ibid., no. 38, p. 71; cf. Sareyko, p. 24.
92. Grudde, *Plattdeutsche Volksmärchen*, no. 23, p. 39.
93. Fox, *Volksmärchen* ("Der feurige Drache"); cf. Woeller, p. 142.
94. Examples in HdM I, 58.
95. Carl and Theodor Colshorn, *Märchen und Sagen* (Hannover: C. Rümpler, 1854), p. 20.
96. Haltrich, no. 11.
97. Wossidlo Archive, Rostock, no. 80 088, cited from Woeller, pp. 134f.
98. Bünker, no. 85, p. 252.
99. Cf. Töpfer, p. 13.
100. MdW, *Deutsche Märchen seit Grimm*, vol. 1, p. 323.
101. Ibid., vol. 1, p. 281.
102. Müllenhoff, *Sagen, Märchen und Lieder der Herzogtümer Schleswig-Holstein und Lauenburg*, no. 22 ("Die gelernten Königssöhne"); cf. Woeller, p. 136.
103. Jahn, *Volksmärchen aus Pommern und Rügen*, no. 1; cf. Töpfer, p. 13.
104. Wossidlo Archive, Rostock, no. 80 644, cited from Woeller, p. 138.
105. Henssen, *Überlieferung und Persönlichkeit*, no. 34, cf. p. 21.
106. Oberfeld, p. 179b.
107. Merkelbach-Pinck, *Lothringer Volksmärchen*, p. 166; cf. Dymke, p. 103, and Karl Spiess, *Das deutsche Volksmärchen*, Natur und Geisteswelt, no. 587, 2nd ed. (Leipzig and Berlin: B. G. Teubner, 1924), p. 10.
108. Merkelbach-Pinck, *Lothringer Volksmärchen*, pp. 166ff.; cf. Dymke, p. 99.
109. Wolf, *Hessen*, no. 6 ("Der Hinkelhirt").
110. MdW, *Irische Volksmärchen*, no. 21, pp. 125ff; cf. Introduction, p. iv.
111. Aphanassjew [Afanas'ev], vol. 1, no. 7, p. 56.
112. Ibid., vol. 1, no. 12, p. 94.
113. MdW, *Neugriechische Märchen*, no. 32, p. 109; cf. p. 331.
114. E. Meier, *Volksmärchen aus Schwaben*, no. 3, p. 13.
115. Jahn, *Volksmärchen aus Pommern und Rügen*, no. 12 ("Vom Königssohn, der noch zu jung zum Heiraten sein sollte").
116. MdW, *Plattdeutsche Volksmärchen*, vol. 2 ("De tru'n Froenn"); cf. Woeller, p. 134.
117. Grudde, *Plattdeutsche Volksmärchen*, no. 80, p. 148. Nos. 13, 16, 19, 20, 40, 49, 86, and 87 are similar; cf. Sareyko, p. 77.
118. Grudde, *Plattdeutsche Volksmärchen*, no. 24, p. 41; cf. Sareyko, p. 76.
119. Oberfeld, p. 63.
120. BP I, 109f.
121. Hahn, no. 10.
122. Oberfeld, p. 166.
123. Merkelbach-Pinck, *Lothringer Erzählen*, pp. 105f.
124. MdW, *Plattdeutsche Volksmärchen*, vol. 1, p. 127. Despite its childish simplicity, the Grimm version (KHM 21) preserves something of the courtly decorum and royal dignity of the eighteenth century: "And when she appeared at the

wedding wearing this dress, everyone marveled at her beauty. The king's son was waiting for her. He immediately took her by the hand and danced with no one but her. When others came and asked her for a dance, he said, 'She is my partner.' " Cf. Heyden, pp. 81f., and Karl Plenzat, "Märchen und Mundart," *Sitzungberichte der Altertumsgesellschaft*, vol. 26 (Königsberg, 1926), p. 299.

125. Zenker-Starzacher, p. 44.

126. Bünker, no. 65, pp. 153f.

127. MdW, *Zigeunermärchen*, no. 24, p. 97.

128. Zenker-Starzacher, pp. 68f.; cf. Dymke, p. 106. Also see Peter Rosegger's wonderful, and folkloristically accurate, description of the "toastmaster" in *Schriften des Waldschulmeisters*, 51st–55th printing (Leipzig, 1904), pp. 18off.

129. Karasek, p. 139.

## VII. THE FOLKTALE'S INNER REALITY

### The Narrator's Ego

1. Russian scholars were the first to illuminate the folktale's significance for individual psychology. For example, Mark Azadovskii devotes an entire study to Natalia Ossipovna Vinokurova from Verkholensk. In the book he says, "the folktale contains deep traces of the [narrator's] personal experience, his occupation with this or that craft, and his personal characteristics. All this has an enormous influence on the performance of the folktale" (p. 14). Gottfried Henssen makes similar observations in *Überlieferung und Persönlichkeit*; also see E. Hoffmann-Krayer, "Die individuellen Triebkräfte im Volksleben," *Schweizerisches Archiv für Volkskunde* 30 (1930), pp. 169–82; A. Vierkandt, "Hervorragende Individuen bei Naturvölkern," *Zeitschrift für Sozialwissenschaft* 11 (1908), 542–53; Richard Viidalepp, "Von einem großen estnischen Erzähler und seinem Repertoir," *Acta Ethnologica* 2 (1937), 158–73; Karl Haiding, "Träger der Volkserzählung in unseren Tagen," *Österreichische Zeitschrift für Volkskunde*, new series 7 (1953), 24–36.

2. Evald Tang Kristensen, *Fra Mindebo, jyske Folkeæventyr* (Aarhus: Forfatterens, 1898), p. 44.

3. Evald Tang Kristensen, *Æventyr fra Jylland*, 4 vols. (Copenhagen: K. Schønberg, 1881–97), vol. 1, p. 263, no. 35.

4. Pol de Mont and Alfons de Cock, *Vlaamsche wondersprookjes* (Ghent: A. Siffer, 1896), p. 220; *Volkskunde (Organe officiel de la Commission Folklore de l'Académie royale néerlandaise des sciences)* 28, p. 138.

5. Cf. BP II, 152.

6. Cf. BP II, 441.

7. Martin Montanus, *Schwankbücher* (1557–1566), Johannes Bolte, ed. (Tübingen: Literarischer Verein in Stuttgart, 1899), p. 547; quoted in BP IV, 20.

8. G. Fr. Meyer, unpublished manuscript collection, cited from E. Andersen, p. 51. Additional examples can be found in *Zeitschrift für Volkskunde* 42 (1933), pp. 228ff. ("Abenteuer eines Gänsemädchens"), and MdW, *Türkische Märchen*, no. 17, pp. 137ff.

9. Haiding, "Träger der Volkserzählung," pp. 3of.

10. Dittmaier, p. 205.

11. Paul Sébillot, *Conte populaires de la Haute Bretagne* (Paris: G. Charpentier, 1880–82), vol. 3, p. 74; translation from BP IV, 19f.

12. Wisser, manuscript collection, no. 82, 1. Text quoted from Andersen, p. 51. The narrator cannot overcome his own nature, even when consciously fabricating the story. Thus even the tale of lying has its inner reality. Maxim Gorky says this quite aptly at one point in his novella *Konowalow*. "You don't believe me, Ljossa?" the offended narrator asked. "Well I believe it. . . . How can one person fail to

believe another? Even if he recognizes that the other is lying, he should still believe him; that is, he should listen to him and try to understand why he is lying. Lies often let us look deeper into a man's heart than the truth. . . . What would we be like if we always told the truth about ourselves? If we lie we make ourselves look nice. . . . Isn't that true?" (Maxim Gorkii, *Gesammelte Werke* [Berlin and Munich, 1923], vol. 1, pp. 448f.).

13. Aarne, *Leitfaden*, p. 34; Aarne speaks of "egomorphism." Angelika Merkelbach-Pinck also reports animal tales in which the animals have the names of well-known and established residents of the village (Merkelbach-Pinck, *Wanderung*, p. 226). Gottfried Henssen has also collected animal tales tied to the local environment (Henssen, "Volkstümliche Erzählerkunst," p. 6, note 9).

14. MdW, *Russische Volksmärchen*, no. 26, p. 151, as well as throughout this and other collections of east European folktales.

15. Henssen, *Überlieferung und Persönlichkeit*, pp. 25f. The Irish collector Danachair clearly had similar experiences with his narrators: "On the evening of the same day, in a farmhouse a few miles inland, another storyteller was so carried away by his telling of the hero-tale ("Tobar Deire an Domhain" = "The Well at the World's End") that he suddenly changed, in the narrative, from the third to the first person and described the hero's adventures as happening to himself" (C. O'Danachair, "Irish Folk Narrative on Sound Records," *Laos* 1 [Stockholm, 1951], 184).

16. Tillhagen, *Taikon*, p. 263.

17. Ibid., p. 264.

18. Busch, *Ut ôler Welt*, p. 4.

19. Henssen, *Überlieferung und Persönlichkeit*, no. 27 and p. 36, as well as Henssen, "Volkstümliche Erzählerkunst," pp. 5 and 28. Regarding the narrator's inner attachment, also see Jacob and Wilhelm Grimm's description of Mrs. Viehmann in the introduction to the 2nd edition of the KHM; also see Jahn's introduction to his collection *Volksmärchen aus Pommern und Rügen*, p. xi, and Wisser, *Auf der Märchensuche*.

20. Merkelbach-Pinck, *Wanderung*, p. 226. "I have seen narrators who perform their tales rather than just telling them" (Zenker-Starzacher, p. 33).

21. Dittmaier, pp. 201f. Danachair describes one of his Irish informants: "His body swayed and his limbs trembled with the earnestness which he put into the telling of the story. His voice rose and fell, like that of an actor on the stage. You got the impression that now he belonged no more to this age, but had gone back to the ancient world of the heroes and was trying to describe that world by means of his story. The King of Spain's son and all the other characters of his tale were to him living persons. Undoubtedly he was a splendid, polished storyteller, and from his mode of telling one could clearly realise how great was the art of the storytellers of long ago" (O'Danachair, p. 183).

22. Tillhagen, *Taikon*, p. 261.

23. Frobenius, *Paideuma*, p. 21.

24. Zender collected French soldier tales that narrators from Lorraine heard during their service in French units ("Quellen," pp. 31f.). "In the French navy," Auguste Jal (*Glossaire nautique* [Paris: Firmin Didot frères, 1948], p. 507) reports, there was a " 'story teller' aboard every ship" (BP IV, 6).

25. Panzer, *Die Kinder- und Hausmärchen der Brüder Grimm in ihrer Urgestalt*, vol. 1, p. xxx. Of course, we must be careful to separate the elements possibly added by editors from the original narratives themselves. The use of military jargon alone does not necessarily allow us to conclude that a soldier narrated the tale. For example, a few such expressions in "The Buffalo-hide Boots" (KHM 199) were added by Wilhelm Grimm, such as the following: "We're looking for a night's lodging and something to line our stomachs. Mine is as empty as an old knap-

sack . . . ; The soldier sat down at the table and began to make a brave attack on the roast. 'Brother Shinyboots, come and eat,' he said to the hunter . . . ; 'Time to strike tents . . . ;' 'Brother Shinyboots,' the soldier said, 'we routed the enemy and got ourselves a good meal. Now let's take it easy and quietly bring up the rear' " (Hamann, *Die literarischen Vorlagen der Kinder- und Hausmärchen und ihre Bearbeitung durch die Brüder Grimm*, pp. 104f.).

26. Uffer, pp. 64 and 241. Goats are also a general's recruits in a Lithuanian folktale. When he calls out, "Fall in!" they form a line, hold their beards high, and do not move; the Russian "Brother Scamp" even gives the devil military instructions (Leyen, *Die Welt der Märchen*, vol. 2, pp. 59ff.).

27. MdW, *Plattdeutsche Volksmärchen*, vol. 2, p. 215; cf. Dymke, p. 76.

28. Henssen, *Volk erzählt*, p. 127.

29. Bünker, p. 140; cf. Dymke, pp. 76f. I. W. Wolf also obtained some of his folktales from soldiers in the Hessian army (cf. the foreword to his collection).

30. Jahn, *Volksmärchen aus Pommern und Rügen*, p. xvi. Of course, this servant never really wore the red hussar's uniform; he only longed to. (Cf. Henssen, "Volkstümliche Erzählerkunst," p. 22.)

31. Cf. Merkelbach-Pinck, *Lothringer Volksmärchen*, p. 12.

32. Ibid., p. 7. "Folktales are not the product of their motifs; they are also not the product of their narrative content. Rather, they are creations of spiritual demeanor; the soul tells these stories" (Werner Spanner, *Das Märchen als Gattung*, Diss. Gießen, 1939, p. 37).

33. Cf. Margarete Wocke, "Ibsen und das norwegische Märchen," *Mitteilungen der Schlessischen Gesellschaft für Volkskunde* 23 (1922), 90f.

34. "Das Klatschgespenst," in Frobenius, *Paideuma*, pp. 26f.

35. Frobenius, *Paideuma*, pp. 24ff.

36. For example, Gottfried Henssen's narrator Gerrits is a rogue, and this is also stamped on his repertoire, which consists of jests about Eulenspiegel, the dumb citizens of Wilsum and other foolish people, the devil getting swindled, parsons and sextons, and Old Fritz, as well as hunting stories, tales of lying, jokes, and anecdotes. In contrast, legends are in the minority. Gerrits strikes the same tone with his songs: Henssen collected mostly dance songs, knavish songs, and light tunes. Like legends among his narratives, ballads and historical songs are of secondary importance among the songs. The narratives reflect the individual more than the songs, which are more constrained by the formal demands of rhythm, melody, and rhyme (Henssen, *Überlieferung und Persönlichkeit*).

37. Anna Birgitte Rooth differentiates "conventional composition" and "individual composition" in *The Cinderella Cycle* (Lund: Gleerup, 1951).

38. Uffer, p. 13.

39. For example, see Zender, *Volksmärchen*, p. xvii.

40. Merkelbach-Pinck, *Lothringer Volksmärchen*, p. 379.

41. Cf. Walter Anderson, *Hessische Blätter für Volkskunde* 30/31 (1931–32), 301, as well as Walter Anderson, "Zu Albert Wesselskis Angriffen auf die finnische folkloristische Forschungsmethode," *Acta et Commentationes Universitatis Tartuensis* 38:3 (Tartu, 1935), 6. The editors of folk narratives from Palestine report: "These folktales were told to adults, not to children, in Bir-Zet. Moreover, one could often observe that, despite the marvelous features, the content was taken to be true, as an event that had taken place in the recent or the distant past. One of our narrators, an old man, began to cry in the middle of the tale when the heroine reached the climax of her sad fate. Another once interrupted his mother's story with the curse 'God burns the liar's father.' This showed that he came expecting to hear something true" (Schmidt and Kahle, pp. 15f.).

42. Haiding, *Österreichs Märchenschatz*, pp. 401f.

43. Ludwig Laistner pointed to the parallels between folk narrative and dreams

long before any modern, psychologically oriented research. *Rätsel der Sphinx*, 2 vols. (Berlin: W. Hertz, 1889).

44. For psychological folktale interpretations, refer to the following publications: G. Jacob, *Märchen und Traum* (Hannover: Heinz Lafaire, 1923); Erwin Müller, *Psychologie des deutschen Volksmärchens* (Munich: J. Kösel & F. Puset, 1928); Erwin Müller, "Traum und Märchenphantasie," *Zeitschrift für pädagogische Psychologie* 31 (1930), pp. 72ff.; Dorith Moers, *Der Traum in vergleichender Betrachtung zu Geisteskrankheiten und Märchen*, Diss. Bonn, 1949; Jung, *Symbolik des Geistes;* Hedwig von Beit, *Symbolik des Märchens. Versuch einer Deutung* (Bern: A. Francke, 1952).

45. Cf. Jacob, p. 60.

46. The motif of flight is taken up in the article "Fahrzauber" in the HdM; also see Müller, "Traum," p. 77; MdW, *Kinder- und Hausmärchen*, p. xi.

47. See HdM II, 31f., for references to this and the preceding examples.

48. BP IV, 16.

49. MdW, *Märchen aus Siberien*, no. 76.

50. MdW, *Japanische Volksmärchen*, Introduction, p. 16.

51. MdW, *Lettisch-litauische Volksmärchen*, no. 41; cf. von der Leyen, *Die Welt der Märchen*, vol. 2, p. 64; Beit, *Symbolik*, p. 28.

52. BP IV, 32; cf. Beit, *Symbolik*, p. 65.

53. Such as Leyen, *Das Märchen*, pp. 62f. and 124. Friedrich Panzer also speaks of the folktale as a "dream put into episodes" (in J. Meier, ed., *Deutsche Volkskunde*, p. 253). The HdM "explains" numerous individual folktales on the basis of dreams, particularly under the entry "Entstehung der Sagen- und Märchenmotive" (Origin of Legend and Folktale Motifs). "The Golden Goose" is traced to the nightmare of not being able to get away from something (HdM II, 314f.; the article is by Hans Honti). In the HdM (II, 158) Aly says the motif of the magic flight "is derived from the nightmare." "Some cumulative tales, particularly the more developed, fantastic ones, are probably dream experiences, i.e., narratives formed according to such dream experiences" (Archer Taylor, HdM II, 166).

54. Cf. Röhrich, "Märchen und Psychiatrie," pp. 44f.

55. For example, A. Lommel reports that for the aborigines in northwest Australia, "dream images and facts are equally real, and it always requires in-depth questioning to determine whether an event took place 'in reality' or 'only' in a dream. . . . It is clear that the daily life of these people, their ability to propagate, and their social bonding depend on psychic processes that are labeled as 'dreams.' Dreams are also significant because these people consider dream experiences equal to experiences during waking consciousness . . ." (Lommel, pp. 187f.).

56. Oberfeld, pp. 31ff.

57. E.g., Aphanassjew [Afanas'ev], vol. 1, no. 21, pp. 151ff. Bolte calls it the "dream of future splendor; cf. BP I, 324, and III, 305.

58. Aphanassjew [Afanas'ev], vol. 2, pp. 1ff.

59. Cf. BP IV, 151; Bolte, *Zeitschrift für Volkskunde* 19 (1909), 289.

60. Hermann and Schwind, no. 11, pp. 120f.

## The Folktale's Themes

1. Cf. Giese's (pp. 138f.) compilation of these formulas. Other formulas of this type include: "It was and it was not. If it didn't happen, it wouldn't be told" (Tillhagen, *Taikon*, p. 158). "It is not completely true, but I didn't make it up, either" (Lambertz, pp. 93f.). "Don't believe it if you don't want to." "Lies or the truth, it is told." KHM 187 ("The Hare and the Hedgehog") begins, "This story sounds like a pack of lies, but it's true just the same."

2. Lüthi, *Volksmärchen*, pp. 108f. The folktale "contrasts with superficial reality but not with actual reality. . . . The folktale regards itself, and presents itself, as a view of the nature of reality" (ibid., p. 110).

3. Wilhelm Grimm, *Kleinere Schriften,* ed. Gustav Hinrichs, vol. 1 (Berlin: F. Dümmler, 1881), p. 333.

4. Cited from Benz, *Märchendichtung,* p. 58.

5. By "theme" we mean the inner point of crystalization, the folktale's, or group of folktales', driving force. (This is actually the original meaning of "motif," i.e., the motive—*movens*—which advances the plot.) The terminological label that we give to constantly recurring basic situations in the folktale is not our primary concern here. Perhaps they are best called "themes," "models," "basic ideas," or "ur-motifs" which mark entire groups of folktales. In contrast to Kurt Wagner's "schema" (*Wirklichkeit und Schicksal,* p. 167, note 2), i.e., the basic motifs with an immanent effect on the plot, the raw materials for a tale type's plot (e.g., fight with the dragon, courtship, marriage to a demonic figure, etc.), we would understand "theme" to refer more to the folktale's inner essence, its psychic, spiritual structure.

In his essay on the categories of prose narrative (in *Volkskundliche Gaben, Festgabe John Meier;* reprinted in *Selected Papers on Folklore*), Carl Wilhelm von Sydow suggested that folktales be grouped into natural clusters rather than according to the method employed in the Aarne-Thompson tale type index. He called for a supplement to Thompson's update of the catalog. Likewise, Friedrich Ranke has urged studies seeking the original psychological "meaning of individual folktale motifs" (F. Ranke, "Märchenforschung. Ein Literaturbericht," p. 300). Also see Kahlo's article "Elementargedanken im Märchen," HdM I, 519ff.; Honti, "Märchenmorphologie," particularly p. 318; Lord Raglan, *The Hero: A Study in Tradition, Myth and Drama,* 2nd ed. (London: Watts, 1948).

6. E. Meier, *Volksmärchen aus Schwaben,* no. 6, p. 29, offers a particularly drastic example.

7. MdW, *Zigeunermärchen,* no. 64, p. 265, and MdW, *Sibirien,* p. 99, offer psychologically illuminating examples.

8. Grudde, *Plattdeutsche Volksmärchen,* no. 49, pp. 93f.

9. Ibid., no. 75, p. 138.

10. In 10 of 22 versions of "The Mongoose"; cf. Hartmann-Ströhm, p. 81.

11. Wolfgang Kayser, *Das sprachliche Kunstwerk* (Bern: A. Francke, 1948), p. 63. Max Lüthi says folktale "situations fit each other perfectly" (*Volksmärchen,* p. 66, with numerous additional examples). Cf. Genzel.

12. Cf. Wagner, *Wirklichkeit und Schicksal,* pp. 180f.

13. Cf. Walter Anderson, "Das chinesische Volksmärchen," *Blick in die Wissenschaft* (June 1948), p. 260.

14. E.g., Jegerlehner, *Sagen und Märchen aus dem Oberwallis,* no. 142, p. 118.

15. Kaarle Krohn, *Übersicht über einige Resultate der Märchenforschung,* FFC no. 96 (Helsinki: Suomalainen Tiedeakatemia, 1931), p. 26.

16. Fox, *Volksmärchen,* p. 45 ("Ringelfest").

17. Cf. Isenberg, p. 146.

18. Cf. Woeller, pp. 278ff.

19. MdW, *Russische Volksmärchen,* no. 42, pp. 251ff.; cf. von der Leyen, *Die Welt der Märchen,* vol. 2, pp. 16ff.

# Selected Bibliography

Afanas'ev, Aleksandr. *Russian Fairy Tales.* Translated by Norbert Guterman. New York: Pantheon Books, 1945.

Azadovskii, Mark. *A Siberian Tale Teller.* Translated by James R. Dow. Monograph Series no. 2. Austin: University of Texas Center for Intercultural Studies in Folklore and Ethnomusicology, 1974.

Bach, Adolf. *Deutsche Volkskunde: ihre Wege, Ergebnisse und Aufgaben, eine Einführung.* Leipzig: S. Hirzel, 1937.

Baumann, Hermann. *Schöpfung und Urzeit des Menschen im Mythus der afrikanischen Völker.* Berlin: Dietrich Reimer, 1936.

Bausinger, Hermann. *Lebendiges Erzählen. Studien über das Leben volkstümlichen Erzählgutes auf Grund von Untersuchungen im nordöstlichen Württemberg.* Diss. Tübingen, 1952.

Bolte, Johannes. *Name und Merkmale des Märchens.* FFC no. 36. Helsinki: Suomalainen Tiedeakatemia, 1920.

Bolte, Johannes, and Georg Polivka. *Anmerkungen zu den Kinder- und Hausmärchen der Brüder Grimm.* 5 vols. Leipzig: Dietrerich'sche Verlagsbuchhandlung, 1913–32.

Bünker, Johann Reinhard. *Schwänke, Sagen und Märchen in heanzischer Mundart.* Leipzig: Deutsche Verlagsactiengesellschaft, 1906.

Dähnhardt, Oskar. *Natursagen.* Leipzig and Berlin: B. G. Teubner, 1907–11.

Dittmaier, Heinrich. *Sagen, Märchen und Schwänke von der unteren Sieg.* Bonn: Röhrscheid, 1950.

Dymke, Anneliese. *Die wirkliche Welt im deutschen Zaubermärchen. Studien zum Märchengepräge.* Diss. Würzburg, 1951.

Friedrich, Adolf. *Afrikanische Priestertümer: Vorstudien zu einer Untersuchung.* Studien zur Kulturkunde, vol. 6. Stuttgart: Strecker & Schröder, 1939.

Geramb, Viktor von. *Kinder- und Hausmärchen aus der Steiermark.* 3rd ed. Graz and Vienna: Leykam, 1948.

Graber, Georg. *Sagen und Märchen aus Kärnten.* Graz: Leykam, 1935.

Grimm, Jacob. *Deutsche Rechtsaltertümer.* 4th ed. A. Heusler and R. Hübner, eds. 2 vols. Leipzig: Dieterich, 1899.

Grimm, Jacob, and Wilhelm Grimm. *German Legends.* Translated by Donald Ward. Philadelphia: Institute for the Study of Human Issues, 1981.

Grimm, Jacob, and Wilhelm Grimm. *Tales for Young and Old: The Complete Stories.* Translated by Ralph Mannheim. Garden City: Doubleday, 1977.

Grudde, Hertha. *Plattdeutsche Volksmärchen aus Ostpreußen.* Königsberg: Gräfe & Unzen, 1931.

Henssen, Gottfried. "Volkstümliche Erzählerkunst." *Westdeutsche Zeitschrift für Volkskunde* 32 (1935), 2–35.

Henssen, Gottfried. *Überlieferung und Persönlichkeit: Die Erzählungen und Lieder des Egbert Gerrits.* Münster: Aschendorff, 1951.

Honti, Hans. "Märchenmorphologie und Märchentypologie." *Folk-Liv* 3 (1939), 307–18.

Jahn, Ulrich. *Volksmärchen aus Pommern und Rügen.* Norden: Soltau, 1891.

Jensen, Adolf Ellegard. *Hainuwele Volkserzählungen von der Molukkeninsel Ceram.* Frankfurt: V. Klostermann, 1939.

Koechlin, Elisabeth. *Wesenzüge des deutschen und französischen Volksmärchens.* Basler Studien zur deutschen Sprache und Literatur, vol. 4. Basel: B. Schwabe & Co., 1945.

Lambertz, Maximilian. *Albanische Märchen*. Akademie der Wissenschaften in Wien: Schriften der Balkankommission, Linguistische Abteilung, vol. 12. Vienna: Alfred Hölder, 1922.

Lefftz, Josef, ed. *Märchen der Brüder Grimm. Urfassung nach der Originalhandschrift der Abtei Oelenberg in Elsaß*. Heidelberg: Carl Winters Universitätsbuchhandlung, 1927.

Leyen, Friedrich von der. *Die Welt der Märchen*. 2 vols. Düsseldorf: E. Diederich, 1953–54.

Littmann, Enno. *Arabische Märchen*. Akademie der Wissenschaften und der Literatur. Abhandlungen der Klasse der Literatur 1955:2. Wiesbaden: Franz Steiner, 1955.

Löwis of Menar, August. *Der Held im deutschen und russischen Märchen*. Jena: Diederichs, 1912.

Lüthi, Max. *The European Folktale*. Translated by John D. Niles. Bloomington: Indiana University Press, 1986.

Meier, Ernst. *Deutsche Volksmärchen aus Schwaben*. Stuttgart: C. P. Scheitlin, 1852.

Meier, John, and das deutsche Volksliedarchiv, eds. *Deutsche Volkslieder mit ihren Melodien*. Berlin: W. de Gruyter, 1935.

Merkelbach-Pinck, Angelika. *Lothringer erzählen*. 2 vols. Saarbrücken: Saarbrücker Druckerei und Verlag, 1936.

Merkelbach-Pinck, Angelika. *Lothringer Volksmärchen*. Kassel: Bärenreiter, 1940.

Naumann, Hans. *Primitive Gemeinschaftskultur*. Jena: Diederichs, 1921.

Okakura, Kakuzo. *The Book of Tea*. London and New York: G. P. Putnam's Sons, 1906.

Page, Eleanor Susan. "The 'Nageltonne': Its Uses in History and Folklore." *Journal of American Folklore* 59 (1945), 20–24.

Panzer, Friedrich. "Märchen." In John Meier, ed., *Deutsche Volkskunde*. Berlin and Leipzig: W. de Gruyter, 1926.

Peuckert, Will-Erich. *Schlesiens deutsche Märchen*. Breslau: Ostdeutsche Verlagsanstalt, 1932.

Peuckert, Will-Erich. *Deutsches Volkstum in Märchen und Sage, Schwank und Rätsel*. Berlin: W. de Gruyter, 1938.

Peuckert, Will-Erich. *Wiedergeburt; Gespräche in Hörsälen und unterwegs*. Berlin: Weidmann, 1949.

Pramberger, Romuald. *Märchen aus Steiermark*. 2nd ed. Seckau: Benediktinerabtei, 1946.

Prestel, Josef. *Märchen als Lebensdichtung; das Werk der Brüder Grimm*. Munich: Max Hueber, 1938.

Ranke, Friedrich. *Volkssagenforschung*. Deutschkundliche Arbeiten, Allgemeine Reihe, vol. 4. Breslau: Maruschke & Berendt, 1935.

Rumpf, Marianne. *Rotkäppchen. Eine vergleichende Märchenuntersuchung*. Diss. Göttingen, 1951.

Rumpf, Marianne. *Ursprung und Entstehung von Warn- und Schreckmärchen*. FFC no. 160. Helsinki: Suomalainen Tiedeakatemia, 1955.

Sareyko, Hans Ulrich. *Das Weltbild eines ostpreußischen Volkserzählers*. Diss. Marburg, 1954.

Sartori, Paul. *Sitte und Brauch*. Handbücher zur Volkskunde, vol. 5. Leipzig: Heims, 1910.

Sydow, Carl Wilhelm von. *Selected Papers on Folklore*. Copenhagen: Rosenkilde & Bagger, 1948.

Thompson, Stith. *The Folktale*. 2nd ed. New York: Holt, Rinehart & Winston, 1951.

Tillhagen, Carl Herman. *Taikon erzählt, Zigeunermärchen und -geschichten*. Zurich: Artemis, 1948.

Uffer, Leza. *Rätoromanische Märchen und ihre Erzähler.* Schriften der Schweizischen Gesellschaft für Volkskunde 29. Basel: G. Krebs, 1945.

Wagner, Kurt. "Formen der Volkserzählung." In *Volkskundliche Ernte. Hugo Hepding dargebracht am 7. September 1938 von seinen Freunden.* Gießener Beiträge zur deutschen Philologie 60. Gießen, 1938. Pp. 250–60.

Wesselski, Albert. *Versuch einer Theorie des Märchens.* Prager deutsche Studien, no. 45. Reichenberg: B.F. Kraus, 1931.

Westermann, Diedrich. *Die Kpelle, ein Negerstamm in Liberia.* Quellen der Religionsgeschichte, vol. 9. Göttingen: Vandenhoeck & Ruprecht, 1921.

Winter, Richard. "Die geschichtliche Wirklichkeit im deutschen Volksmärchen." *Euphorion* 25 (1924), 194–225.

Wisser, Wilhelm. *Auf der Märchensuche: Die Entstehung meiner Märchensammlung.* Berlin: Hanseatische Verlagsanstalt, n.d.

Woeller, Waltraud. *Der soziale Gehalt und die soziale Funktion der deutschen Volksmärchen.* Habilitationsschrift Berlin, 1955.

Wundt, Wilhelm. "Märchen, Sage und Legende als Entwicklungsformen des Mythus." *Archiv für Religionswissenschaft* 11 (1908), 200–22.

Wundt, Wilhelm. *Völkerpsychologie. Eine Untersuchung der Entwicklungsgesetzte von Sprache, Mythos und Sitte.* Vols. 4–6: *Mythus und Religion* (1910–15).

Zender, Matthias. *Volksmärchen und Schwänke aus der Westeifel.* Bonn: L. Röhrscheid, 1935.

Zender, Matthias. *Volkssagen der Westeifel.* Bonn: L. Röhrscheid, 1935.

Zenker, Elli. *Eine deutsche Märchenerzählerin aus Ungarn.* Münich: Hoheneichen, 1941.

# Tale Indexes

## A. THE GRIMMS' TALES (KHM)

(Numbering follows Bolte and Polivka's *Anmerkungen*—see bibliography for full reference.)

## B. AARNE-THOMPSON TALE TYPES

(Only tales Röhrich identifies by their type number are included here.)

# Subject Index

LUTZ RÖHRICH is Professor Emeritus and former Director of the Folklore Institute at the University of Freiburg in West Germany.

PETER TOKOFSKY is a doctoral candidate in Folklore and Folklife at the University of Pennsylvania. He has studied in Freiburg, Göttingen, and Tübingen.

www.ingramcontent.com/pod-product-compliance
Lightning Source LLC
Chambersburg PA
CBHW070449100426
42812CB00004B/1240